# THE WRITTEN WORLD

# THE

# WRITTEN WORLD

*Past and Place
in the Work of Orderic Vitalis*

AMANDA JANE HINGST

*University of Notre Dame Press*

*Notre Dame, Indiana*

*Library of Congress Cataloging-in-Publication Data*

Hingst, Amanda Jane, 1976–
    The written world : past and place in the work of Orderic Vitalis /
by Amanda Jane Hingst.
        p.    cm.
    Includes bibliographical references and index.
    ISBN-13: 978-0-268-03086-5 (pbk. : alk. paper)
    ISBN-10: 0-268-03086-3 (pbk. : alk. paper)
    1. Ordericus Vitalis, 1075–1143?   2. Ordericus Vitalis, 1075–1143?
Historia ecclesiastica.   3. Church history—Middle Ages, 600–1500.
4. Religion and geography.   5. Normandy (France)—History—To 1515.
6. Great Britain—History—To 1485.   7. Crusades.   8. Normans.   I. Title.
    BR252.H56   2009
    270.4—dc22

                                                                    2009004363

*To My Parents*

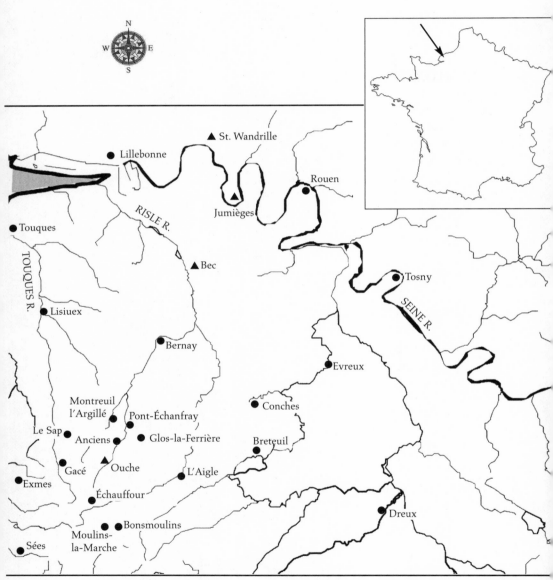

Map of France, twelfth century, detail of the environs of Orderic Vitalis.
Map copyright © 2008 Digital Vector Maps.

# Contents

# Acknowledgments

Monks, Orderic Vitalis said, need only two things to survive: wood and water. Historians need three: money, books, and friends. The first was provided by a Jacob K. Javits Fellowship from the U.S. Department of Education, which supported four years of my graduate study, including two years of work on the dissertation that became this book. The University of California, Berkeley, also provided financial support through the Fletcher Jones Fellowship and the Dean's Normative Time Fellowship.

The books, medieval and modern, needed for this study came from libraries around the world. The Département des Manuscrits (division occidentale) at the Bibliothèque nationale de France, Paris, graciously allowed me access to Orderic Vitalis's autograph manuscript of his *Historia Ecclesiastica* as well as many other treasures. Thanks are also due to the staffs of the Bibliothèque de la ville in Rouen, of the Mediathèque de la communauté urbaine d'Alençon, and of the British Library, all of whom were consistently helpful and understanding. Catherine Hilliard, the librarian at St John's College, Oxford, kindly gave me permission to use images from one of that library's manuscripts and helped to provide me with photographs. Back in the United States, staff members at the many excellent libraries of the University of California, Berkeley, provided me with a wealth of assistance, as did those at the Flora Lamson Hewlett Library at the Graduate Theological Union in Berkeley and at the John M. Olin Library at Washington University in St. Louis. The Robbins Collection in the Law Library of the School of Law at the University of California, Berkeley, gave me a quiet and congenial place to work as well as access to some rare reference materials.

From my California days I must also thank Geoffrey Koziol, my graduate advisor, and Susanna Elm, Steven Justice, Jennifer Miller, R. I. Moore, Maureen Miller, and the participants in the California Medieval History Seminar at the Huntington Library in May 2004, where I presented a version of chapter 1 of this study. From St. Louis, I want to thank Joe Loewenstein and everyone involved in the Interdisciplinary Project in the Humanities at Washington University in St. Louis, where I spent two lovely years teaching as an Andrew W. Mellon Postdoctoral Fellow. I still can't believe how much I learned.

Charity Urbanski has read my work, given me reliable counsel, and was my companion through Normandy; I couldn't have done it all without her (especially since I can't drive a stick shift . . .). David Spafford, Ruth Jewett-Warner (who gave me an invaluable gift at a particularly opportune time), Dan Warner, Rebecca Moyle, Viðar Pálsson, Mike Carver, and Mark Pegg all provided suggestions, hospitality, and support. With Jocelin of Brakelond, the late Robert Brentano taught me how to look for the world in a single text. He died before this study was anything more than a vague idea—my work, and the world, are the poorer for his absence. Thanks also to Barbara Hanrahan at the University of Notre Dame Press for her enthusiasm and support, and Matthew Dowd for his careful attention.

Orderic reminds his readers that "the state of the world is driven by change." My family has cheered me on through many changes over the years, and I owe them more than I can say. My sister Rachel Hingst always reminds me that I have choices, and that the world is wider and more varied by far than medieval geographers could ever have imagined. My parents, Warren and Susan Hingst, have supported me through some unconventional choices, and have never doubted that I could do this, all the more so in those many moments when I *did* doubt. So this book is dedicated to my father and my mother, with love.

# Prologue

"In the year of our Lord 1118, on the vigil of the birth of the Lord, a violent gale leveled many buildings and woods in western regions," the twelfth-century Anglo-Norman monk and historian Orderic Vitalis opened the twelfth book of his *Historia Ecclesiastica*. He immediately went on. "After the death of Pope Paschal, Giovanni of Gaeta, previously chancellor and master of the Roman pontificate, was elected pope as Gelasius and canonically consecrated by the Roman clerics against the wishes of the Emperor. Then Archbishop Bourdin of Braga, called Gregory VIII by his partisans, was intruded into the Church of God with imperial consent. This then grew into a grievous dissension," and, like the storm that chronologically and narratively ushered in the schism, "a fierce persecution rose up and violently disturbed the Catholic people."[1] But this did not exhaust the significance of the gale that had marked the changing of that year. "At that time in Brittany the Devil appeared to a certain woman lying in bed after childbirth, and taking on the image of her husband he brought the food for which she had asked." Deceived by the illusion, she ate. "A little while later her husband returned, heard what had happened, became very much afraid, and came back with a priest. The priest, invoking the name of the Lord, touched the woman, sprinkled her with holy water, and told her what to say if the impostor were to return. Satan came again, and following the instructions she questioned him"—*inquisiuit*, a questioning in search of truth. "'Right before Christmas a very great gale resounded dreadfully, and greatly terrified us,' she said. 'What did it portend? It destroyed churches and homes, flung the tops of towers to the ground, and cut down innumerous oaks in the woods.'" The laywoman's words, remember, were scripted by the Breton priest and devised by the learned priest Orderic as a query into the nature of things obscure. "Satan replied, 'It was decreed by the Lord that a great portion of mankind would perish, but the powerful prayer of the heavenly host persuaded Him to spare the men and command that huge trees fall instead. However, before three years pass there will be terrifying tribulation on the Earth, and very many illustrious people will succumb to destruction.'" Having learned what she wished to know, the woman splashed some holy water on the Devil and he disappeared.[2]

Orderic scraped nineteen lines of his graceful brown script off the parchment surface of what is now folio 157v of MS Latin 10913 in the Bibliothèque nationale de France so that he could squeeze the story of Satan's inquisition by a postpartum Breton woman in at this point in his *Historia*. The erasure is so complete that it is impossible to eke out any glimpse of the previous text, and it can be dated no more precisely than between the mid-1130s and Orderic's death circa 1142.[3] Between the schism that follows immediately in the gale's narrative wake and the appearance of the Devil in Brittany run some twenty-three lines concerning the conflict between England's King Henry I and his rival Louis VI of France and eight more on the fate of Pope Gelasius, who in 1119 "passed quickly away like a morning frost touched by the breath of God."[4] The tale is immediately followed by another evil sign, this one in England at Ely where a mysterious Jerusalemite ordered a pregnant cow to be sliced open to reveal three piglets; the deaths of Count William of Évreux, Queen Edith-Matilda, and Robert, count of Meulan followed, Orderic reported.

Modern historians have tended to pass over these stories, these portents that dot the *Historia Ecclesiastica* as they do so many medieval histories, and hurry on to the portions of Orderic's account alleged to be more accurate, more believable, more real.[5] Even Mark Twain, of all the unlikely critics, scorned the cosmic interpretations offered up by twelfth-century historiography, observing about Orderic's younger English contemporary Henry of Huntingdon, "Sometimes I am half persuaded that he is only a guesser, and not a good one. The divine wisdom must surely be of a better quality than he makes it out to be." The historical inter-

pretation of God's plan was not a skill prized highly by Twain. "I could
learn to interpret," he grumbled, "but I have never tried, I get so little
time."[6] Perhaps Twain would have preferred Orderic's *Historia Ecclesiastica* to Henry of Huntingdon's *Historia Anglorum*. "I am unable to penetrate the divine judgment by which all things happen," Orderic warned
his readers, "and I cannot lay open the secret causes of things, but simply
collect the historical annals requested by my companions. Who can penetrate the inscrutable?"[7]

But the story of the Devil's startling revelation of humanity's escape from the Christmas gale was neither inscrutable nor incidental to
Orderic. It was important to him, important enough for him to go back
in his *Historia* and rub out something else. It was important because
the storm betrayed the consubstantiality among the elements of God's
creation. Trees and men, Earth and humanity—the heavens and Earth
fashioned by God on the first day of His Creation were recognized by Orderic to possess an elemental and persistent involvement with the humans made on the sixth. Human history was not played out *on* the Earth
but *with* it.[8] While people could read the actions of the physical world—
meteorological and astrological, routine and marvelous—as portents
and elements of God's plan, the connections between the mortal and the
terrestrial, though deeply felt and intrinsically sympathetic, were correla-
tive rather than causative. They happened "at intervals of time through
the hidden causes of the world itself," as the redoubtable Augustine of
Hippo wrote, though "nevertheless determined and regulated by divine
providence," of course.[9] "That autumn was stormy in Normandy," Orderic said of the year 1106, "with thunder and rain and war," three parallel symptoms of the chaos affecting the human and earthly elements
of God's creation.[10]

The recording of these portents was a classic element of the medieval historical tradition, but in the twelfth century some writers, like Orderic, relied increasingly on these traditional historical components—
storms, comets, meteor showers—as a way of testifying to the depth of
humanity's historical experience of creation.[11] This historiographical
impulse coincided with the revived interest in natural philosophy that
blossomed in the cathedral schools.[12] The historian, like the philosopher, looked to plot the relationship between the fleeting generations of

humanity and the stability of the world's terrain. The elemental rapport between the Earth and humankind that made omens historiographically significant laid the foundations for the historicized geography that shaped twelfth-century historical writing and is especially pivotal and evocative in Orderic Vitalis's wide-ranging *Historia Ecclesiastica*. The use of geography—the physical terrain of the world, both actual and imagined—as an organizing principle distinguishes the historical narratives that flourished in the twelfth century, and even a few of those from the eleventh, from the annalistic tradition of the earlier middle ages in which the progressive march of years dictated the narrative of events.[13] These earlier, annalistic histories, such as those by Flodoard and Richer of Reims, were by no means unsophisticated, but they were primarily unconcerned with the impact of geographical space on human society through time.

The high medieval historian, on the other hand, was, in his own way, always a geographer. The meaning of geography was not then, nor is it now, found in borders or capital cities or population figures, but rather in the intimacy between human activity and physical space, the ways in which each reciprocally imbues the other with meaning.[14] Human society, made up of three-dimensional material bodies as it is, could not exist without a material space to cradle and shape its eccentricities and intimacies, its diversity and violence.[15] Nor could human memory survive without the strong pull of the spatial to spark recollection at so many levels, from a peculiarly shaped hill reminding a prehistoric hunter of a dangerous animal that lurked nearby to the highly technical topographical mnemonics perfected by professional mnemonists and by medieval scholars.[16]

High medieval historians both explicitly and intuitively recognized geography's significance for the understanding and narration of human affairs.[17] And this organizing geography of twelfth-century chroniclers was not merely historical, not a simple recapitulation of the spatial layout of the past. Rather, these writers *historicized* the places and spaces of their works, recognizing and exploiting the intimacy between human activity and the physical landscape as it developed meaning through time.[18] The exegete and theologian Hugh of Saint-Victor, an exact contemporary of Orderic's and a man of intense historical inclination though not quite a historian himself, set out the essence of this relationship. "There are three things upon which the investigation of things done especially depend," he instructed in the prologue to his very schematic chronicle, "namely, the people by whom things were done, the places in which they were done, and the time at which they were done," a triumvirate that provided a foundation for both historical recollection and historical meaning.[19] The terrain of the Earth, in contrast with the transitory passing of human lives and memories, offered a physical continuity that allowed the passage of time to be plotted on the contours of the Earth's topography through both a cultural memory and written history of place.[20] The Earth's landscape thus provided a persisting structure in the anthropological sense, in that the inertia of the topography of an area, its long-term recognizability, allowed people to attribute a cultural and historical significance to their physical surroundings that could stretch far into the past, even to time mythical and immemorial.[21] But at the same time the inevitable changeableness of human society—"the state of the world is driven by change," as Orderic noted—meant that people continually adapted the meaning imbued in the landscape to their own cultural needs, sometimes by trying to erase the memories linked to certain locations, to wipe the landscape clean, but more often by reinterpreting the terrain's meaningful past in the light of present concerns.[22] It is this complexity, this balance between inertia and change, that gives the word "landscape" its uniquely flexible meaning, encompassing at the same time the material terrain (as in landscape architecture), an artistic representation of that terrain (a landscape painting), and the spatial quality of a human institution (the political landscape).[23]

This history grounded in the terrestrial world recognized no incompatibility between the human soul in its quest for salvation—the fundamental plot of medieval historical narrative—and the material surroundings that shaped, organized, and historicized this quest. "The eternal Creator wisely and beneficially governs the changes of time and events," Orderic explained in his *Historia Ecclesiastica*. "This we see plainly in the winter and summer, and we sense it no less in the cold and the heat; this we weigh carefully in the rise and fall of all things, and we can rightly probe it in the great variety of God's works. Thus manifold histories are produced concerning the many sorts of events that happen on the Earth every day, and sharp-tongued historians are provided with much material for the telling."[24] This, the temporal experience of humanity with God as enacted in the landscape of Christendom, was to Orderic the meaning of historical writing and the motive for his work.[25] In this passage Orderic came very close to Hugh of Saint-Victor's definition, setting out the what (*euenti*, events), where (*in mundo*, in the world), and when (*coditie*, daily) of historical investigation.[26] It was not just the events but their situation on the Earth and in time, their historicized geography, that made up human history. The unraveling of the vagaries of human life in the *Historia Ecclesiastica* required Orderic to envision his world's terrain—past and present, physical and social, natural and architectural, political and ecclesiastic—in all its suppleness and adaptability, its hauntingly spatial embodiment of the past, and also its practical applicability in the recasting of the current geographies of power as seen from his desk in the scriptorium at the Norman and Benedictine monastery that modern historians refer to as Saint-Évroult but that Orderic invariably called by the toponym of Ouche.[27]

"CONSIDERING WHAT HAS HAPPENED IN THE PAST, I STRONGLY believe," averred Orderic in the prologue to his life's work, "that someone will rise up who will be much more astute than I and more able to explore the consequences of the various things that happen throughout the world, and who will perhaps draw something from my slips of parchment, and from others like mine, which he will kindly introduce into his chronicle and narration for the edification of the future."[28] Orderic's vast *Historia Ecclesiastica*, all 602 folios of extant autograph manuscript containing eleven of the work's thirteen books (supplemented by an almost-contemporary copy of the absent two), is considerably more than a few "slips of parchment."[29] These vellum pages are corralled today into three bulging and unattractive modern volumes held in the Département des manuscrits, division occidentale, at the Bibliothèque nationale de France in Paris—two bound in bruised red leather, known as MS Latin 5506, parts I and II, which contain books I and II and books III through VI, respectively; the other encased in battered brown, MS Latin 10913, with books IX through XIII prefaced by four orphaned folios of the *Historia Francorum senonensis* mistakenly bound in.[30] These parchment pages are of unassuming and slightly irregular size, from 14 x 23.5 cm to 15.5 x 24 cm, just slightly larger than a standard sheet of stationery or a largish paperback book. They normally hold thirty-three or thirty-four lines of text, occasionally increasing to thirty-five or thirty-six, and sometimes Orderic even managed to pack in as many as forty-four. The quality of the parchment varies, slightly better in MS Latin 5506 (II) where Orderic began his historical work, a little worse towards the end of the *Historia* when he was writing much more quickly and running through more material. The folios range in color from a deep cream to a tea-stained brown, and throughout they display missing corners and carefully patched tears, often revealing their animal origins by some residual hairiness and the appearance of skin. The original *Historia Ecclesiastica* was, in its quality, the paperback book of the monastic scriptorium, practical and private rather than stylish and intended for display. Orderic's beautiful handwriting, however—in ink tinted most commonly a medium brown though occasionally veering towards orange or black and with intermittent capitals in red, blue, and green—gives the pages a certain unaffected attractiveness that goes beyond the materials themselves.

Orderic's distinctive hand, with its rather angular quality, its peaks and practiced curves, echoes the elaborately knotted Anglo-Saxon and Celtic art of his native England, where he was born on 16 February 1075 in the fortified marcher town of Shrewsbury and where he learned to read and write as a child under the tutelage of the English priest Siward.[31] Half-English himself through his mother, who apparently died while he was still too young for the memory of her to be fixed in his adult mind, Orderic called himself *Angligena*, English-born, for the rest of his life.[32] His father, Odelerius of Orléans, was a Frenchman who had traveled to England after the Conquest of 1066 as a priest in the household of Roger II of Montgomery, one of William the Conqueror's closest friends and allies.[33] Though sent as an oblate to the Benedictine monastery of Ouche in Normandy when he was ten years old, Orderic nevertheless maintained a strong affection for the land of his birth, one evident

throughout his *Historia Ecclesiastica* and also in his copy of another ecclesiastical history, that of his idol Bede, which Orderic himself carefully and lovingly inscribed on large, beautiful, white parchment.[34]

But Orderic was not, like William of Malmesbury and Henry of
Huntingdon, the contemporaries with whom he is often grouped, an
English historian. By his late twenties or early thirties he was already
engaged in a major revision of William of Jumièges's iconic Norman
chronicle, and this work plunged him into the history and myths of Normandy, his adopted home.[35] "Brought here from the furthest reaches of
Mercia," he said from his Norman cloister, "a ten-year-old English-born
boy, an uncultured and ignorant stranger mixed in with knowing natives, inspired by God I have tried to bring forth in writing the deeds and
events of the Normans for the Normans."[36] In the beginning these Normans were just his fellow monks and the patrons of his abbey of Ouche,
for Orderic's *Historia Ecclesiastica* had a modest start as a foundation
narrative of the abbey in its Norman milieu, commissioned by Ouche's
abbot Roger of Le Sap around 1114.[37] But the world outside the cloister
kept intruding, and Orderic, too talented to be bound by the conventions
of monastic institutional history, realized that he had to write more.[38]
In the end even the Norman world, which had for more than two centuries been stretching itself from the moors of northern England to the
Moorish lands of Sicily, was not wide enough for Orderic to achieve his
historiographical vision. And so what began as an account of an obscure
Benedictine abbey hidden away in the forested Norman Pays d'Ouche
grew into a chaotic, intense, monumental yet detailed, politically astute,
and profoundly Christian work in thirteen books that, in its final form,
began with a *Vita Christi*, lingered long with the fractious and roving
Normans, followed the first crusaders to Jerusalem, reveled in the lives
of various saints, critiqued the kings and princes and prelates of the age,
and ended with an intensely personal prayer.

This building up of the Christian world through time did not come
easily or quickly. The Benedictine life, with its relentless communal liturgy, did not allow much personal leisure, and it took Orderic almost
thirty years to complete his thirteen books. The first two (which received their current designations as books III and IV after Orderic re-

organized his work in 1136 or 1137) were composed between 1114 and 1125 and dealt primarily with the abbey and its political surroundings. Orderic next, around 1127, set out in book V the lineage of the archbishops of Rouen, Normandy's only archepiscopal see. The early 1130s saw the composition of the bulk of book VI, again with a focus on the abbey, and also books VII and VIII on the Anglo-Norman world. Book IX, which covered the First Crusade, was written no later than 1135, the year that Orderic also took up again the history of England, Normandy, and the Holy Land in book X. Books XI and XII continue in the same vein, a history of Christendom as Orderic knew it, and were written in large part between 1135 and 1137. At the same time, Orderic compiled the new book I, which began with a *vita Christi* based on the Gospels and continued with a chronicle of ecclesiastical and secular affairs, and also worked on book II on the acts of the apostles and the lineage of the popes. The historian then capped off his *Historia Ecclesiastica* around 1137 with a prologue at the beginning to introduce the work and book XIII at the end, which continued the story of Christendom's history. The bulk of the *Historia Ecclesiastica* was thus complete by 1137, when Orderic was sixty-two years old. He added some material up until 1141, and probably died soon after.[39] The name *Ordricus* appears in memorial in the abbey of Ouche's calender on 13 July, written in a small, clear, trained hand in unfading dark brown ink.[40]

THE MEDIEVAL GENRE OF HISTORY WRITING HAS NOT BEEN NEGLECTED by modern historians. Many scholars, more than it would be possible to list here, have probed the techniques and tropes and reputation of history as literature, and have looked into the medieval historian's understanding of evidence, of precedence, of historicity. They have examined the subjects, subgenres, redactions, continuations, and circulation of histories over the centuries of western historical consciousness, and have provided an intensely detailed and invaluable scholarly tradition on the form, function, and meaning of historiography during the middle ages.[41] As a historian Orderic was, in many ways, typical of his eleventh- and twelfth-century age—typical in that he followed the precedents of the great Christian historians like Eusebius, Jerome, Orosius, and Bede, but also in that he joined some of his contemporaries in reshaping the genre of history writing to make it more responsive to the concerns of the time.[42]

But Orderic did not write his *Historia Ecclesiastica* to provide the future with an example of the genre of history writing. He wrote it to provide the future with a vision of his world, a vision that, he believed, the future could not do without. To Orderic the genre of history was a means, not an end. Historians "reveal the past to future generations un-grudgingly," he wrote, and they "have willingly gathered together writings for the continuing benefit of the future."[43] The fullness of history, Orderic knew, could not be preserved intact; the limitations of writing and of the human spirit prevented it. But he believed that, even so, "benevolent future generations, if they could restore it and could recover the lost pieces, would, briskly shaking off their idleness, rise up and willingly strive after the flower and fruit of the unseen work and ardently search with diligent discernment."[44]

This fiercely optimistic vision of history demands that the modern historian try to reach beyond the *Historia Ecclesiastica* as a representative of a literary genre and into the world of which Orderic's history is a relic, still powerful if sometimes uncooperative and occasionally obscure.[45] Cloistered in his scriptorium in Normandy's hinterlands, Orderic participated in his world by means of written and oral sources, materials that in modern jargon might be boiled down to the word "texts." In this he was no different from present-day historians, whose vision of Orderic's world is also contingent upon texts—often the very same texts that Orderic used and that he anticipated would be read in company with his own textual production.[46] Orderic never doubted that he could know his world to the best of human ability (true knowledge being reserved only for God) by means of texts, that the world of the text, written and oral, was real to one who understood the power and limitations of human language and society. Both the power and the limitations were, and are, great. But within those limitations a real world, a human and physical world, a world of actions and landscape and meaning, could still be made. And Orderic's world can still be found, at least some version of it, in the eight-hundred-year-old parchment pages of his *Historia Ecclesiastica.*

But why should the twenty-first century care about Orderic's world? Why should this obscure Norman monk—who quietly dwelled far from courts or crusades, whose ancestry and life were unremarkable, and whose history was apparently too unwieldy for wide circulation—still matter? Nearly every modern scholar of the high middle ages could no doubt comment on Orderic's usefulness, for the wide and anecdotal nature of his *Historia* has made it a favorite of historians who mine it for information about everything from aristocratic prosopography to battlefield tactics to Church councils. This, though, is utility, not significance. Orderic's significance lies simply in who he was, a man of the eleventh and twelfth centuries—an educated man, yes, an intelligent man, perceptive, eloquent, creative, sympathetic, judgmental, hopeful, worried, joyous, tormented, and at peace, but still just a man. He was not a king, a bishop, a heretic, a criminal, a soldier, or a saint. He was just a man, a monk no different from the rest—"neither better than good men nor worse than bad ones," as Orderic would quote his abbot's saying about another ordinary man who lived through extraordinary times.[47] Orderic was an ordinary person, and that is why he should matter. His thoughts were as complicated, fragmented, and inconsistent as those of any other individual, his loves and hates as arbitrary and as passionate. He may not have been famous in his own day, but neither are most of us, and that doesn't make our views of our age any less meaningful, moving, representative, or unique. Orderic is important because he cared enough to spend a lifetime writing history for anyone who would listen. The fact that people didn't listen then does not mean that we shouldn't listen now.

"I am occupied with probing and laying out the fate of the Christian people in the modern world," Orderic explained, "so I aspire to call this present little book an *Historia Ecclesiastica*."[48] And it is—a history of the Church in the broadest sense of humanity's experience with God on Earth.[49] Despite his isolation in a Benedictine cloister on Normandy's southern marches Orderic's historiographic gaze swept through Christendom from end to end, with long attention to the Anglo-Norman lands that the historian knew intimately as home. Christendom was, for Orderic, not just a community of believers but a meaningful and material landscape, a terrestrial manifestation of God's Church on Earth, a geography of salvation. Orderic wrote this landscape into the narrative of his

*Historia*, sometimes implicitly, sometimes plainly, always with the recognition that space and time were inseparable, that humanity and geography together made up the material of human history. Orderic's *Historia* is one of the most revealing products of an intellectual tradition that increasingly saw Christendom's topography not merely as a stage for human action but as a consequential participant in the world through time. It is a particularly fertile source for the study of this spatial negotiation. As a member of an Anglo-Norman community united through politics and family while unmistakably divided geographically by the English Channel as well as by language, ethnicity, and power, Orderic was well-aware of the entanglements of past and place. Through the uniquely encompassing, intelligent, vibrant, and personal vision of his narrative, Orderic captured the results and also the process of this renegotiation of Christendom's meaningful landscape.

"Geography," says Yi-Fu Tuan, one of the discipline's most influential modern thinkers, "is the study of the earth as the home of human beings."[50] Orderic, at various times and under various circumstances, might have called many things home—his monastery, Normandy, England, the inhabited world as defined by classical geography, Christendom, the cosmos. All of these took part in the geography of the *Historia Ecclesiastica*. And like any home, Orderic built his upon unremarkable foundations: the tropes of desert sanctity that defined Christendom's monastic traditions; the geographical models laid out by classical thinkers and adopted by medieval historians; the cultural trends of crusade and Christology that permeated the intellectual atmosphere of his lifetime. But Orderic then took these commonplace foundations and built a world like no other. It was a world that saw in monastic tradition the building blocks of place, that viewed classical geography as something that could be both manipulated and shattered, that used crusade to talk not about the Holy Land but about a homeland, and that saw in Christ's life and death an all-encompassing model for human history in the material world. Orderic Vitalis's *Historia Ecclesiastica* exposes the ways in which an individual could take the cultural, social, spatial, and intellectual norms of his time and transform them into a geographical vision that is ordinary and unique, traditional and revolutionary, emblematic and eccentric, all at the same time. In most ways Orderic's geographical home was shared by others of his age, with the same hills and streams, the same landscapes, the same limits, and the same conventions. But this shared world abounds with a remarkable color and shimmer, a glory and violence that can be seen only through individual eyes. Yes, Orderic's world, his home, is the idiosyncratic vision of an unusual man, but that is just the point. His geography demonstrates how the cultural and intellectual trends of a society can become the personal and intimate experience of an individual. It is this singular entanglement of heritage and immediacy, and of past and place—a geography of monastery, community, *regnum,* Christendom, and cosmos—that unfolds here as Orderic Vitalis takes his readers on a tour through the history and landscape of his world.

CHAPTER 1

# Ouche

*The History of a Place*

Normandy's characteristic rolling hills grow more pronounced in the Pays d'Ouche. The peaks there are more panoramic, the valleys more thoroughly folded away. Set along the border where in the eleventh and twelfth centuries the duchy of Normandy collided, often violently, with the county of Maine, the forested Ouche boasts the area's highest elevations, some 300 meters above sea-level, and a network of rivers flow down from its heights. Past Gacé to the west and south beyond Mortagne the Ouche's hills slide towards the plains of the Argentan and the Perche where the region's largest rivers, the Orne and the Sarthe, provided the peasants with the only decent agricultural land around. Here in the first centuries of Norman sway, scattered vineyards struggled to produce a palatable wine and apple orchards provided the barely-drinkable genesis of Normandy's famous *cidre*. Vital cereals paved the land with shimmering drifts of verdigris in the spring and, if prayers were answered, with rich gold at the harvest, while underneath the Ouche's tangled forests veins of iron ore were just beginning to surface.[1] L'Aigle was in the twelfth century, as it is still today, the region's largest town. Standing on the Risle roughly eighty-seven kilometers southeast of Caen, eighty-three southwest of Rouen, and seventy-two northwest of Chartres, the hilltop castle provided its lords with a masterful view of their lands and those of their numerous noble neighbors. For L'Aigle was by no means the Ouche's only castle. By 1135 the fortifications at L'Aigle, Bonsmoulins, Moulins-la-Marche, Échauffour, Gacé, Le Sap,

1

Anceins, Pont-Échanfray, Montreuil l'Argillé, and Glos-la-Ferrière domi-
nated the landscape, and a bit further afield the castle at Exmes anchored
the *pagus* of the Hiémois for its lords the Montgomerys, and that at
Breteuil the lordship of William fitzOsbern and his kin.[2]

Tucked away in the Charentonne valley a little more than twelve
kilometers west-northwest of L'Aigle, on the way to Gacé, was the Benedictine abbey of Ouche. This abbey—which Orderic Vitalis entered as
a ten-year-old oblate in 1085, thirty-five years after its foundation—
took its name from the marcher region of Ouche where in 1050 two
linked noble families, the Giroie and Grandmesnil, adopted for their
own Benedictine foundation the place and patronage of the Merovingian
confessor St. Evroul, who had established a monastic community on that
very spot some four hundred years before. The Norman monastery of
Ouche stood in the fee of Bocquencé, which one of the abbey's founding families had held from the Norman dukes before Ouche's abbot
purchased it in 1050.[3] But the monks needed only to look east to the
Charentonne's opposite bank to see the lands held by the barons of La
Ferté-Frênel from the powerful lords of Breteuil. By 1136 the town that
had grown up around the abbey's walls included at least eighty-four
houses—for that was how many, Orderic noted with exquisite precision,
were burned to the ground when the men of L'Aigle sacked the town in
that year.[4]

The abbey of Ouche dangled at the southeastern tip of the diocese of
Lisieux in a region where three influential Norman bishoprics—Lisieux,
Sées, and Évreux—met up not far from the French see of Chartres and
the Manceau diocese of Le Mans. Ouche was actually much nearer to
the episcopal city of Sées, which lay some thirty-one kilometers southwest of the abbey, than it was to Lisieux, a forty-three kilometer trip almost due north, and the monastery's lands straddled the Charentonne,
which, Orderic noted, "divides the diocese of Lisieux from that of Évreux," as well as separating the fee of Bocquencé from that of Le Ferté-
Frênel.[5] Orderic attributed this peculiarity of diocesan geography to a
choice made by the Breton Giroie, the paterfamilias of Ouche's founding
family, when he first acquired the lands of the Norman knight Heugon.[6]
Arriving in the Ouche around 1015, Giroie, Orderic reported, "asked
the inhabitants of that land under whose episcopal authority they were."

Imagine his surprise when his new tenants "declared themselves to be in no one's diocese." Appalled, Giroie "searched out the most reverent prelate in the vicinity and, recognizing the virtues of Roger, bishop of Lisieux, he gave his entire honor over to Roger's authority and persuaded Baudry of Bocquencé and his own sons-in-law Walchelin of Pont-Échanfray and Roger of Le Merlerault to submit their lands, which exercised a similar freedom, to the aforementioned bishop in the same manner."[7] The lands of these four men ran some thirty-five kilometers in length, from the manner of La Roussière in the north to the quarries of Le Merlerault in the south, and would come to comprise the southern tip of the diocese of Lisieux. Orderic's account could be true—there is no other evidence, the Norman sees were notoriously disorganized in the wake of the Viking raids, and the diocese of Lisieux is unusually irregular on its southern border—but Giroie's preference for Roger of Lisieux probably had less to do with the bishop's piety than with the fact that the episcopate of Seés was under the control of the Bellême, a powerful and ruthless family of true marcher lords who held a quasi-independent lordship stretching from Bellême to Domfront and straddling the border between Normandy, France, and Maine.[8] Giroie was already a vassal of William of Bellême, and as a man with pretensions to independence he likely did not want to owe too much loyalty to his ambitious and ruthless lord's family.[9] The abbey of Ouche, like the region, could never escape the tumult on the margins of lordship.

Orderic began his *Historia Ecclesiastica* as an account of the foundation and properties of his monastery, and again and again his history shows how the region's instability shaped the abbey's patrimony, its identity, and its place in the Norman geography of power. But despite its involvement in the secular world, the abbey's modest grey-brown stone buildings, in that way of medieval monasticism, still marked one of the many ordinary places in the Christian landscape where topography, architecture, and above all the history and traditions of monastic life allowed the vast imaginative terrain of Christendom to come to rest in the mundane world.[10] These multiple layers of the abbey of Ouche's historicized geography—the sacred and the secular, the timeless and the contemporary—were Orderic's first and most intimate attempts to elaborate the landscape of his age, and they laid the foundations for his broader work on the religious and political geography of the Anglo-Norman and Christian worlds.

It is for this reason that a study of Orderic's geography must start with that of the abbey and region of Ouche. In the early books of his *Historia Ecclesiastica*, the books that were a part of the original foundation narrative before becoming the cornerstone of the wider work, Orderic recounted the history of a place—a place, as he would show, that had a unique and holy reality before and beyond any human habitation or knowledge or name. This place, the very place inhabited by Orderic for the whole of his adult life, the place where the abbey of Ouche was founded and was lost and was founded again, did not have, for Orderic, a sacred history and a secular. It had one history, one identity, that mixed both sacred and secular elements in ways that made them almost indistinguishable. It was a place marked by revelation and violence and loss, defined by the Norman forest and the Egyptian desert, a home to monks and nobles alike, situated on political and ecclesiastical frontiers, and possessed of a history that was both unremarkable and unique. Through these entangled layers of Ouche's history Orderic demonstrated, in the specific, local, and intensely eloquent landscape of his abbey, how history and geography could come together in ways that he would then apply in the rest of his *Historia Ecclesiastica* to the wider expanse of his known world.

THE SHALLOW CHARENTONNE FLOWS A TRANSLUCENT BROWN PAST the site where for centuries the abbey of Ouche hallowed its west bank only a few kilometers from its source. The river's tea-like color is a result of the tannins picked up on its course through the forest, and it was this forest of oaks, firs, birch, and ferns that, when paired with the river, gave life to the abbey and definition to its landscape. Wood and water— "without these two elements, there can be no monks," as William Giroie, the son of Giroie and a monk at Bec-Hellouin, advised his sister's sons Hugh and Robert of Grandmesnil in a mid-eleventh-century conversation, imagined by Orderic in his revision of William of Jumièges's popular eleventh-century chronicle of Normandy's past, the *Gesta Normannorum Ducum*.[11]

"My dearest nephews, I hear that not only do you hunger for the worship of God but you also want to erect an abbey for monks," William Giroie applauded. "What site have you chosen for this foundation and what have you arranged there for the soldiers of Christ?"[12]

"God willing, we want to establish a fortress to Him at Norrey," Hugh and Robert explained, taking up the common military metaphor— they were knights, after all— "and give it our churches and tithes and everything else we can, so far as we are able in our poverty."[13]

William Giroie—a man of wide experience who had been lord of Échauffour before an unfortunate encounter with his violent neighbor William Talvas, lord of Bellême, left him blind and emasculated and inclined towards a solitary life—offered his nephews a bit of advice.[14] "St. Benedict, the master of monks, ordered that monasteries" (and here Benedict's *Regula* was quoted almost verbatim) "be constructed so that everything necessary—that is, water, a mill, a bakery, a garden, and various trades—may be contained within the abbey so the monks won't need to go wandering abroad, which is not altogether advantageous for their souls. The land at Norrey is certainly fertile enough," he recalled, "but an abundance of wood and handy water, of which monks have the greatest need, are quite distant."[15] William Giroie offered his nephews an alternative, a spot near Échauffour cradled by river and forest that had long ago been consecrated through the life of a Merovingian hermit, St. Evroul.[16]

"Wishing to devote himself only to the contemplation of God," the seventh-century aristocrat Evroul, a saint graced with an exceedingly typical hagiography that Orderic recapitulated in the sixth book of his *Historia*, "eagerly sought out the wilderness with greatest celerity."[17] Evroul and some dedicated companions entered the forest of Ouche in search of a more solitary life and "passed calmly through this most desolate place of solitude on foot."[18] But they could find no spot suited to their needs. And so Evroul prayed to God, "Show us in your mercy a place fit for freedom and for our weakness." Immediately an angel appeared to Evroul and his companions. They followed this divine guide through the forest until "they came to springs most suitable for drinking, which, though small in their origins, were collected into a large pool. There they fell to their knees, and gave great praise to God their guide."[19] They built a simple shelter on this spot, and established what would become, by the end of Evroul's life, a thriving religious community.

The miracle in this story of Evroul's retreat into the forest, called into being by the saint's prayer, is that this perfect location for a monastery had always been hidden there in the Norman Ouche, infused with historical potential and simply waiting to be unveiled as a home for Evroul and his companions. This place was not created out of nothing in its perfection in response to Evroul's prayer—if it had been, there would have been no need for the angel to lead the wanderers there; the miracle would have occurred before their eyes. Rather, this ideal spot was revealed as the preexisting place of the saint's destiny, the proper geographic receptacle for the holiness that Evroul, like all medieval saints, would imbue to the place of his life and death. The idea of a divinely revealed place was by no means unique to Evroul's life; indeed, it was a trope of monastic foundation narratives.[20] But it became a trope, important in Orderic's account as in others, because it enriched the abbey's location with a prehistory of holiness, a meaning that stretched back into time immemorial when historical facts gave way to divine significance. Thus the place of the abbey of Ouche had meaning, historical meaning, before Evroul arrived there, before the place had a name, and long before William Giroie and his nephews discussed the possibilities for a new foundation at that spot in the forest.

"The place in the Ouche to which God directed the venerable Evroul by means of His angel is quite suitable for the poor in spirit to whom the kingdom of heaven is promised," William assured his kinsmen. "For the ancient church of St. Peter still endures there, and ample land surrounds it where a garden and an orchard could be planted. The land is neglected and sterile, to be sure, but the Lord is able to provide a table in the desert for his servants"—a quotation from the Psalms that Evroul also recalled in praise of his wilderness home. "It lacks a fishing stream and fruitful vines, but a dense wood and springs suitable for drinking are close at hand. The bodies of many saints also lie there, which will be resurrected with immense glory on the last day."[21] This juxtaposition of deprivation and necessity, shot through with holiness, was a monastic dream, and in it were entwined the two primary strands of monastic historical and geographical identity: the desert tradition of the earliest

Egyptian monks and the cult of saints that anchored medieval spirituality into the Christian landscape. But all, Orderic knew, was not quite as simple as his William Giroie made it seem in this, the abbey's official story of its past. The Egyptian desert, despite its distance from the forest of Ouche, was available to any monk, as Orderic would show, but the same was not true of the bodies of saints. Orderic would unravel both of these spatial histories of Ouche in his *Historia Ecclesiastica*, and it is within this literary and spiritual tradition of the imaginative landscape of monastic life that Orderic's evocations of his own abbey's place, and also his notions of history as lived and written in the world, must be understood.

EVER SINCE ATHANASIUS'S ANTONY AND JEROME'S PAUL RETREATED into the desert beyond the reach of the flooding Nile the image of the monk in a desert wilderness—*desertus, heremus*—possessed the monastic imagination, in time creating everything from fens to forests and even cities, no matter how lush in reality, as metaphorical realizations of the arid experiences of the first Egyptian hermits.[22] Only in the desert's gaunt landscape could the monk-warrior battle the devil face-to-face in a wilderness at the border of Paradise and perdition.[23] Whether individually or in a community, as an Antony or as a Pachomius—both of whom Orderic held up as models of ascetic rigor—the men who made the western *heremus* their spiritual home sought the purity of heart that was the monk's immediate goal and the most necessary step on the way to the kingdom of heaven.[24] Although the Norman landscape tends to be intimate and satisfying rather than vast and acerbically breathtaking—except at Mont-Saint-Michel-in-Peril-of-the-Sea, where the monastery's perch in the midst of either churning water or a vast sandy plain, depending on the tide, approached the edginess of the Egyptian communities—by the time the confessors strode through the Neustrian countryside in search of a solitary life, the monastic landscape included a forested *heremus* that tended, unlike the Egyptian deserts at the edge of the known world, to be at the sparsely-settled center rather than the ragged hemline of civilization.[25] If northern monasticism, as Orderic said, "did not imitate the customs of the Egyptians who continually burned with the scorching heat of excessive sun, but instead piously introduced cus-toms of the Gauls who often shiver in the west's cold winters," it was only because Normandy was not as hot—appropriate monastic dress, too, would come to be geographically defined.[26] But even in the frostiest climes the desire for the desert did not die away. Hermits could be found in the dense Norman forest of Breteuil, for example, well into the twelfth century. Privileges were conferred on these men by Robert, earl of Leices-ter and lord of Breteuil, in a charter granted between 1121 and 1124, and on 18 April 1125 in the same forest Earl Robert founded a priory named, appropriately, Le Désert.[27]

The refounded Ouche of the eleventh century, though not a hermit-age in any sense, inherited this legacy of the desert, standing according to Orderic *in infructuoso cespite, in tanta heremo, in sterili rure, in regione deserta*—"on unfruitful sod," "in such a wilderness," "in a barren coun-try," "in a desert region."[28] For all the tropes, though, Orderic was not exaggerating. The abbey of Ouche was, quite literally, situated in a soli-tary, barren, unfruitful, wilderness wasteland. Although close enough to Échauffour that Evroul could run the Devil to ground there, around ten kilometers as the crow flies, the narrow Charentonne valley hid the abbey and the adjacent hamlet from the gaze of its neighbors, and those neighbors from that of the abbey's denizens in turn: a situation rather unusual in Normandy, where it is often possible to see from steeple to steeple, and from castle to castle, over the undulating fields.[29] This iso-lation was magnified by the enclosure of the forest. The woods of the Ouche had escaped being turned into farmland because the heavy flint clay paving the hills became a gelatinous mire in the spring after the rains and snows of winter and never entirely dried during the damp Nor-man summer.[30] This unfertile earth in the hills was heavy and intensely difficult for a medieval plow to penetrate, while "the soil in the valley was marshy," Orderic reported, "and whenever it was dug in winter liquid immediately gushed in and a flowing stream filled the hole."[31] In spite of all the moisture the Charentonne—called a *riuus*, a small stream, by Orderic—was not consistently deep enough for boats or even barges (or, for that matter, Vikings) to navigate, and this lack of easy fluvial trans-port further sequestered the community.[32]

The medieval monks' longing for the Egyptian desert and the memories of local confessors' wilderness foundations fortuitously complemented the more practical concerns of wealthy and pragmatic donors. These men and women were pious but were still disinclined to give up their more productive possessions to support the local monks.[33] So although the monastery of Ouche's place in the forest was far from agriculturally ideal, the models of the monastic past meant that as a site for an abbey the valley had other things to offer. "This is a *locus amoenus*," Orderic proclaimed of the surrounding forest, "and well-suited to a solitary life."[34] By drawing on the ancient literary topos of the *locus amoenus* Orderic evoked the forest of the Ouche as an uncorrupted silvan landscape, a place of extreme, even otherworldly beauty, like Eden bounded not by physical walls but by the knowledge that the world outside was somehow second-rate.[35] This monastic conflation of the *heremus* with the *locus amoenus*, the desert wilderness with the silvan paradise, as the image of the transcendent landscape allowed the ascetic imagination to leap over the limitations of earthly space and time and imagine global topography in microcosm.[36] When Orderic and his fellow monks looked beyond the cloister walls they could see in the mundane hills of the Ouche a landscape of tradition that took them beyond the local and the present to link them with the Eden of the past and the Paradise to come.[37]

When Evroul and his companions went to the woods of Ouche to live deliberately, so to speak, the saint immediately faced the desert dilemma encountered by generations of antecedents: the draw of his presence made the desert a city as other *amatores heremi*, lovers of the wilderness, followed both his example and him.[38] For many years his holiness drew people to the remote forest, pilgrims who "sought out Ouche with great difficulty, and," Orderic noted, "the seekers scarcely found it because at that time that place was unknown and a wilderness (*desertus*)."[39] After many years of care for both the pilgrims and his fellow religious Evroul died at peace, and "was wonderfully entombed in marble in the church of St. Peter, chief among the apostles, which he himself had built of stone"—quite an improvement from the hut that Evroul and his followers had originally constructed on the site.[40] And there, in the church, Evroul stayed for a time, in the midst of a thriving foundation at the site.

But sometime in the tenth century this flourishing community collapsed after a trauma that shattered its identity, its past, and its future — the body of its founder, Evroul, was stolen from its midst and once again the perfect site in the forest of Ouche would be lost to the sight of men. But the holiness of this place in the wilderness remained, and it burst out at unpredictable times, quite independently of any saintly relics.

ON 26 MAY 1131 OUCHE'S SEVENTH ABBOT WARIN DES ESSARTS AND two of his most trusted monks, Odo of Montreuil and Warin of Sées, returned to the abbey after an absence of more than half a year. They were not empty-handed. The three men had gone off in pursuit of a rumor that the venerable Benedictine monastery of Rebais-en-Brie in Champagne possessed half the body of St. Evroul, which had been pillaged from its tomb in the Ouche in the tenth century. After months of negotiation, and with the help of Bernard of Clairvaux, Count Thierry of Champagne, and England's King Henry I, the two Warins and Odo carried back to their abbey one arm of its patron along with assorted pieces of his bones.[41] They also, apparently, brought a copy of a sketchy and inelegant eleventh-century account of the relics' translation written by a monk at Rebais, which Orderic dismissed as "having without a doubt been produced by an uninformed author who," he disparaged, "did not demonstrate sufficient knowledge of events and dates."[42]

Orderic did not mention the theft of Evroul's relics in his account of the foundation of the abbey of Ouche. Only after Evroul's posthumous, and partial, return home in 1131 did Orderic apparently feel free to write — and thus interpret and make permanent — his community's memory of this event into his *Historia Ecclesiastica,* in the end fashioning an exceedingly rare narrative of relic theft, *furta sacra,* from the perspective of the losing monastery.[43] Had Abbot Warin not managed to recover some of the remains of the abbey's patron saint, it is likely that Orderic would never have mentioned this traumatic — even shameful — episode in his community's past, and would never have suggested to the reader of his *Historia* that the earthly remains of St. Evroul were not among the "bodies of many saints" that William Giroie had claimed for the site.[44] But the homecoming of St. Evroul to the very spot in the for-

est shown to him by an angel so many years before offered Orderic an
opportunity to recast the more recent history of that place in the Ouche
as one of holiness hidden and revealed, a repetition of the initial revelation of the place to the saint himself. St. Evroul, Orderic believed, had
always remained at that location in the Charentonne valley where the
monastery of Ouche sat. But the Norman refoundation's patron saint
would exist, for the first eighty-one years of the abbey's history, through
the historicized presence of the saint himself and not in the presence of
his mortal relics.[45]

Exactly when the bones of St. Evroul were stolen from his sepulchre
in the Ouche is uncertain.[46] Orderic attributed the theft to the chaos following the assassination of Duke William I Longsword in 942 when the
French king Louis IV d'Outremer encouraged his vassal Hugh the Great
to lead a French invasion into Normandy.[47] Rebais, however, claimed to
have received the bones in the time of a King Robert, which could have
been around 922 or 923 if this meant Robert I, or between 987 and 1031,
during the reign of Robert II the Pious.[48] A comparison of the two accounts, along with a few pieces of other evidence, suggests that the theft
actually took place near the end of the tenth century, probably in the 980s,
but the best that can be known for certain is that the relics of St. Evroul
still graced his riverside church in the Ouche in the year 900 when the
French king Charles the Simple granted a charter to "the monastery of
St. Peter in which St. Evroul rests in body."[49]

In any case, according to the story fashioned by Orderic in his *Historia*, Hugh the Great had come with his troops to Gacé. This town, just
twelve kilometers to the northwest of Ouche, could not house all of
Hugh's soldiers, and the French were forced to fan out over the region.
Hugh's chancellor Herluin and the noble Raoul of Drachy, "both of them
religious and devoted to the fear of God," were welcomed by the small
community on the west bank of the Charentonne and shown every hospitality by the residents.[50] But this proved disastrous, for a dispute between King Louis and Hugh the Great would cause the latter's troops to
sack the region. Herluin and Raoul, remembering the wealth of the establishment in which they had lodged, "returned to that place and unexpectedly forced their way into the monastery." The holy men who had
treated them with such honor as guests stood by in horror as the French

violated the church and "took the three bodies of the saints Evroul, Evremond, and Ansbert from their tombs, and wrapping the bones in deer-
skins they carried them away with other relics of the saints."[51] Hugh the
Great, still furious with King Louis, had set off for his base in Orléans.
Herluin and Raoul fell in with his retinue to head back home with their
sacred booty.[52]

Back at the desecrated church in the Ouche Ascelin, the aged and venerable leader of the community, "had seen that the monks and their servants were mired in so much grief, and that all of them together wished
to leave behind the desolate place to follow their blessed father Evroul
on his pilgrimage with the enemy army."[53] So the old man gave them his
blessing, admonishing them, "Serve faithfully the kind father Evroul,
who has thus far supported you in his own land while you are on pilgrimage with him in a foreign land. However," Ascelin continued, "I will
not leave this place in the Ouche, but I will serve my Creator here where
I have imbibed much good, and I will not withdraw from here so long
as the heat of life is in me. I know that many bodies of saints rest here
and that an angelic vision marked out this place for our saintly father
where he himself should train in spiritual warfare for the inspiration of
many people."[54] In the absence of his patron's body, Ascelin looked back
to the very revelation that originally brought Evroul to the Ouche, to a
place identified and marked very particularly by Ascelin in his speech as
"this place," *hunc locum*.[55] At this place Evroul had had no need of relics,
or patrons, or even buildings. At this place the angelic revelation was
enough, more than enough, for the saint, and it was enough for his successor Ascelin as well.

Ascelin also attempted to interpret the recent sack for his flock. "On
account of our sins and those of our fathers, divine chastisement has descended upon us, and forcing its way into us and our innermost regions
it has fiercely crushed us and cast us down irrecoverably." For God in his
ineffable justice "has rightly humiliated this sanctuary, and through the
hands of Hugh and the Franks He has punished this place by crushing it
in many ways, especially in that which is above all other sorrows, namely
that He robbed us of the bones of the holy father Evroul and of other
relics of the saints."[56] The loss of relics as punishment for a community's sins was typical of accounts of *furta sacra*, holy theft. But Ascelin's

justification—as composed by Orderic—was unusual in that he unambiguously singled out "this place," *hunc locum*, as well as its residents as deserving punishment: not the community, but the place.[57] The relics' loss was inscribed in that particular place in the Ouche, and while the affected people would move away and eventually die, the spot marked by the church of St. Peter would remain to suffer the humiliation dealt out to it by God. Ascelin's choice to remain at the site of St. Evroul's foundation and his continued belief in its holiness bore out his determination to redeem the place's sins, to remain dedicated to the location of his surrender to God's plan for humanity in the same way that God remained dedicated to the redemption of humankind in the created world no matter what chaos or sin might befall it.[58] And the eleventh- and twelfth-century monastery of Ouche, built at the same site, took up this redemptive quest where Ascelin had left off. There was no uninterrupted religious life in that place, no continuous monastic genealogy, to link Orderic's community with the previous foundation and its trauma, or even to link it with St. Evroul. It was the place, and the place alone, that brought the Benedictine abbey of Ouche its patron, and that caused it to inherit the tragedy and the suffering of the relics' loss. But it was also the place that brought the new abbey its holiness, its history, and its links with the fullness of Christendom.

About thirty men accompanied St. Evroul's relics into France, and although the soldiers viewed their new clerical company with some suspicion they left the unwilling pilgrims strictly alone until one of Hugh's jesters (*mimus, ioculator*), having heard of Herluin and Raoul's treasure, joked that the men had been fooled into stealing the bones of peasants, not saints.[59] That night the jester was struck by lightning, the only miracle in the entire narrative and attributed by Orderic to the wrath of God, not the power of the saints. Overall Evroul and his saintly companions were curiously passive throughout their travels; there is no suggestion that the saints wished to be moved, the typical topos of *furta sacra*, or that they cared at all about where their relics ended up.[60] Aside from God's lone lightning bolt, the translation was a human affair, which in the end brought the saint out of his obscure home in the Ouche and into the very human and yet very sacred network of the cult of relics that webbed the Christian world. Greater fame was always one reason that a saint might allow his relics to be stolen, and it was a particularly palatable explanation for a community like Orderic's Ouche, struggling to find meaning in a great loss.[61] The return of some of the relics to their original home allowed Orderic to provide them with an uninterrupted and authenticating chain of custody that more or less replotted the whole sequence as a very protracted *delatio*, those familiar peregrinations in which miracle-working relics were paraded through the countryside to demonstrate the saint's power and increase his renown (and also, of course, to raise money).[62]

And the relics' long *delatio* was successful. The smattering of churches dedicated to Evroul that clustered in the center of the diocese of Chartres may have commemorated the route taken by the relics and their companions on their journey through France, spreading the saint's fame over a larger area. And when the travelers reached Orléans, Orderic explained, the relics were divided.[63] St. Evremond remained in Orléans. So, for a time, did the larger part of St. Evroul's relics, including his head (although if, as Orderic claimed, a church in that city bore the saint's name, no trace of it remains). Evroul's relics were soon translated again, however, to Saint-Mainbœuf in Angers, at the request, according to Orderic, of the Angevin count Geoffrey Greymantle.[64] Raoul of Drachy took the bones of St. Ansbert and the lesser half of St. Evroul's relics to Rebais. The saint remained there in Brie until Ouche's Abbot Warin des Essarts negotiated the return of part of the relics in 1130. This visit created a bond of friendship and prayer between the two communities, one commemorated in Ouche's *liber memorialis* and in the shared body of a saint.[65] And St. Evroul was brought from his isolated tomb into the larger world of Christendom, fixing that place of holiness in the forest of Ouche within the web of saints' cults that had, from the earliest centuries, shaped the geography of the Christian world.[66]

This greater fame was, however, little consolation for the monks who remained behind. The fragmentation and diffusion of St. Evroul's relics was catastrophic for the community in the Ouche, which did not long survive the loss of thirty men and its patron. All that was left of St. Evroul's body at that place was "the dust of the most holy flesh" in the bottom of the tomb, which Ascelin painstakingly swept up and concealed along with a few other small relics in the wall of the church "until," he prophesied, "through the revelation of God they are shown to future worshipers."[67] They never were. The abbey "reverted to loneliness, and far from men huge trees grew up in the oratories and houses, and for a long time it was home to wild animals."[68] But for Orderic the holiness of the abbey did not rest fixedly in bones, nor in hidden if potent dust. Like Ascelin, whose speeches he wrote, Orderic held to the sure knowledge that St. Evroul had never departed from the place in the Ouche where, with the guidance of the angel, he had chosen to serve God.

Some years after the theft of the relics and the community's subsequent collapse, Orderic reported, "a certain priest named Restold from the province of Beauvais was told in a vision 'Go to St. Evroul in Normandy'"— to the saint himself, as if he were alive— "'and there you will enjoy many days and a happy life full of delight.'"[69] Restold was sidetracked for a time at the old church of St. Evroul in Montfort-sur-Risle, where the saint had lived before moving deeper into the Neustrian *heremus,* but a second vision led him to the forest of Ouche and therein to the deserted "dwelling of St. Evroul," *habitationem sancti Ebrulfi,* where he settled and where eventually the church of St. Peter was rebuilt and fell into the hands of Giroie and his descendants.[70] Once again, a revelation brought spiritual life back to this very place in the Ouche, and opened up something, some importance, some holiness, that had been concealed from the eyes of men. Ouche was still believed to be the home of the saint, the place where he lived on, and Orderic made use of Evroul's persistent presence, and the revelation of this presence to Restold, to establish the spiritual continuity and the uninterrupted history of his monastery's place.[71] Evroul's *vita,* his life, over time came to commingle the saint's past lifetime on earth with an experienced and inscribed memory of him at that place in the forest of Ouche.[72] This life of the saint remained present in the Ouche in the same way that the landscape of the Egyptian hermits continued to be real in Orderic's experience of his own abbey's topography.

The power of these past events and past lives could even when forgotten rest hidden in the Christian landscape like the dust of St. Evroul's body and so many other relics that tarried until the proper time for them to be revealed again to the world.[73] St. Evroul's *vita* emerged repeatedly in Orderic's account of Ouche's history, and these versions of the saint's life stepped into the role of his lost relics and continued to draw people, like Restold, to that chosen place. When Robert of Grandmesnil and his brother Hugh came to see their uncle's recommended plot, "a book of the *vita* of the holy father Evroul was given to Robert," who as a child had been more interested in words than war and would later give up his knightly life to become both monk and abbot at Ouche. "He read it very carefully, and thoughtfully explained it to Hugh and his other companions. What more is there to say? The place in the Ouche pleased both brothers."[74] Of course it pleased them, because the site was hallowed not simply by a handful of holy dust hidden in a crumbling wall but, the monks believed, by an accessible and sacred past infused into the place by the life of Evroul himself.[75] Of the twenty-five abbeys founded by the Norman nobles in the great monastic boom of the eleventh century, the monastery of Ouche was one of only five to be associated with a local saint and one of only two to be bound in place and not merely in name with its patron.[76] Orderic Vitalis and his fellow monks had a unique rapport with their father Evroul, one grounded in the place of his life through both human history and divine revelation, diffused into Christendom by his relics' peregrinations, and preserved by Orderic for the benefit of the community at that place.

"NOT LONG AGO I BEGAN WRITING ON THE SUBJECT OF THE CHURCH IN the Ouche," Orderic wrote as he wrapped up the eighth book of his *Historia Ecclesiastica*.[77] It was 1136, and "not long ago," *nuper,* was actually some two decades past.[78] Orderic had celebrated his sixtieth birthday the year before, had passed more than fifty years in the cloister, and the scriptorium in which he wrote his *Historia Ecclesiastica* could be cold and unkind to aging fingers. In the half-century since he had crossed the Channel from his childhood home in England to begin a new life in a Norman world, he had only occasionally ventured from his monastery. Not one of these journeys—though they took him as far north as Thorney in England and as far south as France's Cluny—allowed him to move outside his familiar ecclesiastical milieu. "But," Orderic revealed in an uncommonly candid aside, "I have looked out upon the wide kingdoms of the Earth as if I were caught up in ecstasy, flying far and wide through words," or, even, through prayer, *oratione*, "and traversing many of them I have plowed through very long digressions. Now, however, I will return exhausted to my black-clad life—that is, Ouche—and I will unravel in a plain way some things concerning our own affairs at the end of this book."[79] Ecstasy, *exstasis*—later in the *Historia* the word describes a monk enraptured by a vision of Christ enthroned.[80] The normally down-to-earth Orderic, for one small moment, allowed himself to reveal the flights of imagination, of ecstasy, that provided him a vision of his known world throughout the ages.[81] It was a vision not unlike that experienced by St. Benedict of Nursia, the founder of Orderic's monastic order, for whom one wakeful and prayerful night "the whole world, as if gathered together under a single ray of light, was brought before his eyes."[82]

It is this geographical and historical transcendence that, in Orderic's *Historia Ecclesiastica*, kept the conventional monastic desert imagery and Evroul's stereotypical hagiography from becoming mere tropes of monastic historiography that ultimately severed the rhetorical image of the monastic landscape from the reality of the physical terrain. Orderic Vitalis wrote in a world in which the local could possess an intrinsic identity with the universal and in an imaginative landscape in which space could stretch and fold and blend to make a forest in Normandy into a desert in Egypt and a cloister into a cosmos.[83] This spatial manipulation involved not just the monastic life but the whole of human history, and its importance for Orderic's geography cannot be overstated. Orderic time and again, both painstakingly and just in passing, drew on the traditional techniques of typology to find significance in the events of his own age by locating them within the broad landscape of the past. In Orderic's case, however, this typology did not suggest that the more recent event in this bipartite relationship was more significant, more real, than the other—both Evroul's founding of the original community in the Ouche and the parallel refoundation at the same site were equally significant to Orderic as elements of God's plan for that place.[84]

Returning exhausted and exhilarated to his life as a Black Monk, Orderic would go on to build up Christendom in his *Historia Ecclesiastica* on the historiographic foundation provided by his study of his own monastery's past. Although declaring himself "unable to explore

Alexandrian or Greek or Roman affairs or other things deserving to be told, because as a cloistered cenobite I am confined by my own vow to bear inviolably the monastic observance," through the writing of history Orderic entered a world where geography was defined not by latitude and longitude, not by maps and compasses, not by foreign travel, but by places where things happened.[85] The stability of the Earth's terrain, at this intensely local scale, thus allowed for the medieval experience of a historicity that simultaneously recognized the distance of the past and the transience of humanity's generations while still preserving a pale shadow of the atemporality of human existence in the mind of God. Moving neatly between past and present, local and universal, Orderic found in the terrain of God's creation the places of human history in order to map and memorialize his epoch's Christendom for the benefit of an anticipated though uncertain future. The eleventh and twelfth centuries were a time of increasing preoccupation with humanity's relationship with the physical world. The *Historia Ecclesiastica* of Orderic Vitalis offers an unparalleled contemporary portrait, sweeping yet particularized, of the ways in which people negotiated the geography and materiality of their landscape and lives, with consequences that went far beyond historical writing.

# CHAPTER 2

# Classical Geography
# and the *Gens Normannorum*

Orderic Vitalis was well versed in the writings of the historians who came before him. The library at Ouche possessed the works of "Isidore, Eusebius, and Orosius," Orderic said, whose compositions "beneficially encouraged the young men pursuing similar studies."[1] Orderic himself studied the *Historia Langobardorum* of Paul the Deacon, helped to copy the *Liber Pontificalis*, and referenced Gildas's *De excidio et conquestu Britanniae* (though he believed the *Historia Brittonum*, generally attributed to "Nennius," to be Gildas's as well).[2] In the general prologue of his *Historia Ecclesiastica* Orderic also praised "Dares Phrygius and Pompeius Trogus and other learned historians of the gentiles."[3] The twelfth-century catalog of Ouche's library listed Josephus's *De bello Judaico* and Augustine's *De civitate Dei*, and on a visit to the library at Bec, Orderic might have seen works by Hegesippus, Eutropius, and Gregory of Tours, as well as the compilation of church histories made by Cassiodorus known as the *Historia Tripartita*.[4] Among more recent authors, Orderic was familiar with the Norman historians Dudo of Saint-Quentin, William of Jumièges, and William of Poitiers; the French writers Guy of Amiens, Fulcher of Chartres, and Baudry of Bourgueil; the English chroniclers John of Worcester and Geoffrey of Monmouth; and also Geoffrey Malaterra, who wrote in Norman Sicily.[5] And he lovingly copied Bede's *Historia Ecclesiastica gentis Anglorum* in his own hand.[6] "I consider their accounts with pleasure," Orderic remarked of these authors, "I praise and admire the elegance and usefulness of their books, and I encourage the wise men of our time to follow their remarkable learning."[7] Orderic used these works, classical and contemporary, to shape the vision of history—as a discipline and as a literary genre—set forth in his *Historia Ecclesiastica*. Some of the histories he encountered he excerpted outright, such as the *Liber Pontificalis*, William of Poitiers's *Gesta Guillelmi*, and Baudry of Bourgueil's *Historia Ierosolimitana*. Many others held a more subtle sway in his thought.

But for all his study and imitation of the classics of Christian historiography, Orderic rejected one of the tradition's most common features: the geographical introduction. Early and high medieval historians often began their works by describing the physical space in which the action of their narratives took place.[8] The widely read *Historiarum adversus paganos libri septem* of Paulus Orosius, a student and contemporary of Augustine of Hippo, introduced this topographical trend into Christian historiography, and this model was followed in many of Christendom's historical classics, including Jordanes's *Getica*, Paul the Deacon's *Historia Langobardorum*, Gildas's *De excidio et conquestu Britanniae*, Bede's *Historia Ecclesiastica gentis Anglorum*, and Dudo of Saint-Quentin's *De moribus et actis primorum Normanniae ducum*.[9] And the geographical introduction did not go out of fashion. Geoffrey of Monmouth, Henry of Huntingdon, Gerald of Wales, Otto of Freising, Robert of Torigni, and later Saxo Grammaticus all commenced their histories with a description of the world of the text.[10] These geographical introductions varied widely in length and scope. Some, such as that of Orosius, encompassed the entire *oikoumene*, the known and inhabited world, and went on for pages. Others, like Bede's, limited themselves to a single area but in some detail. And still others, like Otto of Freising's, were very sketchy and derivative indeed.

Orderic admired the work of Orosius, and he idolized that of Bede, but for all his interest in the geography of his world he chose not to imitate their style. The question, of course, is why not? While the omission of a geographical introduction was not necessarily a radical departure from the rules of medieval historiography (William of Malmesbury, the only contemporary chronicler whose historical vision might be considered a match to Orderic's, also dispensed with one), it is nevertheless true that Orderic could easily have included a geographical passage at the beginning of the *Historia* when he reconceived his historical project in the mid-1130s, relying perhaps on Orosius's history as he relied on (or, rather, copied) other traditional texts in the composition of his new books I and II.[11] The omission of a geographical introduction was clearly a conscious choice; it was replaced by a unique *vita Christi* that introduced the Christian world through its savior rather than its landscape.[12]

Orderic, unfortunately, did not justify his decision to forgo this traditional element of the genre in which he wrote, but the historical and spatial currents of his account of "the deeds and events of the Normans for the Normans," as he once characterized it, can demonstrate why no description of the *oikoumene* introduces the *Historia Ecclesiastica*.[13] From the very beginning Orderic's attitude toward the space of the physical world, the space defined and described by other historians' geographical introductions, might best be summed up by his simple assertion that "the state of the world is driven by change."[14] Throughout the *Historia Ecclesiastica*, from his account of the history of Ouche to his discussion of Christendom as a whole, and especially in his history of the Normans as a people, Orderic emphasized the importance of change in the conception and description of human history. And change was something that the geographical outlines of Orosius and even Bede could never fully take into account.

The geography that inaugurated the classic Christian histories was explicitly intended to lay out a static stage upon which human affairs took place.[15] From Orosius in the fifth century to Otto of Freising in the twelfth, geographical introductions depicted the physical world as a changeless arena for humanity, unvarying from the time of Adam to the writer's present. Orosius declared that his history commenced with "the beginning of humanity's wretchedness from the beginning of humanity's sin" in Eden.[16] The account of this continuing historical wretchedness was to be prefaced, however, by a rhetorically tedious tour of "the *oikoumene* itself that humankind inhabits as it has been portioned out into three parts by our ancestors, and then bounded into regions and provinces; so that when the locations of wars and the scourge of diseases are mentioned, anyone interested may gain knowledge not only of the events and the times but also of the places."[17] Orosius then went on to describe the rise and fall of the various empires of world history: the empires came and went, but the geography remained the same. Centuries later Otto of Freising, who followed Orosius's model in beginning his history with Adam, also shared Orosius's understanding of the geographical introduction as an unchanging foundation. "In order to pursue the series of things done from Adam, the first man, all the way up to our own time," Otto began his work, "let us first set out the world itself that humankind inhabits, according to the traditions that we have received from our predecessors."[18] Otto then went on to recapitulate Orosius's discussion of the divisions of the world before telling his reader to "read Orosius" if he wished to know more; the world as described in the fifth century was, to Otto, a perfectly suitable reference for readers and writers in the twelfth.[19]

This tension between geographical stasis and historical change in the universal histories of the Christian tradition, exemplified by Orosius's and Otto's writings, also marks the more national histories of Jordanes, Paul the Deacon, and Bede. The topography described at the beginning of these writers' histories served to frame the movements of various *gentes*, peoples, from one place to another.[20] Jordanes toured the entire *oikoumene* to set the stage for the Goths of his *Getica* to move from the island of Scandza—the classical version of Scandinavia—to Scythia, where they impinged upon civilization and ultimately penetrated the Roman Empire.[21] Paul the Deacon was similarly searching for the origins of the Lombards and their path to Italy. "The region of the North," Paul noted, was "fit for the propagation of peoples," and so "from it have often come *gentes* that have indeed shattered parts of Asia, but even more so the parts of Europe that border upon" this northern clime, including "miserable Italy," which seemed to attract the attention of many of the barbaric tribes from the North, including the Lombards of Paul's history who "came from the island that is called Scandinavia" and ultimately settled in Italy.[22] For both Jordanes and Paul, the static geography of the world helped them to detail the linear migration of peoples from place to place, from the periphery to the center of the *oikoumene*. The Gothic migration began in the second century, and the Lombards moved across Europe in the sixth, but they both came from the same place (Scandza), and they both went to the same place (Italy), navigating through an

unchanging classical vision of the world that neither tribe knew anything about.

Bede also set forth a geography illustrating the migration of peoples,
though he turned the center-periphery *topos* of Jordanes and Paul on its
head. Bede viewed Britain, set like Scandza in the outer Ocean at the edge
of the *oikoumene*, as a destination for rather than an origin of a migrating people—the Anglo-Saxons—and he drew his home island and those
surrounding it to the center of his geographical vision by omitting the
around-the-world tour of Orosius and Jordanes.[23] Bede, in his geography as in so many other things, brought a new and more complex vision
to the writing of history. With his decentering of the classical geographical tradition the Northumbrian historian initiated a transformation of
the relationship between center and periphery, and between geography and history, that Orderic would later adopt and develop further in
his *Historia Ecclesiastica*. For Orderic, like Bede and Paul and Jordanes,
needed to recount the historical movement of a *gens*—namely, the Normans, one of the most recent *gentes* to come on the European scene. But
Orderic realized that, unlike his antecedents, he was not describing a
movement that was complete and in the past, nor one that left the contours of the world, its centers and its peripheries, untouched. It was Orderic's desire to write a history of the Normans for the Normans—a
people who, according to their own stories and myths, had never stopped
migrating, from Troy to Denmark to Normandy, to Sicily and England
and the Holy Land—that showed that the static geographies of classical
Christian historiography would need to be overturned in order to account for the realities of historical and spatial change.

While Orderic could, and did, employ the idea of a spatial "blank
slate" when it suited him, the geographical traditions that he inherited
from earlier writers were only one element in a far more fluid geography, which had multiple centers and multiple scales, and which changed
in conjunction with the changeable nature of humanity.[24] In other, more
modern words, by rejecting the geographical introduction as a historiographical tool, Orderic rejected the notion that geography was a function
of the *longue durée*.[25] Orderic's construction of a geography of change,
one that overturned the notion that landscape structured the social life of
the people who lived in its allegedly changeless contours, appears most

clearly in his history of the Normans, whose constantly changing spatial identity disrupted traditional ideas of geographical space. And it is in the history and myths of these wandering and changing Normans, rather than in some introduction meant to permanently set the stage, that the development and details of Orderic's understanding of geography as a component of written history will be found.

THE NORMANS, ORDERIC REMARKED, "ARE CAPRICIOUS AND EAGER TO see foreign lands."[26] This was not a description of some individual Normans who had a penchant for exotic vacations, but an account of the fundamental nature of the *gens* as a whole as it expanded its domains. The Normans were, the Sicilian chronicler Geoffrey Malaterra agreed, known for "disdaining the fields of their homeland in the hope of something more profitable," and, the Italian writer Amatus of Montecassino added, "they scattered here and there through different parts of the world" though, "they did not follow the customs of many who go through the world placing themselves in the service of others; rather, like the ancient warriors, they desired to have all people under their rule and dominion."[27] No people in medieval Christendom grew to prominence more rapidly than the Normans, and none has sparked more questioning of their communal identity over time and space.[28] Intractability and martial skill were commonly attributed to the Normans by medieval (and modern) writers, but it is not surprising that Orderic, Geoffrey, and Amatus added wanderlust to this list of Norman traits.[29] For the Norman myth, the body of historical and cultural beliefs that structured the Normans' identity as a people, was predicated on the idea that the Normans were always moving, always wandering, always looking for new opportunities to expand their geographic reach—and, in the process, always changing, to such an extent that by the thirteenth century it had become increasingly difficult to define a Norman at all.

Dudo of Saint-Quentin's popular *De moribus et actis primorum Normanniae ducum* contained the seeds of the group's communal identity as a restless *gens*, though written long before the Normans achieved their widest dispersion. The people who would become the Normans, Dudo claimed, once lived on the "island" of Scandza—like the Goths of Jordanes, Dudo's source for his geographical introduction. Like the Goths, Dudo's "barbarians" left Scandza and crossed to Europe, where they settled "in the fertile gap between the Danube and the Scythian Sea" in a region called Dacia.[30] This was not, however, the first time that this *gens* had migrated from place to place. For, as the chronicler William of Jumièges noted—in a section of his work that summarized and clarified Dudo's rather convoluted narrative—the Normans "boast that the Trojans come from their stock, and that Antenor, having gone forth after the fall of the city of Troy (on account of his betrayal of it) with two thousand soldiers and five hundred men, landed in Germany after many digressions by sea." These wandering Trojan exiles eventually ended up "in Dacia, which was called Denmark after a certain Danaus, a king of their stock."[31] But Denmark did not have enough land to satisfy the restless inhabitants, and so, returning to Dudo's account, "according to a very ancient rite, a multitude of young men is gathered by lot and they are thrust out into the kingdoms of foreign nations, in order to acquire through battle a realm for themselves."[32] The first of these exiled Danes to be named by Dudo was Hasting, a mythical figure who along with the various "vagabond nations" that he had gathered into his band laid waste to Francia before deciding to take his chances at "the head of the world," the city of Rome itself.[33] These Vikings ended up in the city of Luna instead, taking it by trickery before they noticed their mistake. They then returned home in disgust after realizing that they had not conquered the city founded by those other, more famous, Trojan exiles.

Hasting, however, was only a prelude.[34] The real story for the Normans began with Dudo's tale of Rollo, another exile from the overpopulated Danish kingdom who sailed off to seek his fortune.[35] He first fought his way to England (which, in Dudo's early history, did not yet prefigure the later Norman conquest of the island), and it was there that the Danish exile dreamed a famous dream.[36] In sleep Rollo saw himself atop a Frankish mountain, where a spring flowed from the earth. He washed in the water, and found himself (like Constantine in legend) cured of the leprosy that had afflicted him for some time.[37] Cleansed of his illness, he looked down from his peak and saw "around the base of it, here in front of him and on the other side, many thousands of birds of different kinds, of various colors, but having red left wings." These countless birds, despite their difference, lived and ate together "without distinction as to genera and species, without any squabbling or contention at all," building their homes together and obeying Rollo's every command.[38] Just in case his readers did not realize the vision's significance, Dudo provided a Christian captive, a new Joseph, to interpret. The hill, of course, was the Church in Francia, and the spring the waters of baptism. The different birds with their matching crimson wings were "men of different provinces with shields on their arms" who would be "joined together in a countless multitude." The captive summed up Rollo's future: "The birds of different species will submit to you; men of different kingdoms will obey you, prostrating themselves in service to you."[39] Rollo's delight at the dream did not keep him from ravaging Francia when he arrived there, but, unlike Hasting, he stayed. As Dudo told the story, the French king Charles the Simple realized that he could not protect his lands, and so in the year 911 he approached the Viking raiders and made them an offer: he would grant Rollo and his men the coastal lands of Neustria, and give his daughter Gisla to Rollo in marriage, in exchange for peace and protection.[40] Rollo, remembering his dream, agreed. He and his men settled in Francia, converted to Christianity, and gathered up his flock of birds, Danes and Franks and Bretons among them, into a community that would in time become the *gens Normannorum.*

This was the story, the origin myth, that Oderic inherited about the Norman past, and it underlay his elaboration of Norman geography as the Normans settled into their new land and subsequently spread out from there. "It is said that the Trojans, in their origins, come from the fierce *gens* of the Scythians," Oderic began his own account of the Normans' wandering ways.[41] This odd association of the Trojans with the Scythians may have simply been a misreading of William of Jumièges's account, but even so it had the result of associating the Trojans, and through them the Normans, with one of the most fierce regions of classical geography—Scythia, which, according to Bede, also gave rise to the fierce Picts.[42] Oderic went on to say that following the destruction of Troy "Antenor the Phrygian entered the territory of Illyria, and with his fellow exiles he searched for a long time and a long distance for a place to live. Finally he settled on the shore of the Ocean sea in the north, and he dwelled in that maritime region with his companions and kinsmen, and from his son Danus this *gens* of Trojan origins took the name Danes."[43] Orderic, ignoring most of the Gothic elements of his sources, produced a pleasant simplification of the Norman origin myth that nevertheless maintained the elements essential to contemporary Norman identity: the distant Trojan origins that placed the Normans on equal historical footing with the other illustrious peoples who claimed Trojan descent, the Franks and the Romans; the more recent Danish past, which served to distinguish the Normans from their French neighbors with whom they shared a land, a faith, and a language; and the image of exile and maritime wandering that would continue to define the Normans as they moved from place to place.[44] "The most ferocious Duke Rollo," Orderic went on to remind his readers, "came from this *gens* with the Normans; he first subjected to himself Neustria, which now bears the name Normandy from the Normans."[45]

This transition from Neustria to Normandy was the first true spatial conversion of the Norman world, and it set in motion Orderic's reinterpretation of the classical geography that Dudo of Saint-Quentin and William of Jumièges, Orderic's sources for the Norman origin myth, had struggled so hard to maintain in their geographical introductions. Named and defined regions stood at the heart of the Orosian view of the world inherited by medieval historiography. Orosius traced out the contours of the world region by region, naming each and defining it by the neighboring regions that made up its borders. "Gallia Lugdunensis," for instance, the ancient province of Gaul that contained the new Norman lands, "partially surrounds the province of Aquitania. It has Belgica on the east and part of the province of Narbo on the south, where the city of Arles is located and the Rhone river is taken into the Gallic Sea."[46] The Normans, with their arrival, disrupted this easily named and delineated classical view of regional geography. In the past this region along Europe's northern edge had been Neustria, but following the settlement of a new people it became Normandy, changing its name and its identity, as well as its contours, for although Normandy overlapped with the Carolingian region of Neustria, the two were not identical.[47] The bursting of the Normans into the classical view of the world can be seen clearly in the tenth-century history of Richer of Reims, who in his attempt to maintain Julius Caesar's vision of a tripartite Gaul described the Norman "pirates who inhabit the province of Rouen, which is part of Gallia Celtica." These Normans, Richer goes on to explain with increasing geographical difficulty, "have attacked furiously nearly the entire part of Gallia Celtica which lies between the Seine and Loire rivers and which is called Neustria."[48]

For Richer, Gallia Celtica, Neustria, and an embryonic Normandy all existed simultaneously in a timeless geography grounded in the classical tradition. But this was not the case for Orderic. The historical transition from Neustria to Normandy, the idea that the geographical space in which he lived and wrote had changed, stood at the heart of Orderic's historical vision from the very inception of his work, and it was a notion that would provide both spatial and temporal expansiveness to his history. At the start of his *Historia Ecclesiastica,* in what are apparently the very first sentences he wrote, Orderic defined his historical mission as the description "of the vineyard of the Lord of Hosts, which over all the world He cultivates and protects with His strong right hand against the evil Behemoth. For truly," Orderic went on, "the tillers having labored here in the region that was once Neustria but is now called Normandy, the vineyard puts up its shoots here and there, and it offers to God a multitude of fruitful men persisting in holiness."[49] At this early point in the *Historia,* the transition from Neustria to Normandy, and the identification between the two regions, helped Orderic to link his abbey's past and its present. The monastery's place might remain constant, remain a site of localized memory for its inhabitants, but this stable place of holiness was set in an ever-changing space of shifting geographical meaning. Neustria was the land of St. Evroul, of the angelic revelation of the place in the Ouche, of the original monastic foundation at the site on the Charentonne. Normandy was the world of the abbey of Ouche, of its founders and their donations, of the monks for whom Orderic wrote his *Historia.* It was the same place, and yet not the same.

Orderic, of course, realized that this geographical rechristening was by no means unique to the Norman experience. Regions changed their names all the time. Neustria was no more a part of Orosius's geography than was Normandy; the region that the Normans called home was named Gallia Lugdunensis in late Roman times, and before that Caesar had famously named it Gallia Celtica.[50] From Bede, furthermore, Orderic knew that "Britain, which was once called Albion, is an island in the Ocean," an island that had become Anglia by the time the Normans came.[51] But Neustria's transition to Normandy was not quite the same as Albion's becoming Britain and Anglia. Bede's northern isle took its label from the *gens* that formed its dominant group.[52] The classical Albion became Britain, Bede wrote, when the Britons "from whom it receives it name" arrived from Armorica.[53] And when those Britons were overcome by the invading Angles the island was transformed into Anglia (in Latin at least, but the vernacular was no different; the land of the *Englisc* was *Engla Lond*).[54]

For the Normans and Normandy, however, the equation between a *gens* and its homeland was somewhat more complicated. As Orderic noted, the land in which he lived indeed took "the name Normandy from the Normans," whose designation derived, as many chroniclers noted, from the words in the Vikings' own language meaning "men of the North"—Northmen, or Normans (an etymology that needed more explanation in Latin than it does in modern English).[55] But while the land took its name from the men from the North who received it from Charles the Bald, very few residents of Normandy were Northmen in any real sense. Only a very small minority of the Norman population was descended from the Scandinavian invaders and the settlers who followed them—and, indeed, even these settlers only truly became "Northmen" after moving south and placing some spatial distance between their origins and new home.[56] As Dudo's account of Rollo's dream made so very clear, the Norman population was notoriously heterogeneous, mixing some men from the North with many more Franks and Bretons. Over time this varied population coalesced into a single group, a group called the *gens Normannorum*.[57] And these Normans were defined not by their common descent from an ethnic group recognized from time out of mind, but by the fact that they lived together in a region called Normandy.[58] The Normans as a people gave their name to their homeland while at the same time this land provided an identity to its inhabitants, a reciprocity that set the Normans and Normandy apart from the Britons in Britain or the Franks in Francia. The transition from Neustria to Normandy was not, therefore, simply a change of name. It gave birth to a new people, one defined by a historical association with a particular place, the duchy of Normandy. For Orderic, Normandy would remain the *patria* of the Normans no matter how far they wandered from the homeland of their heterogenous *gens*.[59] And wander they did, not now as Trojans or Vikings or Danes, but transformed by the land in which they lived into the notorious *gens Normannorum*.

IT WAS ONLY ABOUT A HUNDRED YEARS AFTER THE NORMANS TOOK over, defined, and were defined by their *patria* that expatriates from Normandy—few in number, but identifiably and proudly Norman—began to make their mark elsewhere in Europe, a new migration that would ultimately result in a Norman world of unparalleled spatial fragmentation. Exporting their reputation as fierce and determined fighters, the Normans were much in demand as mercenaries, especially against the Muslims in Spain but also in Italy's internecine wars. Italy had developed a reputation as a land where ambitious young men could fight their way to fame, and it was there that Normandy's wandering knights would leave a permanent legacy.

Beginning around the year 1000 some of the duchy's young nobles left Normandy and, in the tradition of Hasting and Rollo, went off to Italy to seek their fortune.[60] The most notable of these early Norman mercenaries were the sons of Tancred of Hauteville, a petty Norman noble with a dozen boys and a tiny patrimony in the Cotentin. William Iron Arm, Drogo, and Humphrey, Tancred's three eldest sons, all distinguished themselves in the south, but their younger half-brothers Robert Guiscard and Roger would have the more lasting impact on Italian affairs. It was Robert—whose cognomen, Giscard, "the Cunning," was well-earned—who first transformed the Norman practice of receiving land in exchange for mercenary service into a systematic attempt to establish rule over the Lombard regions of Apulia and Calabria in southern Italy. In 1053 Pope Leo IX and his allies finally realized that the Normans had no intention of returning home; they tried to eject the Hautevilles and their men, but by then it was already too late. Though drastically outnumbered, the Normans lived up to their reputation as fierce fighters at the Battle of Civitate on 17 June 1053, decisively defeating their opponents and establishing themselves permanently in their new Italian domains.[61] Six years later the new reforming pope Nicholas II, who needed all the support he could get in the face of a recent schism, called a council at Melfi where in August 1059 Robert Guiscard swore fealty to the pope as the recognized duke of Apulia, Calabria, and Sicily.[62]

Being duke in name was one thing, duke in fact another, and it took Robert Guiscard some time to make his title a reality. Like the Scandinavians in early Normandy, the Normans were thin on the ground in Norman-ruled Italy. Most of the land ruled by Robert and his vassals was inhabited by an amalgamation of Lombards, Greeks, and Muslims, a polyglot population that would in time come to characterize the uniquely cosmopolitan culture of the Norman lands.[63] Robert's marriage to the formidable Lombard princess Sichelgaita, the sister of Prince Gisulf II of Salerno, brought him important ties with the local nobility and helped to shore up his rule in the region, but it was the conquest of Sicily that would firmly establish Robert and his brother Roger as the Rollos, so to speak, of the Normans' southern kingdom. When Robert swore fealty to Pope Nicholas for the island in 1059, Sicily was still in Muslim hands, as it had been for two hundred years. By 1091, however, Robert and Roger had completed their conquest of this isle of ancient fame, and Roger's tireless campaigning earned him the title of count of Sicily.[64] It was not, however, until 1130 and the coronation of Roger II of Sicily by the antipope Anacletus II (the Normans were adept at manipulating papal politics) that the Norman kingdom of Sicily—which ultimately included Calabria and Apulia on the Italian mainland, too—was born.[65]

The Normans in eleventh- and early twelfth-century Italy and Sicily did not allow the lack of a royal title to stop them from working to expand their power. Robert Guiscard had, in fact, not royal but imperial ambitions that looked east toward the weakened Byzantine Empire. Robert and his troops briefly succeeded in taking the important Greek port of Durazzo in 1082–83, and the first duke of Apulia, Calabria, and Sicily ultimately fell ill and died on campaign against Byzantium on 17 July 1085.[66] Roger Borsa, Robert's younger son by his Lombard wife Sichelgaita, inherited his Italian lands—his mixed ancestry made him well suited to govern Italy's mixed populace—but that did not prevent Mark

Bohemond, Robert's eldest son by his repudiated Norman wife Alberada, from having ambitions of his own.[67] Bohemond made a name for himself during the First Crusade.[68] His ancestral cunning won him the city of Antioch, where he and his men, many of them Normans from Italy, established a crusader principality before Bohemond returned home and, like his father before him, set his sights on the Byzantine throne.[69] His so-called "crusade" against the empire was unsuccessful, but the Norman Bohemond nevertheless became, like his father Robert and his uncle Roger, a significant figure in the expanding Norman myth.

In this he was, of course, joined by Normandy's Duke William II, known in his youth as William the Bastard but immortalized as William the Conqueror.[70] A great-great-great grandchild of the Viking leader Rollo, the natural son of Duke Robert I the Magnificent of Normandy and his concubine Herleve, William became duke of Normandy upon the death of his father in 1035 when he was only seven or eight years old. William's minority was not an easy time for the duchy, and the tribulations of his youth were certainly a factor in the Norman migration to southern Italy, where life as a mercenary may have seemed easier than facing the tumultuous political situation back home.[71] But despite (or even, perhaps, because of) these troubles, Duke William was by the mid-1060s the most formidable duke that Normandy had ever seen, and he was looking to translate that rule beyond the bounds of his ancestral *patria*. The result of this ambition is one of the most well-known episodes in all of medieval history. The Norman Conquest of England in 1066 — the mass crossing of the English Channel; the decisive single battle at Hastings on 14 October; the rapid suppression of the remaining English opposition; the Yuletime coronation of William as King of England — continues to have widespread fame.[72] The Norman Conquest did not come out of nowhere. While events leading up to the invasion remain (and probably will always remain) obscure, the Normans sincerely believed that Duke William had been named heir to the English throne by his cousin King Edward the Confessor, and that Harold Godwinson, who had been crowned king upon Edward's death, was a usurper and a perjurer. And so, as Halley's comet raced across the heavens and portended, according to the chroniclers, the transfer of a throne, Duke William gathered together a multinational force of Normans and French, Bretons and Flemings, along with their horses and supplies, and crossed the English Channel to claim what he felt to be rightly his.[73]

William's rapid subjugation of England bore little resemblance to the "other Norman conquest" that, after decades of slow progression, was finally coming to fruition in Italy's south.[74] For the most part the Normans who traveled to Italy had no intention of returning to the lands that they left behind. Many of these exiles kept in touch with their families back in Normandy, but generally speaking the Italian Normans threw themselves into their lives, properties, and quarrels in the south, "forgetting Normandy," as Orderic said of one of those settlers.[75] The conquest of England, on the other hand, was undertaken by those who still maintained close and frequent contact with their families and possessions on the continent. One of the main themes of Orderic's *Historia*—and the author reminds his readers more than once that he was *Angligena*, English-born, despite living in Normandy for decades—was the difficulties the Norman nobles faced in balancing their cross-channel lives, especially during the periods when Normandy and England were in different hands. For while modern historians are accustomed to talk of an Anglo-Norman community, and even an Anglo-Norman *regnum*, the political unity between England and Normandy ebbed and flowed in the eleventh and early twelfth centuries. William's death divided the two lands again in 1085: Robert Curthose, the eldest son, received Normandy, while his younger brother William Rufus inherited the crown of England. A temporary reunification took place while Duke Robert fought in the First Crusade, and a more permanent union (though of questionable legality) existed after 1106 when the third brother, Henry, who had seized the English throne upon Rufus's accidental death in 1100, defeated his brother Robert at the battle of Tinchebray and became duke of Normandy in all but name while Robert lived out his life in a kindly prison. These transfers of authority were difficult for the Norman nobles who held lands and loyalties on both sides of the English Channel, but despite the questions, divisions, and rebellions that marked eleventh- and twelfth-century politics in both Normandy and England, there never was any question for the Normans that their friends and kin in England remained a part of the *gens Normannorum* defined by Norman geography and by the Norman myth.[76]


BY THE BEGINNING OF THE TWELFTH CENTURY THE GREATER NORMAN world had thus achieved, if not its maximum extent, then at least the general contours that it bore in Orderic's *Historia*—Normandy, Sicily and southern Italy, England, and, still important but to a far lesser extent, Antioch (the eventual conquest of Ireland was still well in the future in Orderic's day, though not beyond imagining). And in tune with this growing diaspora, the history of the Normans as a people from the tenth to the twelfth century could be—and, to a certain extent, was—narrated according to the framework of a traditional migration history, similar to that told by Jordanes about the Goths, Paul the Deacon about the Lombards, Bede about the Anglo-Saxons, or, for that matter, Vergil about the Romans or the Pentateuch about the Israelites. But there was a key difference between the geographical framing of these traditional tales of a *gens'* migration and the Norman experience: while Jordanes's Goths, Paul's Lombards, Bede's Anglo-Saxons, Vergil's Romans, and the biblical Israelites all moved from one region to another and left the land of their past behind, the Normans, after their initial settlement in Normandy, migrated to new lands while still maintaining strong ties of family, history, and identity with the *patria* that they had left behind.

That, at least, was the narrative of the Norman migrations set out by Orderic in his *Historia Ecclesiastica*. But this new narrative's geographical impact is contingent, of course, on whether the spatial diffusion of the *gens Normannorum* really took place at all. For modern historians—conditioned both by the model of the more traditional medieval *gentes* that defined themselves by loyalty to a single ruler and residence in a single place, and also by the modern world of the nation-state where national identity is contingent in large part on territorial distinctions—this dispersion, rather than pure migration, of the Normans has long been the most troubling aspect of their communal identity, to the extent that the existence of a *gens Normannorum* that stretched beyond the bounds of Normandy itself has come into serious question.[77] If a *gens* was defined by common descent, rule, and custom, as has traditionally been supposed, how could those Normans who traveled to Italy, who lived under new governments and adopted new political, legal, and social customs, still be a part of the *gens Normannorum*? Was it possible for the Normans to form a community that was not geographically contiguous and that had a reality beyond the *patria* of Normandy itself? In other words, was Norman unity real, or was it simply a construct of the Norman myth?[78]

Orderic has been considered to be—indeed, it wouldn't be too strong to say that he has been accused of being—the primary perpetrator of such a unifying Norman myth. His atypical education and geographical awareness, coupled with his abbey's connections with England, Italy, and the Holy Land, no doubt placed him in an intellectual and social position that was not shared by other Normans, and the popularity of his work with modern students of Norman history has given his *Historia* an incomparable opportunity to impart an idiosyncratic vision of the world.[79] But Orderic's acceptance of a Norman community that stretched beyond Normandy itself has been substantiated by recent work on the Normans in Sicily, the outliers of the Norman world whose sense of identity with the Anglo-Norman community can be said to make or break the argument for the existence of a geographically diverse *gens Normannorum*.[80] These southern Normans undeniably saw themselves as Normans, connected with the Normans to the north in their history, descent, language, and community, although, for obvious reasons, the practical strength of the connections between Sicily and Normandy were no match for those between England and Normandy.[81] While the *gens Normannorum* might not conform to the ideal type of *gens* as defined by modern historians of the period, and it certainly does not meet the criteria of a nation in the modern sense, the Normans across Europe did maintain the emotional, memorial, and cultural connections that served to bind communities together in the premodern world.[82] Orderic may have been unique in his understanding of the connections from north to south, but his awareness that the Normans were Normans in Sicily and England and Antioch just as much as in their *patria*, that a history "of the Normans for the Normans" was more than a history of Normandy, was an element of the Norman myth that was shared by his early twelfth-century contemporaries.[83]

So the Normans indeed remained Normans when they left Normandy to settle along the northern and southern edges of the continent of Europe, and the unique nature and history of this *gens* transformed the way the migration story, and especially its geography, could be told. For the classical stories of migration were predicated on an unchanging geographical stage upon which peoples moved as discrete units, gliding over the surface of a timeless world from north to south, from periphery to center, the geographical introductions of the migration histories setting the scene for their movements. Paul the Deacon's Lombards came from Scandinavia and migrated to Italy in the sixth century, traveling through the very same geography that Jordanes' Goths had traversed four hundred years before, and that had been defined by classical geographers such as Strabo, Pomponius Mela, and Ptolemy. And in Italy the Lombards, forgoing their northern roots, remained—as Orderic and the other Normans knew well, since the Norman migrants to Italy fought with, married with, and ruled the Lombards in the eleventh and twelfth centuries. The migrations of the Lombards and the other so-called barbarian peoples who disrupted the late antique world can be, and have been, set out on a single map—the famous "Map of the Germanic Migrations" found in modern textbooks on medieval history or western civilization, with arrows drawn across the continent to show where the peoples began and where they ended up. These migrations, of course, took time: years, decades, generations, centuries. But when depicted geographically, whether on a modern pictorial map or in a medieval narrative description, the world in which these travels took place takes on a peculiarly timeless quality, as if the Lombards and their fellow migrants marched across the landscape without leaving any traces. The Lombards might have had their origins in Scandza, but when they moved to Italy they left that northern wasteland behind in its timeless isolation.

The Normans were different. The path of Norman migration in the eleventh and twelfth centuries was not linear, and it could not be sketched out as an arrow moving across a timeless geographical stage. To understand the movement of the Normans through time would require not one map with an arrow sweeping across its center but a series of maps upon which the world of the Normans took up an increasing amount of space, first seeping in along Europe's northwestern edge, and then blossoming in the south before moving out from the mainland, more or less simultaneously, to consume two of the continent's major islands. The Normans did not just move from Normandy to Italy or England, from one defined place to another. They moved *out from* the Norman homeland to form a diaspora of unusual geographic diversity, creating new places and new relationships between places as they went. The geography of Norman life was a geography of change through time, and in that way it was fundamentally different from that set out in the geographical introductions of Orosius, Jordanes, Paul the Deacon, and Bede.

From an empirical standpoint, of course, the Norman migrations of the eleventh and twelfth centuries did not change the physical geography of Europe. England and Sicily and Normandy, as landscapes that could be located on the face of the earth, were no different after the Normans came than they were in the time of Ptolemy—or, for that matter, in the time of Adam, according to Orosius and Otto of Freising. What the Normans changed were the ways in which the far reaches of the European continent related to each other, the ways in which they were plotted, geographically and narratively, as places. And these new meta-geographical needs changed the possibility of describing the map of Europe in the traditional Orosian way.[84] Orosius's geography was predicated on physically adjoining regions. "Gallia Belgica has on its eastern border the Rhine river and Germany, on the southeast it has the Poenean Alps, on the south the province of Narbo, on the west the province of Lundunum"—that is, Gallia Lundunensis—"on the northwest the Britannic ocean, on the north the island of Britain."[85] It was a classic and effective (if somewhat tedious) way of outlining the inhabited world, and it was adopted by Jordanes and to a lesser extent by Bede. But this Orosian style of geography was too circumscribed to do justice to the Norman world that Orderic needed to evoke in his Norman history. The conjoining-regions model might work to outline the relationship between Normandy and England, or that of Apulia, Calabria, and Sicily, but it leaves no opening to convey the real and important connections between these far-flung regions, inhabited by the same *gens* but separated by an entire continent. The Orosian model does not allow for the possibility that the relationships between different places might be social and historical rather than geometrical, that time might reshape not the physical earth itself but its human and historicized geography.[86] A history of the Normans for the Normans demonstrated that, for all the timelessness that individual places, like the abbey of Ouche, might be made to bear in the *Historia Ecclesiastica,* the space of the *oikoumene,* the inhabited world made up of the relationships between the people that inhabited it, was defined not by eternity but by change.

But this Norman changeableness went only so far. As the migrating Normans actively replotted European space, they were also inadvertently challenging another fundamental theorem of classical and medieval geography in that they, as a *gens,* did *not* change as they moved from the chilly northern climes to the temperate lands of the south. For it was a truism of medieval geography and ethnography that climate shaped national character.[87] "For the faces and colors of humans, the size of their bodies and the differences in their minds, arise from the differences in the atmosphere," Isidore of Seville wrote in his influential *Etymologiae,* echoing the classical tradition. "Thus we see that Romans are serious, Greeks unreliable, Africans sly, Gauls ferocious by nature and rather quick-tempered, as the nature of the climate makes them."[88] Since ancient times the most penetrating divide in this environmental determinism was drawn between the cold north, the temperate Mediterranean, and the hot equatorial regions. The senator Cassiodorus reminded a friend in the sixth century that "a hot country produces unreliable and sharp people, a cold one sluggish and deceitful ones: it is only a temperate land that puts human nature in order according to its own quality."[89] Furthermore, as Orosius noted, as peoples migrated from one place to another their character was reshaped by their new surroundings. "The Teutons and the Cimbri," Germanic tribes from the frigid North that were challenging the Romans, "with forces intact, having passed over the snows of the Alps, crossed the plains of Italy and there," Orosius explained, "the hard race was made soft over time by the more pleasant air" (though "drink, food, and baths" also had a role in the tribes' defeat).[90]

Given this belief in the interdependence of climate and character, it is striking that Orderic's description of the Normans in the north and those in the Mediterranean region remained remarkably consistent. "The *gens Normannorum* is ungovernable," Orderic reported, writing around 1135, "and unless they are curbed by a stern ruler they are very quick to do wrong. In all communities, wherever they may be, they strive to dominate, and they are often made transgressors of truth and loyalty on account of their surging ambition. This the Franks and Bretons and Flemings and other neighbors experienced again and again; this the Italians and Lombards and Anglo-Saxons have learned to their ultimate destruction."[91] This description of the active and warlike Normans was true, Orderic specified, "wherever they may be," whether in the Mediterranean lands of the Italians or the northern isle of the Anglo-Saxons. The Normans may have changed their climes but they didn't change their character, and Orderic's description was echoed by other chroniclers in both north and south.[92] Geoffrey Malaterra wrote of the Normans in Italy that "unless curbed by the yoke of justice, they can be extremely unrestrained."[93] William of Apulia, another chronicler of the Norman South, remarked that the *gens Normannorum* was "noted for their fierce knights," a characteristic they did not quickly lose in the warm climate.[94] "A *gens* familiar with fighting," William of Malmesbury, a historian from the Normans' northernmost home, called them, "and without war they hardly know how to live."[95] The warlike, restless, ungovernable nature of the Normans was a constant refrain of the chroniclers, echoing equally in frigid England and in temperate Sicily. Of course, change took time. The Normans did indeed change in many ways, and these changes in custom, clothing, and culture were certainly visible to medieval writers. But a certain innate core of character, a certain Normanness, remained constant despite the superficial alterations. By the time Orderic wrote his characterization of the Normans living in "all communities, wherever they may be" the Normans had been in England for some seventy years, and in Italy for more than a century—plenty of time for change to have taken place. But the Normans remained resolutely Norman, despite generations in new climates and under new skies.

The more the Normans changed the political and ethnic topography of Europe, the more they as a *gens* remained fundamentally the same, no matter where their changing patterns of settlement might take them. And this relatively new people, with their unprecedented migration, required Orderic to create for his *Historia Ecclesiastica* a geography that could take into account the historicity of space that the Norman migrations made manifest. The static geographical descriptions of traditional

Christian historiography would no longer do, for they could not fully capture the dynamism of Norman influence as it expanded, in an unusually piecemeal and irregular fashion, over the course of time. Nor did traditional ideas about the inevitable reciprocity between place and character, between climate and peoples, prove to be meaningful when applied to the *gens Normannorum*, for the Normans maintained their unique and fundamental character as warlike, intractable rovers as they spread over the climes from north to south. To a certain extent the migration of the Normans from Troy to Scandinavia, from Denmark to Normandy, and from Normandy to Sicily and England turned the laws of the classical *oikoumene* on their head, disrupting the patterns that had come to be seen as the building blocks of the world and its peoples.

"THE NORMANS ARE ALWAYS RESTLESS," ORDERIC HAD KING WILLIAM the Conqueror tell his son Robert Curthose, "and they thirst passionately for disorder."[96] This disorder that shook Anglo-Norman politics also muddled the tidy classical geography of Europe that so many Christian historians had worked so hard to preserve. The "deeds and events of the Normans" that Orderic took as a theme for his historical work forced him to reevaluate these received traditions about the known world in light of the changes brought about by the *gens Normannorum*. The Norman myth brought this wandering people from Troy to Denmark to Normandy in a more or less traditional fashion—although this was, in a Bedan vein, a migration from the center to the periphery of the *oikoumene*, nearly incomprehensible to classical writers—but the Normans then spread out from their new *patria* as no people had done before. They traveled from northern climes to southern regions without losing their unique identity as a warlike, ambitious, ungovernable people, resisting the geographical determinism that joined climate and character. They took over Britain, the island kingdom at the edge of the known world, without giving up their continental domain, reaching into the outer Ocean while remaining firmly on the shore.

In the end this notion of the Normans as a *gens* that, despite its multiethnic origins, developed a common myth to unify it over space and time would help Orderic to imagine not only the Norman world but also the

Christian. Orderic could construct the multivalent worldview of the *Historia Ecclesiastica*, with all its anecdotes and themes both local and universal, in part because he rejected the stable spatial vision that characterized the geographical introductions of so many late antique and medieval histories. The tour of the world in Orosius's history, or even the more limited vision of Bede, trapped these historians into writing history at a certain scale, within certain predefined boundaries and with only a certain level of detail. Like maps in a modern atlas, where the images' size and scale guide expectations of the maps' content, the shape of a geographical introduction in a work of history conditioned the reader to expect history of a certain range and scale, covering the whole *oikoumene* in a grand sweep in the Orosian style or confined, in the Bedan manner, to a particular place in more detail.[97] By rejecting this model and replacing the traditional geographical introduction with a revolutionary *vita Christi*, Orderic threw off these preconditions and opened up his *Historia* to a range of stories and scales. From the deeply local past of his abbey of Ouche and the intimate places of its cloister, to the experiences of the Normans throughout Europe, to the history of all of Christendom, Christ, in his life and his sacrifice, could embody them all. Orderic did adopt elements of classical Christian geography to tell the diverse historical and spatial stories in his work, but he did so without restricting himself to one view, one scale, or even one world.

# At Sea

The Norman world at its height offered a geographic doubling: Normandy at the northwestern edge of the European mainland, linked to the island of England across the Channel; and Apulia and Calabria near the southwestern corner of the continent, joined with the island of Sicily across the Strait of Messina. This mirror image was a coincidence, but it nonetheless provided for an imagined symmetry that could mitigate the Norman lands' lack of coherence. For someone like Orderic Vitalis, and the many other Normans whose crossing of the English Channel gave them a living knowledge of Anglo-Norman topography, the geographical relationship between Normandy and England could provide a basis for the mental navigation of Norman Italy as well—and vice versa. This symmetry weighed even more heavily in a political and social landscape that was, in both north and south, defined not so much by the land as by the sea.[1] The Viking ancestors extolled by the Norman myth had taken as their domain the world of the outer Ocean, the ring of water that from very ancient times was believed to encircle the world-island of Europe, Africa, and Asia.[2] As these Vikings settled down in Europe's littoral regions and transformed themselves into Normans, the maritime focus of their society, set on the very margins of the medieval *oikoumene*, remained. The Norman world, as an economic, social, and spatial community, would over the course of the eleventh and twelfth centuries look increasingly outward toward the sea, instead of inward toward the classical center of Europe. This change in orientation allowed Orderic once again to turn inside out the traditional geography of the known world.[3]

The Normans in Italy and Sicily, who had taken a terrestrial path to the south, redeveloped the seafaring traditions that had made their Scandinavian forebears so feared, though this renewed "viking" had a distinctly Italian cast.[4] Robert Guiscard employed a formidable navy at Durazzo in 1082–83 and maritime activity, both military and commercial, would by the time of King Roger II of Sicily bring Norman influence as far as Tripoli and Tunis along the North African coast.[5] This broad maritime vision resonated with King Roger's decision to commission one of the most remarkable works of cartography produced in the middle ages, the *Nuzhat al-mushtāq fi'khtirāq al-āfāq* (*The Book of Pleasant Journeys into Faraway Lands*, also known as the *Book of Roger*) by the Arab Muslim scholar al-Idrīsī.[6] According to the preface of this work, which contained a world map as well as seventy detailed sectional maps, Roger "wished that he should accurately know the details of his land and master them with a definite knowledge, and that he should know the boundaries and routes both by land or sea and in what climate they were and what distinguished them as to seas and gulfs," that is, what their coastlines were like.[7] The world map in this collection (the original is lost, but a number of copies exist), placed south at the top in the Islamic fashion, privileging the Mediterranean region in which Roger's kingdom lay.[8]

The Mediterranean enterprises of the Normans in Italy and Sicily were substantial but not unique. Robert Guiscard's navies and King Roger II's traders sailed in a region where the tradition of the sea stretched back into the mythic ages of prehistory.[9] The Mediterranean was *Mare Nostrum*, "Our Sea," at the center of the West's known world. It was the protected sea, where seafaring was, if not entirely safe, at least natural, so long as the sailors remembered not to pass beyond the Pillars of Hercules into the outer Ocean.[10] In light of all this history and myth, the seagoing Normans in Italy and Sicily were not doing anything out of the ordinary. To look for war and trade across Our Sea, to go from Sicily to Greece or from Italy to North Africa, had shaped the western worldview since very ancient times.

For the Normans in Normandy and England, however, it was a different story. The maritime richness of the Anglo-Norman and Scandinavian realms—concentrated in the English Channel and the North Sea but stretching even into the Atlantic—forced a transformation of the classical geography of the North. The island of Britain had long stood in the western imagination at the very edge of the known world. Since ancient times the isle had primarily been defined, quite reasonably, by its place in the Earth's encircling waters.[11] "Britain," Isidore reported in his *Etymologiae*, "is an island in the Ocean"—not just an ocean, but *the* Ocean that bounded the *oikoumene*—"cut off from the whole world by the flowing sea" that has come to be called the English Channel.[12] In other words, as Orderic said in his *Historia*, "England and the other maritime islands" were "removed from the world in the abyss of the roaring waves."[13] While the island was never entirely cut off from the rest of humanity, Britain's isolation, its place in the outer Ocean, gave it a particular meaning in the West's geographic imagination.[14] Unlike Sicily, set in the familiar *Mare Nostrum* just a stone's throw from the Italian mainland, Britain was its own realm, divorced from continental realities. The only historical exception to its isolation was the period of Roman control, but this was the exception that proved the rule—the Romans claimed dominion over the entire *oikoumene*, so Britain's time within the empire simply confirmed that the island was indeed part of the known world, but at the very end of it.[15] Only Ultima Thule, an island that could be seen but never touched, lay beyond it to the north.[16]

Because Britain, like the world-island itself, was completely encircled by the outer Ocean the island could be thought of, as it was by Bede, as the *oikoumene* in miniature, a microcosm of the whole of the inhabited world.[17] And if the Normans had simply come to the island of Britain in 1066 while leaving the land of their past behind, like the Anglo-Saxons portrayed by Bede, they could have adopted and adapted this image from classical geography, placing themselves alongside the Britons, Picts, and Anglo-Saxons in the European geographical imagination as a people isolated on this mini-*oikoumene* at the edge of the earth. Instead, the Normans bridged Britain's isolation. By uniting their new lands in England with their old *patria* of Normandy the Normans broke through the separating ring of the world Ocean and created a political and social community that was anchored both on the island and on the mainland. They were neither an island people nor a continental community. In creating a realm that crossed the sea and jolted the equilibrium between continent and island the Normans turned the classical image of the *oikoumene* inside out.

Instead of inhabiting a world of land surrounded by the Ocean—like the world-island itself, or the insular microcosm of Britain—the Normans traversed a landscape where sea was at the center, and that sea was, in a sense, ringed by land.

Crossing the sea, moving through this watery center to the littoral lands on either side, was a refrain for Orderic's *Historia Ecclesiastica* as he and his fellow Normans struggled to define their community's unconventional geography. William the Conqueror's soldiers, Orderic said, gathered in 1066 "for a transmarine war" in England; rumors flew "from transmarine regions," meaning at one point from England to Normandy and at another from Normandy to England.[18] The Norman rulers were always crossing the sea (*transfretare*) to govern their lands, and this sea-crossing became in the *Historia* a defining characteristic of Anglo-Norman rule. King William Rufus, according to Orderic, upon hearing of the siege of Le Mans while hunting in the New Forest in England, immediately decided, "Let us cross the sea to help our men"—which he did, without any pomp and with little regard for his safety.[19] As Henry of Huntingdon reported, William Rufus answered objectors by proclaiming, "I have never heard tell of a king who sunk into the waves." Henry went on to say that Rufus "crossed the sea, and he did nothing while he lived that had so much fame, so much shining glory" as this.[20] The Anglo-Saxon king Cnut might have given in to the sea, but the Norman kings conquered the waves.[21]

Indeed, it wasn't a king but the son of a king who was taken by the waves in the most defining sea-crossing of Orderic's lifetime, the wreck of the *White Ship* on 25 November 1120, which killed King Henry I's only legitimate son and heir and many other noble men and women, a tragedy that would eventually plunge the Anglo-Norman realm into the chaos of the Anarchy.[22] The families of the drowned, Orderic reported with sympathy, struggled to find the bodies of their loved ones who were swallowed by the "hideous depths"—here they fully realized what it meant to live in a world defined not by the solidity of land but by the changeable waves of the sea.[23] Throughout the *Historia* Orderic, with words like *transmarinus* and *transfretare*, defined the cross-Channel geography of the Anglo-Norman community. He had himself crossed that sea at least three times during his life, first as a boy of ten on his way to enter the abbey of Ouche, then as an adult who traveled to England and back in his role as monastic historian.

THE MARITIME GEOGRAPHY OF THE NORMANS ELABORATED IN THE *Historia Ecclesiastica* also drew on the community's Scandinavian connections, links that were forged through the Norman myth but also in the political reality of Orderic's lifetime. While the Normans did not preserve a real intimacy with their Danish kin beyond the tenth century, they nonetheless, in large part through the influence of Dudo of Saint-Quentin's work, remembered their North Sea origins, and their connections with Norway and Denmark were only strengthened by the Norman conquest of England, an isle that had a long and tangled history with the Scandinavian lands.[24] From the ninth century, when the Viking settlements in northeastern Britain defined the region known as the Danelaw, through the early eleventh century, when King Cnut (whose wife Emma was Norman) and his sons Harald and Harthacnut ruled, England was an outpost of the Scandinavian world. And in 1066 William the Conqueror was not the only leader to take a transmarine force against the island; King Harald Hardrada of Norway landed in Yorkshire in September of that year in an attempt to recreate the North Sea empire of King Cnut, who had ruled Denmark and Norway as well as England.[25] The relations between the Norman kings of England and their fellow Scandinavian rulers were not always peaceful, but the contacts formed by trade and war and history and geography drew the Normans into an oceanic region that was, by the standards of classical thought, at the very edge of the known world, crisscrossing a North Sea that was certainly no Mediterranean.

Norman sovereignty in this North Sea region provoked Orderic to pen some of the most original geographical descriptions in the entire *Historia Ecclesiastica* when a threatening maritime expedition by the Norwegian king Magnus III Bareleg provided an opportunity for the historian to indulge in Scandinavian geography.[26] Magnus, who ruled Norway from 1093 to 1103, "held power over the islands in the Ocean," Orderic remarked—except, of course, for England.[27] It was the king's maritime adventures among these islands that brought him to the chronicler's attention, but Orderic first set the scene by describing more fully the nature of Magnus's realm. "There are," he reported, "five cities situated on the coast of the sea around Norway: Bergen, Konghelle, Kaupanger, Borg, and Oslo. There is also a sixth city, Tønsberg, which is situated to the east in opposition to the Danes. In the middle of the island," that is, Norway, which was, like Scandza before it, considered to be without links to the mainland, "there are large lakes full of fish, and circling the shores of these lakes are country towns. The natives are richly provisioned with fish and birds, and the flesh of beasts of all sorts."[28] This lush and populated—even urbanized—landscape bears little resemblance to the unfertile northern climes that allegedly forced the Goths, the Lombards, and ultimately the Normans to leave in search of survival. King Magnus left Norway out of ambition, not desperation. In 1098, Orderic reported, "traversing the Ocean and blown by the eastern wind, he went to the Orkney Islands, traveled around Scotland from the northwest, and made his way to the other islands that belonged to his dominion all the way to Anglesey" off the coast of Wales.[29] Magnus touched upon Ireland and spent some time on the Isle of Man. "Then he traversed those other Cyclades in the great sea almost beyond the world," Orderic continued, comparing the encir- cling islands in the north to the better-known Cyclades of Greece, "and he compelled many people to settle there by royal command; he himself worked with such enthusiasm for many years to enlarge his kingdom and expand its inhabitants."[30] Orderic was more specific regarding the islands of the north settled by Norwegian subjects. "The Orkney Islands and Finnmark, Iceland and Greenland, beyond which no land can be found to the North, and many other places as far as Gotland are subject to the king of the Norwegians."[31]

As a geographical description of a series of islands there is little to distinguish this passage in form from those of classical writers who island-hopped their way through the outer Ocean in their geographical descriptions.[32] It is the content of Orderic's description that is unusual. For the Scandinavian regions and the islands beyond the North Sea were not a part of the geographical tradition that medieval Europe had inher- ited from the classical world. Britain, Ireland, and the Orkney Islands were known to classical geographers. But to Orosius the Orkneys were the very limits of human habitation in the North, beyond which were only "unbounded Ocean" and "the island of Thule which, separated from the

others by an indefinite space and situated in the middle of the Ocean towards the northwest, is known by only a few."[33] Indeed, Orosius's northern geography was considered so substandard that when the work was
translated into Old English around 900 two interpolations recounting
voyages around Scandinavia and the Baltic were introduced to make the
text more complete.[34] To Isidore of Seville, the Orkneys were, in fact,
"within Britain," not connected to but embraced by the larger island's
northern end, thus preserving Britain's classical place at the northern edge
of the *oikoumene*.[35] Further north was only Ultima Thule "an island in
the Ocean in the northwestern region, beyond Britain, taking its name
from the sun, because there the sun makes its summer solstice, and there
is no daylight beyond (*ultra*) this. Hence its sea is sluggish and frozen"—
not exactly the sort of place a Norwegian king might sail.[36] Orderic knew
about Thule from Orosius and Isidore; in fact, on at least one occasion
he even saw the island marked on a map out beyond Ireland.[37] But Thule,
with its mythical placement and its sluggish seas, had no part in Orderic's
depiction of the actual geography of the North Sea and beyond.

Orderic, in his description of Magnus's realm, took it upon himself
to expand the limits of the *oikoumene*, the inhabited world.[38] He shoved
back the ends of the Earth, placing them not just beyond Britain but beyond Greenland, a place beyond the wildest dreams of classical geographers but nonetheless, as Orderic made clear, inhabited by people who
were subject to a known and renowned Christian king and who were
nothing like the monstrous races believed to inhabit the world's margins.[39] Orderic was not the first continental scholar to mention these
outer islands. Adam of Bremen, a German chronicler who wrote his *Gesta*
of the Archbishops of Hamburg-Bremen in the late eleventh century, told
of Greenland, Iceland, and even Vinland—no doubt the first mainland
European mention of the New World.[40] But Adam's geography, though
far more detailed than Orderic's, was also far more enmeshed in classical and mythological traditions, which he struggled to reconcile with the
details he learned from his Scandinavian informants. Adam quoted Orosius's description of the barely known Thule—noting that "both Roman
and barbarian writers say much worth reporting" about it—before telling his readers that "Thule is now called Iceland, from the ice that binds
the Ocean." He goes on to report this island to be so barren that the in-

habitants "live in underground caves, happy to have shelter and food and blankets in common with their cattle," living lives of eremitic simplicity governed by their bishop.[41] This ascetic account of Icelandic life may have had its origins in stories of Irish monks who sailed north into the Ocean in search of their green martyrdom—Dicuil, a ninth-century Irish geographer writing at the Carolingian court, told a similar story in his popular *De mensura*—but Adam's rather fabulous tales about Icelandic life bore no resemblance to the Scandinavian culture that flourished on the island at the time that he was writing (though Adam assured his readers that "I have ascertained truly these thing about Iceland and Ultima Thule, omitting the fabulous").[42] Similarly, Adam reported that Greenland's inhabitants "are green from the sea, from which the region takes its name"—perhaps they were related to the famous "green children" that appeared in East Anglia during King Stephen's tumultuous rule, according to the historian William of Newburgh's rather skeptical report.[43]

Adam of Bremen's contributions to the historiography of the North were immense and unparalleled, but he nonetheless maintained the classical image of the northern isles as isolated and marvelous places whose recent Christianization had only marginally increased their connections with the civilized world. Orderic, on the other hand, naturalized this region, made it known and inhabited, in a way that had not been done before. True, he provided no ethnographical information about the denizens of Greenland or Iceland, nor did he describe their landscape. But by noting that King Magnus "compelled many people to settle there by royal command" and that "he himself worked with such enthusiasm for many years to enlarge his kingdom and expand its inhabitants," Orderic, however vaguely, connected the inhabitants of these distant isles with the Christian world, without any suggestion that they were monstrous or marvelous or anything other than normal Scandinavian men and women subject to the active rule of a powerful and modern king.[44] In light of Orderic's description of these isles, the northern edge of the world—where Thule might still stand in its frozen sea—was much further off than people had expected. And this placed Britain, traditionally the furthest corner of the *oikoumene,* a little closer to the center. Normandy and Norman England were not, therefore, at the ends of the Earth, but at the heart of a flourishing economic, social, and political realm defined by the not-at-all sluggish waters of the North Sea.


"THE SEA NEVER RESTS, SAFE WITH SURE SOLIDITY," ORDERIC remarked in book IV of his *Historia Ecclesiastica*, "but, swirling with perpetual disorder, it flows on in its way, sometimes appearing calm to the gaze of observers yet frightening sailors accustomed to its waves and instability. Likewise," he went on, "this present age is perpetually rocked by its changeableness, and is plainly changed in many ways both miserable and joyous."[45] This comparison between time and sea might not be Orderic's most original reflection, but the Norman historian knew more than most about the sea, and about change. Orderic's vision of the *oikoumene*, whether he realized it or not, revolutionized the geography of the northern world by expanding it across the sea, binding England to the continent through constant and perilous transmarine crossings while at the same time pushing the bounds of the inhabited world back by thousands of miles. Orderic did not emphasize the ways in which he transformed the geographical tradition that he had inherited from the classical world. He simply did it, because it was natural, because it was necessary for him to portray the world as he and his companions understood it. And this world, the world of the *gens Normannorum*, was a world of water, a world at sea. It changed all that western geographers thought that they knew for sure—that land was in the center; that the island of Britain was at the edge of the *oikoumene*; that monstrous races, not humans ruled by a Christian king, inhabited the farthest reaches of the world. It was the Norman Conquest of England—formerly Britain, "once called Albion," as Bede said—that opened this new, expanded, transmaritime world to Normans, in partnership and conflict with their Scandinavian kin. Orderic Vitalis, a Norman who was *Angligena*, having lived a cross-Channel life, was able to pry open the sealed boundaries of the classical world, letting in the Ocean and the islands within it, manipulating the ancient geography of Europe to tell the story of the Normans as he felt it needed to be told.

# CHAPTER 3

# Albion

*Conquest, Hegemony, and the English Past*

The Norman conquest of England was audacious, stunning, and amazingly quick.[1] Edward the Confessor, the childless king of England, was buried in the newly consecrated abbey church at Westminster on Thursday, 6 January 1066.[2] On the same day Harold Godwinson, earl of Essex and Edward's brother-in-law, was hurriedly crowned king, also at Westminster.[3] But Harold's reign was not to last, for Duke William the Bastard of Normandy, a first cousin once removed of the dead king (though in the female line), considered himself to be the rightful successor to the English throne.[4] According to Norman tradition King Edward had named his continental cousin his heir in 1051. In 1064 or 1065 Harold Godwinson, at that time England's most powerful earl, crossed the Channel to Normandy and with King Edward's blessing allegedly swore on relics to support Duke William's claim to the island kingdom.[5] From William's perspective, therefore, Harold was a usurper and a perjurer on 6 January 1066, and the ambitious Norman duke summoned his allies for battle. The Normans, sailing under the papal standard, landed on the island's southern shore.[6] They defeated the English army and slew King Harold on 14 October 1066 at the Battle of Hastings. Only two months later Normandy's Duke William received England's crown. "At last in the year of our Lord 1067, the fifth indiction, on Christmas Day," Orderic Vitalis reported in his *Historia Ecclesiastica* (using the traditional monastic style of dating that began the new year with the Nativity; in modern notation this would be 25 December 1066), "the English came together at London for the ordination of the king, and a troop of Normans with arms and horses were arranged around the abbey for defense so no trickery and insurrection could rise up"—for William had subdued only a small corner of the island. "And so in the church of St. Peter, chief among the apostles, that is called Westminster and where the venerable King Edward sleeps in the tomb, Archbishop Ealdred consecrated William duke of the Normans to be king of the English and he placed the crown of kings on his head in the presence of the prelates, abbots, and princes of the whole realm of Albion."[7]

This coronation was amply reported in Norman and English sources. For his account Orderic relied in part on that of William of Poitiers, who noted of the Conqueror in his *Gesta Guillelmi* that the archbishop "placed the crown of kings upon him and seated him on the king's throne on the holy feast of Christmas in the year of our Lord 1066, with the support and in the presence of many prelates and abbots in the church of St. Peter the Apostle which enjoyed King Edward's tomb."[8] Guy of Amiens, in the very last extant lines of his *Carmen de Hastingae proelio*, declared that the archbishop "raised the king from the dust, poured out the chrism and anointed the king's head, and consecrated him king through the royal rites."[9] John of Worcester, relying on the *Anglo-Saxon Chronicle*, reported a similar scene, adding that the new king "swore before the altar of St. Peter the Apostle in the presence of the clergy and the people that he pledged by his own will to defend the holy churches of God and their rectors, to rule justly and with kingly providence the whole people subject to him, to institute and uphold just laws, and wholly to forbid plunder and unjust judgments."[10] William of Malmesbury said only that the Norman duke was "without a doubt acclaimed king" and crowned by Ealdred on Christmas Day; Henry of Huntingdon was even more laconic, merely noting the crowning event without fanfare.[11] And Wace in his vernacular version said a bit later that "by the common advice of the clergy, who recommended and advised it, and by the barons, who saw that they could not elect another, they had the duke crowned king and swore fealty to him."[12] These accounts all more or less converge, except for one detail: only Orderic, in his description of William the Conqueror's revolutionary coronation, mentioned the realm of Albion.

To a modern reader of the *Historia Ecclesiastica* this might not seem to be a very significant detail. "Albion," after all, is used widely in contemporary language as a poetic synonym for England. But this everydayness of Albion in current literature has made it easy to overlook the fact that in the middle ages England, as a present-day entity, was almost never called by that name. "Albion" was first and foremost an archaic and obsolete name for the island, which medieval writers employed almost exclusively to refer to Britain as it was before even the British, the archetypal inhabitants, arrived. It was a name drawn from the classical geographers by way of Bede, who explained in the very first sentence of the first chapter of his *Historia Ecclesiastica gentis Anglorum* that "Britain, which was once called Albion, is an island in the Ocean," providing a geographical slate, a spatial prehistory, upon which the history of the English people could be written.[13] Albion was the former name for that isle located beyond the pale, set off from the inhabited world by its place in the outer Ocean.[14]

Orderic, though, in his unprecedented twenty-six references to Albion in the course of the *Historia Ecclesiastica*, never used the name in the Bedan style as a designation of this bygone pre-British yesteryear.[15] Albion was for Orderic a living, inhabited, and governed land of his age, the pan-ethnic and hegemonic kingdom of England. Unlike Bede and those who followed his lead, for whom Albion was fundamentally prehistoric, Orderic found in this ancient name a means of reconciling a disjointed history through the medium of place. The primeval Albion was a name without an ethnic dimension, a place without people. It was not the land of the Britons or the land of the Angles, but a physical place that could both simultaneously and successively be home to many different *gentes*. The Anglo-Saxon kingdom had occupied Albion, as did the Anglo-Norman kingdom in Orderic's day. So, importantly, did the kingdoms of the Welsh (or Britons) and the Scots. But Albion, as pure place, encompassed these various peoples and kingdoms while remaining untouched. It could subsume the kingdoms of the Saxons and Danes and Welsh and Scots and Normans into itself while still being a discrete and undivided "island in the Ocean." Through Albion as pure place Orderic sought a means of reconciling the pre- and post-Conquest kingdoms into a historical and geographical body defined by the *regnum Albionis* and by the king who ruled all the peoples within it.[16]

This was by no means a fully developed theory of territorial kingship, although the Anglo-Saxon kings had propagated a sense of territorial rule that Orderic would reinterpret in his own notion of a loosely imperial *regnum Albionis* embodying the Norman kings' ambitions.[17] For "Albion" was from Bede's day the island from shore to shore, the land free of any political or ethnic boundaries. It was the kingdom as the kings, both Anglo-Saxon and Anglo-Norman, hoped it might be, made natural through the use of a single, island-wide name. Throughout his *Historia* Orderic toyed with this idea of a *rex Albionis* (as he once referred to William the Conqueror's son William Rufus), a king who could more fully rule all the peoples living on an island that was characterized before and after the Conquest by both ethnic diversity and ethnic amalgamation.[18] Orderic's occasional yet intensely expressive use of this single name, Albion, in his *Historia Ecclesiastica*, when placed into the context of the Anglo-Saxon past, the English future, and Orderic's work as a whole, displays the origins of an identity defined by place and by history rather than by ethnicity. Albion was an expression of power through geography, a manifest destiny of a divinely favored king, created by a historian who was himself *Angligena*, English-born, yet French though his father and Norman through his life.

BEFORE LOOKING AT WHAT ALBION WAS FOR ORDERIC, WHAT IT meant for his understanding of Norman sovereignty in England, it is useful to know what it wasn't. This exploration of the name Albion admittedly ranges far from Orderic's usage and era, but it demonstrates the importance of recognizing that place-names have histories. In the case of Albion, the historical and poetic nuances that have accumulated over the centuries have obscured the original importance of the name for the early and high middle ages, and these modern accretions must be stripped away before the medieval meaning can be revealed.

For centuries the idea of Albion has been used to negotiate English identity, unity, power, and place. Albion as an arena for reinterpretation was picked up, not surprisingly, by Geoffrey of Monmouth in the twelfth century, who named Albion as the giant-inhabited island where the Trojan Brutus, the mythic ancestor of the Britons, landed. "At that time the name of the island was Albion," Geoffrey explained, not at all unlike Bede. But then he went on. "It was inhabited by no one except a few giants. It was, however, filled with pleasant places, and the abundance of forests and fishing-streams provoked in Brutus and his companions a desire to live in that chosen place."[19] At first the Trojans were merciful, in a way, for they merely "drove the giants into caves in the mountains" and settled throughout the island. But when the giants fought back "the Britons finally gathered from everywhere, gained the upper hand, and killed all of them except Goemagog," a giant whose name, with its resemblance to the biblical Gog and Magog, evoked any number of mythical, exotic, and biblical connotations.[20] But this last giant would not long survive. The Trojan Corineus (who gave his name to Cornwall, according to Geoffrey; Orderic, on the other hand, attributed it to the hornlike shape of that corner of the island) threw Goemagog into the sea after a wrestling match.[21] With the last giant's death Albion became Britain, named by Brutus for himself, and it passed away as a contemporary land.

This identification of Albion with Brutus's colonization was picked up by Wace and Laȝamon in their vernacular versions of the story, and later by Geoffrey Chaucer, who wrote to King Henry IV, "O conquerour of Brutes Albioun! Which that by lyne and free eleccioun, Ben verray kyng."[22] Geoffrey of Monmouth never explained where the island's prehistoric giants originated; perhaps they were there from the Creation, a part of the land itself. But later writers, drawing on both classical and biblical traditions, filled in this gap. The late thirteenth-century or early fourteenth-century Anglo-Norman poem *Des Grantz Geanz*, and the Latin translation of the 1330s known as *De origine gigantum*, both tell a story of "how and when and from what people came the great giants who originally held England, which at first was named Albion."[23] According to this tale the giants of Albion met by Brutus were the descendants of the thirty daughters of a Greek king who had determined to kill their husbands. The youngest of these sisters revealed the plot and as punishment for their treachery the women were sent to sea on a rudderless ship. They landed on the island "which is today called England; but at that time it was without a name, for it was inhabited by no one."[24]

Albina, the eldest of the sisters, called the land Albion after herself. In time these isolated women were visited by demons, "incubi," and they give birth to the giants who populated the land when Brutus arrived to conquer.[25]

Only since late Tudor and Elizabethan times, however, has the name Albion been a common appellation for the island of Britain in the sense of a present-day and unified land with a unique history that stretched back to the beginnings of time.[26] In 1554 when Queen Mary and King Philip entered London for the first time after their marriage they were met at London bridge by effigies of two giants, Corineus Brittanus and Gogmagog Albionus, representing the two pre-English eras of the island's history.[27] The same two figures, Corineus the Briton and Gogmagog the Albione, greeted Queen Elizabeth in 1558.[28] It was in Elizabeth's reign that Albion would come into its own as a name for a contemporary place. Sir Francis Drake christened the west coast of North America "Nova Albion" in 1579 due to the pale cliffs' resemblance to those at Dover (the name Albion was by this time believed to come from the Latin word *albus,* white); William Warner first published his mythico-historical poem *Albion's England* in 1586; and William Shakespeare used the name to refer to the English kingdom in his plays, though only three times.[29] In Raphael Holinshed's *Chronicles of England, Scotland, and Ireland* (1577), Albion became not only an island but a giant, Geoffrey of Monmouth's Goemagog becoming not only "the Albione," the inhabitant of Albion, but Albion itself.[30]

Since the late 1500s the place-name has only grown in popularity, becoming both more closely associated with the territorial kingship of the British monarchs who claimed hegemony over the whole island and also more fully poetic. In Ben Jonson's play *Masque of Blackness,* first staged in 1605 for King James I of England—who in his person brought England and Scotland into union—the king himself was "Albion."[31] The year before, on the other hand, Sir Francis Bacon—commenting on the appropriateness of "Great Britain" as a name for the kingdom that brought England, Scotland, and Wales together under one king—declared that no name was "known of old but Albion and Britany; but one of these was only poetical, the other true and historical."[32] (Bacon, apparently, did not remember his Bede.) Some two centuries later the French would rail against "perfidious Albion" as a rallying cry during the Napoleonic War.[33] At about the same time the poet and artist William Blake, Albion's most ingenious and prolific commentator, envisioned the giant Albion to be "our Ancestor, patriarch of the Atlantic Continent, whose History Preceded that of the Hebrews & in whose Sleep, or Chaos, Creation began," but also, to the Trojans who landed on the shore of Albion the island, "'our mother, and our nurse,' they said; 'Our children's mother, and thou shalt be our grave.'"[34] Blake brought Albion back around to Geoffrey of Monmouth's Arthurian legend, declaring that "stories of Arthur are the acts of Albion," Albion as a giant, that is, but also Albion as a land, "applied to a Prince of the fifth century."[35] In Blake the land and its unifying personification recombined and reverberated to the present day.

BUT ALL OF THESE LATE MEDIEVAL, EARLY MODERN, AND MODERN meanings of the name, so deeply embedded in the Anglo-American consciousness, must be forgotten when looking at Orderic's use of the word. Orderic wrote long before Albion became popularized into a white land, a poetic evocation, a world of giants, and a dream.[36] In his use of the name Albion in the *Historia Ecclesiastica* to refer to a political reality of the present and the not-so-distant past, Orderic was unique among his contemporaries: no similar meaning emerged in the histories of William of Malmesbury, Henry of Huntingdon, John of Worcester, Geoffrey of Monmouth, Gerald of Wales, Wace, or any other twelfth-century historian of England. But Orderic was not unique in medieval English history. The charters of the unifying Anglo-Saxon and Danish kings of the tenth and eleventh centuries, who created a multiethnic territorial kingship with pretensions to imperial style out of the island's traditionally fragmented peoples, also employed the name Albion to describe a *regnum* of the present rather than an island of the past.[37] It was these charters, apparently, that first inspired Orderic to adopt the place-name in his *Historia*, and the meaning they impart to Albion is vital for interpreting Orderic's use of the term. As early as the 930s the English kings, like Orderic after them, recognized Albion to be a historically legitimate place-name that had no ethnic component and that represented the island as a whole. Albion was a land, complete and undivided, that could be a homeland for people of all ethnic backgrounds, for Angles and Saxons and Danes and Welsh and Scots and later Normans, under the rule of a single king. These Anglo-Saxon charters are not easy to work with.[38] Many alleged to be from the tenth century are forgeries, though often forgeries from the eleventh century, which can still say something about pre-Conquest attitudes towards kingship in England, or from the twelfth, the time at which Orderic was writing. But these Latin documents are, for all their problems, the only body of texts to express fully the meaning of Albion for the English kings, and a careful sorting can sift those with an authentic basis from those that reflect the ideas of a later age.[39]

The earliest ruler of England to style himself king of Albion was Athelstan of the West Saxons, the first English king to control effectively the whole of the island from 925 to his death in 939.[40] Athelstan "governed all the kings who were in this island," the Worcester manuscript of the *Anglo-Saxon Chronicle* explained, "first Hywel, king of the West Welsh, and Constantine, king of Scots, and Owain, king of Gwent, and Ealdred, Ealdwulf's offspring, from Banburgh. And they confirmed peace with pledges and with oaths."[41] Athelstan had hegemony over the whole island as overlord of the lesser kings, and the model he developed would be of continued importance for his Anglo-Saxon, Danish, and Norman successors.[42] It is not at all surprising, given the novel extent of Athelstan's kingly power, that he would feel the need to coin a new title to reflect the unprecedented extent of his rule.[43] The designation "king of the Anglo-Saxons" (*Angol Saxonum rex*), used often by Athelstan's father, King Edward the Elder, was far too limiting, too passé, to suffice at a time when kingship was becoming increasingly territorial and hegemonic rather than ethnic and personal.[44] Beginning in 929, therefore, some of Athelstan's charters proclaimed him to be "king of the English and equally governor of the whole of Albion."[45] Albion was not the only place-name used by Athelstan to express the extent of his rule: as king he used a mixture of terms to define the kingdom geographically, as would his successors on the throne (and as would Orderic for the realm of the Norman kings). Athelstan's coinage, for instance, styled the king *rex totius Britanniae*, king of the whole of Britain.[46] And in a charter of the mid-930s the king declared himself "Athelstan, divine grace smiling upon me, king of the English and equally governor of the whole of Albion" in the body of the text, while witnessing the document as "Athelstan, king of the whole of Britain."[47] The English as a people, and Albion and Britain as the island, all together defined the extent of his rule, and beginning here in the 930s Albion and Britain came to be used interchangeably in Latin documents to indicate that the realm of the king was held to be coterminous with the island as a whole.[48]

It is likely that Athelstan, who was an educated man, found both Albion and Britain in Bede's *Historia Ecclesiastica* and recognized them for what they were, an island-wide designation that could represent his island-wide rule.[49] But in the two hundred years between Bede, writing in the 730s, and Athelstan, who ruled in the 930s, the name Albion had undergone a transformation in the English tradition. It had become the name of a kingdom in the historic present rather than a land of the prehistoric past. It is possible, indeed likely, that Athelstan himself or someone in his chancery effected this connotative transformation in an attempt to celebrate the king's new status as ruler of the entire isle.[50] The place-name Albion would stick, though, and would become a standard evocation in the charters of later English kings, developing in meaning up to the time of the Norman conquest.[51]

Athelstan's successors Edmund and Eadred both maintained the title "king and ruler of the whole of Albion," but it was with Eadwig and especially Edgar, kings and brothers, that the place-name Albion developed a fully articulated sense of a pan-ethnic kingdom. Eadwig styled himself "by the grace of God king not only of the Anglo-Saxons but also of the whole of the island of Albion" in 956, and in the same year as "king of the English and of all peoples of Albion."[52] It was a vain boast on Eadwig's part: the next year the Northumbrians and Mercians would rebel and declare his brother Edgar king. After 957 Eadwig was no longer king of the whole of Albion, and he never again styled himself as such. The final charters in which Eadwig was called ruler of Albion or of Britain are dated to 957, and although Eadwig continued to rule south of the Thames until his death in 959 no charter of his ever again made an island-wide geographical claim.[53] By the late 950s the title of ruler of Albion was clearly restricted to a king who was recognized to rule the entire isle. It was not a casual boast of royal grandeur, but a specific indication of a particular type of rulership, one defined by the island itself.

The rule of Eadwig's brother King Edgar marked the true turning point in the development of England's territorial hegemony and also in the use of the name Albion to refer to this political reality. Edgar's reign—which began in 957 when Mercia and Northumbria declared him king in opposition to his brother Eadwig, solidified in 959 with Eadwig's death, became glorious with his elaborate formal coronation at Bath on 11 May 973, and ended with his death two years later at the age of only thirty-two—was seen as the golden age of tenth-century England.[54] "His deeds are celebrated with great splendor even in our own day," William of Malmesbury exclaimed in the mid-twelfth century. "Divine love and favor shone upon his years, which he purchased diligently through the devotion of his spirit and his forceful policies."[55] Many of Edgar's charters referred to him as ruling Albion, a minority of his total diplomas to be sure but nonetheless a significant proportion. He was "governor and ruler (*rector*) of the whole of Albion," "king and emperor (*primicerius*) of the whole of Albion," "king (*basileus*) of the whole of Albion."[56] A number of the charters attributed to the anonymous scribe known as Edgar A begin the proem by extolling the king's "sovereignty over the whole of Albion with the approval of the Ruler who is seated on high," a strong statement of divine sanction for Edgar's island-wide kingship that relied on the hegemonic associations of the name Albion.[57]

Even more interesting than the use of Albion in Edgar's authentic charters is its employment in those that were forged. For it was in these inauthentic charters, usually of uncertain date but often suggested to be post-Conquest documents from the late eleventh or early twelfth century, that the name Albion was truly and explicitly framed as a multi-ethnic and island-wide imperial *regnum*. The idea of Edgar's kingdom as one that unified all the peoples of the island under his aegis continued to evolve in English writings, including forged charters, through the eleventh and twelfth centuries, developing a historical precedent and ideal for the Norman kings.[58] To Henry of Huntingdon, a historian normally rather given to pessimism, he was "Edgar the Peaceable, the magnificent king, the second Solomon, in whose time a foreign army never came into

England, to whose dominion the kings and princes of England were subject, to whose power even the Scots bent their necks."[59] To the Cistercian Aelred of Rievaulx, writing later in the twelfth century, Edgar "joined peoples of many languages under the compact of one law."[60] This same movement towards an image of semi-imperial unity was displayed in the forged charters. In a document addressed to Alfric, abbot of Malmesbury, dated to 974 in the text but more likely to be a late eleventh- or early twelfth-century forgery, Edgar was said to declare himself to be "ruler of the whole of Albion, having subjected the kings of the surrounding coasts and islands to a greater extent than any of my forefathers."[61] It was a sentiment, no doubt, that the Norman kings could appreciate.

The same view was expressed in a forged Ely charter, which exists in both Latin and Anglo-Saxon versions and was likely composed no later than the end of the eleventh century.[62] In this charter, dated to 970 in the document, Edgar was styled "king of the cherished island of Albion, having subjected to us the sceptre of the Scots, and of the Welsh or Britons, and of all the regions round about."[63] This was most likely a reference to King Edgar's activities at Chester in 973 where, according to the Peterborough manuscript of the *Anglo-Saxon Chronicle*, "there 6 kings came to meet him, and all pledged that they would be allies on sea and on land."[64] These kings were first identified as those of Wales and Scotland in Ælfric of Eynsham's *vita* of St. Swithun in the very late tenth or early eleventh century.[65] By the late eleventh century, as the forged documents make clear, the place-name Albion had found meaning as the name for a kingdom that not only stretched across the island from shore to shore but that encompassed a number of different kingdoms and peoples—including the Scots and the Welsh—under the rule of a single overking. At least some of the counterfeited charters of King Edgar in which he was styled as the ruler of Albion date from Orderic's lifetime, and they suggest the image of Albion that Orderic would adopt for England's Norman kings.

But where did Orderic, in his isolated Norman monastery, learn of the Albion of the Anglo-Saxon rulers? The most likely source is the ancient English abbey of Crowland. Orderic traveled to Crowland sometime in the second decade of the twelfth century at the invitation of Abbot Geoffrey of Orléans, previously a monk at Ouche.[66] Crowland,

Abbot Geoffrey thought, was in need of a new history, and he invited
the historian from his former abbey to journey to England and write a
chronicle of the Fenland monastery. In the process of learning all that
he could about the monastic community's past Orderic would undoubtedly have turned to the abbey's charters, as he did when composing the
history of his own monastic home at Ouche.[67] At least two of the charters
at Crowland, both dated to 966 and almost certainly forged, proclaimed
Edgar to be the king of Albion.[68] Orderic explicitly mentioned one of
these documents in the history of Crowland that he included in his *Historia*, the first attestation to the charters' existence and proof that at least
one of them was composed prior to his visit.[69] The extant document differs slightly from Orderic's chronicle account, but it is nevertheless
clearly the same charter that, according to Orderic, Crowland's Abbot
Thurketel confirmed "under the seal of the most vigorous King Edgar
son of King Edmund"—namely, "Edgar, monarch of the whole of Albion" as the king was said to have attested this charter.[70] Orderic's reference to this document strongly suggests that the Norman historian had
experience with the Albion of the Anglo-Saxon kings, the island kingdom
complete and undivided in which a single king held hegemonic, though
not absolute, rule over the inhabitants, no matter what their national
backgrounds. And, with his inquisitive and flexible understanding of history and historical identity, he adopted and adapted the word to fit the
new yet old *regnum* of the Anglo-Norman kings.

"IN THE YEAR OF OUR LORD 1066, THE FIFTH INDICTION, WILLIAM DUKE
of the Normans crossed to England with many armed soldiers—the
lineage of the vigorous King Edgar, which had been capable of holding
the royal sceptre, having died out—and on the field at Senlac Harold,
usurper of the kingdom of Albion, was slain in battle."[71] Thirteen of the
twenty-six times Orderic mentioned Albion in his *Historia Ecclesiastica* he linked it with the word *regnum*, kingdom, both with reference
to the Norman kingdom of Orderic's own experience and to the Anglo-
Saxon realm of the recent past. Harold had usurped, in Orderic's words,
the *regnum Albionis*, and lost his life for that. This was an important moment in the Conqueror's progress, and Orderic used an important phrase.

The kingdom that William of Normandy had gained through the death of Harold was not the kingdom of the English, made up of the English people and belonging to them, but the kingdom of Albion, a place that existed before and beyond all peoples. The *regnum Albionis* served in the *Historia* as a bridge between the pre-Conquest and post-Conquest kingdoms on the island, linking the Norman kings to their English predecessors not through genetic but rather through geographic means.[72] In 1066 "the prelates, abbots, and princes of the whole *regnum* of Albion" attended the crowning of William the Conqueror as the island kingdom changed hands.[73] By using this expression, rather than referring to the illustrious men of England, Orderic implied a coronation that was not a rupture in the kingdom of the English but rather a continuation of the realm of Albion, a place that had existed from time out of mind. To Orderic this link through place meant, for one thing, that King William did not have free reign to do whatever he wanted in his new land, without regard for tradition, history, or virtue. Two rebels against the king would claim, in Orderic's words, that they merely wanted "the state of the kingdom of Albion to be restored in every way to the way it was in the time of the most pious King Edward"—and they were Normans.[74] William the Conqueror, the ruler of Albion, did not create but inherited something: a community and history defined through its link with a primordial land and available to both Norman and English alike, including rebels from both parities who objected to William's new powers.

Orderic had encountered a present-day Albion, perhaps for the first time, in the forged Crowland charter attributed to King Edgar, who, in Orderic's words "had been capable of holding the royal sceptre." It was this Anglo-Saxon king whose territorial power William the Conqueror no doubt hoped to equal. And it was Edgar's lineage that Orderic mentioned as having died out, passing on the glorious king's sceptre—and his power—to the Norman kings. Guy of Amiens, whose *Carmen de Hastingae proelio* Orderic had known before writing his own account of the Norman conquest, said of that sceptre that it "signified the interests of the realm. For by the sceptre the holders of the kingdom control uprisings."[75] This image of the sceptre, and its association with the hegemonic and even imperial Anglo-Saxon kings of Albion, would return to Orderic's history. Later in the *Historia*, in one of Orderic's famous invented speeches, King William would defend his possession of Edgar's sceptre to his son Robert Curthose, who had been angling for a piece of the *regnum Albionis* while his father still lived.[76] "The holy crown was publicly placed upon my head by the vicar of Christ, and the royal sceptre of Albion has been entrusted to me alone to bear," William informed his greedy son. "Therefore it would be inappropriate and completely unlawful if, so long as I enjoy the breath of life, I should allow anyone to be equal to or greater than me in my dominion."[77] Orderic similarly referred to William the Conqueror's son Henry, king of England, as *Albionis sceptriger*, the sceptre-bearer of Albion (Henry of Huntingdon used the same word, *sceptriger*, to describe Edgar).[78] In the *Historia*, Orderic wove his vision of the Albion of England's post-Conquest kings, asserting through the place-name not only the legitimacy of the Norman rulers but the type of rule that they might be expected to have, a hegemonic rule like King Edgar's before them, stretching from sea to sea and subsuming the Welsh and Scots within.

Orderic's mention of the "sceptre of Albion" echoed, most likely unknowingly, the forged Ely charter that described Edgar as "king of the cherished island of Albion, having subjected to us the sceptre of the Scots, and of the Welsh or Britons, and of all the regions round about," a charter that Orderic could, just possibly, have seen.[79] But whether he saw this document or not, Orderic believed that the Norman kings inherited from their Anglo-Saxon predecessors not only the rule of the English but the hegemony over the other kingdoms that existed on Albion's shores.[80] It was a notion shared by the Peterborough author of the *Anglo-Saxon Chronicle*. William the Conqueror "ruled over England," the chronicler said, and "Wales was in his control and he built castles there and entirely controlled that race of men. So also Scotland he made subject to him by his great strength." What was more, "if he could have lived two years more he would have won Ireland by his shrewdness and without any weapon," a conquest that would not occur until the reign of his great-grandson, Henry II.[81] Henry of Huntingdon echoed the same sentiment. "He alone reigned over the whole of England," Henry said of the Conqueror. "He also subjected Scotland to himself, and, having inspired awe, took Wales."[82] King William not only wished to hold the sceptre of Edgar, he also wanted to hold the lands that Edgar had held, not necessarily outright, through absolute conquest, but through an expression of sheer authority that would bring the other kings of the island to their knees to swear featly to him, the same type of promise believed to have been given to Edgar at Chester in 973.[83]

Orderic was in a position to understand the relationship between the English kings, their Norman successors, and the other peoples living on the island, for he had been born in the Welsh marches and, though only a child at the time, had seen the extension of Norman hegemony first-hand. Orderic's father had been a priest in the service of Roger of Montgomery, earl of Shrewsbury on the Severn where it divided the lands of the English from Wales, who, according to Orderic, "vigorously subdued the Welsh and others who opposed him, and pacified the whole province committed to him."[84] William fitzOsbern, another close ally of the new king (and, like Roger of Montgomery, a neighbor of the monastery of Ouche in Normandy), was similarly set on the marches "to fight the war-like Welsh."[85] And Robert of Rhuddlan, whose brothers were monks at Ouche and well-known to Orderic, was established near Chester to subdue the rebellious Britons.[86] Orderic did not approve of all of the techniques of power used by these men—the Welsh were Christian, after all—but he did not consider Wales to be rightfully free of Norman rule. Like the English kings before them, and Edgar in particular, the Normans could expect to have dominion over the lands of the Welsh.

Orderic's belief in Norman hegemony in Albion shows more clearly in his discussion of the English kings' relations with their northern neighbors, the kings of Scotland. Shortly after William the Conqueror's ascent to the English throne, Malcolm king of the Scots, by means of proxy, "faithfully swore obedience to King William," Orderic claimed.[87] The Worcester manuscript of the *Anglo-Saxon Chronicle* defines this further: "King Malcolm came and made peace with King William, and was his man, and gave him hostages."[88] Later however, in the reign of William Rufus, Orderic wrote that Malcolm "rebelled against the king of the English and refused to do the service owed to him," a phrase that clearly suggests that Orderic viewed Malcolm as the English king's subordinate.[89] This is reinforced by a speech that Orderic placed in the Scottish

king's mouth, delivered not to King William Rufus but to Robert Curthose, William the Conqueror's eldest son and the duke of Normandy. "I
acknowledge that when King Edward,"—that is, the Confessor, the last
of the Anglo-Saxon rulers—"handed over to me his great-niece Margaret in marriage he gave me the county of Lothian," Malcolm confided
in Robert. "Then King William," the Conqueror, not the Red, "confirmed
those things that his predecessor had given to me."[90] The Norman kings,
Orderic believed, had inherited the relationship that the Scottish rulers
had had with their Anglo-Saxon predecessors. In Orderic's mind the English kings continued to have hegemony over the kingdoms on Albion's
northern and western shores that their Anglo-Saxon predecessors had enjoyed, to the extent that, as John of Worcester explained, by 1093 "kings
ceased to reign in Wales," replaced by the lordship of Normans.[91]

ORDERIC NEVER EXPLICITLY DEFINED THE PLACE-NAME ALBION IN HIS
*Historia Ecclesiastica.* This was not the case with, for instance, Henry
of Huntingdon, who expanded slightly on Bede's definition to refer to
"the most noble of islands that was formerly called Albion, after that
Britain, and now England," or Wace, who explained that "England was
called Britain and was first called Albion."[92] Orderic used the name without clarification, without justification. Albion was presented as a fait ac-
compli in the *Historia,* a natural geographic entity that needed no explanation. This could imply, of course, that Orderic's audience at Ouche
simply knew their Bede. But this seems an unlikely explanation, given
that even Bede only mentioned Albion once in his history of the English
and that no Norman writer, other than Orderic, employed the name
Albion to refer to present-day England at all. It could also be the case
that Orderic merely used the word for his own pleasure, as he did with a
great deal of unusual vocabulary sprinkled throughout the *Historia.* In
any case, the name *Britannia,* used interchangeably with Albion by the
Anglo-Saxon kings, was to the continental historian "Brittany," not Britain, which might have forced Orderic to use the less-common name
Albion for the island. But, despite all of these cautions and caveats, the
name Albion simply held too consequential, too careful, a place in Orderic's narrative to have been used casually. By leaving Albion undefined

Orderic seems to have intended a subtle commentary on the *regnum* of the Anglo-Norman kings. He left the nature of the kingdom of Albion open and flexible, deeply meaningful to those who had read Bede or the ancient geographers and yet available to the imagination of that majority of people who were not so widely learned.

William the Conqueror established his rule over England, and, to a lesser and more fragile extent, over Scotland and Wales as well. It was not quite the Albion of Edgar and the other Anglo-Saxon kings, though it was a kingdom strongly defined by the island's shores. This was the kingdom William passed on to his sons, first to William Rufus, the *rex Albionis,* and then to Henry, the *Albionis sceptriger.* This king, Orderic said of Henry, "flourishing fully, was raised up in every good fortune; his fame hastening far and wide through the four corners of the Earth, he was named among the greatest of kings. No ruler," Orderic declared, "has been more powerful than he in the realm of Albion, nor more enriched with a wealth of lands on the island, nor more fortunate in an abundance of all things that suit mortal men."[93] Henry was determined to extend his authority from shore to shore, and, in Orderic's eyes, he worked to maintain the territorial rulership, the hegemonic authority, encompassed in the name Albion since the time of King Athelstan. Henry married the Scottish princess Edith-Matilda, sister of King David who had been raised in part at Henry's court and remained closely allied with England and its king.[94] Edith-Matilda, moreover, was not only of Scottish royal blood but also, through her mother, of the royal lineage of King Edgar, the great sceptre-bearer of Albion. Henry, therefore, killed two birds with one stone. He affiliated himself not only with the contemporary kingdom of the Scots but with the lineage of England's hegemonic kings, kings who, Orderic noted in his account of Henry and Edith-Matilda's marriage, "having conquered or wiped out those who are now called the Welsh, named the island that they had occupied through war England."[95] In a roundabout way, therefore, Henry's marriage also associated him with the defeat of the Welsh. And in truth Wales, without a royal family of an ancient and accommodating nature, did not fare so well under Henry as Scotland did. Henry was ruthless in exercising his power over the Welsh lands, through administration as much as violence.[96] He was declared by a Welsh chronicler to be "the man who had subdued

under his authority all the island of Britain," and this was as close to
being true as anyone since Edgar had achieved.[97] Orderic did not go
into detail about Henry's Welsh campaigns, but the Norman chronicler's statement that no man was "more powerful than he in the realm of
Albion, nor more enriched with a wealth of lands on the island," and that
included lands in Wales, goes far in stating the true position of Henry as
*Albionis sceptriger,* sceptre-bearer of Albion, in the tradition of Edgar
before him.[98]

It was this drive for legitimate and firmly exercised dominion that set
Henry I apart from his older brothers and that would cause Orderic to
extol his legitimacy in both England and Normandy. For Orderic, drawing more fully on the Anglo-Saxon image of the *primicerius* than on
the *rex* of a sort familiar to continental historians, envisioned a post-
Conquest England joined inherently to the island's past not through William the Conqueror's circuitous genealogical claims but through the island itself. Albion, a place without people, a name without lineage, served
for Orderic as it had for Bede: a blank geographical slate upon which
English history could be written. William the Conqueror's hegemonic
vision—one supported by Orderic so long as it did not involve an un-
necessary imposition of violence and suffering on the innocent—was not
only an expression of Norman indefatigability but an attempt to recap-
ture territorially a version of the English past in which the kingdom was
coterminous with the island and the *rex et primicerius tocius Albionis,*
the king and emperor of the whole of Albion, ruled over all the island's
peoples together. These subjects of the king, defined by the island, could
then become the *propago de Albione,* the offspring of Albion, a term Orderic used just once to describe some of England's saints, men of both
Danish and Saxon ancestry.[99] It's a curious phrase, a way to bring together men of different ethnicity as offspring of the same land, of Albion.
And this was what Orderic hoped to achieve overall with his twenty-
six references to Albion in his *Historia,* a sense of common community
derived through the inseparable landscape, *regnum,* and king. Orderic
did not revolutionize English identity by any means, and Albion in the
Anglo-Saxon sense of a hegemonic political community reached a temporary dead end with the *Historia Ecclesiastica.* But the rebirth of the kingdom of Albion in the late 1500s and its persistent and flexible presence

ever since shows just how powerful a concept with which Orderic alone experimented in the mid-twelfth century. Orderic's hesitant insular geography did not find an audience in his own age, but it is nonetheless essential to a study of the trials and errors of the Anglo-Norman community.

Orderic was writing in Normandy at a time when the island across the Channel was unsettled in its communal and geographical identity.[100] It was simultaneously England, Britain, and Albion, home to the English, Welsh, Normans, Scots, even Danes. Given this flexibility it is not surprising that a historian like Orderic, a man with an unusually broad vision of the historical landscape, would experiment with place as a way of talking about society. Throughout the middle ages talking about place in the past and the present was one way of talking about communal identity and kingly power.[101] Spatial genealogies were just as important as the establishment of familial lineages for the assertion of political power over a land or over a people.[102] The historicized landscape was an essential element of medieval origin myths.[103] England could be Albion for Orderic because in the twelfth century, in the face of the influx of Normans, the island's persistence as England was not yet entirely certain. England, and Englishness, would ultimately win out as the unifying identity for the land and its people.[104] But this was not inevitable, and the ultimate victory of England as a national concept does not make Orderic's experimentation with Albion as an alternative any less intriguing in the investigation of why English national, geographic, and historical identity resolved itself as it did.[105] Apparently, in his construction of a kingdom of Albion, Orderic was simply before his time.

# CHAPTER 4

# Jerusalem and the Ends of the Earth

Alongside the year 1099 in the annals of the monastery of Ouche, Orderic Vitalis (who kept this chronological record for much of his adult life) noted three events: "Jerusalem was taken on 15 July by the holy pilgrims, the heathens who had held it for a long time having been conquered. Pope Urban died in this year; Paschal succeeded him. The church of St. Evroul at Ouche was dedicated."[1] The same items appear in Orderic's hand, in an almost identical form, on a stray scrap of parchment bound into MS Latin 10062 in the Bibliothèque nationale in Paris, quite possibly the earliest piece of Orderic's historical work still extant.[2] From one perspective, this entry exemplifies the apparent lack of historical scale typical of medieval annals: a local church dedication was given the same billing as an event that shook both the Christian and Muslim worlds. But such a perspective is far too narrow. These two events marked a real and potent conjunction for the monks at Ouche: the altar in the new church became, in a sense, a new Jerusalem, the place where the body of Christ was present anew in the Eucharist, in the same year that the earthly Jerusalem, the place of Jesus's historical and bodily life, was taken by the crusaders, the "holy pilgrims."

Orderic was twenty-four years old in 1099 when the crusaders took, and the altar at Ouche embraced, the Holy City. He was becoming the historian who would some thirty-five years later claim that "never has more glorious material been provided for those who tell the tales of war than God has now given our poets and writers when He triumphed over the pagans in the East by means of a few

Christians."[3] Jerusalem as the City of God was the epitome of a historically meaningful place in the middle ages and was the key to finding
meaning in topography, and in history, at any scale. If Ouche, with its
new stone church, was the intimate landscape of Orderic's monastic
home, Jerusalem, encircled by its own stone walls, was his Christendom
and his cosmos. Everything else fell in between.[4] But while Orderic's
vision of Ouche can be found near the surface of the *Historia Ecclesiastica*, Jerusalem—and all that it implied for the relationship between
space, time, and humanity—is much more deeply embedded in the narrative of Orderic's work and in the *Historia's* relationship to the intellectual world in which its author took part. Orderic was always modest
when it came to his learning and his *Historia's* connections to a wider
philosophy of Christian life. "I see many things in the divine scriptures
that when subtly considered seem similar to events of our time," he remarked, referring to the common practices of historical exegesis that
could bring Jerusalem's scriptural meaning to bear on the events of the
medieval world. "But I leave to the learned the eager probing of allegori-
cal revelations and the proper interpretation of human ways, and I will
occupy myself with bringing forth a little more of the simple history of
Norman affairs."[5]

Orderic declined to indulge in explicit philosophizing in his work,
but he was nonetheless influenced by the body of philosophical thought,
increasingly discussed in the twelfth-century schools, that gave history
a prominent place in the unified cosmos of Christian life. This increasing focus on the city of Jerusalem, and the cognate images of Christendom and cosmos, were what provided Orderic with the knowledge that
he was writing a *Historia Ecclesiastica*, a history of the pilgrim church
on Earth, and that this history had a meaning beyond his local community, even at the times when it *was* simply a history of his local community. In the eleventh and twelfth centuries Jerusalem was the place that
gave meaning to all places, from the consecrated altar in each and every
church, no matter how small, to the far-off ends of the Earth. It was this
synthesis of altar and city, and the intensely organic vision of geography
it implied, that allowed the leap from the monastery of Ouche, where
Orderic participated in the consecration of the new church, to Jerusalem,
the *axis mundi*, the center of the world.[6]

For Christians, Jerusalem stood beyond normal temporality, and in this it could anchor a particular medieval approach to place and time, to geography and history, that privileged a sense of cosmic meaning over the more conventional (and, to modern readers, more palatable) historical components like story, causality, and scale. Annals, born of Easter tables and framed by the progression of years, embodied the cyclical return of Christ's death and resurrection in the Holy City while at the same time emphasizing Christendom's ever-increasing distance from the life of Jesus on Earth. Maps—which were in the middle ages as much about history as about geography—were also centered on the eternal city, arraying an atemporal, graphic, and spatial Christian past around Jerusalem at their heart. Even the *annus-mundus-homo* diagram, that peculiar medieval figure in which the connections of the year-world-man were geometrically displayed, could have Jerusalem at its center. When Orderic's *Historia* is set in parallel with these other types of historical record—when his accounts of the holiness of Europe's lands and of the apostles' foreign wanderings are set next to maps, for instance, and his description of Ouche's new church is seen in the *annus-mundus-homo* tradition—it becomes clear how much Orderic absorbed, exemplified, and reinterpreted the systems of thought that shaped the twelfth-century's theology of God's creation and that placed a Christian geography, with Jerusalem at its center, at the very heart of human and cosmic history.

Jerusalem had always been a center of Christian devotion and pilgrimage, but the passing of the first millennium of Christ's human life and the destruction of the Church of the Holy Sepulchre by the Fatimids at the same significant moment seems to have brought Jerusalem more firmly into the western historical consciousness.[7] The early eleventh-century monastic historian Raoul Glaber, a Cluniac who had come of age with the millennium and who wrote an entertaining and expressive if not always accurate history of his times, suggested as "a matter worthy of meditation" how "it very often happened that the infidels were converted to the faith of Christ in both the northern and western parts of the world, but we do not chance to have heard of the same thing happening in the East and the South." This Raoul attributed to the position of Christ's cross, which marked out Jerusalem as the hub of the Christian world. "When He was hung from the cross," Raoul explained, "the immature people of the East were hidden behind His head, but the West was before His eyes, ready to be filled with the light of faith. So too His almighty right arm, extended for the work of mercy, pointed to the North, which was to be mellowed by the holy word of the faith, while His left was the lot of the South, which swarmed with barbaric people."[8] To Raoul Glaber the nature of the historical conversion of the world to Christianity was guided by the correlation between geography and the body of Christ at Jerusalem. In His moment of sacrifice Christ had turned His back on the East and cast His gaze on the West, a sign of the course of the sixth age of human history. The East and South were not entirely cut off from Christendom, but—like the ages before the incarnation— they had meaning only when paired with significant events and places of the Christian West.[9]

Raoul Glaber's narrative structuring of global geography through a cross centered at Jerusalem found a far wider graphical representation in the medieval world maps, the *mappae mundi*. These maps depicted a landscape of time as much as space, illustrating a tradition of Christian geography that stretched back to the faith's formative years and saw places become holy, and therefore significant, through their links with a past in which God's actions were visible in the world.[10] The classic and diagrammatic T-O maps of the middle ages—a circle inscribed with a T to divide the globe into the three known continents, Africa and Europe represented by the smaller sections, Asia by the larger—were centered at Jerusalem. The intersection of the T, the shape of the cross, marked out the Holy City.[11] This style of map had ancient, indeed pre-Christian, origins and gained currency during the middle ages due to its frequent inclusion in Isidore of Seville's *Etymologiae* alongside the passage that declared the world to be "divided into three parts, of which one part is called Asia, another Europe, and the third Africa," though these three parts were not equal, since "it is plain that one half" of the world-island "holds both Europe and Africa, but the other half only Asia."[12] A similar map would sometimes accompany another of Isidore's texts, the *De natura rerum*.[13]

By the early middle ages the map's T gained its association with the cross of Christ's crucifixion.[14] The known world was thus divided geographically by means of the sacred instrument of Christ's sacrifice for

humanity's sins, as in Raoul Glaber's speculative account of Christianization. This locating of Christ's crucifixion at the cartographic center
would become even more explicit in the elaborately illustrated *mappae
mundi* of the thirteenth century and later.[15] The famous Hereford map,
for instance, explicitly located a crucifix, not merely a cross, above the
small sketch of the walled city of Jerusalem at its center.[16] Christ's crucifixion defined not only Christendom's history but its geography as well.
This notion of Christian geography as history is especially evident in the
accounts of pilgrims to the Holy Land, including those pilgrims who went
armed and would later be known as crusaders.[17] Pilgrims to the Holy Land
did not normally describe the contemporary landscape; rather, they re-
lived the past, describing the events of sacred history as if being in the
place where they occurred broke down the nature of time and the events
were occurring eternally at that spot.[18] The crusaders did not simply
want to reconquer the land of the Bible; in a sense they believed themselves to be taking back history itself, for the events of sacred history remained vivid in the deserts of Palestine. The world of the Old and New
Testaments came alive in Jerusalem; the geography of the past, both
actual and metaphorical, overlay the land with an almost crushing in-
tensity.

No copy of Isidore's *Etymologiae*, the traditional vehicle for
a T-O map, survives from Orderic's library at Ouche, nor is there any
evidence that he read Raoul Glaber's meditation on the geographical
impact of the crucifixion. But Orderic did know the stories of pilgrims,
and he was by no means unaware of Jerusalem's profound place in the
coalescing of history and geography as it had developed through ten
centuries of Christian thought. During a trip to England, Orderic had
the opportunity to lay his hands—and his pen—on one of the most elegant expositions of this body of thought still extant today, a manuscript
from the English abbey of Thorney.[19] This compendium, completed in
1110, has at its core the mathematical and astrological texts and diagrams
necessary for the reckoning of time and the making of calendars, a science
known as *computus* originally developed to determine the correct date
for Easter.[20] *Computus*, in its purest and most rarified form, is simply

mathematics applied to astronomy and cosmology, the analysis of time as a calendrical constant rather than as a matter for philosophical speculation. But *computus*, like all sciences, had a social context that went beyond its technicality, and—thanks to Christendom's most famous computist, Bede—that social context was primarily spatial. Christendom, as both a community and a geographical entity, was defined by the notion that everyone, everywhere, from the northernmost island of Britain to the Holy Land itself, was doing the same thing on the same day.[21] *Computus* thus identified Christian space as much as it did Christian time.

The Thorney manuscript exemplifies the broader context that this temporal reckoning had come to embody. A planned collection rather than a miscellany, Thorney's technical works of *computus* sit alongside a wide variety of affiliated texts and images intended to find order and meaning in the Christian concepts of time, space, and humanity.[22] These include grammatical treatises, medical lore, texts and illustrations on cosmology, Thorney's calendar and annals, an unusual *annus-mundus-homo* image known as Byrhtferth's diagram, a number of other diagrams dedicated to astrology and time, and very near the beginning of the volume, on folio 6r, a large *mappa mundi* of a striking and unususal design.[23] This map's most eye-catching feature is its adaptation of the traditional T-O form, with the name "Jerusalem" written all the way across the circle in a horizontal band, the word split by a small cross at the exact center where the two bars of the T meet at the *axis mundi*—or the *medium mundi*, as another, smaller map in the same volume labeled it.[24] In the case of the large *mappa mundi*, however, the traditional T-O design quickly breaks down, for *EVROPA* is not in the lower left-hand quadrant of the circle but rather in a second, shorter horizontal bar that runs across the stem of the T. Through this small change the cartographer effected a large shift in meaning, for this new bar created a second cross on the map and thus designated not only Jerusalem but Europe as a land signed by the cross, turning the classical continent of Europe into the land of Christendom. *HIERUSALEM* and *EVROPA* are also written in capital letters of equal size, further emphasizing the equivalence between the two and their priority over all the other places of the globe. Europe, as Raoul Glaber pointed out, was the region in front of the cross, the region saved by the cross, and it thus integrated into itself the meaning

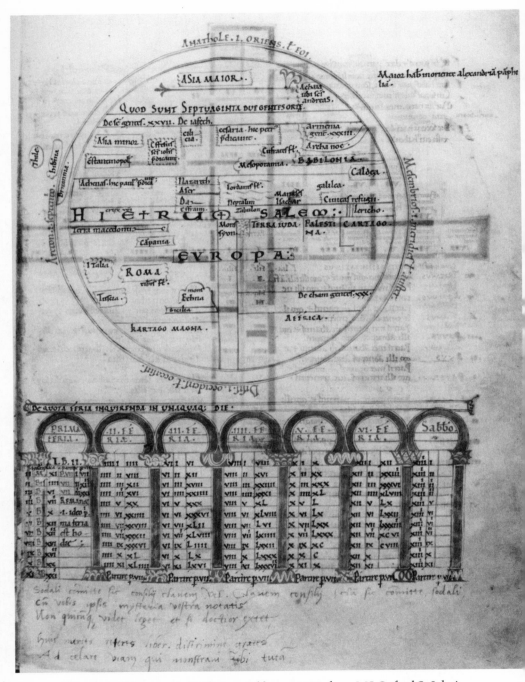

FIGURE 1. *Mappa mundi*, Thorney Abbey, c. 1110, from MS Oxford St John's College 17, fol. 6r. By permission of the President and Scholars of the College of Saint John Baptist in the University of Oxford.

imbued to Jerusalem by the cross. The existence of Jerusalem as a holy place made Europe a holy place as well.

Orderic visited Thorney only a few years after this extraordinary compendium had been completed, probably between 1115 and 1120.[25] He had come to that isolated region of England at the invitation of Geoffrey of Orléans, abbot of Crowland near Thorney and previously a monk at Ouche, who had invited Orderic, the English-born historian from his previous home, to write an updated history of the ancient foundation of St. Guthlac at Crowland.[26] Orderic had only recently begun his work on the *Historia Ecclesiastica*; at that time it was still ostensibly an institutional history of the foundation and properties of the abbey of Ouche, though it was already showing signs of growing beyond its original plan.[27] An institutional history, however, was what Abbot Geoffrey needed, and he called on Orderic to provide one. It was during this visit to Crowland that Orderic took the opportunity to call on another former brother from Ouche, Robert of Prunelai, named abbot of Thorney in 1113 or 1114.[28] While at Thorney Orderic was apparently drawn to the computistic and historical works contained in Thorney's beautiful codex. And in reading and studying it, he left his mark on folio 21v: "On this day the pious father Evroul ascended above the stars" is written in Thorney's martyrology next to 29 December in Orderic's hand, his fine and elegant writing standing out from the surrounding text.[29] It was an appropriate epitaph to include in a work centered around the astrology of time.

Orderic was a dedicated son of his monastery's patron Evroul, of course, but he would not have delved into a prized volume of Thorney's scriptorium only to check on and make corrections to the English community's liturgical commemorations. Orderic was, from all appearances, studying this important manuscript when he ran across the calendar and its lack of Evroul's name and decided to make a small and appropriate addition. There is no doubt that Orderic would have been attracted to such a book, with its maps and *computus* paired with the monastery's annals — in fact, this unusual collection might have rivaled Robert of Prunelai as a reason to visit Thorney.[30] Orderic's hand in the manuscript proves that he saw it, and his interests and later work suggest that he studied, and indeed absorbed, the history, theology, and geography drawn into Throney's texts and images. It may well have been this book of *computus* that inspired Orderic to make his own copy of one of the classics of medieval chronological learning, Bede's *De temporum ratione*, a copy that survives today in MS Latin 10062 of France's Bibliothèque nationale, complete with the indispensable (but, to the modern reader, nearly unintelligible) multicolored diagrams and charts used to calculate the solar, lunar, and zodiacal positions, as well as the dates of various feasts.[31] It is extremely unlikely that this manuscript from Thorney was Orderic's only exposure to the long-standing theory of everything— geography, cosmology, astrology, time, humanity, and God—that stood at the heart of Christian learning. The library at Ouche had other books, many of which unfortunately no longer survive, that covered some of the same material, if not to the same extent.[32] But the survival of the Thorney's *computus* (now known as MS Oxford St John's College 17) provides a unique opportunity to consider Orderic's historiography in light of an important—and in many ways representative, despite its idiosyncrasies—collection of philosophical works on time and place and to show the ways in which, in this as in many things, Orderic took these core notions of Christian philosophy, embraced them, and then, though only implicitly, turned them inside out in his *Historia*, changed symbol into narrative, and adapted the schematic forms of philosophy to the temporal and mundane realities of human life in the world.

BY THE EARLY TWELFTH CENTURY THE CROSS THAT CARTOGRAPHICALLY identified Jerusalem and Europe on the Thorney *mappa mundi* had come to have a very public role as the mark of a vowed crusader.[33] A man who was signed by the cross, who wore it on his clothes, was among the "sons of Jerusalem" who at the urging of Pope Urban were determined to take back the Holy Land.[34] But as the draw of crusading spread throughout Europe the notion of the cross as an expression of terrestrial sanctification bled beyond the Holy Land's boundaries. The cross was suddenly everywhere, not simply in consecrated churches or at the site of Christ's death but on the bodies of people who moved through the profane world with a new sense of purpose, a new sense of holiness, that took over their worldly lives. This spread of the cross throughout Christendom made it available in unprecedented ways to writers looking for a new engagement with Christian space, including those whose interest was grounded more fully in the mundane world than in the holy. In one notable case, Orderic not only noticed but manipulated this proliferation of crosses in the daily life of Christendom to turn the crusaders' sign around and, like in the Thorney *mappa mundi,* reinterpret it to signify not the lands of Jerusalem but European lands, lands much closer to home.

Helias, the count of Maine, a man greatly respected by Orderic for both his Christian piety and his lordly dedication, had in 1095 taken up the cross to go to Jerusalem as a crusader. But when the security of Maine was threatened by England's King William Rufus, Orderic placed a speech in Helias's mouth that presented an alternative role for the crusader. "I will not give up the cross of our Savior with which I am signed in the way of a pilgrim," the count proclaimed in the *Historia,* "but I will place it on my shield and helmet and on all of my arms, and I will fasten the sign of the holy cross on my throne and my horse. Protected by such a symbol I will proceed against the enemies of peace and rightness and with my arms I will defend the lands of Christians," the lands of Maine, his own lands, not the lands in the East, not the terrestrial Jerusalem. "And so my horse and my arms will be signed with a holy mark and all adversaries who will rise up against me will be fighting a soldier of Christ," a *miles Christi,* the term commonly used to designate a crusader to the Holy Land. "I have faith in Him who rules the world," Helias concluded, "that He knows the secret of my heart, and through His mercy I will wait for a suitable time when I will be able to accomplish the desired vow."[35]

In this speech Orderic rhetorically transformed all the land of Christendom into holy land and the crusading vow into an expression of native commitment.[36] Of course Orderic, like many of his contemporaries, saw the defense of Jerusalem and the historical land of Christ's life and death as the heart of the crusading impulse.[37] In the *Historia's* account of the pope's famous speech at Clermont (a speech which, for all its fame, exists only in the subjective accounts of various writers) Urban wept "on account of the trampling of Jerusalem and of the holy places where the Son of God lived in the flesh with his most holy disciples" and called for Christian action.[38] Jerusalem was the place signed by the cross, and it was therefore right that the defenders of the Holy City should also be so signed. But Jerusalem, as Raoul Glaber and the Thorney *mappa mundi* both indicated in their way, was not the only land to find its meaning in the instrument of Christ's death and resurrection. Through the speech that he wrote for Helias, Orderic turned the crusading impulse inward toward Christendom itself, emphasizing the sign of the cross again and again—on the shield and helmet, arms and throne and horse—as the symbol of commitment to "the lands of the Christians" no matter where those lands might be. By reinterpreting Helias's crusading vow as a vow to protect the independence and integrity of Maine and its people, Orderic transformed a local patrimony into an image of the Holy Land and established a Christian leader's duty to protect his lands in the same way he, or any Christian, would wish to protect the land of Christ's bodily and historical life by means of the crusade. Christ was himself a lord, the crusaders believed, who had lost his patrimony to the Saracens; He would understand Helias's desire to protect his own lands and people.[39] Orderic's speech for Helias transformed the sign of the cross affixed to the crusader's body and armaments into a symbol of just authority, an indication of what it meant to be a truly Christian leader. It meant, to Orderic, to treat one's land in Europe as if it were the Holy Land itself, just as vital, just as meaningful, just as geographically central as the landscape of Christ's historical life.

In the wake of Pope Urban's call to take up the cross for the liberation of Jerusalem the sign of the cross took on added meaning for Christendom's self-identity. It was still a sign of Jerusalem's profound centrality for the community's geography, a relic of a real and marvelous past. But the ubiquity of the cross at the time of the crusade, and the success (however short-lived) of the crusaders in reintegrating Jerusalem, the land of the cross, back into the fold of Christendom, broadened the symbol's power. The cross no longer simply marked Christendom's edge, as it did for Raoul Glaber at the very beginning of the eleventh century; rather, with the crusade, it encompassed the whole of a Christianized geography. The *EUROPA* cross on Thorney's *mappa mundi*, plotted shortly after the success of the European *crucesignati*, proclaimed this broadened significance. The cross stood in Europe as well as in Jerusalem, and the whole of Maine, through the sign of the cross, could become Holy Land. Orderic's speech for Helias and the Thorney cartographer's European cross both, in their different approaches to history, manifested a larger awareness of the identity between Europe and Jerusalem, one strengthened though by no means created by the profusion of crosses that marked the crusaders as they massed throughout Europe and brought the cross's topographical fame, its *fama,* to all corners of the Christian world.[40]

STRANGE IT AS MAY SEEM, *FAMA*—FAME, RUMOR, REPORT, RENOWN, "than which nothing on the Earth moves faster," Orderic averred— could be a superb measure of geography.[41] King Henry I of England's *fama* "flew through the four parts (*climata*) of the world."[42] The Sicilian-Norman Mark Bohemond was acclaimed "in the three parts (*climata*) of the globe."[43] (The numeric inconsistency is not a sign of Orderic's geographical ignorance but merely the effect of the very flexible meaning of *clima,* climate or region or part, a word that could refer to one of the three continents or four corners of the Earth, or even to the northern *clima* of the church at Cluny where the short-lived second Abbot Hugh was buried.[44]) *Fama* was that rare intangible that made the known world known. The *oikoumene,* the inhabited world, was defined in the middle ages by how far a story could travel, how far a thing could be told.[45] It was, to the Church in the West at least, how far Christendom could shout and still be heard. To Orderic, it was the extent of the "true vine," the *uitis uera,* which God had spread "through every *climata* of the world."[46] And this true vine in the *Historia Ecclesiastica* had a character of particular holiness—it was the *fama* of the apostles, whose evangelical wandering brought the ends of the Earth home for medieval Christians, and whose names or faces sometimes traced the boundaries of the known world on medieval *mappae mundi.*

Defining the contours of the Christian *oikoumene* by means of the apostles had an important place in medieval cartographic practice, associated most closely with the body of glorious maps that illustrated the commentary on the Apocalypse attributed to the eighth-century Spanish monk Beatus of Liébana.[47] These maps of Beatus's end-time vision, fourteen of which survive, were in part intended to interpret a section of text that Beatus drew from a poem entitled *De Ortu et Obitu Patrum,* "On the Origin and Death of the Fathers," often attributed to Isidore of Seville (a man with diverse cartographic associations). "These are the twelve disciples of Christ, preachers of the faith and teachers of the people," the text explains. "While they are all one"—one in Christ, that is—"still each of them received his own lot for preaching in the world: Peter, Rome; Andrew, Achaia; Thomas, India; James, Spain; John, Asia; Matthew, Macedonia; Philip, Gaul; Bartholomew, Licaonia; Simon Zelotes, Egypt; James the brother of the Lord, Jerusalem."[48] In his work Beatus described the Gospel mandate of the risen Jesus to the apostles: "Go into all the world and proclaim the good news to the whole creation."[49] This mandate is depicted graphically in the maps that accompanied the text, which marked out the inhabited world, the potentially Christian world, by placing the apostles in the regions where they preached. This apostolic sense of geography was realized most strikingly in the late eleventh-century Beatus map from Burgo de Osma, which plotted the bounds of the world by placing the haloed and labeled heads of the apostles in the appropriate realms.[50]

The Thorney *mappa mundi* may have contacted this Beatus tradition, back in the distant past of its sources, for the preaching of the apostles also defined the contours of the historical world on this English chart, with Paul's preaching in Athens, John's in Ephesus, Peter's in Caesarea, and Andrew's in Achaia located graphically throughout the East. At Thorney it was not Andrew's head that appeared at the top of the map (far from Achaia's actual Greek home) but merely the inscription "Achaia, where St. Andrew [preached]."[51] "This man," Orderic explained much more fully in the *Historia Ecclesiastica*'s narrative localization of the apostles' *fama*, "received Scythia and Achaia as his lot for preaching, where he died suspended from a cross in the city of Patras on 30 November."[52] Orderic went on to detail the life, death, and legends of Andrew and his role in the preaching of the gospel to the world. Then he did the same for all of the other apostles whose evangelizing filled the Earth. In fact, the majority of the second book of the *Historia*, some sixty-nine manuscript folios, is taken up with a chronicle, much of it based on apocryphal texts, of the apostles' travels to spread the gospel throughout the Earth.[53] In this book, near the beginning of his *Historia*, Orderic used the apostles to map out the extent of the Christian world and to find the boundaries of the *oikoumene* by tracing the edges of Creation. If the apostles were given the charge of preaching to all the world, then the stories of the apostles could define that world in full.[54] Orderic's account of the apostles' wanderings was narrative and devotional but above all intensely geographic. Peter was first at Antioch and then Pontus, Galatia, Cappadocia, Asia, and Bithynia before heading to Rome, from whence he sent the evangelist Mark to Aquileia and then Alexandria, Martial to Limoges, Apollinaris to Ravenna, and Valerius to Treves.[55] Of Paul's followers, Luke preached at Bithynia, Titus in Crete, Carpus at Troas, Timothy and Archippus in Asia, Trophimus at Arles, Onesimus at Ephesus, Sosthenes at Corinth, Tychicus at Paphos, Dionysius the Areopagite at Athens, Epaphras at Colosse, and Erastus at Philippi.[56] There is more detail about Andrew's life in Achaia, Matthew's in Ethiopia, Simon and Jude's in Persia, and Thomas and Bartholomew's in India—in fact, "it is said by historians that there are three Indias," the first "stretching to Ethiopia, the second to the Medes, and the third to the end, where it has on one side the region of darkness and on the other the Ocean."[57] Orderic even followed the European journey of the pseudo-apostle Martial of Limoges, whose ancient life had been forged at the beginning of the eleventh century by the talented but unstable historian Ademar of Chabannes, whose work was then exposed as a fraud; Orderic's access to this carefully constructed apostolic sham is a mystery.[58] The *fama* of the apostles, the stories told about them, served to define the important world, the inhabited world, the world intended to be a part of God's plan.[59] The world became coterminous with the extent of Christian texts and Christian stories. "Truly the priests and deacons situated personally at the church at Achaia saw" the martyrdom of St Andrew, Orderic's *Historia* announced, "and they wrote it down usefully and elegantly for the universal church founded throughout the four *climata* of the world."[60]

The preaching of the apostles was an essential part of Christian geography for Orderic. As depicted both in the Thorney *mappa mundi* and, more famously, in the illustration of Beatus's commentary, the emissaries of the Christian gospel served to define not just medieval Christendom, the lands inhabited by professed Christians during the middle ages, but the entire spatial expanse of the new covenant brought by Christ. This included both those who, as Raoul Glaber suggested, were before the eyes of Christ and therefore more inclined to accept His sacrifice as theirs, and those who were behind His back, those in the Muslim lands and in the three Indias that stretched to the region of darkness, to the ends of the Earth. The gospel proclaimed that the apostles were to travel through the *mundus universus,* the entire Earth, and to preach to the whole of Creation, *omnis creatura.*[61] A belief in the truth of this statement allowed medieval thinkers to chart the world as coterminous with the apostolic peregrinations, to find the extent of the *mundus* through the medium of historical texts rather than through personal exploration. The dedicated wanderings of the apostles established an authoritatively Christian geography for the entire world.

In detailing the travels of the apostles with far greater historical and geographical detail than the canonical Acts of the Apostles provided, Orderic created a second book for his *Historia Ecclesiastica,* which mapped the contours of the world in which the rest of the events took place, from the consecration of the new church at Ouche to the great movement of the First Crusade.[62] Orderic may not have known what went on beyond the Holy Land held by the Latin crusaders, behind Christendom's back so to speak, but because of the travels of the apostles he was aware that lands were there and that they were meaningful, however populated by destructive barbarians they may have been in his day. Jerusalem could be known to be the center of the world because the apostles' wanderings had rippled out from there in all directions. And the gospel imperative defining the *mundus* went even further than these terrestrial boundaries. For the medieval *mundus* was more than just the Earth's landscape. It was, according to Isidore of Seville in his *De natura rerum,* "the entire universe, which consists of the heavens and the Earth," a definition Bede borrowed in his work of the same title.[63] The apostles did not in their lifetimes travel to the heavens and preach, but they did through their carrying of the Christian word ensure the continued meaning of the *mundus* in full.

"MAN," ISIDORE OF SEVILLE SAID IN HIS *DE NATURA RERUM,* "IS called a microcosm, that is a *minor mundus,*" the universe writ small.[64] Isidore was speaking of man as an individual, *homo,* but the same could be said for humanity as a whole as it existed through time. As the Devil revealed to the Breton woman in Orderic's story of the Christmas gale of

1118—for Orderic, always a reluctant philosopher, found his expression of humanity's *minor mundus* in events rather than words or images—the turbulence of the Earth was intimately connected with the state of humankind.[65] The Thorney *computus* illustrated this identity between the microcosm and macrocosm, between humanity and the cosmos, throughout its entire corpus, medical texts paired with works on time, cosmology with grammar.[66] The explicit historicity of the *mappa mundi*, too, embodied this synthesis, history told through geography, place defined by past. But the geography of the world in the Thorney *computus* was possessed even more subtly by humankind. The circle of the *mappa mundi* is embraced on its folio by the shadow of what seems to be a large cross, but, when the page is turned, reveals itself to be a tree-shaped diagram detailing degrees of kinship.[67] This family tree—for it is nothing else—links the impersonal passage of time inherent in *computus* to the human progress of generations.[68] Each generation led humanity further through God's historical plan, branching out and filling the Earth, the form of the tree merging with the cross of Christ's sacrifice. Medieval scribes had more than enough experience to know that back-to-back images could haunt each other on the page; dark ink on one side of the folio, especially in the thick lines of illustrations, could often bleed through to the other side. To look at the map of the world in the Thorney manuscript, with its explicitly plotted human and historical events, was to see the shadow of the generations of humanity who made the Earth historically meaningful as a part of God's temporal plan.[69]

These associations were drawn even more explicitly through the elaborate chain plotted out in another diagram in the Thorney manuscript, an elaborate *annus-mundus-homo* (year-world-man) image on folio 7v usually called "Byrhtferth's diagram."[70] Reading out from the inside, this emblem begins in the inner diamond with the name Adam, representing the four cardinal directions in Greek—*Anathole, Disis, Arcton, Mesembrios*—that form the acrostic ADAM when read according to the sign of the cross—East, West, North, South—the first man surrounding and defining the history and geography of the inhabited world.[71] This acrostic was popularized by St. Augustine in his commentary on the Gospel of John (a commentary that Orderic knew and used in the first book of his *Historia*), and it appears again, with reinforced meaning, around the edge of the *mappa mundi* in the same volume.[72] Each letter, and each cardinal direction, is then associated in Byrhtferth's diagram with one of the four elements—earth, air, fire, and water—each of which shares its defining circle with the names of three of the twelve terrestrial winds.[73] Dissecting the ribbons linking these four elements into the outer diamond are four more circles, containing the dates of the equinoxes and solstices and the associated stages of human life—the childhood of spring, the adolescence of summer, the prime of life in autumn, and the old age of winter.[74] Surrounding these two diamonds are two joined but incomplete circles with the signs of the zodiac representing the cosmos, encircling and providing meaning to the joining of the temporal, the spatial, and the human. This might seem to be just a contrived academic exercise, an isolated scholar's geometric game with the repetitive fours of medieval science.[75] This, however, would be to underestimate the power and meaning of visual images in the middle ages. Byrhtferth's diagram is able to reconcile the elements of Creation with a simultaneity, an indivisibility, that would be impossible to achieve through language alone.[76] The historical, human, terrestrial, temporal, and cosmological came together into an image that provided meaning to the Thorney codex as a whole with its various texts and diagrams, its maps and medical lore, its *computus* and cosmology, which together built up an image of the cosmos.

This knowledge of time, space, and humanity shaped not only *computus* manuscripts and *annus-mundus-homo* diagrams but also, on an entirely different scale, Christian churches. If the Eucharistic celebration made the altar into the city of Jerusalem, the center of the world, the enclosing church was, by association, a microcosm of Christendom that flowed out spatially from the heart.[77] The building was, like man, a *minor mundus.* When Ouche's new church was dedicated in 1099, when it became the embodiment of the earthly and heavenly Jerusalems, it came to encompass an image of the cosmos that, while not as elaborate or as schematic as Byrhtferth's diagram, still took this geometric picture of a temporal and human Creation and rendered it architecturally real. "With God's aid the church at Ouche was dedicated on 13 November," Orderic remembered his own monastery's experience of 1099. "Gilbert bishop of Lisieux consecrated the principal altar in honor of Mary the Holy Mother of God, St. Peter the prince of the apostles, and St. Evroul the confessor;

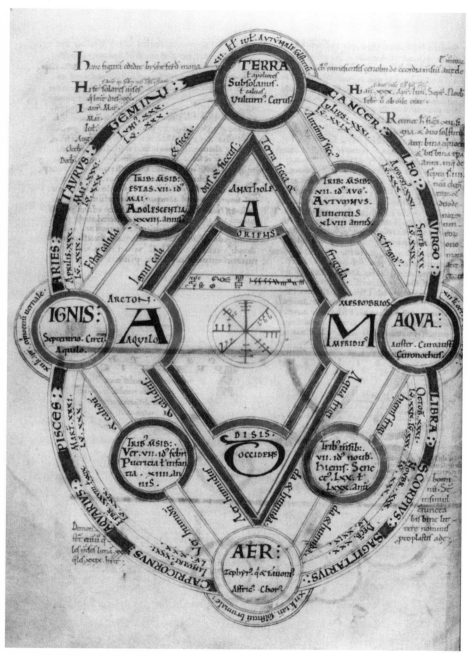

FIGURE 2. Byrhtferth's diagram, Thorney Abbey, c. 1110, from MS Oxford St John's College 17, fol. 7v. By permission of the President and Scholars of the College of St. John Baptist in the University of Oxford.

Gilbert bishop of Evreux the altar to the South in honor of all the apostles; and Serlo," who had been abbot of Ouche before being named bishop of Sées, "the altar in honor of all the martyrs. Then on the following day Serlo blessed the crucifix and its altar in honor of the Holy Savior and St Giles the Confessor, and Gilbert of Evreux the altar of the Morrow Mass in honor of all the saints. Finally on 15 November the bishop of Evreux sanctified the altar in the south transept in honor of all the confessors." The delineation of the church's spatial holiness was still not quite finished, and so "Serlo of Sées dedicated the altar in the north transept on 31 December in honor of all the virgins."[78]

When the twenty-four-year-old deacon Orderic Vitalis witnessed and participated in the consecration of his monastery's new church, he saw the main altar set at the eastern end consecrated to St. Peter, Mary the mother of God, and St. Evroul. There at Ouche's altar occurred a re-interpretation of space that brought together the Jerusalem of Jesus and His Mother with the Rome of Jesus's chosen apostle and pope, all at the place in the Ouche consecrated by the living St. Evroul. The altar was both of the crosses on the Thorney *mappa mundi*, Jerusalem and Europe (the latter represented by the Church of Rome), made present in Ouche not uniquely but in conjunction with countless other churches and altars throughout the whole of Christendom. This center altar, which marked all Christian time and space, was then surrounded by the sacred geography of the Christian world in the form of all the saints, martyrs, virgins, and confessors who together in life and death plotted the contours of Christendom and whose altars marked out the sacred space of Ouche's church.[79] The church itself faced east, as was the case almost without exception in medieval Europe, each sacred sanctuary aligned alike along the sacred axis of the rising and setting sun, looking east in the direction of Jerusalem.[80] Orderic, in his account of the church's consecration, then plotted the location of the rest of the altars not through a personal experience of the space, not by the subjective means of left and right, but in relation to the cardinal directions—the south altar of the apostles, the north altar of the virgins. The church was a space where humanity touched the divine, and it was therefore melded into the fundamental structure of the cosmos. The anonymous ninth-century commentary on the rite of church dedication known as *Quid significent duodecim candelae*—a text known at Orderic's Ouche, for it survives in an important twelfth-century copy from that abbey, now held in Rouen—explained that "it must be known that the four corners of the church represent the four regions of the *mundus* that have been reached by ecclesiastical doctrine, which is signified by the letters written in the Earth," the letters of the *abecedarium*, the ritual of consecration in which the Latin alphabet was written on the floor of the church from the left-east corner to right-west corner, and then the Greek letters from the right-east corner to the left-west corner.[81] The church building thus was one and the same with the *mundus*, and Abbot Hugh of Cluny's tomb, for instance, could be *in aquilonali climate*, in the north region, as Orderic said, of his community's church.[82]

The church building, like Byrhtferth's diagram, was a geometric manifestation of both Christian time and Christian space, though on a more specific, more concretely named scale. In it Orderic plotted spatially the cosmic connections epitomized by the saints, who embodied the intimate links between space, time, and humanity in the Christian world. At the same time the church was to some extent an architectural *mappa mundi*, plotting Jerusalem and Rome and Ouche, and the places of all the saints, within the confines of a building meant to represent the known world. This plotting may not have been precise—the floor of the church of Ouche was not a map with the altars of saints set at accurate sites—but like the *mappae mundi* this ecclesiastical space encompassed Christian history. It was in the church that the cyclical liturgy of Christianity was proclaimed, where the masses for the holy days, especially the mass for the all-important Easter, were celebrated. So the church building, in its plotting out of Christian time and space, was the ultimate embodiment of the convoluted and pregnant science of *computus*.

"IN THE YEAR OF OUR LORD 1095, THE THIRD INDICTION, ON 4 APRIL, the fourth day of the week, in the twenty-fifth day of the moon, countless eyewitnesses in France saw such a shower of stars that except for their light one would have thought them hail on account of the thickness," Orderic began the ninth book of his *Historia Ecclesiastica*, the book detailing the course of the First Crusade. This starfall was an event that needed to be explained. "Gilbert bishop of Lisieux, an old man and a physician, most skilled in many arts, had for a long time been in the habit of observing the stars every night and, as a wise astrologer, skillfully plotting their course. So the physician carefully watched this astral prodigy, and he called out to the watchman who was guarding his court while the others slept." The guard saw the hail of stars and was baffled, but the learned Gilbert suddenly understood. "The old man said, 'In my opinion it prefigures a transmigration of people from kingdom to kingdom. Many will go forth and never return until the stars return to their own orbits, from where, as we see clearly, they are now falling. Others will remain in a high and holy place like stars shining in the firmament.'"[83] This transmigration of people manifest in the heavens was nothing less than the First Crusade, the journey to Jerusalem that would bring Christianity's holiest city back into the orbit of Christendom. Orderic's account of the shower of stars embraced without effort the lessons of *computus* taught explicitly by Thorney's manuscript and lived implicitly in the daily lives of Christendom's most conscious citizens, the Benedictine monks. The stars, whose cyclical course represented the cyclical liturgical year, prefigured in their movement a movement of peoples, a change in the human geography of the Earth. The exacting chronology defined by the year and the date and the moon, the sympathy between the heavens and humanity, the expectant tension surrounding the journey to the city at the center of the world, these were the elements of Christian cosmology and geography made real in human history. Orderic's *Historia Ecclesiastica* shows that the disciplines of *computus* and cosmology and even cartography were not restricted to the philosophical sphere. It's not that Orderic intentionally sought to integrate theology into his work—in fact, he explicitly declined to do any such thing. He was simply writing a history of the Church in an intellectual atmosphere suffused by the potent sign of the cross, with Jerusalem's centripetal pull, with the apostles' definitive wanderings, with the sympathy of the heavens and Earth and humankind, all of it surrounded by the consciousness of God's plan inherent in the cardinal name ADAM.

By placing Orderic's *Historia* next to the most intellectually revealing extant source he is known to have read, the parallels between the Norman historian's careful crafting of human affairs and the wider trends of Christian thought suddenly leap from the chronicle. Helias's passionate speech about being signed by the cross is, when read alongside the dual crosses of Jerusalem and Europe, no longer merely an expression of mutiny against his avaricious neighbor William Rufus but Orderic's statement of a sacred identity between lands that would widely shape his notions of lordship. The inclusion of the apocryphal acts of the apostles in the *Historia* becomes in the context of the *mappa mundi* not an act of uncritical redaction but a conscious mapping of the historicized contours of Christian geography that brought the sphere of the new covenant far beyond the traditional borders of Christendom. Byrhtferth's diagram shows Orderic's description of the layout of Ouche's new church, with its expression of Christendom's sacred history and geography, to be joined through the cardinal directions into the great unity of God's plan for humanity, time, and space. "In the year of our Lord 1095, the third indiction, on 4 April, the fourth day of the week, in the twenty-fifth day of the moon, countless eyewitnesses in France saw such a shower of stars that except for their light one would have thought them hail on account of the thickness." Orderic wrote this about forty years after the fact. And he was, about the indication and the day and the moon, about all of elements derived from the science of *computus,* absolutely correct.[84]

CHAPTER 5

# Haunted Landscapes

"I reckon," Orderic Vitalis reflected in the mid-1130s, "that I must not neglect or keep silent about something that happened to a certain presbyter from the diocese of Lisieux on 1 January" in 1091. The story that follows is one of the most famous passages in the entire *Historia Ecclesiastica*.[1] "There was a priest named Walchelin," Orderic began, "in the town of Bonneval," known today as Saint-Aubin-de-Bonneval, about eighteen kilometers north of the abbey of Ouche, well within Orderic's local and familiar landscape. "In the year of Our Lord 1091, on 1 January, this man was summoned by night, as his vocation demanded, to visit a certain ill person at the furthest limits of his parish. As he was returning alone, and passing through a remote place far from human habitation, he heard a great noise that he took to be that of a huge army moving through the countryside."[2] Well-aware, as were all of his neighbors, of the violence that shook Normandy under the rule of Duke Robert Curthose, Walchelin assumed this to be the knights that Robert of Bellême was known to be bringing to besiege the nearby town of Courcy.[3] "Indeed," Orderic went on to explain, "the eighth moon shone brightly in the sign of Aries at that time, and the road was shown clearly to travelers," making it possible for a troop to move at night and for a priest to see what was coming.[4] But it wasn't an army, at least not in the way that Walchelin had expected. On an average winter night, while traveling down a nondescript road that passed through Normandy's deserted winter fields, Walchelin encountered those who suffered for the sins of their lives in the purgatorial ride of the dead. He would recognize many of the roaming shades as his friends and neighbors and kin in life, and he would live to tell the tale.

Some years later Orderic heard the story of Walchelin's very local encounter with this ghostly army from the shaken priest himself and in turn included the tale in his *Historia Ecclesiastica* as just one of many examples of the intimacy between the worlds of the living and the dead.[5] Orderic, as might be expected, interpreted Walchelin's experience as a lesson given by the dead to the living. "I have written these things down for the edification the reader," he explained, "so that the just might persevere in good, and the perverse may turn away from evil."[6] By means of this journey of souls, Orderic explained, "every base impurity committed in the flesh is melted away in purgatorial fire and will be purified through various purgations just as the eternal Judge determines."[7] Walchelin's experience, as related by Orderic, touches upon the medieval tradition of visions of the Otherworld. The most famous of these include Dryhthelm's journey through heaven and hell and two levels in between as told by Bede in his *Historia Ecclesiastica gentis Anglorum*, the Carolingian accounts of Wetti and Charles the Fat, the twelfth-century Irish visions recounted in the *Visio Tnugdali* and the *Purgatorium Sancti Patricii*, and Dante Alighieri's famous reveries.[8] In these accounts the protagonists, in a sleeping dream or a waking vision, in life or in a short-term death, travel to and through the world beyond, seeing the eternal suffering of those in hell, the unending joy of the saints in heaven, and, sometimes, the temporary torments of those whose confessed but unexpiated sins were still being burned away in the purgatorial fire. But the vision reported by Orderic, though related to these, had an important difference: Walchelin did not go anywhere, not even in his mind. He remained at the side of a Norman road, fully awake, fully alert, while the purgatorial ride passed through the very physical landscape in which he lived his daily life.

Orderic's account of Walchelin's vision shows how intensely local, and intensely physical, the geography of death was in the Norman world of the eleventh and twelfth centuries. The young priest did not need to travel anywhere, even in dreams, to catch a glimpse of the Otherworld.[9] It was right there, sharing the space of the living, occasionally breaking through into the here and now.[10] Throughout the *Historia Ecclesiastica*

Orderic would map out the world of the dead at the same time and in the same places as he unfolded the geography of the living. These two worlds were concurrent, intertwined both spatially and temporally, though the living and the dead could have only infrequent, incomplete, and often unanticipated access to the others' reality.[11] This entangling of the living present with the Otherworld made both places equally part of the fullness of Christian history for a historian like Orderic.[12] The past and the present, the tombs of the dead, the world beyond—Orderic set out in his *Historia Ecclesiastica* a geography of death that folded these together in the local landscape in such a way that the experiences of the departed were still intimately accessible to the community of the living.

"THIS PRIEST WHOM I MENTIONED WAS YOUNG, BOLD AND STRONG, sturdy in his body and agile," Orderic noted of Walchelin, who was at this point in the story still standing on the road and considering the problem of the approaching company.[13] The presbyter was not the sort of man to run away, even if he was only a cleric armed with nothing but a walkingstick when faced with a roving nighttime army. He was also, Orderic was pointing out to the reader, not aged, ill, or near death, often the state of those who were touched by visions of the Otherworld.[14] But despite his good physical condition Walchelin concluded that if the savage Robert of Bellême were involved—for it was Robert's army the priest mistakenly believed to be approaching—discretion might be the better part of valor, so he darted off the road, hoping to hide behind a stand of four medlar trees that he saw across the field. But suddenly "a certain figure of enormous stature carrying a huge mace stood before the priest as he ran, and holding his weapon raised above his head he cried, 'Halt! Do not move any further.'"[15] Walchelin froze. Then he stared in horror as the rest of the troop came into view.

"Behold," Orderic recounted, "a huge crowd of people passed by on foot, carrying on their backs and shoulders cattle and clothing and all sorts of furnishings and various utensils of the sort that plunderers are accustomed to carry off. Truly, all were lamenting and encouraging each other to hurry."[16] This was not, however, the dangerous but merely earthly army that Walchelin had anticipated. "The priest recognized many of his neighbors who had recently died, and heard them mourning the great suffering with which they were wracked on account of their sins."[17] These figures were followed by a thousand individuals carried on biers, tormented by "men as small as dwarfs" who had "great heads like barrels." They were in turn succeeded by a "cohort of women" riding on side-saddles fixed with burning nails that pierced the riders repeatedly as punishment for their lusty sins.[18] "In this troop the priest recognized certain noble women, and he saw small horses and mules with the saddles of women who still enjoyed the breath of life"—though apparently not for long.[19] Behind the women strode monks and clergy, the abbots and bishops still carrying their staffs, all of them, not just the Benedictine monks, clothed in black. "They groaned and lamented, and some of them called out to Walchelin and begged him for the sake of past friendship to pray for them." Indeed the young man saw there "many men esteemed to be truly great" including those "human opinion had added already to the saints in heaven."[20] Walchelin (and Orderic) went on to name names—Hugh, bishop of Lisieux, "a man unequaled in our age," as Orderic had described him elsewhere; Mainer, abbot of Ouche, who had welcomed a frightened ten-year-old Orderic into the monastery; Abbot Gerbert of Saint-Wandrille, who was numbered by Orderic as a star "shining in the firmament of heaven."[21] These three men had all died recently—Hugh of Liseiux in 1077, the abbots Mainer and Gerbert both in 1089—and they were well-known, at least by reputation, to Orderic and others at Ouche.

To see the lasting torment of those who were, if not exactly saints, at least far better than the average Christian, was an unexpected shock to Walchelin and those to whom he told his story. But these men were not the only ones in the tormented troop who were recognized by the young priest, as Orderic noted again and again. This purgatorial ride was an intensely local affair. On the one hand, it was widely believed in the middle ages that revenants, the reanimated bodies of the recently dead, would linger near home and, in their violent moods, confront those who had been closest to them in life.[22] But revenants, who returned from the dead to possess the very bodies that they had had when they were alive, were bound by those bodies and were thus restricted in their movements and their abilities to wander in the world of the living. Revenants

were an entirely different genre of the dead, so to speak, than those encountered by the priest Walchelin. Walchelin saw, not the risen bodies of
the dead (although, as he would learn, the riders did possess a physical
reality), but their eternal souls that had passed into the Otherworld and
its purgatorial cleansing. Like the revenants, however, these spectral men
and women continued to dwell in the landscape of their living world,
the purgatorial fire burning away their sins in the very places where
those sins had been committed. The dead, at least those who were not
consigned directly to hell, continued to be a part of the local community,
visible and recognizable to those who might pass them on the street.

Walchelin, though, after catching sight of those suffering clerics
whom he had believed to be in heaven, was in for a still greater and more
intensely personal blow. Following these clerics came the knights, the
"third order" of medieval society, pushing the overloaded peasants
and the black-clad prelates before them, men on horseback "in whom no
color could be seen except blackness and the gleam of fire."[23] Again, the
young priest recognized some of the recently dead, including Richard
of Bienfaite, Richard's brother Baldwin of Meules, and Landry of Orbec,
local knights from the area of Ouche, men living out their purgatory in
the lands and among the people they knew well.[24] "Walchelin, after an
enormous cohort of many thousands had passed, began to think to himself, 'This is without a doubt the troop of Hellequin,'" the hellish hunter
of legend who, at least in this version of the tale, led a throng of the dead
on a purgatorial march through the countryside.[25] The appearance of a
ghostly army was common in medieval stories of the wandering dead.[26]
Walchelin, who was apparently well versed in the tales of haunting, knew
exactly what he was seeing. He muttered on to himself, "I have heard
about this vision from many people, but I was skeptical and sneered at
the tellers because I had never seen any dependable evidence of such
a thing. Now, however," he averred, "I have truly seen the ghosts of the
dead, but"—remembering his own response to the tales—"no one will
believe me when I report the vision, unless I offer definite proof to living men. Therefore I will seize one of the empty horses that follow the
crowd, mount it without delay, lead it home, and show it to my neighbors, bringing them to faith."[27] Walchelin tried to put his plan into action, grabbing onto a passing horse, but "immediately he felt under his

foot a great heat like a raging fire, and an unspeakable cold seeped into his heart through the hand that held the reins."[28]

Any reader of modern ghost stories would expect Walchelin's hand to pass right through the spectral horse. Ghosts, after all, are incorporeal shades, the mere intangible echo of a soul or of a life. Their insubstantiality, their inability to be grasped by the hand or by the mind, is a primary mark of their character. But not for Walchelin. The suffering ghosts of Hellequin's traveling purgatory possessed a physical and material being.[29] Even those knights who were merely blackness and fire still had a painfully tangible presence (as Walchelin would learn and never forget). It was in their physicality that these shades of the dead suffered their torment; as the flesh had to be subdued in the living, the shadow of the flesh—and exactly what this post-demise body consisted of was a matter of serious debate—required similar suffering in the purgatorial fire of the next world.[30] This material existence had more meaning than merely suffering, however. It was in their physicality that the ghosts of the past still haunted the landscape of the present. The world of the dead as seen by Walchelin was strangely congruent with that of the living. These phantasms of Hellequin's troop did not drift through solid stone walls or cut across the center of a field or engage in any other behavior that implied that they were not aware of and bound by the landscape of Walchelin's present. They traveled down a road like any other person, or army, on a journey. The terrain of their posthumous world, their paths of movement, was the same as that of living men in the local landscape.

Walchelin managed to seize the physical body of the ghostly horse, but his escapade didn't last long. Four of the fiery knights converged angrily on the man who dared to interrupt their journey, but one of them suddenly seemed to recognize the young priest. "Leave him alone, and let me talk to him," the shade said to his ghostly companions. Then he turned to Walchelin. "Hear me," he begged, "and take back to my wife what I tell you."[31] The knight identified himself as William of Glos, the son of Barnon, who had been steward to William fitzOsbern and his son William of Breteuil while alive.[32] Here was another man who still haunted the world of his life, trapped in the local landscape of his sins yet for the most part tantalizingly unable to touch those who still lived and might help relieve him of his suffering. Walchelin was reluctant to become the messenger of the dead—"they will deride me as a madman," he fretted—and William of Glos raged at him in fury (it was exactly the sort of behavior that had landed the knight in the fire of purgatory in the first place).[33]

The young presbyter once again feared for his life, but another knight unexpectedly stepped in. At first the priest did not recognize this new figure, but the man immediately revealed himself to be Walchelin's brother Robert, a Norman by birth who had gone to England and ended his life there. Again, in this momentary disjunction of recognition, Walchelin was playing out a trope of the middle ages' ghostly literature. The world of the living and the world of the dead, although coterminous, did not fit together so seamlessly that vision could instantaneously acknowledge what the eyes saw. It might seem odd that Walchelin could immediately identify such people as William of Glos and Abbot Mainer of Ouche while being unable to recognize his own brother. Perhaps it was not inability but unwillingness, the reluctance to accept that one's own kin suffered so.[34] But this disjunction could also have been another result of the intense localization of the Otherworld. For Robert had died not in the Ouche but in England, where he had lived out the last years of his life. For Walchelin it would have been like unexpectedly seeing a close friend in a foreign city, that moment of confusion where the mind cannot locate a person out of place. But Robert's spirit, in his afterlife, had returned to his patrimony in the Ouche, further reinforcing the intensely embedded localization of the world of the dead.[35] Walchelin and Orderic were able to place so many of the ghosts because for them the history of the Ouche was rooted so deeply in the local landscape and the families who lived there. Recognizing these shades by name, like repeating the appellations in a monastic *liber memorialis,* was an exercise in *memoria,* a confirmation that the dead who were associated with the religious and secular life of the region had not been forgotten.[36] The presence of the ghosts in Hellequin's hunt historicized the landscape. It was a literal possession of the present terrain by the past, a continuing link between the dead and the living. And it was not just any past but the local past, the local dead, who used the local landscape of the Ouche to mediate and communicate with the present.

Robert went on to explain to his cleric brother the suffering that he and his fellow warriors endured. "The arms that we carry are fiery, and they infect us with a foul stench; they weigh us down beyond measure with their immense weight"—it was "as if carrying Mont-Saint-Michel upon me," he explained, an intriguing allusion to one of Normandy's most distinctive local landscapes—"and they burn us with their inextinguishable flame."[37] The many masses Walchelin said as a priest, Robert revealed, had lifted the burden of suffering slightly, and in only one more year he hoped to be free to move on from the purgatorial ride. Robert then galloped away, the last of the parade, leaving the young priest trembling by the side of an empty, moonlit road. Walchelin "was gravely ill for a full week" following his run-in with the ghostly troop, as might be expected after such a shattering encounter.[38] But he lived and thrived for at least fifteen years following his otherworldly confrontation— astoundingly, since an encounter with a spirit of the dead was widely believed to bring death in its wake.[39] Walchelin himself told the local historian Orderic Vitalis his tale, and, Orderic said, he still bore the scar on his face where the hand of one of the fiery knights had seared his skin, a souvenir of the apparitions' physical reality.[40]

Unlike the many visions of purgatory that would come after his—and even some that came before, such as Dryhthelm's in Bede— Walchelin's vision on a lonely Norman road was not an experience of purgatory as a separate, unique place in the Otherworld. It was not *purgatorium*, the Latin noun, parallel to the places of heaven and hell.[41] But just because purgatory was not *a place* in Orderic's account of Walchelin's vision does not mean that it was not *emplaced*. Rather than consigning the very average dead to a distant Otherworld, a foreign place in the extreme, the *Historia Ecclesiastica*'s story of purgatorial fire found the spirits of the departed in the very same places where they had lived out their imperfect but redeemable lives.[42] This local purgatory emphasized the continuing relationship between the living and the dead.[43] They both dwelled in the same places, the same landscape. Although the sporadic encounters between the two were not voluntary, in certain circumstances the barriers between the dimensions broke down so that a single spot, such as a moonlit road in the Ouche, displayed to the living the continuing proximity of those who had passed on. And the dead, as Walchelin's brother Robert told the frightened priest, could still be touched by the prayers, the *memoria*, of the living. The ghosts of the dead of the fairly recent past still possessed the present, possessed it in the modern sense of haunting it, but also in that they laid claim to their right to be remembered, to be prayed for, to be released from suffering, to be a part of the local history.[44] Identifiable ghosts, like those portrayed by Orderic in his account of Walchelin's vision, were a statement that the local past had not been forgotten.[45] It could still speak to the world of the living, in the messages uttered by the shades of those still bound up in the penance they had not completed in life.

In narrating the purgatorial ride of Hellequin's hunt in his *Historia Ecclesiastica*, Orderic first placed familiar people within the terrain of their earthly lives and then shattered the provincial nature of that terrain by making the isolated region of Ouche one and the same with the immeasurable expanse of the Otherworld. This turning inside-out of intimate space to show the infinite that lurked just beyond the edges of ordinary human experience provided the largely unrecognized subtext for many monastic ghost stories of the high middle ages, not just Orderic's singular account of Walchelin's vision.[46] Raoul Glaber, for instance, told the story in his eleventh-century *Historiarum libri quinque* of a monk named Wulferius from the monastery of Réome in the diocese of Langres, who had remained in the abbey church after matins for some private prayer. Suddenly "the whole church was filled with a procession of men wearing white robes and striking purple stoles." These men "were led by a man who carried a cross in his hands. He said himself to be a bishop of many peoples and asserted that they were obligated to celebrate the sacred mass there on that day."[47] The ghostly prelate then moved to the altar of St. Maurice the Martyr and began the service. "But meanwhile the aforementioned brother asked who they were, from whence, and for what cause they had come to that place." They told him that they were Christians killed by the Saracens, martyrs on their way to "the lot of the blessed. But for that reason," they continued, "it has fallen to us to have to pass through this province, since many from this region will be added to our fellowship in a short period of time"— again, local prayers were needed for the local dead. The ghostly congregation then finished their mass and one of their number gave Wulferius the kiss of peace and told him to follow. He tried, but they disappeared, and Wulferius died soon after.[48]

A similar tale was told by Cluny's abbot Peter the Venerable in his *De miraculis*. On the night of 24 December in the mid- to late 1130s, a young novice lay awake in the dark dormitory at Charlieu (a dependency of Cluny) when, towards dawn, the boy saw a man walking towards him. It was his uncle Achard, a former prior of the community. But Achard had died some years before, as had the man who accompanied him, another former prior by the name of William. "Although the boy had known neither of them when they were alive," Peter explained, "he had heard about them from those who had, and he recognized them without any doubt when he saw them." Suddenly William disappeared, and Achard led the frightened boy through the silent abbey and into the community's cemetery. "The boy observed that innumerable chairs filled the whole perimeter of the cemetery, and upon these chairs sat men dressed in the fashion of monks." In the center of this circle, on a stone platform that the boy remembered from previous and licit visits to the graveyard, sat a man who appeared to be a judge. Achard prostrated himself before the figure in penance for his lateness as he would have in life in the monastic chapter-house. Then the entire group rose to leave through a gate on the far side of the cemetery. The boy saw "a great deal of fire right in front of that portal," and as he watched "many of that troop passed through it, some delaying for a long time in it, others moving through quickly." When the cemetery was again empty Achard led the boy back to the dormitory, and disappeared.[49]

In both Raoul's story and Peter's, the intimate space of the living in the monastery was rent to reveal the expanse of the Otherworld.[50] Peter even noted the importance of that moment of recognition, the supernatural realization of the presence of the local dead, that Orderic emphasized so much in his account of Walchelin's vision of Hellequin's hunt. Orderic's narrative revelation of the world beyond was not constrained within explicitly ecclesiastical space. For Orderic, it was not just the consecrated places of the monastery that allowed the living and the dead to touch. But the story of the ghostly ride in the *Historia Ecclesiastica* served the same purpose as the tales recounted by Raoul Glaber and Peter the Venerable.

In transforming the visionary genre of otherworldly travel into an extremely localized experience, Orderic and the other Benedictine writers folded the world beyond into the landscape of their own and their readers' lives, demanding that in every place and at every time a person be aware of all that went on just beyond his senses.

ORDERIC DID NOT WRITE OF GHOSTS IN OUCHE'S CLOISTER. RATHER, he used the tombs of the dead to embed the local landscape in the nooks and crannies of his monastery. Peter the Venerable's story about a ghostly chapter meeting in a monastic cemetery explicitly communicated the links between the tombs of the dead, the community of the living, and the imminence of the world beyond in the mid-twelfth century. Orderic, writing in the context of history rather than the miraculous, saw in the same enclosed environment not the Otherworld but the wider expanse of this one. Though rather more familiar than frightening, the tombs that paved the chapter-house and cloister at the abbey of Ouche, with their engraved white slabs marking and memorializing the various posthumous members of the monastic community, haunted the living in much the same way as the ghostly dead seen by Walchelin, their recognizable and continuing presence a confirmation of the intimate persistence of the past. Both ghosts and tombs named those whose lives defined the historicized geography of Normandy, and both linked the very local landscape into the broader space of Christian life.

For almost thirty years Orderic probably labored at his *Historia Ecclesiastica* in view of the cloister garden at the abbey of Ouche if, as at Cluny, the scriptorium's monks sat under the arcade at the cloister's north side against the church wall.[51] When he looked up from his manuscript to rest his aching eyes, Orderic would not have been able to help but notice the arched and varicolored painted stone tomb of Robert of Rhuddlan on the cloister's north side with its long epitaph composed by Orderic himself.[52] "Here in this tomb Robert of Rhuddlan is buried, in the womb of the earth after the way of humankind," Orderic wrote as a favor to Robert's brother Arnaud, who was a monk at Ouche. It was a phrase that linked the body of the dead very intimately to the ground in which it rested. Orderic then went on in the epitaph to give an account of the life and death that had brought Robert to this place, reminding the reader that "Gruffydd cut off his head with a sword and it was thrown into the sea, but the rest of the body dwells in this small place," this *loculus*, a little place or tomb, a word that emphasized the localization of the sepulchres of the dead.[53] Robert's body had originally been buried in Chester, near the place of his death on the Welsh frontier, but his brother Arnaud had traveled to England sometime in the 1090s to bring Robert's remains back home to be buried in the cloister at Ouche.[54] Other benefactors' less-elaborate mausoleums also stood in the cloister garden: Robert Giroie, poisoned by an apple he had playfully grabbed away from his wife; Arnaud of Échauffour, also allegedly poisoned; and Raoul of Montpinçon (his son Hugh and grandson Raoul rested nearby in the chapter-house).[55]

When Oderic and his fellow monks gathered daily in the chapter-house, which may have curved like a church's apse on the east end in the peculiar Norman fashion, they did so also in the presence of the past, keeping company with, among others, former abbots and a founder.[56] The body of Abbot Osbern (d. 1066) had been translated there by Abbot Mainer of Échauffour (d. 1089), who rested nearby. Abbot Roger of Le Sap (d. 1126) and Abbot Warin des Essarts (d. 1137) were entombed alongside.[57] Warin's tomb was covered by a white stone engraved with an epitaph composed by his friend and monastic brother Oderic, who was himself quite an old man when he wrote it. "The dust and bones of Warin, who was a monk of Ouche for four times eleven years, are covered by this stone," the slab stated. "He was chosen for governance from among the flock by the bothers on account of his merit, so that he might bring special aid to his companions."[58] Hugh of Grandmesnil (d. 1094), one of the founders whose body had traveled from England in salt and an ox-hide, lay on the south side of the chapter-house beside Abbot Mainer, covered by a memorial stone placed by his nephew Arnaud of Rhuddlan and bearing another of Oderic's poems.[59] "Behold, the vigorous Hugh rests under this inscription," the monks could read. "In the time of William, the strong king of England, among distinguished nobles, he was a hero."[60] Hugh, the patriarch of the Grandmesnil family, was surrounded in death as in life by his kin: his wife Adeliza of Beaumont; his son Robert and two of Robert's three wives, Agnes of Briquessart and Emma of Estouteville; his knightly son Hugh, who died young; his son-in-law Hugh of Montpinçon and grandson Raoul.[61] Some of these sepulchres in the chapter-house would still lay there, mutilated and bramble-encrusted, for a roaming antiquary to stumble upon in the early nineteenth century.[62]

These graves of Ouche's revered founders, fathers, and benefactors were part of the essential fabric of the monastery, making its history visible in the intimate and familiar places of the community's everyday life. The abbey's past was very much underfoot at Ouche, and the community's historian, Orderic, was also the one who wrote the epitaphs inscribed on the abbey's graves.[63] The entombment of favored patrons within the monastic enclosure has long been recognized as one of the most fundamental expressions of the relationship between monastic communities and the secular world. Burial *ad sanctos,* near the potent relics of the saints, had its roots in the early Christian period. As the cult of saints became increasingly monopolized by Benedictine monks and the *sancti* moved into the sanctuary, burial in the abbey became the surest promise of salvation.[64] This relationship between the monks and their donors has recently been depicted mainly as a political and economic exchange in which the monastery received money and property and the donors benefitted from their posthumous proximity to the monastery's relics as well as the prayers and commemoration of the monks.[65] In this picture the monastic communities through the ages are portrayed as prayer-machines, repositories of the memory of their patrons' families; the monks' participation in *memoria* was merely mechanical and mediating.[66] As some more recent studies have shown, however, monastic communities—including those founded by noble and royal families— were not just tools for transforming property into prayer and salvation.[67] Monks actively constructed and maintained their own communal *memoria,* in cooperation with that of their patrons, and the abbey's donors and founders and abbots participated along with the monks in the work of evoking heaven through time. The burial of patrons and abbots within the sanctuary of the monastic precinct not only assured that the memorialized dead would be that much closer to the saints in heaven, it also strengthened the connections between the community's place and its past.[68] The tombs grounded a historical topography that continued to be a part of the abbey's identity, a spatial *liber memorialis* in which the names of the dead were engraved in the terrain of the monastery and in the permanence of stone, continuing to make the dead present and part of the community at that very sacred place.[69]

Orderic himself, as Ouche's designated historian and also the abbey's most important provider of epitaphs, showed just how intimately history writing and personal commemoration were linked in the minds of the monks. Orderic often included descriptions of his community's sepulchres in the *Historia Ecclesiastica*. He situated the memorials of Ouche's patrons and fathers very explicitly within the monastery's layout, and he included transcriptions of the epitaphs, many of which he had written himself.[70] These memorial poems were not merely pious reflections on the mercy of God or heartfelt pleas for posthumous prayer (although they included these, too). Rather, they were often lengthy accounts of the person's life, including family background, military achievements, pious donations, and personality. In other words, the epitaphs were brief poetic histories. Robert of Rhuddlan's campaigns against the Welsh were recounted in great detail in his forty-four lines of verse, and his gravestone even noted that his head did not rest underneath with the bulk of his bones since it was never recovered after Robert's decapitation by King Gruffydd.[71] Hugh of Grandmesnil's fourteen lines noted his luster in William the Conqueror's England.[72] Abbot Warin des Essarts did his fighting for forty-four years in the monastery, for fourteen of them as abbot.[73] Glowing epitaphs were not restricted to men, either. Avice of Auffay, who was interred under a stone vault in the cloister at Ouche's priory of Auffay (which had been founded by her family) was praised in twenty-two lines by Orderic for her beauty, piety, generosity to the Church, and twelve children. Her husband Gautier, on the other hand, who died soon after, got a mere six lines noting his name and his death with a couple of pious sentiments.[74]

These epitaphs etched on the tombs were not intended simply to coax the readers to pray for the souls of the dead. As brief histories they reminded the living community of their past, a past that with each burial became more firmly grounded in the site of the monastery itself.[75] Like the ghosts who rode through the countryside in the purgatory of Hellequin's hunt, these epitaphs provoked a type of memory, a recognition of a cumulative local history that was embedded in the local landscape. Both the tombs and the specters spoke to the living, demanding prayers, recounting stories, reminding the present of the past. By including copies of these epitaphs in his *Historia,* Orderic took this remembering one step further, placing the individual and local lives within a larger historical and geographical context, thereby forming a three-part chain linking universal history to personal history and then to localized tomb. By linking the graves with living stories Orderic thus created both in his *Historia* and in his abbey a *lieu de mémoire* where history and locality came together to animate the monastery's past within the community's home and memory.[76] It was a celebration of local continuity. Not only were the dead still remembered but the living were still remembering, the two worlds linked through a geography of the dead that remained aligned with the landscape of the living.

Most of the people whose tombs graced the monastery of Ouche died good deaths, slowly and with time to deplore their sins, beg forgiveness from God, maybe even become a monk, as Hugh of Grandmesnil had done six days before he died.[77] Some died bad deaths, violently and with no time for repentance.[78] Curiously, the manner of death, whether good or bad, may have served to locate not only one's place in the afterlife—heaven, purgatory, or hell—but also one's place of burial in the topography of the abbey, at least within the precinct of Ouche built during the time of Abbot Mainer in the late eleventh century. Of the four men singled out by Orderic as buried in the cloister rather than the chapter-house—namely, Robert of Rhuddlan, Robert Giroie, Arnaud of Échauffour, and Raoul of Montpinçon—three are known to have met violent and unexpected ends.[79] Robert of Rhuddlan, as his epitaph described, was beheaded by the Welsh king Gruffydd ap Cynan ap Iago. Robert Giroie was poisoned (but allegedly by accident). Arnaud of Échauffour met his death in the same way, though, according to Orderic, he lingered long enough to repent and become a monk before he passed away.[80] The manner of Raoul of Montpinçon's death is unfortunately unknown, but he was the steward of William the Conqueror and as such may not have gone peacefully.[81] Those buried in the chapter-house, on the other hand, all died good, peaceful, tame deaths, at least according to the information contained in the *Historia*: the abbots of Ouche (including Osbern, whose body had been moved from the cloister to the rebuilt chapter-house seventeen years after his death), Hugh of Grandmesnil and his family, Raoul of Montpinçon's son Hugh, who was married to Hugh of Grandmesnil's daughter Matilda, and their son Raoul in turn.

The exclusion from the chapter-house of at least two of those interred in the cloister probably had little or nothing to do with their means of death. Robert Giroie and Arnaud of Échauffour both died before the new abbey, with its new stone chapter-house, had been built. Abbot Osbern himself, who died reconciled and cleansed of a controversial investiture, was buried in the cloister at about the same time. But Abbot Osbern's body, Orderic specifically noted, was translated to the chapter-house once the new structure was complete; the same was never said of the earthly remains of Robert and Arnaud, both members of Ouche's founding family who might have expected to rest in a place of honor with their kin.[82] Raoul of Montpinçon and Robert of Rhuddlan were not part of this original founding coterie, and it could be argued that it was this, rather than the way in which they died, that excluded them from the posthumous community in the chapter-house. But Robert of Rhuddlan, at least, was Hugh of Grandmesnil's nephew, an important relationship by medieval standards, and he was a generous benefactor of the monastery of Ouche.[83] In addition, Robert's brothers Arnaud and Roger were monks at Ouche, and his parents, Humphrey of Tilleul and Adelina of Grandmesnil were buried in the abbey; Orderic, unfortunately, did not indicate where in the precinct their tombs lay, but given Adelina's place in the founding family (she was Hugh and Abbot Robert's sister) she and her husband probably rested in the chapter-house.[84] Why then exclude Robert of Rhuddlan—one of England's most illustrious marcher lords, patron of the abbey, kin to the founding family, brother to two of Ouche's monks—from the family of tombs in the chapter-house? The violence of his bad death must have set him apart, dictating his eternal place in that microcosm of the world, the precinct of the monastery of Ouche.

This segregation at Ouche of those who died a good death from those who suffered a bad one is too distinct to be a coincidence, though the reasons for this can only be guessed at.[85] Perhaps the monks of Ouche, all too accustomed to violence, did not want the disturbance of a bad death, a death without the chance of repentance, to be brought into their community as represented spatially by the monastery's community room, the chapter-house. Robert of Rhuddlan's headless body passively represented the shedding of blood, something that was actively believed to pollute a consecrated place.[86] The persistent presence of this violence could have been a disruption to the community of the living and the tame dead who came together in the chapter-house.[87] In the middle ages, as still today, it was people who died violently or suddenly who were believed to disturb the living as ghosts.[88] Moreover, Robert of Rhuddlan was beheaded, and his head was never recovered. Beheading was one of the worst of the bad deaths.[89] Perhaps the monks at Ouche believed that the power of the cloister, more cosmic but less intimate than that of the chapter-house, would help those who had died rough and sudden deaths to overcome their unconfessed sins in the afterlife; on the other hand, maybe they hoped that the same claustral power would keep the possible disturbance brought about by bad death at bay and away from the serenity of monastic life.[90] In either case, the topography of death at Ouche, the layout of the graves of those who took posthumous refuge in the walls of the monastery, was apparently dictated not only by the relationship of the dead with the monastic community but also by the way, good or bad, these individuals met their worldly deaths.

By means of the historical epitaphs that he wrote for the tombs of those buried within the walls of Ouche, Orderic could link the intimate geography of the dead within his abbey into the course of human history as narrated in his *Historia Ecclesiastica*. The little places, the *loculi*, that enclosed the material bodies of the dead came, through the invocation of their names and histories in stone, to take part in the glorious or tragic past. Calling out the names of the dead as part of the monastic liturgy was believed to make these people present again in the world of the living. The tomb and its epitaph did the same, not just for the individual but for the meaning of the person's life in the world. And this past did not die with the body, as those suffering in the purgatorial fire for sins they had committed but not been cleansed of in life knew all too well. The persistence of the past was the reason that Robert of Rhuddlan's violent and corporeally disruptive death would dictate not only his experience of the Otherworld, whatever that might be, but also his corpse's place in the landscape of the living. For the earth was, in a very real way, the medium through which the body buried within it interacted with the history embedded in that place.

"Blessed are those who died a good death," Orderic remarked piously.[91] Good deaths, bad deaths, they all made up the geography of death that was just beneath the feet and beyond the senses of the living. It was the dead who linked the living to the past and to the places of their lives. The materiality of the landscape and of the body came together in the places of burial to continue to anchor the experiences of past lives into the communities of the living. At least, so long as the living remembered. Walchelin's encounter with the ghostly ride of Hellequin's hunt was so important for Orderic because it allowed him to unravel in a shockingly potent way the importance of remembering, of recognizing, the local past. For Orderic history continued to possess the landscape of the present, to claim it by means of the entombed bodies and the wandering spirits of the dead.[92] And by means of the writing of history. Orderic wrote his *Historia Ecclesiastica* in conversation with ghosts, and in it he memorialized not just the local dead of the Ouche but generations of Christians who had come before him and had shaped the geography of Christendom. Ultimately history's intense incarnation in the materiality of the physical landscape and in the corporeality of the human experience would find meaning far beyond the geography of the dead. For there was one body, in life and in death, that more than any other defined the meaning of Christian time and space, and that was the body of Christ. Christendom's geography and history were defined overall by that single death, and it was that body, the body of Christ, that brought the intimacy of the local into the boundless expanse of God's plan.

# CHAPTER 6

# Historians, Heretics,
# and the Body of Christ

On 29 August 1070, four years after Normandy's William the Bastard crossed the Channel and conquered England, the scholar and administrator Lanfranc, formerly abbot of St. Stephen's in Caen, was consecrated archbishop of Canterbury.[1] The previous prelate, Stigand, had been deposed the April before, allegedly for ecclesiastical irregularities (although the English chronicler John of Worcester asserted that England's new Norman ruler "took pains that very many English were deprived of their honors and he substituted individuals of his own *gens* in their place, in the interest, no doubt, of confirming his newly acquired kingship").[2] When Orderic Vitalis turned to write of Lanfranc's archepiscopal appointment in his *Historia Ecclesiastica,* he selected from the many glories of the new bishop's career one epitomizing episode. "Assuredly, at synods in Rome and Vercelli," Orderic told of Lanfranc, "with the sword's point of his spiritual eloquence he pierced Berengar of Tours, who some people considered a heresiarch and damned for his dogma concerning the saving host, a dogma through which souls imbibed death."[3] This dogma that Berengar proclaimed, his heresy, was that the Eucharist was merely a sign of the body of the Christ, not the actual, material body of the Savior who had walked upon the Earth.[4] At these synods, which took place in 1050, Lanfranc "set out in a most holy way and confirmed in a most true," Orderic declared, "that the bread and wine that are placed on the altar of the Lord are, after the consecration, the true flesh and true blood of the Lord Savior."[5] Later Lanfranc

returned to the subject of the Eucharist and Berengar's heretical con-
tentions and in the 1060s "published a book in a clear and graceful style,
weighty with sacred authorities and unbreachably firm in the natural sequence of reason, rich with an accumulation of proofs of the true meaning
of the Eucharist, splendid in the eloquence of its discourse but not tedious
in its prolixity."[6] This was Lanfranc's *De corpore et sanguine Domini*, his
famous tract against Berengar, which Orderic had evidently read.[7]

Orderic's evocation of the eucharistic heresiarch Berengar of Tours
comes at a moment in the *Historia* when the unity of the Anglo-Norman
community hung conspicuously in the balance. And this was not an accident. The English historian William of Malmesbury, one of Orderic's
most probing contemporaries, also, and independently, associated Berengar's thought with the question of Anglo-Norman solidarity, juxtaposing the heresiarch's life and doctrines with the divisive death of William
the Conqueror in 1087.[8] And elsewhere in the *Historia* Orderic again
recalled Berengar and another *De corpore et sanguine Domini*, this one
by Lanfranc's student Guitmund of Aversa, who had also been offered
a bishopric in England.[9] Orderic brought up Guitmund's opposition to
Berengar immediately before he placed into the cleric's mouth a scathing
speech that set out the *Historia*'s most critical indictment of the Normans'
destructive post-Conquest activities in England.[10] "Study the Scriptures,"
Orderic's Guitmund demanded as he refused the episcopal see, "and see
if any law allows to be violently imposed on the Lord's flock a pastor who
is chosen by their enemies."[11] Division, both political and ecclesiastical,
again brought the question of the Eucharist to the surface in the *Historia
Ecclesiastica*.

The body of Christ, in contexts such as these, has long been recognized to have provided medieval Christendom with a model for understanding and enacting community.[12] As the apostle Paul wrote to the
Corinthians, "you are the body of Christ and individually members of
it."[13] But for medieval historians the body of Christ came to be a potent
realization of Christian society in ways that went beyond the metaphoric
or symbolic.[14] In the postmillennial climate of the eleventh and twelfth
centuries the eucharistic and historical body of Christ—and these were
not at all separate—provided a model for understanding and enacting
human history in the material world.[15] Heresy, history writing, and the

devotion to Christ all blossomed in a new and more emotionally complicated way in the early eleventh century and flourished through the eleventh, twelfth, and into the thirteenth, as Orderic's work and that of his
contemporaries demonstrate. In conversation with contemporary philosophers and theologians, the most talented historians of Orderic's age
would find in the historical body and blood of Christ a perpetually real,
material, and unifying sacrament that served as the model for an intensely physical and human historicity in the created world.[16] This historiographic Christocentrism provided a set of related ideas about the
historical life and body of Christ, the spatial and material structure of
the Christian world, and the way in which the individual Christian could
participate in this world's history—ideas that explored and responded to,
even if only implicitly, the very issues that preoccupied the heretics and
scholastics of the age.

Orderic's involvement in the insistent Christocentrism of his world
began sacramentally in 1107 when, he remembered, "in the thirty-third
year of my age, William archbishop of Rouen charged me with the priesthood on 21 December."[17] He performed the mass daily "with an eager
mind" for the rest of his life.[18] This ever-present sacramental imperative has in the case of Orderic long been overlooked.[19] The meditative
conventual life of monk-priests was punctuated daily by the moment
of unfathomable holiness when, through their own words and the rituals performed by their own consecrated bodies, the historical moment
of the crucifixion became present and the bread and wine on the altar were
changed into the very body and very blood of the historical Savior.[20] The
sheer power of this moment cannot be overestimated, and it gave the
question of the Eucharist's nature a more than merely academic importance for Orderic and others like him who found the very meaning of the
sacerdotal priesthood called into question by the heretics of the age.[21] Orderic's liturgical meditations on the life and body of Christ undoubtedly
influenced his decision to begin his *Historia Ecclesiastica* with the temporal life of Jesus, a choice that he made in 1136 or 1137 when he reorganized his historiographical project to give it its final form and meaning.
For Orderic the foundations of Christendom were found not in an ahistorical geographical introduction but in the very historical and deeply material life of Christ on Earth. This *Vita Christi*, a harmony of the Gospel

narratives, is immediately followed in book I by a chronicle that leads the reader briefly from Jesus's historical life through the events of the world's sixth age and up to Orderic's present, highlighting and providing context to materials dealt with in more detail in the *Historia*'s next twelve books.[22] By arranging his project in this manner Orderic demanded that his *Historia Ecclesiastica* be read in the light of, and be historicized by means of, the human life, death, and resurrection of Christ in the world. The interdependence between humanity and the physical world implicit in Orderic's conception of history as a meaningful whole relied fundamentally on the eleventh and twelfth centuries' historicization of Christ, a historicization that found its material basis first and foremost in the eucharistic miracle.

Berengar of Tours's eucharistic challenge was one aspect of a dramatic restatement of the nature of Christian space and time, the relationship between the material and the spiritual, and the orthodoxy of a non-dualist vision of the created world. These ideas would be articulated most fully by the people of the eleventh and twelfth centuries through a belief in the material and historical reality of Christ's participation in the world. A Christological model for both history and geography allowed Orderic and his contemporaries to find in the person of humanity's Savior a consistent geographical model that could be applied across scales from the very local and individual to Christendom as a whole and that could bring these various levels of spatial understanding together into a single Christian world. Through this Christocentric lens Orderic's geography of the Christian world became far more than merely a map of the places of human events, as Orosius's, for instance, had been.[23] The miracle of the Eucharist in human history demonstrated that the spiritual and the material, the human and the terrestrial, were deeply intertwined in the pilgrimage towards salvation. A study of Orderic's geography must therefore end where the *Historia Ecclesiastica* begins, with Christ.

"I, BERENGAR, BELIEVE IN MY HEART AND CONFESS WITH MY MOUTH that the bread and wine that are placed on the altar change in their substance"—*substantialiter*, the most controversial word of this statement—"through the mystery of sacred prayer and the words of our Savior into the true and authentic and life-giving flesh and blood of Jesus Christ our Lord. And I also believe them to be after the consecration the very body of Christ that was born of the Virgin, hung on the cross as an offering for the salvation of the world, and is seated at the right hand of the Father, and also the true blood of Christ that flowed from His side."[24] Berengar, archdeacon of Angers and *scholasticus* at Tours, was forced to swear this at a council held by Pope Gregory VII at Rome in February 1079. This oath represented the core eucharistic belief of the eleventh and twelfth centuries, the Real Presence of Christ in the Eucharist (a belief that, though deeply held, would not take on a firm, consistent, and fully enforceable form for some centuries, the attempts of the Fourth Lateran Council of 1215 notwithstanding).[25] Berengar of Tours had challenged this belief, and he was not alone. The heretics tried in Orléans in 1022 were alleged to have gone even further than Berengar, denying completely the efficacy of the Eucharist, as did, to much more effect, Peter of Bruis from around 1119 to 1139, or so Peter the Venerable reported in his *Contra Petrobrusianos.*[26] But Berengar of Tours's opinions were the most articulate, vehement, and widely known. "My position," Berengar explained in a letter to his former schoolmate at Chartres, Adelmann of Liège, "or rather that of written authorities, has been that the bread and wine at the table of the Lord are changed into the body and blood of Christ not physically (*sensualiter*), but intellectually, not by being taken away but by being taken on, not in small portions of flesh, against the authorities, but, in accordance with written authorities, in full."[27] For Berengar the full presence of Christ in the Eucharist could only be accomplished as a sign, a figure, not *substantialiter,* in substance, the word that Berengar despised in the oath of 1079.

Berengar of Tours's challenge to the Real Presence and the historicity of the eucharistic body brought to the fore a matter more commonly associated with the heresies of the later twelfth and thirteenth centuries. For beneath its emphasis on scholastic reason and its polemical rhetoric the Berengarian debate over the Eucharist was a debate over matter and spirit, over body and soul, over God's participation in the physical world: in other words, it was a debate over dualism.[28] This Berengarian dualism was not the absolute sort commonly associated with the Bogomils and Manichees and the perfidious heresy of the Albigenses, which posited the existence of competing good and evil gods. Rather, it was a weaker form of dualism that saw matter and spirit, body and mind, earthly and divine, to be fundamentally incompatible. Berengar's argument against the Real Presence of Christ's body in the Eucharist rejected the idea that humanity could be saved through the coarse materiality of a body—even Christ's redemptive body—rather than though the spirit, the mind, the soul.[29] "Man is composed of two substances," Berengar maintained, "soul and body, the superior and the inferior: the superior is restored to eternal life by Christ's body as an inner bread, a spiritual bread; the inferior to temporal life by physical bread."[30] Or in other, more complicated words (Berengar never quite knew when to leave well enough alone), in the Eucharist there was "physical bread, by which the substantial body is restored, and spiritual bread, which is the body of Christ, through which the supersubstantial soul," the soul that is beyond earthly substance, "is restored."[31] Berengar's view of reality, which saw the material world as merely a lesser and impotent shadow of the divine reality, was countered by Lanfranc's emphasis on a fundamentally material eucharistic miracle in which the essence of the bread was replaced by Christ's body while the appearance remained the same. Or, in more Aristotelian terms, the substance of the bread changed while the accidents such as color, taste, smell, and texture endured.[32]

Berengar of Tours, by his own assertion, never strayed so far into dualism as to doubt the reality of the historical Incarnation through which the Son of God became man and was born, suffered, died, and rose again in the real body of a man (as allegedly did, for instance, the heretics of Orléans in 1022). But he was nonetheless accused of advocating a dualist view of the world and Christ.[33] Berengar, in his letter to Adelmann of Liège, declared that he "never agreed with the position of the Manichees. For I have held and do hold the body of Christ to have been true and human, while they held and do hold it to have been a phantasm."[34] This invocation of the Manichees was intended to implicate the accused—Berengar—in the late antique dualist faith of Mani as described by the one-time Manichee Augustine of Hippo.[35] Despite his avowed rejection of the Manichees's dualist beliefs, however, Berengar's challenges to the Eucharist's redemptive physicality nevertheless brought the spectre of heretical dualism into the relationship between the superior human soul and the inferior human body, between the divine and the material. The soul was, of course, generally considered to be superior in medieval thought but only insofar as it was able to subdue the flesh and lift up the human person as a united whole, both soul and body, to a level of union with God that would come to fullness in the bodily resurrection at the end of days.[36] Berengar thus went too far when he denied the material world any continuing role in the process of salvation. The bread and wine became the body and blood of Christ, Berengar asserted, "not physically, but intellectually" and it was only "by faith and intellect" that the Eucharist saved.[37] This attitude denied not just the bread and wine of the Eucharist but the material and created world as a whole a role to play in humanity's salvation and relationship with God.

On the other side of this debate over dualism stood the antiheretical Christian philosophers and clerics and also, importantly, the Christian historians who developed a more material, imaginative, and intense vision of history as played out in the physical world at exactly the same time as heterodox visions called the importance of that physical world, and of history as a whole, into question. For to place an emphasis on history—to believe, as Orderic did, that "it is necessary to write truthfully about the course of the world and human affairs, and to compose a chronicle in praise of the Creator and just Governor of all things"—was to give the physical world meaning for human salvation.[38] The material and historical body of Christ as present in the Eucharist created an actual, physical bond between the past and the present, between Christ's bodily Incarnation and the Christian believer, between the content of the *Vita Christi* and that of the next twelve books of Orderic's *Historia*. This eucharistic bond linked the moment at which Christ held up the bread at the Last Supper and said *Hoc est corpus meum*—"This is my body"—with the moment at which the priest said the same words. It also embraced every moment in between that then and this now, for all of that intermediate time was also made real by the repetition of the same ritual and the presence of the same sacred body. Thus the Eucharist did not only sanctify the history of Christ's life as told in the Gospels. It made all of Christian history—past, present, and future—holy because it all shared in the miracle of the past becoming materially present in the world through the physical and historical body of Christ.[39] Furthermore, this link created by the Eucharist between the material and the historical made not just time holy, but space as well. Since at least the fourth century pilgrims to the Holy Land had known that in gazing upon the landscape of Christ's life they linked themselves to the reality of the historical Jesus's existence on Earth.[40] The materiality of the present could make real the events of the past.

BERENGAR WAS, ORDERIC SAID, A "HERESIARCH," A PIED PIPER OF apostasy, but Berengar himself would no doubt have scoffed to find himself associated with heresy's hoi polloi. He was a grammarian, arrogant and jealous of his dignity, a scholar who (as described by Guitmund, one of his decided critics) walked pompously in and sat on a high platform in front of everyone, the hood of his cloak pulled over his head while he sat in meditation before speaking "for a long time in a very slow voice as if he were daily in mourning."[41] Berengar's heresy is typically classified as "intellectual" rather than "popular" by modern scholars, which has for the most part removed it altogether from discussions of medieval dissent.[42] If "popular" is given its, well, popular meaning, though, Berengar of Tours's heresy was, on the basis of the number of tracts, professions, and passing condemnations produced against him and his ideas, far more popular than any other heresy before the thirteenth century. The fundamentals of Berengar's alleged heresy were widely known and understood during his lifetime and in the centuries that followed—a fact that the excessively intellectualizing studies of Berengar's doctrines in modern historiography have largely obscured.

For historians of the twelfth century such as Orderic and William of Malmesbury, however, the thought of Berengar of Tours was certainly not considered to be beyond the average reader. Nor was its invocation merely a pious reference to the social unity desired in the body of Christ that was the Church (a unity disrupted by heretics in general and eucharistic heretics in particular). For these historians the condemnation of Berengar reflected a particular understanding of this sacramental and social body as a unity unmixed, material, even miraculous, and above all historically real. The orthodox statements about the nature of the eucharistic body of Christ asserted over and over again that the bread and wine became the *historical* body of Jesus, the very same flesh and blood of the Incarnation that had ushered in the sixth age of the world.[43] With a formula similar to that recited by Berengar at Rome in 1079, the Council of Poitiers in 1075 professed that the bread and wine "changed in their substance into the true body and into the true blood of Christ—that is to say, into the body that was born of the Virgin Mary, suffered and was crucified for us, rose from the dead, and is seated at the right of God the Father, and into the very same blood that flowed out from His side while He hung on the cross."[44] In this statement, as in Berengar's oath at Rome, historical events defined the nature of the eucharistic body. When Guitmund of Aversa accused Berengar of a belief in impanation (*impanatio*), "the intermingling of Christ with the bread and wine" in a heretical parallel of Christ's Incarnation—God made bread rather than God made flesh—it was perhaps the lack of physical historicity that bothered the Norman scholar so much.[45] If impanation were true, the Eucharist was not the actual historical flesh of the crucified Christ made real again in the world, but the person of Christ made visible in the material of the bread.[46] Even the accusation that Berengar was a Manichee was a supremely historicizing act that recognized the continued reality of the past—as the historical Christ could still be real in the Eucharist, and the historical saints in their relics and the places of their lives, the historical enemies of Christ could continue to exist in the enemies of the present.[47]

For Guitmund, as for others, the Eucharist was not simply the real and physical body of Christ, but the historical body, the body that walked on the Earth at a time memorialized both in the first book of Orderic's *Historia Ecclesiastica* and in the ritual life of Christendom. The Church's cyclical liturgy, lived out most fully by those in the cloister, was dedicated to the revival of the past in the places of the present world.[48] The yearly celebration of the birth, death, and resurrection of Christ not only reenacted the past, it made it real in the places of the present. The Eucharist was only the most material and miraculous element of this persistent folding of time. Orderic exemplified this meditative and historicizing view of the Eucharist through the *Vita Christi* that he placed at the beginning of his *Historia Ecclesiastica* as a lens through which human history had to be read. Adopting a passage from Bede's *Chronica Maiora*,

Orderic went out of his way to place the miracle of the Incarnation within a fully human and historical frame before moving on to a full account of Jesus's life and miracles. "And so in the forty-second year of Caesar Augustus, twenty-eight years after the ruin of Cleopatra and Antony when Egypt turned into a province, in the third year of the 193rd olympiad, the 752nd year from the foundation of the city of Rome, that is, in the year in which Octavian Caesar had established a most firm and true peace by the order of God, having suppressed the rebellions of peoples in all the lands of the Earth, Jesus Christ the Son of God consecrated by His coming the sixth age of the world."[49] With this passage, Orderic placed into the context of human history the primary miracle of God becoming Man, His taking on flesh in the world. And it was this very same body born in the age of Octavian that became repeatedly real throughout the following generations of human history by means of the eucharistic consecration.

By celebrating the Eucharist Orderic and every other consecrated priest condensed the passage of time into the sacramental bread when it became in substance the historical body of Christ. Each individual Christian who shared in the Eucharist experienced this sacramental time machine that made the historical miracle of the Incarnation alive again and again in the world.[50] But this chronological condensation was not complete, for the nature of the eucharistic miracle relied in part on the fact that it occurred despite the passage of time, that it bridged time so that the historical body could be celebrated in its substantial form by each subsequent generation. The eucharistic celebration proved that the past had not disappeared. It still existed for the human world in a perpetual reality materialized by the priest's repetition of the transforming words of Christ, who embodied the creative Word of God.[51] For a historian-priest such as Orderic, as for all the monastic and clerical writers who recognized this transformative potency of words, the combination of language and the material reality of history provided a powerful sacramental undercurrent to their own historical works.

This binding consequence of the body of Christ in its historical reality allowed the Christocentric historians of the eleventh and twelfth centuries to broaden the scope of historical significance to include not just saints and kings but average Christians as well. For the Eucharist was not like sainthood or royal anointing, restricted to a select few. It was obtainable by every Christian, and the historicity it created thus encompassed the entire Christian community.[52] This historical inclusiveness brought about by the age's eucharistic focus included the writers of history as well, and these authors, in their historiographic presence, exemplify the more inclusive scope that high medieval histories were beginning to take on. Historians of the eleventh and twelfth centuries stepped personally into the worlds that they inscribed in their works in a way unknown in earlier ages.[53] It is true that Gregory of Tours, for instance, was a character in his own *Historiarum libri decem*, but his participation was as bishop of Tours, as a representative of a clerical office, not as an individual man.[54] Bede emerged only at the end of his *Historia Ecclesiastica gentis Anglorum*, and then self-consciously and primarily through the list of his writings, a reporter of history rather than an actor in it.[55] Orderic followed Bede in this style, adding his most complete autobiographical moment at the end of his *Historia Ecclesiastica*, but this was not his only personal intrusion into the history that he recounted. Bede's uncomfortable retreat behind his writings or Gregory's episcopal mold contrasts strikingly with Orderic's statement at the beginning of his fifth book. "It seems right to begin the present book in the aforementioned year," Orderic explained, meaning 1075, "in which I came forth from the womb of my mother into the light on 16 February, and was reborn at the sacred font the following Holy Saturday at Atcham through the ministry of the priest Orderic," who christened the historian Orderic with his own name, "in the church of St. Eata the confessor which is situated on the river Severn."[56] The year of his own birth, not the year in which a new king ascended to the throne, provided Orderic with a chronological marker for his history, an intensely personal participation in the course of his larger narrative. Orderic linked his personal emotions into his history on frequent occasions. "I beg your pardon, good reader," he wrote after a digression on the founding of the abbey in his hometown of Shrewsbury, England, "and I entreat you not to mind that I set down in writing some memory of my father, for I did not see him after he sent me into exile for love of the Creator as if I were a hated stepson."[57] (The comparison was not, perhaps, as cruel as it sounds; Orderic remembered also that his father cried as he sent his eldest son away.[58])

Orderic was by no means unique in creating a bond between the personal experiences of the historian and the grander events of the world that made up the traditional material for historical works.[59] Ademar of Chabannes, for instance, a monk at Saint-Martial in Limoges writing around 1027, was not quite so intimate in his grammar as Orderic—he referred to himself in the third person—but his link with history was very intimate. Ademar told how in the year 1009 or 1010, just when the Church of the Holy Sepulchre was destroyed by the Fatimids, "he saw high in the southern sky a great crucifix, as if fixed in the sky, and the figure of the Lord hung on the cross, weeping a great river of tears." Ademar, who had just been peeking outside on a starry night in a moment of insomnia, was transfixed. "Indeed he saw both the cross itself and the figure on the crucifix, with the color of fire and very much blood, fully for half an hour in the night."[60] Ademar's early eleventh-century vision of Christ crucified—in addition to being one of the earliest portrayals, literary or artistic, of such an emotionally intense crucifixion figure— provides a key insight into the greater historiographic intimacy that grew in the eleventh and twelfth centuries. The monk and historian Ademar of Chabannes became a part of history through his vision of the suffering and historical body of Christ that linked him to the suffering of the fallen Jerusalem and thus also into the great course of the sixth age of history. Thus, though a mere individual who just happened to be awake in the middle of the night, he became by means of Christ as legitimate a part of history as any king or bishop. Most other historians (at least so far as is known) did not have such frighteningly intimate visions of the crucified body of Christ fixed in the sky, but they did see the consecrated body of Christ held up in the Eucharist, the very same body of Christ that hung on the cross in Jerusalem. Many, like Orderic, consecrated and held it up themselves. The historicization of the eucharistic body and its intimacy as a sacrament brought each individual into union with Christ and His Church and created a more intimate, more personal, more individual sense of historical importance that drew the historian himself and many other minor, nonroyal, nonepiscopal men and women into the sphere of historical meaning for the first time.

As evident in Ademar's vision, the Eucharist in the eleventh and twelfth centuries became more and more closely paired with another concentrated point of Christological import: Jerusalem, the *axis mundi*, the center of the world.[61] The geography of the Holy Land, like the bread and wine on the altar, was a material realization of the historical life of Christ. Ademar of Chabannes's vision of the fiery, bloody crucified Christ coincided with the catastrophic fall of Jerusalem to the Saracens in 1009, suffering body and suffering place coming together in his mind.[62] Attention to the fall of Jerusalem was rare overall in western thought of the eleventh century, but Ademar and also Raoul Glaber, the age's most historiographically conscious and innovative chroniclers, latched on to the image of the fallen city, bearing out the historian's link with the city's Christological framing.[63] The material reality of the eucharistic miracle, the presence of the real and historical Christ at the altar, came together with the eschatological awareness prompted by the millennium and also Pope Urban II's call for an armed pilgrimage to the Holy Land, and awoke in people the desire to see the land where Jesus had lived and died.[64] This came to a head, of course, with the massive armed pilgrimage that came to be called the First Crusade. "I consider the heart of these things," Orderic wrote as he began his account of the holy war, "and I commit my meditations to writing, since an unexpected change has happened in our time, and a theme, eminent and marvelous to tell, has been prepared to be studied as a lesson. Look! A divine journey to Jerusalem has been undertaken by many people from western parts brought together in a marvelous way into a single group, and a single army has been led against the pagans in eastern parts." A mass of people driven to the land of Christ's life was an irresistible theme for historians, both those who participated and those who made their pilgrimage vicariously through stories. "Never, I think," Orderic vowed, "has more glorious material ever been provided for military authors than God has now given to our poets and writers when He triumphed over the pagans in the East by means of a few Christians, summoned from their own homes by the sweet desire to be pilgrims."[65]

These pilgrims, most of them nameless, without any other distinction in their lives, were drawn by the historical land of Jesus and through it became, like Ademar, a part of Christian history by means of their continued connection with the life, death, and body of Christ. The crusade, like the Eucharist, allowed the historian to draw the mass of common

Christians, not just kings and saints, into the course of history. This unifying product of the crusade, the inclusive historiographical and geographical model created by the shared eucharistic body, helps to explain why the First Crusade was always portrayed in consciously historical texts as a movement with far more popular support and participation than seems to have actually been the case.[66] The crusade's potency as a model for Christendom that allowed historiographic and geographic horizons to be broadened within a Christological context—its reflection, in other words, of the Eucharist—caused it to draw all Christians into its symbolic realm, Christians who traveled to the Holy Land or who simply wrote about such travels and who hoped, or perhaps feared, that this expansion of Christendom's boundaries might bring Christ back to usher in the end of days.

The magnetic pull that drew the crusaders to the Holy City demonstrated the centering power of the body of Christ for medieval Christianity, and this functioned so strongly that the land of Christ's life could be experienced at places far from the earthly Jerusalem. If the Eucharist celebrated at the altar was the true and historical body of Christ who had made the supreme sacrifice in Jerusalem, the city believed to mark the center of the world, then the altar itself became this center and the enclosing church, a microcosm of Christendom.[67] The eucharistic creeds articulated under the pressure of Berengar of Tours's challenge consistently emphasized "the bread and wine that are placed on the altar." This very particular locating of the material and historical body of Christ within liturgical space created a historicized geography of Christendom that was mapped and recentered at each altar throughout the Christian world.[68] The main altar in Ouche's new church, set at the eastern end, was dedicated to St. Peter, Mary the mother of God, and St. Evroul. At that sacred and particular place, along with the eucharistic collapsing of time present in the body of Christ, occurred a collapsing of space that brought together the Jerusalem of Jesus and His Mother with the Rome of Jesus's chosen apostle and pope, all at the place in the Ouche consecrated by the living St. Evroul. But this bridging of space at the altar, like the bridging of time in the eucharistic bread, did not negate the meaning of distance or the reality of the material world in its spaciousness.[69] Rather, the altar was a place where distance (like time) could be miraculously overcome, where space could be folded and far-flung but still very real places could be simultaneously present in the sacramental reality. This bridging was a necessary and wondrous part of the Eucharistic miracle, a way of making historicized space as well as historical time present and accessible to all the Christian community.[70]

The Eucharist as the material and historical body of Christ was one of the things that made Orderic's Christian geography possible. At one level the sacrament epitomized a particular place, Jerusalem, at a moment in time, the moment of Christ's sacrifice. But it was also all places and all times where the Eucharist was, had ever been, or would ever be celebrated. The Eucharist became Christendom, the material and earthly geography that embraced the Christian community through time, particularly when placed in the context of the cyclical and commemorative liturgical year and when performed within the church building, a microcosm of the Christian world.[71] This conflation of the body of Christ with the geography of the *oikoumene* was depicted most clearly on the now-destroyed Ebstorf *mappa mundi* from the mid thirteenth century, which depicted a circular map of the world with Christ's head at the top edge, his hands at the left and right borders, and his feet at the bottom of the frame; the world, with the whole of history upon it, was literally, in this depiction, the body of Christ. The life and body of Christ, for Orderic, could do something that the geographical introductions of the other writers could not: embrace Christendom at all scales and at all times, from the local to the universal, from Greenland to the Holy Land, from a specific moment in an individual's life to the grand sweep of human history in the mind of God.

The Church's view of historicized Christian space was challenged by some, such as the twelfth-century heretic Peter of Bruis who, Peter the Venerable reported, preached "that the building of temples or churches ought not to be done, and moreover those built ought to be torn down. Sacred places are not necessary for Christians to pray, since God hears appeals equally in a tavern and in a church, in a market and in a temple, before an altar or before a stable, and He listens to those who are deserving."[72] There was, of course, a potent and popular strand of anticlericalism in this statement. But there was also a more fundamental denial. To reject the localization of holiness through buildings was to reject the

Christian notion of both geography and history. Denying the special
holiness of the altar or of Jerusalem was not just to make every place the
same as every other, it was to make every moment in time the same, too.
For the church buildings that the heretical preachers spoke out against
were microcosms of Christian space and time—embracing Jerusalem,
the cosmos, the lives of the saints, and the singular yet repeated moment
at which God became Man. The stone walls marked out the boundaries
between Christendom and damnation. While Peter of Bruis and others
were condemning the vision of Christian space and time manifest in
the churches and in the eucharistic sacrifice that took place within—for
Peter also denied the efficacy of the Eucharist—Orderic and other historians were writing in implicit but vigorous opposition to their views. The
historians narrated human history as the realization of the eucharistic
miracle and of the historicized Christian geography that it placed at the
center of God's plan for His creation.

    "The sea never rests, safe with sure solidity," Orderic wrote in 1125,
"but, swirling with perpetual disorder, it flows on in its way, sometimes
appearing calm to the gaze of observers yet frightening sailors accustomed to its waves and instability. Likewise, this present age is perpetually rocked by its changeableness, and is plainly changed in many ways
both miserable and joyous."[73] For all the stability that the Eucharist provided to Christendom's vision of space and time, it is impossible to ignore
Orderic's frequent comments on the volatility of his world. Orderic and
his fellow historians of the eleventh and twelfth centuries could not help
but recognize that they wrote in a world of change: countries changed
their kings; monks changed their orders; Jerusalem changed hands; the
Church changed its customs; the Eucharist, once and for all, was known
to change from bread to the very body of Christ; and some people, mostly
labeled heretics, even tried to change the meaning of Christianity itself.[74]

    Orderic's unsettled age has been honored, however problematically,
as a "renaissance," in large part because of its changes in mentality and
practice.[75] It was the time of Peter Abelard and Bernard of Clairvaux and
Suger of Saint-Denis, men whose effervescent passions led to new ways
of thinking and new ways of praying, and new styles of buildings in
which to pray. It was also the age of Berengar of Tours, Peter of Bruis,
Henry of Lausanne, and many other more anonymous dissidents whose

challenges to the mainstream of Christian tradition did far more than merely force the Church into a greater and ultimately more brutal articulation of its theology and its authority. The heresies of the eleventh and twelfth centuries, both those called popular by modern historians and those that took place among Europe's theological elite, were part of a fundamental shift in the way Christians understood the meaning of space and time, of geography and history, in their world. Historians, philosophers, and theologians articulated and disseminated as orthodox a fundamentally nondualist vision of God's creation in which the material and the spiritual, the physical and the intellectual, substance and meaning, were all inextricably linked into a powerfully redemptive understanding of human life in the world based on the notion of Christ's historical Incarnation and his historical body's continuous eucharistic presence, called into being by the mimetic words of the priest.[76]

But how could the twelfth-century historians reconcile this relentless change with the unchanging reality of Christ's sacrifice, made materially and historically real in His body? Once again, they could look to the Eucharist for answers. For the changing of bread and wine into the body and blood of Christ provided a model for change that, for all its miraculous incomparability, demonstrated which elements of change were important and which were incidental. The definition of the eucharistic change that came out of the Berengarian controversy maintained that while the substance of the eucharistic elements changed, the accidents remained the same. Within the Eucharist the substance was essential, the accidents were not, and it was this model that allowed the historian to understand the changes in human history. For—in an inversion of the singular eucharistic change, though one that nonetheless retained the eucharistic notions of important substance and unimportant accidents— the vital substance of human history, namely God's plan for His creation, remained the same while the accidents produced by human action and free will changed.[77] "Look," Orderic said, "the wheel of fortune," which, for him, represented the natural variability of the world as established and overseen by God, "turns daily and the state of the world is driven by change," and this was the way that God had planned for the world to work.[78] Orderic and others like him wrote about the changes that took place in their age not to glorify diversity but to show how this escalating variability conformed to the unchanging substance of God's created world.[79] "The eternal Creator," in Orderic's words, "wisely and beneficially sets in order the changes of times and circumstances. He does not arrange and change human affairs at the fancy of fools, but benevolently preserves them, and fitly promotes and regulates them, with a powerful hand and the arm of the divine."[80]

Paradoxically, however, the historians in this time of change could only affirm the world's invariability by creating a new style of historiography that embraced change and broke out of the rhetorical molds of the past. The swift intellectual and social currents of the eleventh and twelfth centuries gave birth to historians who might best be styled "exploratory." Working alongside the philosophers and theologians, these exploratory historians—who included Ademar of Chabannes and Raoul Glaber in the eleventh century, and in the twelfth Orderic Vitalis, William of Malmesbury, Otto of Freising, Galbert of Bruges, William of Newburgh, Gerald of Wales, and also Geoffrey of Monmouth and Henry of Huntingdon—searched for the truth about their world; but where the scholastics relied on reason and texts, the historians found their material in the events of human history. They explored "the secret causes of things," to use Orderic's phrase, by laying out events, juxtaposing them in new ways, asking *sic* or *non* about the truths of human life.[81] They made the past available for future explorers, whether in the next generation or the next millennium, "so that," Orderic explained, these future historians "might unravel the past happenings of the declining world for the instruction or pleasure of their contemporaries."[82] Filled with miracles and marvels and metamorphoses, burning heretics and Saracen princesses, Crusaders and Cistercians, storms and stories, and as always kings and saints, these exploratory histories are complicated, probing, inconsistent, even, by modern standards, ahistorical. Though individually fascinating, they jar with the genres and subjects through which medieval historiography has traditionally been approached by modern scholars.[83] But they fit perfectly with the character of their age. With their style and method and content, the things that they included and those that they ignored, these exploratory historians depicted a world that was, and was determined to remain, fundamentally nondualist, both materially and socially. Orderic Vitalis and his fellow historians participated, sometimes implicitly and sometimes openly, in the fundamental questions of their age: the relationship between body and soul, between matter and spirit, between humanity and God. And, unlike the philosophers with their abstractions, the historians engaged with these issues concretely, grounding them in the actual events of human history as located and played out in the physical, created world. Within a context that increasingly saw the historical and material body of Christ, made present in the Eucharist, as the unifying body of Christendom, the writing of history in the eleventh and twelfth centuries brought the ideas of the age together with the events and showed how the changes lived out in the created world were governed inalterably by God.

# Epilogue

"The time of Antichrist draws near," Orderic Vitalis wrote in 1127 in a mid-work dedication to his abbot and friend, Warin des Essarts, "whose form, as the Lord made known to the blessed Job, will be preceded by a lack of miracles, and a great frenzy of vices will proceed from those who take pleasure in their own carnal delights."[1] Orderic was, in this passage, drawing on the *Moralia* of Gregory the Great, and like Gregory he kept writing for many years despite his conviction that the end was not far off.[2] In part, this unremitting literary activity was for Orderic an element of monastic discipline. "Following eagerly the examples of our masters," Orderic began his dedication to Abbot Warin, "we ought perpetually to shun deadly leisure and to labor in useful study and salutary exercises by which the eager mind might be cleansed of its faults and armed with glorious discipline against every sin of life (*vitali*)," or, if Orderic intended a curious pun on the word *vitalis*, every sin of his own.[3] This discipline, in Orderic's case, came from writing history, and he believed that his efforts, however small, were added to humanity's exploration of God's plan for the world. "Our ancestors from earliest times have skillfully looked into the course of the declining ages and as a warning to mankind have noted the good and the bad befalling mortals," Orderic wrote in the prologue to the *Historia Ecclesiastica*, "and they have willingly gathered together writings for the continuing benefit of the future."[4] And "since new things happen daily in the world," he continued, "it is fitting that they diligently be committed to writing for the praise of God, and just as past deeds have been conveyed to us by our ancestors, present happenings should

129

likewise be set down by the present in the form of written signs for future generations," just in case the signs of Antichrist were simply meant to mislead.[5]

Future generations again and again materialize in the *Historia Ecclesiastica* like ghosts in reverse, haunting the past and demanding that it answer for that which is to come.[6] There was a strong messianic undercurrent to medieval historical writing.[7] Just as Christians of each generation had the obligation to pray for the souls of their ancestors, they needed equally to provide the material necessary for future generations to further humanity's struggle to find God's meaning in the world. In this way, each point in the continuum of Christian history looked both back and forward. Henry, archdeacon of Huntingdon, in one of the most hauntingly personal passages in all of medieval historiography, dramatically illustrated this consciousness of time in his *Historia Anglorum*. "Now then, I speak to you who will exist in the third millennium around the 135th year," wrote Henry, addressing the world in the year 2135, a thousand years after he wrote these words. "Think of us who seem just now to be famous (for, to be sure, certain piteous people revere us). Think, I say, about what will become of us. Tell me, I beg, what good will it do us if we are great or famous? Nothing, in short, except what we have made clear in God." And so it was God's mercy upon which Henry relied as he spoke directly to his future readers. "Now, however, I who will be dust in your time have made mention of you in this work, such a long time before your birth. So if my work has reached you—which my soul desires greatly—and has been placed in your hands, I beg that you will prevail upon the incomprehensible mercy of God on my behalf in my misery," Henry entreated. "In the same way, may those who walk with God in the fourth or fifth millennium, if mortal generations are prolonged so long as that, pray and obtain the same for you."[8] Henry went on to tell those who would argue that "we are daily trembling with expectation of the end of the world" that they had too little faith.[9] Although the day and hour of the end was hidden, it would not be unreasonable to expect that the Christian era in its greatness would be at least equal to the inferior pre-Christian age that had lasted some 5000 years. Contempt for the world runs through Henry of Huntingdon's *Historia Anglorum*, but still history's redemptive potential for both the present and the future served to anchor its meaning for the Christian community through time. Historians, Orderic said, "labor out of goodwill, and they manifest the past for future generations unenviously," a gift from one generation to the next.[10]

Despite his belief in the necessity of history for future generations, however, Orderic's allusions and pointed references to the possible end of days were not merely rhetorical flourishes. To say that he believed the end to be near would be putting it too strongly. But he did, most certainly, believe in an end, and it shaped his vision of both the present and the past.[11] By invoking Antichrist, the most talented of the medieval historians—like Orderic and also Otto of Freising, whose last book of his *Historia de duabus civitatibus* was entirely occupied with Antichrist, the resurrection of the dead, and the last judgment—projected into the future the periodization and meaning of their world based on Christ's human life, Antichrist (Christ's explicit opposite), and the Savior's promised return.[12] Medieval history was not open-ended, and the general character of the end, the anticipated "history" of the future, could be used by the historian to further establish the Christological order of human affairs. Orderic trusted, as the scriptures promised, that both the human and physical worlds in their sympathetic blossoming of good and evil would manifest visibly the signs of this end, which could happen at any moment or a thousand years hence. In his *Vita Christi* Orderic summed up the Gospels' teachings about the end of days. "When asked about the end Jesus responded that many evils would come forth, wars among nations, earthquakes in many places, pestilence and famines, and great and fearful signs in the heavens."[13] Well, the eleventh and twelfth centuries certainly had more than enough famine and plagues and wars to provoke worry, and brilliant signs in the pitch-black night sky could be seen far more often and more vividly than the modern stargazer could ever imagine in a light-polluted sky. The wrenching movement of an earthquake, the stars streaming from the sky in brilliant rivers of light, scorched and barren fields, wretchedly emaciated bodies of the starving or those trembling with fever, these were the signs of the end and they could be seen and recorded by the historian. This eschatology, again, reflected the fundamental antidualism expressed in the work of the eleventh and twelfth century historians. The Gospels and the Church fathers assured that "about the day and hour no one knows," but Christ's return, which would bring about the resurrection of the physical body, would be manifest in physical signs visible in the material world and in human history.[14]

The drying up of miracles that Orderic drew from Job via Gregory the Great was one of these visible signs in the world, and it provided a running thread for Orderic throughout the *Historia Ecclesiastica.* "Concerning miracles and marvels of the saints," Orderic pointed out caustically in the sixth book, "since there is now a great lack of them in the world it isn't necessary for writers to sweat over reporting them at all."[15] And at the beginning of the *Historia's* eleventh book, in a pessimistic and palpably apocalyptic poem in which he declared that "the evil beast bearing ten horns now has dominion" and listed the many scriptural names of Satan, Orderic affirmed that "the light of the saints has now justly ceased in great things. Sinners who transgress the law deserve the punishment of heavenly wrath, not signs."[16] These declarations about the dearth of miracles in the world might seem out of place in a history abounding with miraculous events, from St. Evroul's springing of a man from prison at the castle of Domfront to the astounding discovery of the Holy Lance during the crusade. But none of these miracles was performed by a living holy man or woman of the time.[17] All the miracles of the *Historia Ecclesiastica* were brought about through a residual holiness drifting up through time from the past. This lingering sanctity, so very often localized in Christendom's sacred landscape, provided the most pressing reason that history had to be conveyed to future generations. For if the landscape of medieval holiness were lost, if the people of the future could not find the places where the miraculous power of the saints continued to dwell, then in a world devoid of miracles all sacred power could be lost. In his *Historia Ecclesiastica* Orderic Vitalis set out the historicized geography of his world—from the ends of the Earth known only through the travels of the apostles to the landscape of the Norman Ouche where Orderic and his fellow monks participated in and remembered an intensely local past—so that future generations would not forget the places where individuals, both good and bad, lived out God's plan on Earth.

THE SITE OF ORDERIC'S MONASTERY OF OUCHE, SO CAREFULLY located by its historian in a landscape both local and cosmic, has not been forgotten. But no scrap of the Romanesque abbey of Ouche built by Abbot Mainer of Échauffour, the abbey in which Orderic wrote the whole of his *Historia,* has survived. The picturesque ruins that today adorn the Charentonne's banks and in a somewhat less ruined state graced the sketchbooks of romantically inclined nineteenth-century artists are Gothic remnants from the thirteenth century.[18] But yet Ouche "is essentially a place of pilgrimage," E. A. Freeman, the great nineteenth-century historian of the Anglo-Norman world, wrote in his *Sketches of Travel in Normandy and Maine,* "not a Canterbury pilgrimage, but a pilgrimage to the cell of a hermit, to the *scriptorium* of a chronicler of whom we get more personally fond than any other."[19] Of the town of St.-Evroult-Notre-Dame-du-Bois, the modern name for the site of Ouche, little more can be said in the twenty-first-century than Freeman said in the nineteenth. "Not a word could we find in any guide-book to say whether the abbey was living or ruined or desecrated or wholly swept away." And, as Freeman noted, "a monastic site from which everything monastic has been swept away is not so instructive as a fortified site from which the fortifications are gone. We should be best pleased to find at Saint-Evroul a church in which Orderic may have worshipped, but it would be better to find a later church" than to find "no church at all."[20] And find a church he did, at least of a sort, as does the twenty-first-century pilgrim. "The church of the monastery is a mere ruin; but at least it stands open to the sky; it is not desecrated and disfigured by being put to any profane use." But still there is for the traveler, as Freeman said, "perhaps a slight feeling of disappointment at finding that here at Saint-Evroul there is nothing directly to remind us of the man for whose sake we have come thither. We would fain to see something that had met the eyes of the island-born child in the first years of his coming to his foreign home," the Romanesque walls guided by Abbot Mainer.[21]

But Mainer's church apparently went out of style. In place of the Romanesque church, Freeman found the ruins of a Gothic structure—which are still there, though a little more ruinous than in Freeman's time. This building was launched in 1231 and was apparently little if any longer or wider than its predecessor at the site, although quite a bit more grand.[22] This later edifice, in its pre-Revolutionary splendor, can be admired in the Maurist *Monasticon Gallicanum* in an engraving dating from 1683 (although the skewed perspective causes the church in particular to seem larger than life, especially when compared to the minuscule church of St. Mary hidden in the upper right-hand corner of the plate and rendered not much bigger than the ducks floating in the dammed and widened Charentonne).[23] When Frédéric Galeron, the *procureur du roi* at nearby Falaise and a native of L'Aigle, returned to his childhood stomping ground on a glorious autumn day in the late 1820s he saw the death throes of this basilica as he gazed down from the hills to find in the abbey's ruins "an enormous lime kiln, built within the walls of the ancient choir," its noxious smoke blackening the pale stones. "It is into this maw that the untiring entrepreneur of this destruction calmly feeds, at all hours, the rich capitals, the cornices with their delicate indentations, the graceful ribs of the vaulting, and even the debris of the statues of those saints and martyrs who were venerated for so long by our fathers."[24]

The nineteenth-century musings of Galeron and Freeman continue to strike a chord with the traveler, for the landscape of modern Normandy— still blanketed by the fields and forests described by Orderic, still spotted with Romanesque churches whose steeples lead the traveler from town to town—allows one to slide easily from the present into the past, to believe oneself to be one of Orderic's "future generations," seeing the geography of the medieval Norman landscape in the modern terrain. But often this time travel, before it can reach the middle ages, stops jarringly in 1944. Normandy today is haunted not so much by the shades of dukes and knights and monks as by those of too-young heroes fighting and dying in a war which by medieval standards would have been considered more than just.[25] The devastation suffered by Normandy and its people during the two World Wars makes the cheerful prewar descriptions of the Norman countryside and people, such as those by Freeman in his *Sketches* and by Charles Homer Haskins in the first chapter of his *The Normans in European History,* seem as distant as the Viking invasions.[26] Today every road sign pointing the way to a medieval church or chateau is matched by one leading to a battle of the Denouement, and every statue of Rollo or William the Conqueror is outnumbered one hundred to one, perhaps one thousand to one, by memorials inscribed with dozens of names and the epitaph *Mort pour la France.* The great medieval cities of Caen and Rouen, today thriving once again, were six decades ago piles of smoldering rubble. The abbey of St. Stephen's in Caen, William the Conqueror's foundation, has undoubtedly listened to millions of prayers in its millennium of existence, but few were likely to be as fervent as those uttered by the citizens of the city who took refuge in its red-cross-marked sanctuary as bombs rained down upon their homes outside. This war, like those described by Orderic, is marked and memorialized in the Norman landscape, a historicized geography of a more recent history. Normandy's recent trauma serves to remind the historian why it is so vital to learn from the past, as Orderic and other medieval chroniclers wished and warned, no matter how close or how distant that past might be.

"HOW CHANGEABLE ARE THE VICISSITUDES OF THE PRESENT LIFE," Orderic reflected in the thirteenth and final book of his *Historia Ecclesiastica*. "Temporal joys pass quickly, and they abandon in an instant those who strive after them exceedingly. Worldly honor, like a bubble, bursts and disappears, and taunts and deceives those who pant after it."[27] Henry I of England, both king and duke for much of Orderic's adult life, was dead. The reign of Stephen, known in modern historiography as the Anarchy, had begun. And Orderic was reflecting on the meaning of his age, and of his work. "And so the omnipotent Creator prepares those born on Earth and profitably teaches them in many ways, so that they might not fasten the anchor of their hope in the sea of this fragile world, nor fatally cling to transitory delights or gains. We do not have here a lasting city, as the apostle said, but we seek the one to come."[28] It is fortunate that Orderic did not have much use for earthly fame, for that of his *Historia Ecclesiastica* did not spread far outside the walls of his abbey for hundreds of years. The *Historia*, in both size and content, was apparently too weighty to circulate widely, though it did have some limited appeal. For all Orderic's talk about future generations it was the modern world, not the medieval, that would be touched by his words and would thank him for daring to record both the good and bad of his age.

No one in the middle ages recorded an epitaph for Orderic Vitalis. Probably no one ever wrote one. Orderic was not, in his own age, famous. He probably would have considered himself to be "neither better than the best men nor worse than the worst ones," Abbot Warin's description of an exceptionally average English man.[29] Orderic was not a patron of his monastery, and he was not from a wealthy family. So he would have been buried anonymously in the cemetery of the monks, without a memorial stone, and so far as anyone knows he has never come back to haunt the living, at least not outside of the pages of the *Historia Ecclesiastica*. His only medieval memorial was his name in Ouche's calender on 13 July.[30]

But in 1912 the Société historique et archéologique de l'Orne arranged for a memorial obelisk to be erected outside the ruins of the monastery of Ouche in memory of Normandy's most famous historian. The list of subscribers to the monument and the accompanying volume of studies is a fascinating read. Albert I, the Prince of Monaco, was among those interested in Orderic Vitalis's *memoria*, as were a Rothschild, a Seigneur Comte David de Montgomery (although it seems unlikely that he was a direct descendant of Roger of Montgomery), and, more predictably, Charles Homer Haskins and R. L. Poole.[31] The Latin inscription on this monument, Orderic's modern epitaph, makes a particularly apt conclusion to a study of Orderic's history and geography:

> *Orderici Vitalis*
> *Angligenae*
> *Coenobis Vticensis*
> *Saecvlo XII Monachi*
> *Normannicae Historiae*
> *Solertissimi Indagatoris*
> *Memoriae Sacrvm.*

> Sacred to the Memory of
> Orderic Vitalis
> English-Born
> Monk at the Abbey of Ouche
> in the Twelfth Century
> A Most Skilled Explorer
> of Norman History.

An explorer, indeed.

# Notes

Prologue

Orderic Vitalis's *Historia Ecclesiastica* is peculiarly complicated when it comes to citations. Marjorie Chibnall's recent definitive edition contains the text of books III through XIII, but not the complete text of books I and II. For those books the older, but still solid, edition by Auguste Le Prévost must be used, although it is not always easy to find. To make things even more complicated, Chibnall's definitive edition does not mark the standard section divisions in books III and IV, though it does begin to do so with book V. To navigate these editorial issues, Orderic's *Historia Ecclesiastica* is cited here as *HE*, with the book and (when available in Chibnall's edition) the section number, followed in parentheses by the editor's name, volume number, and page number. So, for example, *HE* xii.1 (Chibnall 6:184) refers to Orderic's book XII, section 1, which can also be found on page 184 of volume 6 of Chibnall's edition. Also, the Latin text of Chibnall's edition appears on the even number pages, with the English translation on the odd, so cited quotations might appear to stretch over an unnatural number of pages.

In addition, Chibnall's edition preserves Orderic's use of punctuation that does not exist today, including pitch marks designed to facilitate reading the text out loud. For the sake of simplicity, I have modernized these marks as appropriate when quoting Orderic's Latin.

While Chibnall's translation of Orderic's work is invaluable in opening this monumental work up to new readers, all translations in this study are my own unless otherwise indicated.

1. *HE* xii.1 (Chibnall 6:184): *Anno ab incarnatione Domini* M°C°XVIII° *indictione xiª, uigilia Natalis Domini uehemens uentus ædificia et nemora in partibus occiduis plurima prostrauit. Defuncto Paschali papa Iohannes Caietanus Romanorum pontificum antiquus cancellarius et magister in Gelasium*

*papam electus est, et contradicente imperatore a Romano clero canonice con-
secratus est. Tunc etiam Burdinus Bragarum archiepiscopus qui suis a fau-
toribus Gregorius VIII uocatus est, imperatore coniuente in æcclesia Dei
intrusus est. Tunc grauis inde dissensio inoleuit, seua persecutio inhorruit, et
katholicam plebem uehementer perturbauit.* The storm took place on 24 December 1117 in modern dating; Orderic began the new year at Christmas, and
the vigil began the feast day (Chibnall 6:184n1). The storm was significant
enough that Orderic also mentioned it in his continuation of Bede's *Chronica
Maiora*, contained in book I of the *Historia* (*HE* i.24 [Chibnall 1:160; Le
Prévost 1:188]), again in *HE* xii.8 (Chibnall 6:209) and *HE* v.19 (Chibnall
3:196–98), and in the *Annales Uticensis* (Le Prévost 5:160).

2. *HE* xii.1 (Chibnall 6:186): *Tunc in Britannia cuidam mulieri post
partum decubanti diabolus apparuit, et in specie uiri sui a quo petierat escas
detulit. . . . Paulo post uir eius uenit, quod contigerat audiuit, nimis expauit, ac
presbitero retulit. Presbiter autem inuocato nomine Domini feminam tetigit,
aqua benedicta aspersit, et si rursus delusor accederet, docuit quid diceret.
Iterum Sathan uenit, et illa quod edocta fuerat inquisiuit, 'Nimius' inquit
'uentus qui nuper ante Natale Domini terribiliter personuit, et nos grauiter
perterruit, quid portendit? Templa domosque detexit, et fastigia turrium
deiecit, et innumera siluarum robora prostrauit.' At ille ait, 'Decretum fuit
a Domino ut magna periret hominum portio, sed efficax superorum optinuit
supplicatio, ut parceretur hominibus et lapsus ingens immineret arboribus.
Formidanda tamen ante tres erit annos in terra tribulatio, et quamplurimæ
sullimes personæ succumbent excidio.'* I agree with Chibnall that *Britannia*
means Brittany and not Britain in this case; Orderic in fact rarely employed
the name Britain for the island (see chapter 3).

3. Orderic's erasures were not always so thorough. On folio 107r of
the same manuscript, at the beginning of book XI, Orderic seems to have
immediately disliked the last few lines of the verse he was writing, for he
quickly rubbed them out and reorganized. The original verses can be made
out underneath the revised version. The completeness of the erasure on folio
152v suggests that Orderic went back at a later date with the sole and determined intention to revise the text.

4. *HE* xii.1 (Chibnall 6:186): *cito instar gelu matutini flante Deo per-
transiit.*

5. The role of omens and portents as elements of high medieval historical thought has received little attention. Richard W. Southern treated them
briefly to demonstrate the lack of a notion of historical causation in medieval
histories (Southern, "Aspects of the European Tradition: 1. The Classical Tradition," 180). Nancy F. Partner sees them as manifestations of Christian con-

sciousness (Partner, *Serious Entertainments*, 214–23). Chris Given-Wilson views them as simply another form of historical "evidence" (Given-Wilson, *Chronicles*, 31).

6. Twain, "As Concerns Interpreting the Deity," 118 and 117.

7. *HE* xiii.16 (Chibnall 6:436): *Diuinum examen quo cuncta fiunt discutere nescio, latentes rerum causas propalare nequeo, sed rogatus a sociis annalem historiam simpliciter actito. Inscrutabilia quis perscrutari potest?* Cf. Gerald of Wales, *Topographia Hiberniæ* II.8, p. 90, who used Vergil to say much the same thing about the wonders of the world. The "secret causes of things" lay just as much in the mundane and the tragic as in the marvelous to Orderic and his contemporaries. Caroline Walker Bynum has rightly dissociated portents and omens from the emphasis on medieval alterity in recent historiography. Orderic's work stands at the leading edge of the self-conscious naturalization of the marvelous that Bynum has identified (Bynum, "Miracles and Marvels," and *Metamorphosis and Identity*, 59–71).

8. Gurevich, *Categories of Medieval Culture*, 56–57, 60–61; Brague, *Wisdom of the World*, 105. Cf. Merrills, *History and Geography*, 50, for a similar comment about Orosius.

9. Augustine of Hippo, *De civitate Dei* x.16, p. 290: *interuallis temporum occultis ipsius mundi causis, uerum tamen sub diuina prouidentia constitutis et ordinatis.* The historiographical significance of astronomical and meteorological portents in Orderic's *Historia*, and in other chronicles written before the early twelfth century, must be considered in light of Augustinian ideas about God's participation in worldly affairs, not anachronistically through the lens of later astrological sciences, as has often been the case.

10. *HE* xi.20 (Chibnall 6:82): *Autumnus tunc in Normannia tonitruis et imbribus atque bellis tempestuosus fuit.*

11. Early medieval writers, on the other hand, depicted portents not as a natural and sympathetic correlation between the earthly and the human, but rather as interruptions in the natural order of the world provoked by God as a message to humankind. See Dutton, *Charlemagne's Mustache*, 93–127, for the early medieval perspective.

12. William of Conches (d. after 1154), a slightly younger contemporary of Orderic's who grew up very near the historian's Norman abbey, exemplified this new interest in the natural world. The revival of both historiography and natural philosophy during the late eleventh and twelfth centuries has been a commonplace of high medieval historiography at least since the publication of Haskins's *Renaissance of the Twelfth Century* in 1927, but these two disciplines' renaissances have only rarely been considered in relationship to one another.

13. For the medieval and modern differentiation between annals, chronicles, and histories, see Galbraith, *Historical Research,* 2–3. The writing of annals certainly did not die out in the twelfth century. Orderic himself maintained his abbey's annals while working on his narrative history and he also, in imitation of Bede, included an annalistic summary of the Christian era from the birth of Christ up to his own age at the end of the *Historia's* first book. Nor was narrative history entirely absent before the eleventh century, as Bede's *Historia Ecclesiastica gentis Anglorum* demonstrates. But the eleventh and especially the twelfth century did see a clear shift away from the schematic chronology of annals and chronicles and towards a form of narrative history that did not use chronology as a single organizing principle.

14. A number of works in recent years have explored medieval geographical ideas, including Dalché's collected studies in *Géographie et culture;* N. Howe, *Writing the Map;* Lozovsky, *Earth is Our Book;* Remensnyder, "Topographies of Memory"; Smail, *Imaginary Cartographies;* and the papers in Hanawalt and Kobialka, *Medieval Practices of Space;* J. Howe and Wolfe, *Inventing Medieval Landscapes;* Tomasch and Gilles, *Text and Territory;* Westrem, *Discovering New Worlds.* The classic study by Wright, *Geographical Lore,* is still essential.

Modern ideas about geography, on the other hand, are not so easily summarized. The discipline of geography—with its subdisciplines of historical geography, cultural geography, human geography, humanistic geography, physical geography, economic geography, political geography, etc.—defies any attempt to list a standard corpus of scholarly literature. I have, however, found certain general works helpful in formulating my ideas about geographical theory as developed in this study, including Baker, *Geography and History;* Dodgshon, *Society in Time and Space;* Gregory, *Geographical Imaginations;* Pred, "Place as Historically Contingent Process," and others cited throughout.

15. Pred, "Place as Historically Contingent Process," 279–80. The importance of space as a framework for human society through time has also been discussed by cultural theorists such as Bachelard, *Poetics of Space;* Certeau, *Practice of Everyday Life;* and Lefebvre, *Production of Space;* as well as the city planner Lynch in *Image of the City.* These scholars, though not geographers by trade, still add much to the study of the human experience of physical space.

16. For the medieval use of spatial mnemonics, see Carruthers, *Book of Memory,* 122–55, and for a modern discussion, Luria, *Mind of a Mnemonist,* 31–38.

17. To date the best discussions of the relationship between space and historical narrative in medieval Europe can be found in many of the papers

contained in Tomasch and Gilles, *Text and Territory,* and in Otter, *Inventiones.* The relationship between geography and historiography in the ancient world has been studied in detail in Clarke, *Between Geography and History,* and Merrills, *History and Geography.*

18. The conceptual framework of this chapter draws on Basso, *Wisdom Sits in Places,* in particular, and also Certeau, *Practice of Everyday Life,* 91–130.

19. Hugh of Saint-Victor, *De tribus maximis circumstantiis gestorum,* p. 491, ll. 16–18: *Tria igitur sunt in quibus praecipue cognitio pendet rerum gestarum, id est, personae a quibus res gestae sunt, le loca in quibus gestae sunt, et tempora quando gestae sunt.* This work, which Hugh wrote more as a handbook of historical structure than an actual historical text, has not been edited in full. Hugh of Saint-Victor's historical thought is treated by Southern, "Aspects of the European Tradition: 2. Hugh of St Victor."

20. In this, as in other things, Orderic was following in the tradition of Bede. Nicholas Howe argued that place was for Bede just as significant as his much-appreciated sense of time, noting that "place becomes setting in Bede's work because it allows him to contain the layers of the past that he must register to achieve his ends as historian and exegete. Place becomes a device for ordering narrative because it enables the writer to establish the necessary relation between events from different periods. Put more reductively, a sense of place allows the historian to contain the vagaries of chronology within the framework of a fixed, identifiable location" (N. Howe, "From Bede's World to 'Bede's World,'" 36–37).

21. For geography as an inertial structure that resists change, but that is by no means unchanging or unchangeable, see Dodgshon, *Society in Time and Space,* 6–7, 10–16, in conjunction with Pred, "Place as Historically Contingent Process," 281–82. This stability (or inertia) of the physical landscape comes together with the human ability to manipulate both the physical and symbolic nature of geography, allowing for a historicized and mythicized approach to landscape that has received the attention of scholars most concretely and intriguingly in the study of the Dreamtime of Australian Aboriginal culture. See, for instance, Rumsey, "Tracks, Traces, and Links to Land"; Stewart and Strathern, "Origins versus Creative Powers"; and Morphy, "Landscape."

22. *HE* viii.24 (Chibnall 4:290): *mundi status uariabiliter agitatur.*

23. For the multivalent meaning of landscape, see Barnes and Duncan, "Introduction: Writing Worlds"; Daniels and Cosgrove, "Introduction: Iconography and Landscape"; Hirsch, "Landscape"; Ingold, "Temporality of the Landscape"; Olwig, *Landscape, Nature, and the Body Politic*; and idem, "Recovering the Substantive Nature of Landscape."

24. *HE* ix.1 (Chibnall 5:4): *Vicissitudines temporum et rerum æternus conditor sapienter salubriterque ordinat. . . . Hoc in hieme et estate palam uidemus, hoc nichilominus in frigore et caumate sentimus, hoc in omnium rerum ortu et occasu perpendimus, et in multiplici uarietate operum Dei rite rimari possumus. Inde multiplices propagantur hystoriæ, de multimodis euentibus qui fiunt in mundo cotidie, et dicacibus hystoriographis augmentantur copiose fandi materiæ.* This type of thought had its origins in early Christianity (Glacken, *Traces on the Rhodian Shore,* 178).

25. For the significance of historical writing to Orderic, see Chibnall 1:35; idem, *World,* 177–78, 181; Blacker, *Faces of Time,* 13; Gransden, *Historical Writing,* 154–55; Shopkow, *History and Community,* 202; Wolter, *Ordericus Vitalis,* 73.

26. The importance of *cotidie,* the everydayness of God's action in the world, for Orderic is discussed by Mégier, *"Divina Pagina,"* 123 and n. 91.

27. This monastery has been known as Saint-Évroult, after the name of its patron, since the late twelfth century. However, Orderic always called the community by its earlier name, Ouche, *Vticum* in Latin. I've chosen to maintain this usage, rather than to defer to modern conventions, because for Orderic this place-name represented a cascade of connections that linked his abbey into the geographical and family matrix and defined its place in the Norman community. This is discussed more fully in chapter 1 and throughout this book.

28. *HE* prologue (Chibnall 1:130, 32): *Firmiter ex coniectura preteritorum opinor, quod exurget quis me multo perspicacior, ac ad indagandos multimodarum quæ per orbem fiunt rerum euentus potentior, qui forsitan de meis aliorumque mei similium scedulis hauriet, quod chronographiæ narrationique suæ dignanter ad notitiam futurorum inseret.*

29. The autograph manuscripts are described briefly here. For more detail about the manuscript tradition and publication history of the *Historia Ecclesiastica,* see Chibnall, 1:115–23.

30. The twelfth-century catalogue of the library at Orderic's monastery of Ouche (now in Bibliothèque nationale in MS Latin 10062, fol. 80v) lists *Quattuor uolumina Vitalis,* so although the bindings are modern the divisions of the thirteen books into four volumes (one now lost) dates back to the twelfth century.

31. *HE* v.1 (Chibnall 3:6).

32. In fact, Orderic never referred to himself as "Vitalis," the Latinate name he was given when he entered his continental monastery, without also remarking that he was *Angligena,* English-born (Stein, *Reality Fictions,* 100). For him, his Latin name needed an English qualifier.

33. *HE* iv (Chibnall 2:262); v.14 (Chibnall 3:142–50). The fact that Odelerius vowed to enter the new monastery of Shrewsbury in 1083, without mentioning the consent of his wife, strongly suggests that Orderic's mother was dead by the time he was eight years old.

34. This manuscript is now in the Bibliothèque de la ville, Rouen, MS 1343, ff. 34r-121r.

35. Orderic's interpolations into William of Jumièges's *Gesta Normannorum Ducum* are included in Elisabeth M. C. Van Houts's edition and translation of the text. Van Houts dates this redaction to c. 1095 – c. 1113 (William of Jumièges, *Gesta Normannorum Ducum* 1:xviii). Orderic's autograph manuscript of this work is preserved on ff. 116r–139v of MS 1174 at the Bibliothèque de la ville, Rouen. A facsimile of the manuscript is available in Lair, *Matériaux*.

36. *HE* v.1 (Chibnall 3:6): *ego de extremis Merciorum finibus decennis Angligena hunc aduectus, barbarusque et ignotus aduena callentibus indigenis admixtus, inspirante Deo Normannorum gesta et euentus Normannis promere scripto sum conatus.*

37. *HE* v.1 (Chibnall 3:6); prologue (Chibnall 1:130).

38. For monastic institutional history, see Remensnyder, *Remembering Kings Past.*

39. For a more detailed account of the dating and contents of these books, see Chibnall 1:45–48, and her introductions to the individual volumes.

40. BN MS Latin 10062, fol. 19v.

41. Many of these studies of medieval historiography are cited in the following chapters. Grundmann, *Geschichtsschreibung im Mittelalter*; Guenée, *Histoire et culture historique*; and Southern's four presidential addresses on "Aspects of the European Tradition of Historical Writing," are particularly influential.

42. The new trends in eleventh- and twelfth-century historiography are discussed in chapter 6. Orderic's *Historia Ecclesiastica*—its sources, models, genre, style, function—has been extensively and skillfully examined in the context of the medieval tradition of historical writing in, to note the major studies, Albu, *Normans and their Histories*, 180–213; Blacker, *Faces of Time*, 10–17, 153–60; Chibnall, *World*, 169–220; Delisle, "Notice sur Orderic Vital"; Gransden, *Historical Writing*, 151–65; Ray, "Monastic Historiography"; Shopkow, *History and Community*; Wolter, *Ordericus Vitalis*; and Chibnall's introductions to her edition of the *Historia*, both the general introduction in vol. 1 and those of the individual volumes.

43. *HE* vi.1 (Chibnall 3:212): *preterita posteris sine inuidia manifestant. HE* Prologue (Chibnall 1:130): *futuris semper prodesse uolentes scripta scriptis accumulauerunt.*

44. *HE* vi.1 (Chibnall 3:212): *beniuola posteritas si posset restaurare, et intermissa recuperare, alacris excusso insurgeret torpore, et inuisi operis florem fructumque obnixa expeteret uoluntate, et ardenter perscrutaretur sedula perspicacitate.*

45. In other words, to use Gabrielle Spiegel's term, this is to look for "the social logic of the text" (Spiegel, "History, Historicism"). See also Glenn, *Politics and History,* 9–16, for a particular focus on the difficulties of working with a single, idiosyncratic work.

46. *HE* iii (Chibnall 2:189).

47. *HE* vi.10 (Chibnall 3:346): *nec optimis uiris melior neque malis deterior.*

48. *HE* prologue (Chibnall 1:130): *modernos Christianorum euentus rimari et propalare satago, unde presens opusculum æcclesiasticam historiam appellari affecto.*

49. The impact of the monastic *lectio divina* on Orderic's historical conscious is discussed by Ray, "Monastic Historiography," chapters 1 and 2.

50. Tuan, "Foreword," ix.


CHAPTER 1   Ouche: The History of a Place

1. A topographical map of the region can be found in Desloges and Bernouis, "Milieu naturel," 44, and, for agriculture, 46–47. The geology and topography of the region is also discussed in Bauduin, *La première Normandie,* 42–45. Léopold Delisle plotted the location of Norman vineyards in *Études sur la condition de la classe agricole,* 418–70, esp. 432–42, and commented on the quality of early Norman cider on 471–72. The iron industry in the Ouche is unearthed in Arnoux, *Mineurs,* passim, but note especially the map of the Ouche on 62.

2. These castles are mapped by Chibnall, *World,* 19. See Louise, "La mise en place," 9–24, for the waves of castle-building along Normandy's southern frontier in the eleventh and early twelfth centuries, and also Yver, "Les châteaux-forts," 28–76. Orderic did not consistently differentiate between a *castrum* (castle) and an *oppidium* (fortified town). The larger, older, and more formidable castles, which were probably stone by the twelfth century, stood at Exmes, Breteuil, L'Aigle, Gacé, and Moulins-la-Marche. The other sites possessed less substantial fortifications.

3. *HE* iii (Chibnall 2:34).

4. *HE* xiii.23 (Chibnall 6:460).

5. *HE* iii (Chibnall 2:76): *Luxouiensem episcopatum ab Ebroicensi dirimit.*

6. Giroie had been betrothed to the only daughter of Heugon, but when both the girl and her father died before the marriage took place the duke assigned Heugon's lands in the Ouche to Giroie at the encouragement of Giroie's lord William of Bellême (*HE* iii [Chibnall 2:22]). Pierre Bauduin dates Giroie's acquisition of his Norman lands to c. 1015 (Bauduin, "Une famille châtelaine," 313), although Orderic is not so specific (*HE* iii [Chibnall 2:22, 26]). For a map of these lands, see Maillefer, "Une famille aristocratique," 200.

7. *HE* iii (Chibnall 2:26): *incolas illius patriæ de quo episcopatu essent inquisiuit. Illi autem dixerunt se nullius episcopatus esse. . . . Deinde quis uicinorum præsulum religiosior esset inuestigauit. Agnitisque uirtutibus Rogerii Luxouiensis episcopi, ei totum honorem suum subiugauit, et Baldricum de Balgenzaio generosque suos Wascelinum de Ponte Erchenfredi et Rogerium de Merula terras suas quæ simili libertate abutebantur præfato pontifici similiter submittere persuasit.* The tenth- and early eleventh-century Norman episcopal lists are vague. Roger apparently ascended to the bishopric of Lisieux before c. 980, when he was noted to be present at the translation of the relics of St. Ouen in Rouen, and he probably died in 1022 (Deshays, *Mémoires,* 14–16). The bishop of Sées was probably Sigefroy (c. 1007–17), about whom little is known (Hommey, *Histoire,* 403).

8. The eleventh-century Norman episcopacy is discussed in Douglas, "Norman Episcopate," 101–15. For the Bellême, see Louise, *La seigneurie de Bellême,* and Thompson, "Family and Influence." Though often spoken of as a Norman see, the diocese of Sées—like the Bellême lands—was never fully contained within Normandy's political bounds. A large part of the bishop's domain stretched into the independent county of Perche (Power, *Norman Frontier,* 116–17, 317; Thompson, *Power and Border Lordship,* 20).

9. Chibnall, "Ecclesiastical Patronage," 106.

10. For the importance of space for medieval monastic life, see Cassidy-Welch, *Monastic Spaces,* and Noisette, "Usages et représentations de l'espace." Both of these studies focus more on the architectural space of monasticism than on the natural landscape that will be my focus here, though interior and exterior space are certainly intertwined in the monastic imagination. The following discussion found inspiration in Wagner, "Condensed Mapping."

11. *HE* iii (Chibnall 2:14): *absque istis duobus elementis, monachi esse non possunt.* For Orderic's imagined conversations and speeches, see Chibnall 1:79–84 and Chibnall, *World,* 197–99. The practical process of founding

a monastery is reviewed by Remensnyder in *Remembering Kings Past,* 19–41, with a discussion of aristocratic initiation on 24–27.

12.  Orderic Vitalis, interpolations in William of Jumièges, *Gesta Normannorum Ducum* vii.23: *"Audio uos, o karissimi mei nepotes, erga Dei cultum feruere, quin etiam monachile monasterium uelle erigere. . . . Sed tamen ad hanc fabricam quem locum elegistis et quid ibidem Christo militantibus collaturi estis?"*

13.  Orderic Vitalis, interpolations in William of Jumièges, *Gesta Normannorum Ducum* vii.23: *"Apud Nuceretum, iuuante Deo, castrum ei stabilire cupimus et ecclesias decimasque nostras, et alia que poterimus, pro posse paupertatis nostre dabimus."*

14.  For William Giroie's life, see *HE* iii (Chibnall 2:14).

15.  Orderic Vitalis, interpolations in William of Jumièges, *Gesta Normannorum Ducum* vii.23: *"Sanctus Benedictus, monachorum magister, iubet monasterium ita constitui, ut omnia necessaria, id est aqua, molendinum, pistrinum, ortus uel artes diuerse infra monasterium exerceantur ne sit monachis necessitas ita uagandi foras, quia omnino non expedit animabus eorum. Nucereti uero rura quidem satis fertilia sunt, sed copia silue ac habilis limpha, quibus monachi maxime indigent, procul absunt."* From *ut omnia* through *animabus eorum* Orderic followed the *Regula S. Benedicti* 66, with only very minor variations.

16.  The various ways in which saints and their hagiographies came to define the medieval landscape have been studied by D. Harvey, "Constructed Landscapes"; J. Smith, "Oral and Written," 337 and passim; and others. The particular case of Evroul and his relationship to the Ouche is unraveled below.

17.  *HE* vi.9 (Chibnall 3:268): *solius Dei contemplationi uolens incumbere, summa cum uelocitate studuit heremum expetere.*

18.  *HE* vi.9 (Chibnall 3:270): *intrepidis gressibus uastissima loca solitudinis peragrarent.*

19.  *HE* vi.9 (Chibnall 3:270): *"locum libertatis et nostræ fragilitati opportunum clementer ostendere." . . . peruenerunt ad fontes habilissimos ad potandum, qui paulum diriuati colligebantur in magnum stagnum. Vbi genua flectentes, monstratori Deo immensas referunt laudes.*

20.  For the importance of divine revelation in determining the monastic site, see Remensnyder, *Remembering Kings Past,* 43–65, esp. 52–53. In its foundation and its refoundation combined, Ouche manifested nearly every sort of "revelation" discussed by Remensnyder.

21.  Orderic Vitalis, interpolations in William of Jumièges, *Gesta Normannorum Ducum* vii.23: *"Vticensis locus, ad quem Deus uenerabilem Ebrulfum per angelum suum direxit, pauperibus spiritu, quibus regnum celorum*

*promittitur, satis congruit. Nam uetusta sancti Petri basilica ibidem adhuc permanet, et amplus ager, ubi hortus et uiridiaria fieri possunt, circumiacet. Terra quippe inculta et sterilis est, sed Dominus seruis suis parare mensam in deserto potens est* [Psalm 77 (78).19]. *Piscosa quidem flumina et uberes uinee desunt, sed densum nemus et habiles ad bibendum fontes presto sunt. Multorum quoque sanctorum corpora ibidem requiescunt, que cum ingenti gloria in extremo die ressurrectura sunt."* At the site of the abbey the Charentonne river was very close to its source and quite shallow, which probably accounts for its lack of fish.

22. Athanasius, *Vita Antonii*; Jerome, *Vita S. Pauli eremitae*. Modern scholars have been almost as enamored with the image of the ascetic desert as the monks themselves. See Chitty, *Desert a City*, Goehring, "Dark Side of Landscape," Merrills, "Monks, Monsters, and Barbarians," and Miller, "Jerome's Centaur," for the late antique understanding of the desert as a place of spiritual power and for its ambiguous relationship with the city. Le Goff's study of the desert/wilderness motif in history, theology, literature, and reality is found in "Wilderness in the Medieval West." B. Ward looks at the Cistercian *topos* of the desert in "Desert Myth." G. Williams, *Wilderness and Paradise*, examines the theme from biblical to modern times.

23. G. Williams, *Wilderness and Paradise*, 38–39.

24. *HE* viii.26 (Chibnall 4:312).

25. In his *Vita* of the Cluniac-inspired reformer William of Volpiano, the early eleventh-century Benedictine hagiographer and historian Raoul Glaber employed the word *heremus* to describe the body of land held in common by a monastic community, demonstrating how closely the *heremus* had become associated with a monastery's property (Raoul Glaber, *Vita Domni Willelmi Abbatis* v and 266n3).

26. *HE* viii.26 (Chibnall 4:316): *non mores Ægiptiorum qui nimio solis ardore iugiter estuant imitatus est, sed ritus Gallorum qui sepe brumali gelu in occidente contremiscunt pie intuitus est.*

27. Crouch, *Beaumont Twins*, 109.

28. *HE* iii (Chibnall 2:20); *HE* iii (Chibnall 2:14); *HE* v.13 (Chibnall 3:124); *HE* v.12 (Chibnall 3:118).

29. *HE* vi.9 (Chibnall 3:288–90) for Evroul and the Devil.

30. Dabon, "Saint-Évroult en pays d'Ouche," 2; Pelatan, "Milieu naturel," 312.

31. *HE* vi.9 (Chibnall 3:286): *quia in ualle palustris humus erat, et in hieme passim dum foderetur limpha mox scaturiebat, manansque foueam fons adimplebat.* See also Deslogus and Bernouis, "Milieu naturel," 45–66.

32. *HE* iii (Chibnall 2:76).

33. Greene, *Medieval Monasteries*, 57.

34. *HE* iii (Chibnall 2:76): *Locus ipse est amenus et solitariæ uitæ satis congruus.*

35. The classic discussion of the medieval *locus amoenus* is Curtius, *European Literature*, 192–202. See also Constable, "Renewal and Reform," 48; J. Howe, "Creating Symbolic Landscapes," 210–12; Leclercq, *Love of Learning*, 55.

36. Miller, "Jerome's Centaur," 215–16 and n. 34; Remensnyder, *Remembering Kings Past*, 23.

37. Wagner, "Condensed Mapping," 77

38. *HE* vi.9 (Chibnall 3:270) for Evroul's fellow *amatores*. Referencing also Athanasius, *Vita Antonii* 14 for "making the desert a city," and Henry David Thoreau's *Walden*, 66.

39. *HE* vi.9 (Chibnall 3:276): *Vticum cum summa difficultate quesierunt, et uix quia tunc locus ille obscurus erat uti desertus indagantes inuenerunt.*

40. *HE* vi.9 (Chibnall 3:302): *in basilica sancti Petri apostolorum principis quam ipse ex lapidibus ædificauerat, in saxo marmoreo mirifice sepultus est.*

41. Orderic's account of this journey is in *HE* vi.10 (Chibnall 3:338–42). A concise and thorough summary of the theft and return of the relics can be found in Lauer, *Le règne de Louis IV,* 120n4. François Dolbeau has commented on the rarity of *translationes* in which stolen relics were returned through the agency of secular authorities rather than that of the saint (Dolbeau, "Un vol," 173). Although Orderic's account of the relics' return, set in the midst of his *Historia,* might seem to confirm Dolbeau's assertion that accounts involving secular intervention belong to the genre of history rather than hagiography, I believe that Dolbeau's argument differentiates too firmly and anachronistically between notions that were not so clearly separated in the middle ages. See also Jankulak, *Medieval Cult of St Petroc,* 196–97, and Lifshitz, "Beyond Positivism and Genre."

42. *HE* vi.10 (Chibnall 3:306): *edita nimirum ab auctore ignaro, cui non plene . . . patuit rerum et temporum certitudo.* This account, known as the *De translatione SS. Ebrulfi abbatis Uticensis et Ansberti,* is contained in the seventeenth-century *Acta Sanctorum ordinis S. Benedicti.* The only other source for the theft, a fourteenth-century vernacular poem apparently written at Ouche, follows Orderic's version extremely closely and adds no further information (Sandqvist, *La Vie de saint Évroul*). Unfortunately, since the feast of St. Evroul is celebrated on 29 December, the Bollandists' *Acta Sanctorum* has not turned a critical eye to the texts involving Orderic's patron saint.

43. The classic studies of the translation—forced or voluntary—of medieval relics are Heinzelmann, *Translationsberichte,* and, for theft in particular, Geary, *Furta Sacra.* The meaning of a community's relics was inextricably intertwined with the narratives surrounding the community's possession of those relics; the transition of relics from one place to another thus changed not only the relics' place but also their meaning (Geary, "Sacred Commodities," 208).

I have found only two other narratives describing the theft of relics from the perspective of the losing monastery. The most thoroughly studied is the twelfth-century theft of the Cornish St. Petroc, whose theft and recovery shows certain parallels to Orderic's account of St. Evroul. See Jankulak, *Medieval Cult of St Petroc,* esp. chapters 5 and 6, and J. Smith, "Oral and Written," 316–17. Dobleau, "Un vol," 172n4, discusses the other case, that of St. Metro.

44. Orderic Vitalis, interpolations in William of Jumièges, *Gesta Normannorum Ducum* vii.23: "*Multorum quoque sanctorum corpora.*"

45. Julia Smith has noted instances in which the cults of Breton saints focused on places rather than relics (J. Smith, "Oral and Written," 325–29).

46. Although Orderic initially attributed the destruction of Ouche to the Vikings, further research convinced him that the Norsemen were not to blame for the dispersal of St. Evroul's relics, as he knew to be the case at Jumièges and Saint-Wandrille, where the monks took up their relics and fled before the advancing Vikings. He was almost certainly correct. But modern historians have consistently treated the theft of St. Evroul's relics in the context of the so-called "relic exodus" from ninth- and tenth-century Neustria, ignoring the significant difference in context and meaning. For Orderic's revised opinion of his monastery's past, see the speech attributed to William Giroie in *HE* iii (Chibnall 2:16) and also in Orderic Vitalis, interpolations in William of Jumièges, *Gesta Normannorum Ducum* vii.23, in which he associated the destruction of Ouche with that of Jumièges, Saint-Wandrille (Fontenelle), and Marmoutier, and his later expanded version of the same events in *HE* vi.10 (Chibnall 3:302–6), in which Ouche is omitted. Orderic clearly stated that the community in the Ouche had survived the ravaging of Hasting and Rollo in *HE* vi.10 (Chibnall 3:326), attributing the abbey's good luck to its isolation.

The common label for the "relic exodus" is taken from Legris, "L'exode des corps saints." See also Musset, "L'exode des reliques," esp. 14–16 for the translation of Evroul, and idem, "Les translations de reliques." For a new perspective on the reality of this "relic exodus," much needed though I disagree with the conclusions, see Lifshitz, "'Exodus of Holy Bodies' Reconsidered," and idem, "Migration of Neustrian Relics." Lifshitz believes the Viking relic exodus to be a later myth devised to explain away the movement of relics from Neustria to central France by means of outright theft. In response to this suggestion, see Potts, *Monastic Revival*, 18n19, who points out that the large-scale hagiographic conspiracy needed to sustain this myth was really beyond the abilities of Normandy's fledgling monastic revival.

47. Lauer, *Le règne de Louis IV*, 118–28; Flodoard of Reims, *Annales*, ann. 944–45; Richer of Saint-Remegius, *Historiarum* II.42–43; William of Jumièges, *Gesta Normannorum Ducum* iv.5–6. There is conflicting evidence as to whether Duke William died in December 942 or 943, but 942 is now generally accepted. See Lauer, *Le règne de Louis IV*, 88n1, and William of Jumièges, *Gesta Normannorum Ducum* 1:95n2.

48. *HE* vi.10 (Chibnall 3:306); *De translatione* 3. Robert the Pious's reign is here dated from the time he was associated with his father on the throne in 987, not the traditional date of 996 when his father died.

49. *Recueil des actes de Charles III le Simple* XXXV: *monasterio sancti Petri, in quo Ebrulfus sanctus corpore quiescit.*

Lucien Musset has suggested that the temporary Hun-related flight of the monks of Rebais to Marcilly-sur-Eure around 935–38 may have brought St. Evroul to the French monastery's attention, but neither account of the translation suggested that there was any previous contact between the two communities (Musset, "Évroul," 219; idem, "L'exode des reliques," 16). Mabillon, in his edition of the *De translatione*, identified the King Robert of the text as Robert I, which places the events in 922–23, but he provided no justification for his choice of kings. Mabillon may well have had information that current scholars lack; internal evidence in the *De translatione* makes it clear that the work as printed is an except from a longer text, but whether it was excerpted by Mabillon himself is unclear. (Unfortunately I have been unable to track down the original manuscript; it may no longer survive.) However, I believe that details from both the *De translatione* and Orderic's account of the theft suggest that the theft of Evroul's relics actually took place at the end of the tenth century, during the time of Hugh Capet (whom Orderic also called "Hugh the Great"), which would make the King Robert of the Rebais account Robert II, who became king in association with his father Hugh Capet in 987.

50. *HE* vi.10 (Chibnall 3:308): *ambo religiosi, et in timore Dei studiosi.* Geary has noted how the moral character of the perpetrators reflected upon the meaning of the theft (Geary, *Furta Sacra*, 115). Orderic's positive description of Herluin and Raoul softened the trauma of the theft. The identity of these two men has never been established. Herluin the chancellor appears only in Orderic's version of events, and there is no corroboration for the sug-

gestion that he was lay abbot of Saint-Pierre-en-Pont. Orderic probably took his information about Raoul of Drachy from the Rebais text, which may have had more reliable connections with this donor to the foundation. He was, according to Rebais, "equally most powerful and most noble of all citizens of the city of Soissons" (*ditissimus pariter & nobilissimus omnium Suessionensis urbis civium; De translatione* 3). This description was probably meant to flatter rather than to inform, but it does provide one possible lead. Raoul, the son of Gautier I count of Valois, Vexin, and Amiens, was bishop of Soissons in the late tenth century (d. after 992); his brother Guy succeeded him in the office, establishing that the family had more than merely a casual connection with the city. For this Raoul and his family, see Grierson, "L'origine des comtes d'Amiens, Valois et Vexin," 96–97 and the genealogy in between.

51. *HE* vi.10 (Chibnall 3:314): *illuc reuersi sunt, et ex insperato cum suis in cœnobium irruerunt. . . . tria corpora sanctorum Ebrulfi et Ebremundi atque Ansberti de mausoleis sustulerunt, et coriis ossa ceruinis inuoluta cum aliis sanctorum reliquiis asportauerunt.*

52. *De translatione*, the text from Rebais, much shorter than Orderic's version, differs in a number of ways from this account. In addition to placing the events in the reign of a King Robert (with no mention of Louis d'Outremer or Hugh the Great), Herluin the chancellor is absent, as is St. Evremond, leaving Raoul of Drachy, a nobleman from Soissons, to steal the relics of St. Evroul and St. Ansbert. *De translatione* also makes no mention of any monastic hospitality, claiming that Raoul wished "to steal the bodies of any saints whatsoever" (*quorumlibet rapere corpora sanctorum*). So when the king "ordered the churches of that land, which were meeting places for mercenaries, to be razed to the ground, and whatever pertained to them was to be destroyed by fire, iron, and all manner of ravaging," Raoul snatched the first relics he found and returned to France with his king (*De translatione* 3: *Jussit illius terræ ecclesias, quæ latronum erant conciliabula, solotenus destrui; & quicquid ad easdem pertinebat, igne, ferro, ac omnimoda vastatione pessumdari*). Relics were considered a legitimate target of plunder throughout the middle ages.

53. *HE* vi.10 (Chibnall 3:316): *Hic dum uidisset monachos et eorum uernulas in nimio constitutos merore, et omnes uelle locum pariter desolatum derelinquere, patremque beatum peregre sequi cum hostili agmine.*

54. *HE* vi.10 (Chibnall 3:316): *benigno patri qui uos hactenus aluit in sua regione, fideliter seruite cum eo peregrinantes in aliena regione. Ego autem Vticensem locum non relinquam, sed hic ubi multis bonis potitus sum creatori meo seruiam, nec inde quamdiu uitalis calor in me fuerit recedam. Scio quod multa hic sanctorum requiescunt corpora, et hunc locum sancto*

*patri designauit uisio angelica, ubi se deberet ad multorum ædificationem in spirituali exercere militia.*

55. "Place is a special kind of object," Yi-Fu Tuan has said. "It is a concentration of value, though not a valued thing that can be handled or carried about easily; it is an object in which one can dwell" (Tuan, *Space and Place*, 12). Ascelin's valuing of that particular location, his inability to carry that meaning with him elsewhere, and his continued dwelling all defined that spot in the Ouche as "place" for Ascelin and Orderic.

56. *HE* vi.10 (Chibnall 3:316): *"Pro peccatis nostris et patrum nostrorum diuina percussio super nos descendit, et terribiliter irruens nos et nostra penitus contriuit, irreparabiliterque deiecit. . . . sanctuariumque suum iuste humiliauit, sic per manus Hugonis atque Francorum hunc locum pluribus modis affligendo puniit, precipue quod super omnia dolendum est ossibus sancti patris Ebrulfi aliisque sanctorum reliquiis nos priuauit."*

57. Cf. *HE* ix.2 (Chibnall 5:14) for a similar idea concerning the Holy Land under the Saracens.

58. The parallel between the monastic commitment to a stability of place and God's commitment to humanity is drawn by Sheldrake, *Spaces for the Sacred*, 109.

59. *HE* vi.10 (Chibnall 3:318).

60. Dolbeau, "Un vol," 181; Geary, *Furta Sacra*, 113–14.

61. The author of the late-twelfth-century *furta* narrative of the Cornish St. Petroc, also written by the losing side after the relics' recovery through political means, attributed the theft to Petroc's desire for greater fame, especially in Brittany where the relics ended up. Jankulak suggests that viewing the theft in this manner made it more palatable to the losing but ultimately triumphant community by emphasizing the saint's power and prestige. Petroc, like Evroul, was for the most part a passive passenger during his theft; understanding the theft as a successful move for greater renown for the saint himself and for his monastery allowed the writer to attribute a motivation to the saint that did not require any miraculous intervention (Jankulak, *Medieval Cult of St Petroc*, 199–200).

62. One of the fundamental objectives of *translationes* as a genre was to provide a convincing narrative proof of the authenticity of the translated relics. This was even more vital in the case of Ouche, which recovered long-lost relics stolen from a previous foundation. The meaning of medieval *delationes* is discussed in Bozóky, "Voyages de reliques"; Héliot and Chastang, "Quêtes et voyages de reliques"; Koziol, "Monks"; Sigal, "Les voyages de reliques."

The relics recovered in 1131 were not the first fragments of Evroul's bones to find their way back to the monastery. A tooth was recovered between

1066 and 1084/5 by Fulk, Ouche's prior, and sometime after 1108 William of Montreuil, who headed Ouche's French priory at Maule, received one of Evroul's vertebrae from a canon of Paris named Fulbert, possibly the uncle of Heloise (*HE* vi.10 [Chibnall 3:336]). The official and negotiated return of the relics from Rebais, however, clearly meant more than these other haphazardly acquired fragments.

63. See the map in Hincker, "Histoire," 21, for the sites of veneration that may be associated with the translation of the relics.

64. *HE* vi.10 (Chibnall 3:320, 320n3, 324, and 325n3).

65. Chibnall, *World*, 69.

66. For the early relationship between the cult of saints and medieval geography, see Markus, *End of Ancient Christianity*, 139–55.

67. *HE* vi.10 (Chibnall 3:326): *puluerem sanctissimæ carnis. . . . Alias quoque preciosas reliquias . . . donec reuelante Deo manifestentur futuris cultoribus.*

68. *HE* vi.10 (Chibnall 3:328): *in solitudinem rediit, et remotis hominibus in oratoriis et domibus ingens silua creuit, et habitatio ferarum multo tempore ibidem extitit.*

69. *HE* vi.10 (Chibnall 3:328): *In prouincia Beluacensi Restoldo cuidam presbitero per uisionem tunc dictum est, 'In Normanniam ad sanctum Ebrulfum uade, ibique perfrueris dierum longitudine, et felicis uitæ iocunditate.'*

70. *HE* vi.10 (Chibnall 3:328).

71. Sharon Farmer has looked at the ways in which a monastic community might use texts and history to provide a sense of continuity in *Communities of Saint Martin*, 151–67. Also see Remensnyder, *Remembering Kings Past*, 6–7, for a discussion of monastic continuity at a place.

72. Sofia Boesch Gajano discusses the shift away from "places of saints" defined by their tombs to "spaces of sanctity" consecrated in both life and death in "Des *Loca Sanctorum*," 69. See also, for the connections between relics and *vitae*, Ashley and Sheingorn, "Translations of Foy," and Bourgne, "Translating Saints' Lives."

73. The *Historia* is full of stories of lost, forgotten, and found relics. Athanasius of Alexandria, for instance, allegedly hid the relics of John the Baptist in the wall of a church, much like Ascelin was said to have done with Evroul's dust (*HE* i.23 [Le Prévost 1:117]; Orderic took this passage directly from Bede, *Chronica Maiora*, an. 4316). The body of St. Judoc lay forgotten until it was revealed again by a layman (*HE* iii [Chibnall 2:164]). During the First Crusade Ilger Bigod discovered some relics that included hair of the Virgin. A few strands made their way to Ouche's priory at Maule (*HE* ix.15 [Chibnall 5:170]).

74. *HE* iii (Chibnall 2:16): *libellus uitæ sancti patris Ebrulfi Rotberto oblatus est. Quam diligenter legit et Hugoni aliisque sociis suis prudenter exposuit. Quid multa? Vticensis locus placuit ambobus fratribus.* For Robert's childhood education, see *HE* iii (Chibnall 2:40).

75. "Places became sacred as the past became localized in the present," R. A. Markus noted of early Christian sacred space. "It was always the past that really mattered, and it was the impact of past human action that gave places their significance" (Markus, "How on Earth," 271).

76. The five communities founded by Norman nobles in the eleventh century with local patrons were the three monasteries of Ouche (St. Evroul), Saint-Vigor-de-Bayeux (St. Vigor, bishop of Bayeux), and Saint-Sever (St. Severus, bishop of Avranches), and two nunneries, both of which stretched the local association a bit: Notre-Dame-de-Pré had a secondary dedication to St. Desiderius, a monk at Fécamp, and Préaux was dedicated to St. Leger, who was imprisoned briefly at Fécamp although he was primarily associated with his bishopric at Autun. Only Saint-Vigor-de-Bayeux and Ouche were geographically linked with their patrons. A few of the tenth-century ducal monasteries were also associated both in name and in place with their patrons, such as Saint-Taurin of Evreux. See Potts, *Monastic Revival*, for many but not all of these abbeys.

77. *HE* viii.27 (Chibnall 4:334): *Materiam scribendi nuper ab Vticensi æcclesia cepi.*

78. This passage occurs at the very end of Orderic's commentary on the new monastic orders, which circulated independently of the bulk of the *Historia* (Chibnall 4:xl–xlii). Chibnall dates this work to 1135 or possibly 1136, but Christopher Holdsworth has noted additional internal evidence for the date of 1136 (Chibnall 4:xix; Holdsworth, "Orderic, Traditional Monk and the New Monasticism," 25). Orderic began work on his *Historia* around 1114.

79. *HE* viii.27 (Chibnall 4:334, 6): *sed ampla terrarum regna uelut in extasin raptus prospexi, longe lateque oratione uolitaui, et per plura perlustrans longissimam epanalempsim protelaui. Nunc autem stratum meum quod est Vtici fessus repetam, et quiddam de rebus ad nos pertinentibus in libri calce liquido retexam.* See Chibnall 4:279n2 for the derivation of the unusual word *epanalempsim*.

80. *HE* x.25 (Chibnall 5:284). The word *extasis* is extremely uncommon in the *Historia*. In addition to these two instances, it occurs twice in passages based on the Acts of the Apostles which Orderic included in *HE* ii.1 (Le Prévost 1:196; Acts 3:10), and *HE* ii.1 (Le Prévost 1:209; Acts 11:5). For the medieval meaning of *extasis*, see Newman, "What Did It Mean to Say 'I Saw'?" 9.

81. Nicholas Howe sees a relationship between physical emplacement and spiritual journeying in the historical work of Bede. Bede, Howe contends, "demonstrates that a sense of place need not depend on wide travel, as is thought necessary in our time, but rather can be based on a contemplative regimen by which the observer detaches himself from the immediate circumstances of physical reality. . . . *Stabilitas loci*," the Benedictine ideal of geographical stability, "meant focusing on the essential matter of place by abjuring the distractions of travel or aimless wandering in the mapped world" (N. Howe, "From Bede's World to 'Bede's World,'" 24).

82. Benedict's *vita* was written by Gregory the Great in the *Dialogues* II.35.3: *omnis etiam mundus, uelut sub uno solis radio collectus, ante oculos eius adductus est.*

83. For the manipulation of spatial scale, see Gaddis, *Landscape of History*, 25–26, 81–84, and Certeau, *Practice of Everyday Life*, 101–2. For the folding of space see Wagner, "Condensed Mapping," 77.

84. Mégier, "*Divina Pagina*," 122, argues that Orderic's typological relationships "have nothing to do with prefiguration in the sense of a historical process. They connect happenings at the same level, the more recent episode is not more 'fulfilled' than the more ancient in time. There is no reason not to admit the historicity of this relationship: history can be a succession between two different positions, it can also be the continuity between two similar ones, and God can be acting either way." See also, for a more general statement of the importance of typological thinking for medieval history writing, Spiegel, "Political Utility," 92.

85. *HE* preface (Chibnall 1:130): *res alexandrinas seu grecas uel romanas aliasque relatu dignas indagare nequeam, quia claustralis cenobita ex proprio uoto cogor irrefragabiliter ferre monachilem obseruantiam.* For topography as "places where" see, from very different but complimentary perspectives, M. Campbell, "Object of One's Gaze," 6, and Basso, *Wisdom Sits in Places*, 7.

CHAPTER 2    Classical Geography and the *Gens Normannorum*

1. *HE* iii (Chibnall 2:50): *Isidori, Eusebii et Orosii . . . ad simile studium secuturam iuuentutem salubriter cohortati sunt.* Orderic also mentions Orosius, "the priest who wrote the book *De ormesta mundi*" (*presbiter qui librum de ormesta mundi scripsit*) in *HE* v.9 (Chibnall 3:52).

2. Orderic's narrative sources are discussed in Chibnall, 1:48–63. Orderic mentions Paul the Deacon in *HE* v.9 (Chibnall 3:68), and he frequently

refers to Paul's *Historia* in the same book (see the "Index of Quotations and Allusions" in Chibnall 3:370 for the citations). For Orderic's work with the *Liber Pontificalis*, see Chibnall 1:59–60. This papal chronicle formed the framework for part of the chronicle in book II of the *Historia Ecclesiastica* (*HE* ii.18 [Le Prévost 1:382–456; Chibnall 1:191–98]. Gildas, in conjunction with Bede, is mentioned in *HE* x.16 (Chibnall 5:298) and again in *HE* xii.47 (Chibnall 6:382), where he is apparently conflated with "Nennius." Orderic's error regarding Nennius is understandable; it remains unclear whether the "Nennius" mentioned in the preface of some later manuscripts of the *Historia Brittonum* was the author of the work, a scribe who copied it, or, indeed, an entirely made-up figure. The majority of extant medieval manuscripts attribute the *Historia Brittonum* to Gildas (Dumville, "Nennius," 78).

3.  *HE* prologue (Chibnall 1:130): *Darete Phrigio et Pompeio Trogo comperimus aliisque gentilium historiographis.* The *De excidio Troiae historia* was attributed to Dares Phrygius; it served as a source for Benoît de Sainte-Maure's popular *Roman de Troie.* A copy of most of the work (lacking the very end) was made at Ouche in the twelfth century, and is now in BN MS Latin 6503, fols. 53r-58v. Pompeius Trogus, from southern Gaul, was a historian of the first century BCE. His *Historiae Philippicae* was the only Latin universal history written by a non-Christian in antiquity. The original has unfortunately been lost, but it is preserved in a third-century *Epitome* by Justin.

4.  BN MS Latin 10062, fol. 80v, for the catalog from Ouche, and Nortier, *Les bibliothèques*, 209, 212, 214 for Bec's library. Orderic never said outright that he visited Bec, but his first-person comment on Bec's hospitality suggests that he spent some time there, and he does say that Eadmar's *Life of St. Anselm*, which he had clearly seen, was available in the library at Bec (*HE* iv [Chibnall 2:296] and x.9 [Chibnall 5:252]). A discussion of the works available to Normandy's twelfth-century monastic historians can be found in Shopkow, *History and Community*, 158–60.

5.  Orderic mentions nearly all of these writers by name in his *Historia*: Dudo (*HE* iii [Chibnall 2:2], vi.10 [Chibnall 3:304]); William of Jumièges (*HE* iii [Chibnall 2:2, 78], vi.10 [Chibnall 3:304]); William of Poitiers (*HE* iii [Chibnall 2:78, 184], iv [Chibnall 2:258–60]); Guy of Amiens (*HE* iii [Chibnall 2:184–86]); Fulcher of Chartres (*HE* ix.1 [Chibnall 5:6]; Baudry of Bourgueil (*HE* ix.1, 18 [Chibnall 5:6, 188–90]); John of Worcester (*HE* iii [Chibnall 2:186–88]); Geoffrey Malaterra (*HE* iii [Chibnall 2:100]). The exception is Geoffrey of Monmouth. Orderic included Geoffrey's *Prophetia Merlini* in the *Historia*, but did not mention Geoffrey by name (*HE* xii.47 [Chibnall 6:380–88]).

6. Bibliothèque de la ville, Rouen, MS 1343, ff. 34r–121r.

7. *HE* prologue (Chibnall 1:130): *Horum allegationes delectabiliter intueor, elegantiam et utilitatem sintagmatum laudo et admiror, nostrique temporis sapientes eorum notabile sedimen sequi cohortor.*

8. A. H. Merrills has studied four of the most influential geographical introductions—those of Orosius, Jordanes, Isidore of Seville, and Bede—in his *History and Geography.* My discussion of the classical tradition owes much to his study. See also Lavezzo, *Angels on the Edge,* 80–83, and Lozovsky, *Earth Is Our Book,* 68–101.

9. Jordanes, *Getica* I.4–V.46; Paul the Deacon, *Historia Langobardorum* I.1–2; Bede, *Historia Ecclesiastica* I.1; Dudo, *De moribus* I.1. Translations of the geographical introductions of Orosius, Jordanes, Isidore, and Bede are also in Merrills, *History and Geography,* 313–31.

10. Geoffrey of Monmouth, *Historia regum Britannie* 5; Henry of Huntingdon, *Historia Anglorum* I.1–3; Gerald of Wales, *Topographica Hibernica* I.1–4; Otto of Freising, *Historia de duabus civitatibus* I.1; Robert of Torigni, interpolations in William of Jumièges, *Gesta Normannorum Ducum* i.(2); Saxo Grammaticus, *Gesta Danorum,* preface.ii.1–10.

11. Books I and II, composed primarily of a patchwork of excerpts from classical and biblical texts, are by far the most derivative of the entire *Historia.*

12. The significance of Orderic's *vita Christi* is discussed in chapter 6.

13. *HE* v.1 (Chibnall 3:6): *Normannorum gesta et euentus Normannis.*

14. *HE* viii.24 (Chibnall 4:290): *et mundi status uariabiliter agitatur.*

15. Merrills notes that the geographical portions of the histories of Orosius and his imitators were characterized by "a descriptive stasis" (Merrills, *History and Geography,* 10). Lozovsky refers to Orosius's geography as "generalized and timeless" and that of Jordanes as "hard to locate in time," and comments on the "timeless world" of classical geography (Lozovsky, *Earth is Our Book,* 72, 84, 100). Walter Goffart, too, mention Orosius's "timeless geography"(Goffart, *Narrators of Barbarian History,* 348).

16. Orosius, *Historiarum adversus paganos libri septem* (hereafter *Historia*) I.i.4: *initium miseriae hominum ab initio peccati hominis.*

17. Orosius, *Historia* I.i.16–17: *ipsum terrarum orbem quem inhabitat humanum genus sicut est a maioribus trifariam distributum, deinde regionibus prouinciisque determinatum, expediam; quo facilius cum locales bellorum morborumque clades ostentabuntur, studiosi quique non solum rerum ac temporum sed etiam locorum scientiam consequantur.* For *orbis terrarum* as *oikoumene,* see Nicolet, *Space, Geography, and Politics,* 38–41; Romm, *Edges of the Earth,* 121–22.

18. Otto of Freising, *Historia* I.1: *Gestarum rerum ab Adam protoplasto usque ad tempus nostrum seriem executurus primo ipsum, quem habitat genus humanum, orbem, sicut a maioribus accepimus breviter distinguamus.*

19. Otto of Freising, *Historia* I.1: *legat Orosium.*

20. The Latin word *gens* (pl. *gentes*) had a range of meaning that is difficult to convey with any single English word. A medieval *gens* was, as defined by Susan Reynolds, "a natural, inherited community of tradition, custom, law, and descent" (Reynolds, *Kingdoms and Communities,* 251). Traditionally, the word "race" was often used as a translation of *gens,* but the modern resonances of the term no longer match (if they ever did) with the medieval connotations. The papers in the special issue "Concepts of Race and Ethnicity in the Middle Ages" of the *Journal of Medieval and Early Modern Studies* 31, no. 1 (2001) demonstrate, quite unintentionally I expect, how deeply flawed the idea of race, and even simply the word, can be when applied to the middle ages (see Jordan, "Why 'Race'?," for perceptive comments on this problematic historiography). For the meaning of *gens* from a particularly Norman perspective — which, as will become clear below, was to some extent unique within medieval Europe — see Loud,"*Gens Normannorum,*" 110–11; Jordan, "Why 'Race'?" 165–66; Bartlett, "Medieval and Modern," 42–44.

21. See Merrills, *History and Geography,* 100–169.

22. Paul the Deacon, *Historia Langobardorum* I.1: *Septemtrionalis plaga . . . propagandis est gentibus coaptata . . . saepe gentes egressae sunt, quae nihilominus et partes Asiae, sed maxime sibi contiguam Europam adflixerunt . . . miserae Italiae . . . ab insula quae Scandinavia dicitur adventavit.*

23. Yi-Fu Tuan sees this tendency to center the world around one's self and one's people as a nearly universal human trait (Tuan, *Topophilia,* 27–44).

24. Orderic did use the idea of a geographical "blank slate" in his adoption of the classical term "Albion" to refer to the island of Britain, which is discussed at length in chapter 3.

25. Fernand Braudel exemplified this perspective in his monumental study of *The Mediterranean and the Mediterranean World in the Age of Philip II,* where he described the picture drawn in the first, geographical part of his work as "one in which all the evidence combines across time and space, to give us a history in slow motion from which permanent values can be detected. Geography in this context is no longer an end in itself but a means to an end. It helps us to rediscover the slow unfolding of structural realities, to see things in the perspective of the very long term (*le plus longue dureé*). Geography, like history, can answer many questions. Here it helps us to discover the almost imperceptible movement of history" (Braudel, *Mediterranean,* 1:23).

26. *HE* vii.8 (Chibnall 4:40): *leues et extera uidere cupidi sunt.*

27. Geoffrey Malaterra, *De rebus gestis Rogerii* I.3: *spe alias plus lucrandi patrios agros vilipendens. . . .* Amatus of Montecassino, *Historia Normannorum* I.2. The original Latin version of Amatus's history has been lost, and the work is extant only in a French translation of the fourteenth-century, which contains some problems, comments, and omissions. See pp. 18–23 of Dunbar and Loud's translation of Amatus, and also Wolf, *Making History*, 89. All quotations from Amatus are from Dunbar and Loud's work.

28. The issue of Norman identity is briefly touched on in many studies, but for focused attention see: Albu, *Normans and Their Histories*; Davis, *Normans and Their Myth*; E. Johnson, "Normandy and Norman Identity"; Loud, "*Gens Normannorum*," 104–16, 205–9; Potts, "*Atque unum ex diversis gentibus populum effecit*"; Thomas, *English and the Normans*; and Webber, *Evolution of Norman Identity*.

29. Orderic frequently described the Normans as an untamed *gens*, difficult to govern and inclined towards violence. See, for instance, *HE* v.10 (Chibnall 3:98), vii.15 (Chibnall 4:82), ix.3 (Chibnall 5:24), xiii.21 (Chibnall 6:456). Orderic was not alone in characterizing the Normans in this fashion, however. See Loud, "*Gens Normannorum*," 111–13, for the construction of the Norman character.

30. Dudo, *De moribus* I.1: *In copiosa igitur intercapedine a Danubio ad Scythici ponti.* The "Scythian Sea" is the Black Sea. It was William of Jumièges who would first make the identification between Dacia and Denmark (*Danamarcha*) explicit (William of Jumièges, *Gesta Normannorum Ducum* i.3[4]). Dudo's reliance on the traditions of classical geography, with its Mediterranean biases and lack of knowledge about the northern lands, made his descriptions of the Danish migrations rather confused.

31. William of Jumièges, *Gesta Normannorum Ducum* i.3(4): *Iactant enim Troianos ex sua stirpe processisse, Antenoremque ab urbis exterminio cum duobus milibus militum et quingentis uiris ob proditionem illius ab eo perpetratam euasisse, ac per multimodos ponti anfractus Germaniam appulisse . . . eamque a quodam Danao, sue stirpis rege, Danamarcham nuncupasse.* Cf. Dudo, *De moribus* I.3, who tells the same story but with rather less clarity.

While the Norman historical tradition asserts that the Normans traced their mythical origins to the Trojans, Dudo's and William of Jumièges's attempts to insert this Norman origin myth into the orthodox northern geography set out by Jordanes were not entirely successful. Dudo, generally more interested in rhetorical effect than historical accuracy, simply tossed the Trojan reference into his text with little context (Dudo, *De moribus* I.3). William returned once again to Jordanes's original description, apparently attempting to sort out Dudo's narrative, but his diligence produced little; it is unclear in the *Gesta Normannorum Ducum* whether William meant that the Danes were descended from the Goths who were descended from the Trojans, or whether he believed that the Danes were descended from an intermingling of the Goths and Trojans (William of Jumièges, *Gesta Normannorum Ducum* i.2[3]–3[4]; see also Van Houts's introduction to William's work, 1:xxxvi).

32. Dudo, *De moribus*, i.1: *collecta sorte multitudine pubescentium, veterimo ritu, in externa regna extruduntur nationum, ut acquirant sibi præliando regna.*

33. Dudo, *De moribus* I.3: *profugas . . . gentes*; and I.7: *caput mundi.* The full story of Hasting's journey is in Dudo, *De moribus* I.3–7, and another version of his exploits (which makes him a traitorous Frank rather than a Dane) appears in Raoul Glaber, *Historiarum libri quinque* I.v.19. This desire of northern peoples to conquer Rome returns in Geoffrey of Monmouth's *Historia* (Wright §§ 43–44, pp. 28–30; Thorpe iii.9–10, pp. 97–99), with Belinus and Brennius (Lavezzo, *Angels on the Edge*, 21–24).

34. It is important to emphasize that this is the Norman origin *myth.* Reality was, of course, quite different. However, the facts of Norman origins as teased out by modern historians with better source materials and a developed historical method did not affect the ways in which the Normans of Orderic's age understood the history and development of their community.

35. While it was Dudo's account of Rollo and his Danish origins that lived on in Norman writings, Norwegian legends preserved a different set of traditions about Rolf Ganger (Rolf the Walker). For Rollo, see Douglas, "Rollo of Normandy," and Musset, "L'origine de Rollon."

36. The dream is recounted in Dudo, *De moribus* II.6.

37. The story of Constantine's leprosy comes from the "Donation of Constantine," now known to be forged but widely accepted as genuine in the middle ages.

38. Dudo, *De moribus* I.6: *circum basim illius hinc inde et altrinsecus, multa millia avium diversorum generum, varii coloris, sinistra alas quin etiam rubicundas habentium . . . sine discretione generum et specierum, sine ullo contentionis jurgio.*

39. Dudo, *De moribus* I.6: *homines diversarum provinciarum scutulata bracchia habentes . . . innumeram multitudinem coadunatam. . . . Tibi aves diversarum specierum obtemperabunt; tibi homines diversorum regnorum serviendo accubitati obedient.*

40. Dudo's account, with its mythological contours, is deeply oversimplified. See Chibnall, *Normans*, 9–14, for a good brief summary. Bauduin,

*La première Normandie,* 128–41, and Le Patourel, *Norman Empire,* 3–15, go into more detail.

41. *HE* ix.3 (Chibnall 5:24): *De feroci gente Scitarum origio Troianorum uti refertur processit.*

42. The idea of the Trojans' Scythian origins apparently stems from William of Jumièges comment that the Goths migrated from Scandza in two waves, the first of which went to Scythia and the second to Germany and Denmark; Orderic seems to have taken William's account to mean that the Goths who went to Scythia later became the Trojans, who, following the fall of Troy, reunited with the Danish branch of the *gens* (William of Jumièges, *Gesta Normannorum Ducum* i.2[3]–3[4]). The region of Scythia figured prominently in the geography of both Orosius and, especially, Jordanes (Orosius, *Historia* I.ii.47; Jordanes, *Getica* I.v.30–38). Bede names Scythia as the Picts' homeland in his *Historia Eccleisastica* i.1 (cf. Merrills, *History and Geography,* 284–85). For the classical anthropology of the Scythians, see G. Campbell, *Strange Creatures,* 93–105.

43. *HE* ix.3 (Chibnall 5:24): *Frigius Antenor Illiricos fines penetrauit, et cum uicinis exulantibus diu longeque locum habitationis quesiuit. Denique super littus oceani maris in boreali plaga consedit, et sibi sociisque et heredibus suis maritimam regionem incoluit, et a Dano filio eius gens illa e Troianis orta Danorum nomen accepit.*

44. For the archetypical Roman origin myth, which found its fullest expression in Vergil's *Aeneid,* see Bickerman, "*Origines Gentium,*" 65–68.

45. *HE* ix.3 (Chibnall 5:24): *Rollo dux acerrimus cum Normannis inde genus duxit, qui primus Neustriam sibi subiugauit, quæ nunc a Normannis Normanniæ nomen optinuit.*

46. Orosius, *Historia* I.ii.64–65: *Gallia Lugdunensis . . . Aquitanicam prouinciam semicingit. Haec ab oriente habet Belgicam, a meridie partem prouinciae Narbonensis, qua Arelas ciuitas sita est et mari Gallico Rhodani flumen accipitur.*

47. Geoffrey Malaterra also noted that the region "was not always called Normandy," though he claims that before the Normans came it "was thus called France as a general name" (*non semper Normannia dicta fuit . . . generali nomine Francia et sic vocabatur*) (Geoffrey Malaterra, *De rebus gestis Rogerii* I.1). For the relationship between Normandy and Neustria, see Bauduin, *La première Normandie,* 100–107. For the political and geographical nature of pre-Norman Neustria, see Werner, "Qu'est-ce que la Neustrie?"

48. Richer of Reims *Historiarum libri quinque* I.4: *piratę qui Rhodomensem provinciam incolebant, quę est Celticę Gallię pars . . . Gallię Celticę*

*partem quae Sequanae Ligerique fluviis interiacet quę et Neustria nuncu-*
*patur, totam pene insectati sunt.* See Lozovsky, *Earth is Our Book,* 94–100,
for Richer's geography.

49. *HE* iii (Chibnall 2:4): *de uinea Domini sabaoth, quam ipse forti dex-*
*tera colit et protegit in toto mundo contra insidias Behemoth. Hæc nimirum*
*in regione quæ olim Neustria, nunc uero uocatur Normannia, laborantibus*
*colonis sparsim suas propagines emisit, et multiplicem fructum hominum in*
*sanctitate permanentium Deo obtulit.* This later became the beginning of
book III of the *Historia;* for the order of writing of the books, see the preface.
As Chibnall notes, Orderic apparently left room for a preface on fol. 1r of
what is now BN MS Latin 5506 (II) and went back to fill in the space at a later
time. Therefore, the text on fol. 1v, the beginning of the narrative proper, appears to be the very first lines Orderic wrote in the *Historia.*

50. Lozovsky, *Earth is Our Book,* 97 and n. 139.

51. Bede, *Historia Ecclesiastica* I.1: *Brittania Oceani insula, cui quon-*
*dam Albion nomen fuit.*

52. The island, of course, was never ethnically homogenous. Bede noted
that in his own day English, Welsh (British), Irish, and Pictish were all spoken on the island, and his *Historia Ecclesiastica* lays out the interactions between these groups (Bede, *Historia Ecclesiastica* I.1).

53. Bede, *Historia Ecclesiastica* I.1: *a quibus nomen accepit.*

54. P. Wormald, *"Engla Lond,"* 10–11. The balance between the island,
its name, and the groups that inhabited it—which is more complex than is set
out here—is discussed in chapter 3.

55. *HE* ix.3 (Chibnall 5:24): *a Normannis Normanniæ nomen.* Orderic
gives this explanation immediately following the above comment. See also
Robert of Toringi, interpolations in William of Jumièges, *Gesta Normanno-*
*rum Ducum* i.3(4); Geoffrey Malaterra, *De rebus gestis Rogerii* I.3; Davis,
*Normans and Their Myth,* 12–13.

56. The extent of Scandinavian settlement in Normandy, and therefore
the extent to which the Normans were "ethnically" different from their French
neighbors, has been a long-standing question. The current consensus asserts
that while the ruling class of Normandy had a strong Scandinavian component,
the Norman population in general remained largely made up of Franks and,
in the northwestern regions, Bretons. Furthermore, the Norman nobles almost
immediately began intermarrying with their Frankish and Breton counter-
parts, further "diluting" the Scandinavian "blood." For some discussions of
this issue, see Musset, "Essai," and Davis, *Normans and Their Myth,* 19–27.

57. For the idea of a *gens Normannorum,* see Loud, *"Gens Norman-*
*norum."*

58. For the importance of Normandy to Norman identity, see Davis, *Normans and Their Myth,* 57–59 (though I disagree with his interpretation of Orderic's use of the word "Neustria"), and, for a slightly different perspective, Loud, "*Gens Normannorum,*" 108–9.

59. The word *patria* used in the classical sense of "homeland" or "country" experienced a revival in the twelfth century. See Iogna-Prat, "Constructions chrétiennes"; Kantorowicz, "*Pro Patria Mori*"; Koht, "Dawn of Nationalism," 266–67; Monnet, "La *patria* médiévale"; Post, "Two Notes on Nationalism," 281–96.

60. The discussion of the Normans' settlement in Italy offered here is meant simply to set the stage for Orderic's geographical vision, and is by no means a complete account of events. For much more detailed accounts of the Normans in Italy, see Chibnall, *Normans,* 75–93; Loud, *Age of Robert Guiscard*; France, "Occasion of the Coming of the Normans to Southern Italy"; Cowdrey, *Age of Abbot Desiderius*; and the various papers reprinted in Loud, *Conquerors and Churchmen.* Loud, "How 'Norman,'" 16–18, gives a good account of the political and social conditions in Normandy that provoked emigration.

61. Loud, *Age of Robert Guiscard,* 118–20.

62. Loud, *Age of Robert Guiscard,* 128–30, 186–93, with the text of Robert's oath of fealty on 188–89. Also Loud, "Papacy," 153–58.

63. Despite their common government, these groups would maintain not only their religious identity—they were Muslim, Greek Christian, and Roman Christian—but also an awareness of their ethnic diversity. See Drell, "Cultural Syncretism," 187–202, and Loud, "How 'Norman,'" 24–30, for different perspectives on the diverse nature of the community, both emphasizing Norman-Lombard assimilation. For the Muslim population, see Metcalfe, "Muslims of Sicily."

64. Loud, *Age of Robert Guiscard,* 146–85.

65. Loud, "Papacy," 162–69. For a good concise account of the kingdom, see Chibnall, *Normans,* 85–93. Roger II of Sicily was arguably one of medieval Europe's greatest kings; see Houben, *Roger II of Sicily,* for his personality and rule.

66. Loud, *Age of Robert Guiscard,* 209–23, for Robert's Byzantine campaigns.

67. For the significance of Roger's ancestry, see Drell, "Cultural Syncretism," 198–99.

68. Bohemond figures most prominently in the *Gesta Francorum,* an account of the crusade believed to be written by an anonymous Norman from southern Italy, and his reputation spread with the popularity of the *Gesta*

*Francorum.* For the Normans on crusade and elsewhere in the East, see Chibnall, *Normans,* 94–103.

69. Loud, "Norman Italy and the Holy Land," 49–52; Murray, "How Norman was the Principality of Antioch?" The best study of crusader Antioch is Asbridge, *Creation of the Principality of Antioch.*

70. There are, of course, a number of biographies of William the Conqueror. The standard account remains Douglas, *William the Conqueror,* complemented recently by Bates, *William the Conqueror.*

71. For the troubles of William's minority, see Bates, "Conqueror's Adolescence"; idem, *Normandy Before 1066,* 175–77; Douglas, *William the Conqueror,* 15–80; Loud, "How 'Norman,'" 16–17; Searle, *Predatory Kinship,* 179–89.

72. Again, as was the case above with Norman Sicily, the discussion of the Conquest here is designed simply to lay the foundations for Orderic's geographical understanding, and it in no way does justice to the complexity of the Conquest and its aftermath. A more thorough discussion of the Conquest, with more extensive citations, can be found in chapter 3.

73. *HE* iii (Chibnall 2:144); William of Poitiers, *Gesta Guillelmi* ii.2, for the various peoples who joined William in the Conquest.

74. Loud, "How 'Norman'," 15–16, 30. The phrase "the other Norman Conquest" became popular with John Julius Norwich's *The Normans in Sicily: The Magnificent Story of 'the Other Norman Conquest'* (Harmondsworth: Penguin, 1992), which contains both his *The Normans in the South* (1967) and *The Kingdom in the Sun* (1970).

75. *HE* iii (Chibnall 2:126): *Normanniam oblitus.*

76. Wace's *Roman de Rou,* or "Romance of Rollo," a vernacular history of the Normans written for England's King Henry II in the 1160s and 1170s, clearly demonstrates that the Norman myth was alive and well in England well into the twelfth century.

77. The most influential articulation of the argument that the Normans were not a *gens* beyond Normandy is that of Davis, *Normans and Their Myth,* 13–17, and passim. This view has been seriously challenged by Loud, "*Gens Normannorum.*"

78. In Davis's words, the question is "whether the Normanness of the Normans was an objective reality, or merely a myth which remained effective only so long as people believed in it" (Davis, *Normans and Their Myths,* 17).

79. Davis argued that "by writing the way he did, Orderic has persuaded almost all subsequent historians of the reality of the Norman world. . . . It is a frightening thought that one eloquent historian might impose an idiosyn-

cratic view on all his successors, compelling them to consider that disparate conditions and disjointed events were really part of an inherent unity" (Davis, *Normans and Their Myths*, 15).

80. Loud's article "*Gens Normannorum*" specifically engages with and disproves Davis's argument regarding Orderic's unique perspective.

81. See, for instance, Loud, "*Gens Normanorum*," passim, for discussion of some of the Norman Sicilian historians, and Drell, "Cultural Syncretism," 198–201 for the ethnic memory of the Normans in Italy. Drell's study demonstrates that the Normans in Italy maintained one of the markers of communal identity that Anthony D. Smith, the great historian of the nation, has identified as significant, namely, "a common self-image, including a collective proper name, which symbolises 'us' as opposed to others around us" (A. Smith, "Were There Nations in Antiquity?" 39). The Normans, as Drell notes, persisted in calling themselves "Normans" for generations after their migration to Italy.

82. See, for instance, Smith's suggestion that pre-modern "nations" might better be defined as *ethnies*, that is, "as named human communities, with myths of common descent, shared memories and one or more elements of common culture such as language, religion and customs, and a sense of solidarity, at least among the elites. While they are often linked to specific territories, *ethnies* may continue to function outside any homeland as diasporas, and remain resilient over centuries" (A. Smith, "Were There Nations in Antiquity?" 38–39). A number of the main elements that Smith associates with the ideal-type of the premodern nation can be seen among the Normans in Normandy, Italy, and England. Particularly notable were the Normans' "distinctive shared memories, myths, symbols and traditions of the historic culture community formed on the basis of one or more ethnic categories and communities," and also "the occupation, residence in and development of a common ancestral homeland," namely, Normandy (Smith, "Were There Nations in Antiquity?" 39).

83. *HE* v.1 (Chinball 3:6): *Normannorum gesta et euentus Normannis.* This was true through the first half of the twelfth century, but over time, of course, the nature of the connections between the various groups of Normans changed. As the Normans who lived in Sicily and in England became generationally distant from their origins in Normandy, the nature of the *gens Normannorum* fundamentally changed. For this changing identity, see Drell, "Cultural Syncretism," passim; Short, "*Tam Angli quam Franci*"; and Thomas, *English and the Normans*.

84. The term "metageography" was coined by Martin W. Lewis and Kären E. Wigen to describe "the set of spatial structures through which

people order their knowledge of the world; the often unconscious frameworks that organize studies of history, sociology, anthropology, economics, political science, or even natural history" (Lewis and Wigen, *Myth of Continents*, ix). As Lewis and Wigen argue, metageographical structures are deeply ingrained and very difficult to change.

85. Orosius, *Historia* I.ii.63: *Gallia Belgica habet ab oriente limitem fluminis Rheni et Germaniam, ab euro habet Alpes Poeninas, a meridie prouinciam Narbonensem, ab occasu prouinciam Lugdunensem, a circio oceanum Britannicum, a septentrione Britanniam insulam.*

86. In the early middle ages geography was in fact included in the quadrivium as an element of geometry (Lozovsky, *Earth is Our Book*, 23–28).

87. Bartlett, "Medieval and Modern," 45–46; Friedman, *Monstrous Races*, 35–36, 50–55; Glacken, *Traces on the Rhodian Shore*, 80–115 for ancient thought, and 254–87 for medieval.

88. Isidore of Seville, *Etymologiarum libri xx* (hereafter *Etymologiae*) IX.ii.105: *Secundum diversitatem enim caeli et facies hominum et colores et corporum quantitates et animorum diversitates existunt. Inde Romanos graves, Graecos leves, Afros versipelles, Gallos natura feroces atque acriores ingenio pervidemus, quod natura climatum facit.*

89. Cassiodorus, *Variae* XII.xv.3: *Patria siquidem fervens leves efficit et acutos, figida tardos et subdolos: sola temperata est, quae mores hominum sua qualitate componit.*

90. Orosius, *Historia* V.xvi.14: *Teutones autem et Cimbri integris copiis Alpium niues emensi Italiae plana peruaserant ibique cum rigidum genus diu blandioribus auris, poculis, cibis ac lauacris emolliretur.*

91. *HE* ix.3 (Chibnall 5:24): *Indomita gens Normannorum est, et nisi rigido rectore coherceatur ad facinus promptissima est. In omnibus collegiis ubicumque fuerint dominari appetunt, et ueritatis fideique tenorem preuaricantes ambitionis estu multoties effectu sunt. Hoc Franci et Britones et Flandrenses aliique collimitanei crebro senserunt, hoc Itali et Guinili Saxonesque Angli usque ad internecionem experti sunt.*

92. For the similar characterizations of the Normans, see Loud, "*Gens Normannorum*," 111–12.

93. Geoffrey Malaterra, *De rebus gestis Rogerii* I.3: *nini jugo justitiae prematur, effrenatissima est.*

94. William of Apulia, *Gesta Roberti Wiscardi* I.4: *Gens Normannorum feritate insignis equestri.*

95. William of Malmesbury, *Gesta regum Anglorum* iii.246.1: *Gens militiae assueta et sine bello pene uiuere nescia.*

96. *HE* v.10 (Chibnall 3:98): *Normanni semper inquieti sunt, et pertur-bationes ardenter sitiunt.*

97. For the significance of cartographic scale and its manipulation of perception, see Lewis and Wigen, *Myth of Continents*, 2–3, 131–33.


ENTR'ACTE   At Sea

1. The idea of the sea as geographically binding is certainly not new, but it has recently gained prominence as a field of historical and geographical inquiry. When John Le Patrourel suggested that "the English Channel, set in the midst of the lands and lordships of the Norman kings, served to bind those lands and lordships together, as the Mediterranean and the Irish Seas have served in other times and contexts," he may have been thinking about Braudel's classic *The Mediterranean and the Mediterranean World in the Age of Philip II*, which brought the notion of that sea as a unifying force to the fore of European historiography (Le Patourel, *Norman Empire,* 172). Braudel's Mediterranean has been revisited recently by Peregrine Horden and Nicholas Purcell's *The Corrupting Sea,* but the so-called "maritime turn" or "new thalassology" now reaches far beyond the Mediterranean, as demonstrated by the papers included in Finamore, *Maritime History as World History.* In the past decade three journals have published special issues or forums looking particularly at the unifying nature of the sea: "Oceans Connect," *Geographical Review* 89, no. 2 (1999); "Historical Geographies of the Sea," *Journal of Historical Geography* 32, no. 3 (2006); and "AHR Forum: Oceans of History," *American Historical Review* 111, no. 3 (2006). These dialogues have been influential in my thinking about the sea, and individual articles from these journals are cited when appropriate.

2. See Romm, *Edges of the Earth,* 12–17, for the classical development of the circular Ocean. Orosius, *Historia* I.ii.1, and Isidore of Seville, *Etymologiae* XIII.xv.1 and XIV.ii.1, helped to perpetuate this idea.

3. See chapter 2 for other ways in which Orderic undermined the geographical traditions of European historiography. Also, Lewis and Wigen, "Maritime Response," 165, for the geographical significance of looking outwards towards the sea.

4. Bennett, "Norman Naval Activity."

5. Abulafia, "Norman Kingdom of Africa."

6. See Ahmad, "Cartography."

7. Quoted in Ahmad, "Cartography," 159.

8. Copies of the world map can be found in Ahmad, "Cartography," 161–62. For a general discussion of medieval Islamic world maps, see Edson and Savage-Smith, *Medieval Views of the Cosmos*, 75–84.

9. The scholarship on the historical meaning of the Mediterranean is vast. For a recent overview, see Horden and Purcell, "Mediterranean and 'the New Thalassology.'"

10. Horden and Purcell, *Corrupting Sea*, 11; Romm, *Edges of the Earth*, 17–18.

11. Lavezzo, *Angels on the Edge*, 2–8, and passim.

12. Isidore, *Etymologiae* XIV.vi.2: *Brittania Oceani insula interfuso mari toto orbe divisa.* Cf. Orosius, *Historia* I.ii.76; Bede, *Historia Ecclesiastica* I.1.

13. *HE* ix.4 (Chibnall 5:30): *Angliam quoque aliasque maritimas insulas . . . undisoni maris abissus illas remoueat ab orbe.*

14. Britain's location also gave the sea a particular meaning for the island's inhabitants, as the Anglo-Saxon poems *The Wanderer* and *The Seafarer* demonstrate (N. Howe, *Writing the Map*, 70–72).

15. Romm, *Edges of the Earth*, 121–23, 140–41; Lozovsky, *Earth Is Our Book*, 74–75; Nicolet, *Space, Geography, and Politics*, 29–47; Clarke, *Between Geography and History*, 308–13.

16. For the ancient idea of Thule, and its ambiguous place in Roman manifest destiny, see Romm, *Edges of the Earth*, 156–71. Ireland, of course, might also figure into this equation, and it was indeed known to classical geographers, but often placed further south than it is in actuality. Orosius, for instance, locates it "between Britain and Spain" (*inter Britanniam et Hispaniam*) (Orosius, *Historia* I.ii.80).

17. Merrills, *History and Geography*, 272–73.

18. *HE* iii (Chibnall 2:144): *ad bellum transmarinum*; iv (Chibnall 2:208): *ad transmarinis partibus* (from England to Normandy); viii.9 (Chibnall 4:178): *de transmarinis partibus* (from Normandy to England). This is only a sampling of Orderic's use of this word. See Chibnall 1:378 for more occurrences.

19. *HE* x.10 (Chibnall 5:256): *'Eamus trans mare nostros adiuuare.'*

20. Henry of Huntingdon, *Historia Anglorum* vii.21: *'De rege fluctibus submerso loqui non audiui.' Ergo mare transiens, nichil dum uiueret egit, unde tantam famam, tantum glorie decus, haberet.* The same story is told by William of Malmesbury, *Gesta regum Anglorum* iv.320.2, and Robert of Toringi, interpolations in William of Jumièges, *Gesta Normannorum Ducum* viii.8. See also Greenway, "Authority, Convention and Observation," 105 and n. 3.

21. For Cnut's capitulation to the sea, see Henry of Huntingdon, *Historia Anglorum* ii.20.

22. The story of the *White Ship* is told by Orderic in *HE* xii.26 (Chibnall 6:294–306). Orderic's account is the fullest, but see also Henry of Huntingdon, *Historia Anglorum* vii.32; Robert of Torigni, interpolations in William of Jumièges, *Gesta Normannorum Ducum* viii.12; William of Malmesbury, *Gesta regum Anglorum* v.419.

23. *HE* xii.26 (Chibnall 6:304, 6): *tetra uorago*. William of Malmesbury also mentions the search for bodies (*Gesta regum Anglorum* v.419.8).

24. As mentioned in chapter 2, the question of Scandinavian influence in Normandy has been a thorny one. See Abrams, "England, Normandy and Scandinavia"; Musset, "L'image de la Scandinavie"; and Van Houts, "Scandinavian Influence," for some perspectives on the continued political and cultural connections between the Normans, Norwegians, and Danes.

25. Bennett, *Campaigns of the Norman Conquest*, 24–37.

26. For a brief discussion of this section of the *Historia*, see Musset, "L'image de la Scandinavie," 223–25. Orderic's source for his Norwegian information is uncertain. Chibnall rejects the idea that Orderic was familiar with Adam of Bremen's *Gesta Hammaburgensis ecclesiae pontificum* and suggests that he relied on a now-lost Latin source (Chibnall 5:221n5). But certain geographical flourishes found in both Orderic and Adam's descriptions suggest that some common tradition lay behind both of their works.

27. *HE* x.6 (Chibnall 5:218, 20): *potentiam in insulis Oceani habebat.*

28. *HE* x.6 (Chibnall 5:220): *Quinque ciuitates in circumitu Northwagiæ supra littus maris sitæ sunt, Berga, Cuneghella, Copenga, Burgus et Alsa. Turesberga uero sexta ciuitas est, quæ contra Dacos ad orientem sita est. In meditullio insulæ piscosi lacus et ingentes sunt, et uillæ campestres in marginibus stagnorum circumsitæ sunt. Indigenæ uero piscibus et uolucribus, omniumque ferarum abundant carnibus.* Musset notes that this is "the first satisfactory list of Norwegian towns that can be found in western historiography" (Musset, "L'image de la Scandinavie," 223).

29. *HE* x.6 (Chibnall 5:222): *subsolano flante Oceanum perlustrans Orcades insulas adiit, Scotiam a parte Circii circumiuit, et alias insulas quæ ad suam ditionem pertinent usque in Angeleseiam penetrauit.*

30. *HE* x.6 (Chibnall 5:222): *Alias quoque Ciclades in magno mari uelut extra orbem positas perlustrauit, et a pluribus populis inhabitari regio iussu coegit, seseque per plures annos ad augmentum regni et dilatationem plebium tali studio exercuit.* Adam of Bremen says that the Orkneys, like the Cyclades, are "scattered through the Ocean" (*dispersae per occeanum*) (Adam of Bremen, *Gesta* IV.35).

31.  *HE* x.6 (Chibnall 5:220): *Orcades insulæ et Finlanda, Islanda quoque et Grenlanda, ultra quam ad septentrionem terra non reperitur, aliæque plures usque in Gollandam regi Noricorum subiciuntur.* For *Finlanda* as Finnmark rather than Finland, Musset, "L'image de la Scandinavie," 223.

32.  Orosius, *Historia*, I.ii.75–82; Jordanes, *Getica* I.4–III.19; and especially Isidore, *Etymologiae* XIV.vi.1–44, all provide descriptive catalogs of islands.

33.  Orosius, *Historia* I.ii.78–9: *oceano infinito. Deinde insula Thyle quae per infinitum a ceteris separata, circum uersus medio sita oceani, uix paucis nota habetur.*

34.  Gilles, "Territorial Interpolations"; N. Howe, *Writing the Map*, 114–15.

35.  Isidore, *Etymologiae* XIV.vi.5: *intra Britanniam.* Cf. Orosius, *Historia* I.ii.78.

36.  The sea's sluggishness at Thule was a classical trope (Romm, *Edges of the Earth*, 148).

37.  This map, and Orderic's engagement with it, is discussed in much more detail in chapter 4.

38.  In this he was rather like the English translator of Orosius, although there is nothing to suggest that Orderic ever read the Old English Orosius.

39.  Friedman, *Monstrous Races*, 84–85.

40.  Adam of Bremen, *Gesta* IV.35–39.

41.  Adam of Bremen, *Gesta* IV.36: *tam a Romanis scriptoribus quam a barbaris multa referuntur digna predicari. . . . Thyle nunc Island appellatur, a glacie, quae oceanum astringit . . . in subterraneis habitant speluncis, communi tecto [et victu] et strato gaudentes cum pecoribus suis.*

42.  Adam of Bremen, *Gesta* IV.36: *Haec de Island et ultima Thyle veraciter comperi, fabulosa preteriens.* Dicuil mentioned the eremitic inhabitants of the northern isles in his *Liber de mensura orbis terrae* VII.11–15.

43.  Adam of Bremen, *Gesta* IV.37: *a salo cerulei, unde et regio illa nomen accepit.* William of Newburgh, *Historia rerum Anglicarum* I.27.

44.  *HE* x.6 (Chibnall 5:222): *et a pluribus populis inhabitari regio iussu coegit, seseque per plures annos ad augmentum regni et dilatationem plebium tali studio exercuit.*

45.  *HE* iv (Chibnall 2:302–4): *Sicut mare nunquam tutum certa soliditate quiescit, sed inquietudine iugi turbatum more suo defluit, et quamuis aliquando tranquillum obtutibus spectantium appareat, solita tamen flucuatione et instabilitate nauigantes territat, sic præsens sæculum uolubilitate sua iugiter uexatur, innumerisque modis tristibus seu lætis euidenter uariatur.*

CHAPTER 3    Albion: Conquest, Hegemony, and the English Past

1. The extremely complicated and, despite an astounding amount of scholarly research, still rather obscure circumstances that led to William of Normandy's conquest of England following the death of King Edward the Confessor in 1066 are beyond the scope of this study. A brief overview is given here to set the stage for Orderic Vitalis's vision of post-Conquest life. Additional details will be provided as needed, but for more complete information see, among countless others, Bennett, *Campaigns of the Norman Conquest;* Chibnall, *Debate on the Norman Conquest;* Freeman's legendary but flawed *History of the Norman Conquest of England;* Loyn, *Norman Conquest;* Van Houts, "Norman Conquest through European Eyes." Biographies of William the Conqueror include Bates *William the Conqueror,* Douglas, *William the Conqueror,* and Freeman, *William the Conqueror.*

2. For the circumstances of Edward's death, including the confusion over whether he had designated Harold Godwinson his deathbed heir, see Barlow, *Edward the Confessor,* 247–55.

3. Barlow, *Edward the Confessor,* 254–55. King Edward was married to Harold's sister Edith.

4. Edward the Confessor's mother Emma was the daughter of Richard I duke of Normandy and therefore Duke William's great aunt.

5. Barlow, *Edward the Confessor,* 106–9, 220–29. The Norman sources for this story include William of Poitiers, *Gesta Guillelmi* i.41, ii.8, ii.12; William of Jumièges, *Gesta Normannorum Ducum* vii.13(31); *HE* iii (Chibnall 2:134–36). There are a number of inconsistencies in this Norman tradition, which was used by the Normans after 1066 to justify the conquest of England; the problems are discussed by Barlow and also Beckerman, "Succession"; Douglas, "Edward the Confessor"; John, "Edward the Confessor"; Oleson, "Edward the Confessor's Promise." Sheppard, *Families of the King,* 124–31, discusses both the Norman tradition and the English perspective as set out in the *Anglo-Saxon Chronicle.*

6. Duke William's appeal for papal support for the invasion, apparently based on Harold's perjury, is noted in William of Poitiers, *Gesta Guillelmi* ii.3 and *HE* iii (Chibnall 2:142). See also Douglas, *William the Conqueror,* 187–88; Van Houts, "Norman Conquest through European Eyes," 832, 850–52.

7. *HE* iii (Chibnall 2:182, 4): *Denique anno ab incarnatione Domini MLXVII indictione quinta, in die natalis Domini, Angli Lundoniæ ad ordinandum regem conuenerunt, et Normannorum turmæ circa monasterium*

*in armis et equis ne quid doli et seditionis oriretur præsidio dispositæ fuerunt.*
*Adelredus itaque archiepiscopus in basilica Sancti Petri apostolorum prin-*
*cipis quæ Westmonasterium nuncupatur ubi Eduardus rex uenerabiliter hu-*
*matus quiescit, in præsentia præsulum et abbatum procerumque totius regni*
*Albionis Guillelmum ducem Normannorum in regem Anglorum consecrauit,*
*et diadema regium capiti eius imposuit.*

    8. William of Poitiers, *Gesta Guillelmi* ii.30: *imposuit ei regium di-*
*adema, ipsumque regio solio, fauente multorum praesentia praesulum et ab-*
*batum, in basilica sancti Petri apostoli, quae regis Edwardi sepulchro gaude-*
*bat, in sacrosancta solemnitate Dominici natalis, millesimo sexagesimo sexto*
*Incarnationis Dominicae anno.*

    9. Guy of Amiens, *Carmen de Hastingae proelio*, ll. 833–35: *regem de*
*puluere tollit; / Crismate diffuso regis et ipse caput / Vnxit, et in regem regali*
*more sacrauit.*

    10. John of Worcester, *Chronica* an. 1066: *ante altare sancti Petri apos-*
*toli coram clero et populo iureiurando promittens se uelle sanctas Dei eccle-*
*sias ac rectores illarum defendere necnon et cunctum populum sibi subiectum*
*iuste et regali prouidentia regere, rectam legem statuere et tenere, rapinas*
*iniustaque iudicia penitus interdicere.* Cf. *Anglo-Saxon Chronicle* Worcester
MS D 1066, p. 200; *Anglo-Saxon Chronicle* Peterborough MS E 1066, p. 198.
This three-fold promise was at the heart of the English coronation oath (Loyn,
*Governance*, 85; Nelson, "Rites of the Conqueror," 120, shows the place of
the promise in the Third English Ordo, which Nelson demonstrates to be the
one used to crown the Conqueror).

    11. William of Malmesbury, *Gesta regum Anglorum* iii.247.3: *haud*
*dubie rex conclamatus.* Henry of Huntingdon, *Historia Anglorum* vi.30.

    12. Wace, *Roman de Rou* iii.8977–82: *Par commun conseil del clergié, /*
*qui l'out loé e conseillié, / e par les barons, qui veeient / que altre esliere ne*
*poeient, / ont le duc fait rei coroné / e feelté li ont juré.*

    13. Bede, *Historia Ecclesiastica* i.1: *Brittania Oceani insula, cui quon-*
*dam Albion nomen fuit.* Merrills, *History and Geography*, 255. The name
Albion in medieval texts seems to be traced to Pliny the Elder, *Naturalis his-*
*toria* iv.xvi.102: *Albion ipsi nomen fuit.*

    14. For more about the classical geographical tradition, and Britain's
place in particular, see chapter 2 and the Entr'acte.

    15. Twenty-six mentions in a work of thirteen books might not seem
very significant until it is put into context. This can be done through a quick
search of the online version of Migne's *Patrologia Latina*, which finds the
word Albion used only fifty-eight times in the entire massive corpus, and

that number *includes* the twenty-six occurrences in the *Historia. (Patrologia Latina Database,* http://pld.chadwyck.com. In my search I excluded apparatus and included medieval authors only). Orderic Vitalis's *Historia Ecclesiastica* is contained in *PL* 188.

Albion is mentioned in *HE* iii (Chibnall 2:184); iv (Chibnall 2:214, 216, 240, 254, 258, 314); v.10 (Chibnall 3:96, 100); vi.2 (Chibnall 3:214); vii.5 (Chibnall 4:16); vii.8 (Chibnall 4:40); viii.2 (Chibnall 4:126); viii.7 (Chibnall 4:178); viii.23 (Chibnall 4:282); x.4 (Chibnall 5:210); x.10 (Chibnall 5:254); x.14 (Chibnall 5:284); x.18 (Chibnall 5:304); x.19 (Chibnall 5:320); xi.2 (Chibnall 6:16); xi.3 (Chibnall 6:30); xi.23 (Chibnall 6:100); xi.33 (Chibnall 6:150); xii.18 (Chibnall 6:234); xiii.24 (Chibnall 6:462).

16. The word *regnum,* kingdom, had territorial as well as regnal connotations (Loud, "*Gens Normannorum,*" 206–7) and, when the kingdom included more than one *gens,* a *regnum* could also be an *imperium* (Fanning, "Bede, Imperium, and the Bretwaldas," 14).

17. Loyn, *Governance,* 81–82. William the Conqueror was determined to establish power to the widest extent using every historical and military claim possible (Chibnall, *Anglo-Norman England,* 44–45). Many of the ideas about Norman kingship elaborated in this chapter, though not the idea of Albion, are discussed in Davies, *First English Empire.*

18. *HE* viii.7 (Chibnall 4:178): *Guillelmus Rufus Albionis rex.* Chibnall obscures the uniqueness of this title by translating it as "king of England," the same translation she often uses for the Latin *rex Anglorum.*

19. Geoffrey of Monmouth, *Historia* 21: *Erat tunc nomen insule Albion que a nemine exceptis paucis hominibus gigantibus inhabitabatur. Ameno tamen situ locorum et copia piscosorum fluminum nemoribusque preelecta affectum habitandi Bruto sociisque inferebat.*

20. Geoffrey of Monmouth, *Historia* 21: *gigantes ad cauernas montium fugant . . . Britones undique tandem confluentes preualuerunt in eos et omnes preter Goimagog interfecerunt.* The name of this giant is often rendered in studies and translations of Geoffrey as Gogmagog, and, whatever the spelling, it was almost certainly intended to evoke the biblical images. See Scherb, "Assimilating Giants," esp. 64–67; Westrem, "Against Gog and Magog," 58.

21. Geoffrey of Monmouth, *Historia* 21; *HE* iv (Chibnall 2:228).

22. Wace, *Roman de Brut,* pp. 18–19, 30–31; Laȝamon, *Brut,* vol. 1, ll. 975; Geoffrey Chaucer, "Compleint," ll. 22–24.

23. *Des Grantz Geanz,* ll. 2–5: *coment / E quant e de quele gent / Les grantz geantz primes vindrent / Qi Engletere primes tindrent, / Qe primes fu nomé Albion.* The equivalent passage from *De origine gigantum* runs: "What

is now called England was once called Albion and was inhabited by giants. How this name was given to it and how it came to be inhabited by such a *gens* will now be set out" (*Anglia modo dicta olim Albion dicebatur et habebat inhabitatores gigantes. Qualiter hoc nomen sibi inditum fuerit et qualiter tali gente inhabitata extiterit iam patebit*) (*De origine gigantum*, ll. 3–6).

24. *Des Grantz Geanz*, ll. 239–42: *est hurté / Qe Engletere est ore nomé; / Mes en ceo tens sanz noun estoit, / Pur ceo qe nul home n'i manoit.*

25. For a more detailed analysis of this narrative, see L. Johnson, "Return to Albion."

26. The Elizabethan era provides the first widespread use of the term Albion to refer to England that I have been able to find. See, "Albion," in *The Oxford English Dictionary*, 2nd ed.

27. Scherb, "Assimilating Giants," 72.

28. Scherb, "Assimilating Giants," 73.

29. Warner, *Albion's England*; Shakespeare, *Third Part of King Henry VI* iii.3.7: "Great Albion's queen in former golden days"; *King Henry V* iii.5.14: "that nook-shotten isle of Albion"; *King Lear* iii.2. 84: "Then shall the realm of Albion / Come to great confusion."

30. Holinshed, *Chronicles*.

31. Bindoff, "Stuarts and Their Style," 200. The importance of Jonson's *Masque of Blackness* as an articulation of James I's ideology is discussed in Olwig, *Landscape, Nature, and the Body Politic*, 62–79.

32. Quoted in Bindoff, "Stuarts and Their Style," 200.

33. Schmidt, "Idea and Slogan of 'Perfidious Albion.'"

34. W. Blake, *Vision of The Last Judgment*, 609; idem, *King Edward the Third* vi, ll. 15–16. For Blake's complicated creation of Albion, see Ashe, *Camelot and the Vision of Albion*, and Damon, *Blake Dictionary*, 9–16.

35. Blake, *Descriptive Catalogue*, 578.

36. Although Orderic was writing at the same time as Geoffrey of Monmouth and knew some of the insular historian's work, the *Historia Ecclesiastica* gives no sense that Orderic knew of Geoffrey's elaboration of the Albion myth when adapting the word to refer to England.

37. Anglo-Saxon notions of hegemony and imperialism, and their territorial basis, will be discussed in more detail below, but see in general Campbell, "United Kingdom of England"; Gillingham, "Foundations of a Disunited Kingdom," 94–97; John, "*Orbis Britanniae*"; Loyn, *Governance*, 81–82; Nelson, "Inauguration Rituals." It is important to note, though, that the use of imperial language by the Anglo-Saxon kings of the tenth and eleventh centuries did not mean that these kings ruled, or even wanted to rule, in a way

that shared characteristics with the Roman, Carolingian, or German notions of empire. See Loyn, "Imperial Style."

38. The charters of the Anglo-Saxon kings have a complicated publication history. First, there are two comprehensive and classic editions that overlap to some extent. The older edition, which contains charters from the earliest times up through King Edward the Confessor, is *Codex Diplomaticus Aevi Saxonici* (henceforth to be called *CD*). Much of this edition has been superceded by Birch's *Cartularium Saxonicum* (henceforth *CS*). Birch's *CS*, however, only goes up to the end of Edgar's reign in 975; for the period of 975 to 1066 the *CD* must still be used. More recently the British Academy has put out a number of excellent new editions of the charters of various monasteries in the series Anglo-Saxon Charters. In addition to these, Sawyer, *Anglo-Saxon Charters*, does not contain the text of the charters, but its numbering of the documents has now become the standard. I will cite all Anglo-Saxon charters using Sawyer's standard number and, if quoting, also the charter number of the edition used.

39. Unless noted, all the charters I cite are proven or believed to be authentic at their core.

40. Albion was mentioned in at least seven charters attributed to Athelstan: Sawyer 401, 404, 408, 410, 411, 434, 437. Some of these (408, 410, possibly 401) are probably spurious, but no later than the twelfth century; see *Charters of Abingdon Abbey*, 1:113–15, for commentary on Sawyer 408 and 410. For Athelstan's reign, see Dumville, "Between Alfred the Great."

41. *Anglo-Saxon Chronicle*, Worcester MS D, an. 926, p. 107. For Athelstan's rise to power, see A. Williams, *Kingship and Government*, 84–85.

42. Stenton, *Anglo-Saxon England*, 340–42; John, "*Orbis Britanniae*," 44–45; Le Patourel, *Norman Empire*, 52–61.

43. Dumville, "Between Alfred the Great," 149.

44. See for example *CS* no. 600 (Sawyer 368), among many others, for King Edward *Angul Saxonum rex*. This style was used almost exclusively for the kings Edward the Elder and Alfred (John, "*Orbis Britanniae*," 46–47).

45. *CS* no. 712 (Sawyer 437): *rex Anglorum et eque totius Albionis gubernator.*

46. Williams, *Kingship and Government*, 85. This style was related to the Old English title "Bretwalda," most clearly translated as "Britain-ruler," though the practical and symbolic significance of this old title is still not fully clear. The earliest known use dates to the eight century, but the title was probably older. See John, "*Orbis Britanniae*," 7–8, 10–11; Stenton, *Anglo-Saxon England*, 34–35; P. Wormald, "Bede, the *Bretwaldas*," esp. 101–17;

and, more recently and comprehensively, Fanning, "Bede, Imperium, and the Bretwaldas" 1–6, 22–26.

47. *Charters of Abingdon Abbey*, no. 29 (Sawyer 411): *ÆÐLSTAN, diuina mihi adridente gratia rex Anglorum et eque totius Albionis;* and *Ego ÆÐLSTANUS rex totius Britannie.*

48. This was a practice that developed among the Latin-writing elite; Albion as a place-name does not occur in documents originally written in Old English.

49. Dumville notes of Athelstan that "there is a very great self-consciousness about his diplomas" in their "extravagant but by no means wholly insubstantial claims to quasi-imperial standing" (Dumville, "Between Alfred the Great," 153).

50. Athelstan was the first king to have a chancery that produced his royal charters (Dumville, "Between Alfred the Great," 153; John, "*Orbis Brittaniae*," 48).

51. For Athelstan's influence on tenth-century royal styles, see Dumville, "Between Alfred the Great," 154.

52   *CS* no. 976 (Sawyer 598): *ego EADWIG non solum Angul Saxonum basileus verum etiam totius Albionis insule gratia Dei sceptro fungens. Charters of Abingdon Abbey*, no. 55 (Sawyer 597): *ego Eaduuig, largiflua summitonantis prouidentia rex Anglorum et cunctigenarum Albionis populorum.* The year 956 saw a flood of charters by Eadwig, for reasons that have never been fully established; it is likely that they were part of the new king's attempt to establish his authority, but the exact situation is unclear (Williams, *Kingship and Government*, 87).

53. Sawyer 574 (a very questionable charter), 644, 1291, and possibly 661 (which is also questionable). The one exception to this post-957 rule, Sawyer 658 (*Charters of Abingdon Abbey*, no. 83), which is witnessed by *EADWIG Britannie Anglorum monarcus*, has extenuating circumstances. This document is a grant of privileges to Abingdon Abbey, dated 17 May 959, and is probably authentic. To the same year, and in many of the same manuscripts, is attributed another grant of privileges to Abingdon Abbey, this one by Eadwig's brother and rival Edgar, which is witnessed by *Eadgar Britannie Anglorum monarcus* (Sawyer 673; *Charters of Abingdon Abbey*, no. 84). The identical forms of the title in the list of witnesses in charters of the same year for the same abbey, contained in the same twelfth-century cartulary, suggests that the title was a standard form given by the abbatial scribe rather than a choice made by the king or his court. Another charter, Sawyer 586, extant only in a fourteenth-century copy, is of uncertain date. It declares Eadwig to be "king of the English and Britons" (*rex Anglorum atque Bryttanorum*),

which is as close to a wider geographic claim as Eadwig's post-957 charters come. Sawyer dates this charter to 959 and Birch to 958, although the charter itself contains the date of 956. The body of the document is probably authentic, but the uncertainty in dating and the late manuscript copy make this charter too uncertain to weaken my point about the narrow geography of Eadwig's post-957 charters. Note also that none of Edgar's charters from the time before his brother Eadwig's death refer to him as king of Albion or king of Britain.

54. See Stafford, *Unification and Conquest,* 50–56. For Edgar's delayed consecration, see Nelson, "Inauguration Rituals," 63–67.

55. William of Malmesbury, *Gesta regum Anglorum* ii.148.1: *Res eius multum splendide etiam nostro celebrantur tempore. Affulsit annis illius diuinitatis amor propitius, quem ipse mercabatur sedulo deuotione animi et uiuacitate consilii.*

56. *CS* no. 1051 (Sawyer 680): *tocius Albionis gubernator et rector; Charters of Abingdon Abbey,* no. 85 (Sawyer 682): *rex et primicerius tocius Albionis,* and no. 89 (Sawyer 689): *tocius Albionis basileus.* For *basileus* as "king" rather than "emperor" in Anglo-Saxon thought, see Loyn, "Imperial Style," 111.

57. *CS* no. 1101 (Sawyer 717): *Annuente altithroni moderatoris imperio totius Albionis.* The same proem appears in Sawyer 709, 720, 729, 746. For "Edgar A," see *Charters of Abingdon Abbey,* cxv–cxxi and, for a political interpretation, Insley, "Where Did All the Charters Go?" 114–15.

58. Davies, *First English Empire,* 10.

59. Henry of Huntingdon, *Historia Anglorum* v.26: *Edgarus pacificus, rex magnificus, Salamon secundus, cuius tempore numquam exercitus aduenarum uenit in Angliam, cuius dominio reges et principes Anglie sunt subiecti, cuius potentie Scoti etiam colla dedere.*

60. Aelred of Rievaulx, *Genealogia regum Anglorum, Patrologia Latina* 195:726C: *multarum linguarum gentes, unius foedere legis conjunxit.*

61. *CS* no. 1301 (Sawyer 796): *tocius Albionis basileus necne maritimorum seu insulanorum meorum sujectione regum circum habitancium adeo ut nullus progenitorum meorum.* The Malmesbury charter is printed in a number of places, in often confusingly different forms. In addition to *CS,* see *CD* no. 584, and William of Malmesbury, *Gesta regum Anglorum* ii.153.1. The authenticity of this charter has been questioned by some, but in any case it certainly dates to no later than the late eleventh or early twelfth century.

62. Sawyer 779. As David Thornton notes, it has been argued that Ælfric was responsible for the Old English version of the document and that it was possibly composed around 1006 (Thornton, "Edgar and the Eight Kings," 52).

E. O. Blake disagrees with the attribution to Ælfric but agrees that the charter was composed after 970 (*Liber Eliensis*, appendix D, 414). Simon Keynes
suggests that the active abbacy of Ely's Abbot Simeon produced the charter
during the 1080s (Keynes, "Ely Abbey," 50). Eric John takes the opposite view,
arguing for the charter's authenticity (John, "Some Alleged Charters"). John
is distinctly in the minority, although some recent opinion is turning his way.
Overall the opinion on this charter is too divided to treat it as authentic.

   63. *CS* no. 1266 (Sawyer 779): *EADGARUS basileus dilectæ insulæ Albionis subditis nobis sceptri Scotorum, Cumbrorumque, ac Brittonum, et omnium circum circa regionum.* In accordance with the practice mentioned above,
the Old English version of the charter does not refer to Albion.

   64. *Anglo-Saxon Chronicle*, Peterborough MS E, an. 972, p. 119. See
also Thornton, "Edgar and the Eight Kings," 50; my summary of the evidence for the events at Chester relies heavily on Thornton's analysis. A legendary story grew up around this event which claimed that Edgar had the
other kings row him in a boat along the river Dee as a display of his mastery
over them (see, for instance, William of Malmesbury, *Gesta regum Anglorum* ii.149.2). For a discussion of this legend, which appeared in the post-
Conquest period, see, in addition to Thornton's analysis of the sources, J. Barrow, "Chester's Earliest Regatta?"

   65. Ælfric of Eynsham, *Lives of Three English Saints*, 80; Thornton,
"Edgar and the Eight Kings," 51.

   66. *HE* iv (Chibnall 2:324). This visit is discussed in more detail in chapter 4.

   67. For Orderic's use of charters in the composition of his history, see
Chibnall 1:63–76.

   68. Sawyer 741 and 1294.

   69. *HE* iv (Chibnall 2:342).

   70. *HE* iv (Chibnall 2:342): *inde sigillo strenuissimi regis Edgari filii
Edmundi regis.* Also *CS* no. 1178 (Sawyer 741): *datæ sunt vel acquisitæ*; and
*Edgarus totius Albionis monarcha.* The *Historia Ecclesiastica* is the first independent attestation to the existence of this forged charter. Orderic's talent
for history—which brought him to Crowland in the first place—might justly
provoke speculation that the Norman historian participated in the forgery of
the charter and, therefore, that Orderic's penchant for the name Albion worked
its way into the Crowland text rather than the reverse. This, however, is extremely unlikely, if only because Orderic's knowledge of Crowland's local geography would have been insufficient to the task.

   71. *HE* vi.2 (Chibnall 3:214): *Anno ab incarnatione Domini M°LXVI°
indictione quinta, Guillelmus dux Normannorum deficiente strenui regis*

*Edgari stirpe, quæ idonea esset ad tenendum sceptrum regale, cum multis milibus armatorum ad Anglos transfretauit, et in campo Senlac inuasorem regni Albionis Haraldum bello peremit.*

72. For this practice, see L. Johnson, "Etymologies."

73. *HE* iii (Chibnall 2:184): *præsulum et abbatum procerumque totius regni Albionis.*

74. *HE* iv (Chibnall 2:314): *status regni Albionis redintegretur omnimodis, sicut olim fuit tempore Eduardi piissimi regis.*

75. Guy of Amiens, *Carmen de Hastingae proelio* ll. 784–85: *Commoda . . . significant patrie; / Nam sceptro tumide regni moderantur habene.* Orderic mentioned Guy's *Carmen* in *HE* iii (Chibnall 2:184–86), and his reference to the work was the only attestation to its existence before two manuscripts of Guy's work were discovered in 1826 (Guy of Amiens, *Carmen de Hastingae proelio*, xiii–xiv).

76. See *HE* v.10 (Chibnall 3:96), where Robert's friends goad him: "Come on then, rise up like a man, demand part of the kingdom of Albion from your father" (*Eia uiriliter exurge, a genitore tuo partem regni Albionis exige*).

77. *HE* v.100 (Chibnall 3:100): *Capiti meo a uicariis Christi sacrum diadema celebre impositum est, et regale sceptrum Albionis ferre michi soli commissum est. Indecens igitur est et omnino iniustum, ut quandiu uitalibus auris perfruar, parem michi seu maiorem in ditione mea quempiam patiar.*

78. *HE* xii.18 (Chibnall 6:234); Henry of Huntingdon, *Historia Anglorum* v.26.

79. *CS* no. 1266 (Sawyer 779): *EADGARUS basileus dilectæ insulæ Albionis subditis nobis sceptri Scotorum, Cumbrorumque, ac Brittonum, et omnium circum circa regionum.* It is not out of the question that Orderic visited Ely in 1119 when he was in residence at Crowland. Ely, like Crowland, was in the fens, and Orderic's *Historia* occasionally converges with Ely's *Liber Eliensis*, though no doubt through similar sources rather than direct borrowing (*Liber Eliensis*, xxviii).

80. For the Norman kings' (and chroniclers') belief in English hegemony, see Davies, *First English Empire*, 9–10; Le Patourel, *Norman Empire*, 61–73.

81. *Anglo-Saxon Chronicle*, Peterborough MS E, an. 1086, p. 220. For Henry II in Ireland, see Warren, *Henry II*, 194–206.

82. Henry of Huntingdon, *Historia Anglorum* vi.39: *Super Angliam solus totam regnauerat. Scotiam quoque sibi subiugauerat. Waliamque reuerendus in suam acceperat.*

83. Davies, *Domination and Conquest*, 66–67.

84. *HE* iv (Chibnall 2:263): *Gualos aliosque sibi aduersantes fortiter oppressit, et prouinciam totam sibi commissam pacificauit.* See also Chibnall, *World*, 5; Le Patourel, *Norman Empire*, 73; Davies, *Conquest, Coexistence*, 30.

85. *HE* iv (Chibnall 2:260): *pugilibus contra Britones bellis.* Davies, *Conquest, Coexistence*, 28–29.

86. *HE* viii.3 (Chibnall 4:138). See also Lloyd, "Wales and the Coming of the Normans," 150–58; Davies, *Conquest, Coexistence*, 31. For the life and death of Robert of Rhuddlan, see chapter 5.

87. *HE* iv (Chibnall 2:218): *Guillelmo regi fidele obsequium iurauit.* See also Davies, *Domination and Conquest*, 56.

88. *Anglo-Saxon Chronicle*, Worcester MS D, an. 1073 (1072), p. 208; the same was said in the Peterborough MS.

89. *HE* viii.22 (Chibnall 4:268): *contra regem Anglorum rebellauit, debitumque seruitium ei denegauit.*

90. *HE* viii.22 (Chibnall 4:270): *Fateor quod rex Eduardus dum michi Margaritam proneptem suam in coniugium tradidit Lodonensem comitatum michi donauit. Deinde Guillelmus rex quod antecessor eius michi dederat concessit.*

91. John of Worcester, *Chronica* an. 1093: *regnare in Walonia reges desiere.* This was not actually true, but it demonstrates how much the Normans had infiltrated Wales even by the end of the eleventh century.

92. Henry of Huntingdon, *Historia Anglorum* i.1: *insularum nobilissima cui quondam Albion nomen fuit, postea uero Britannia, nunc autem Angia.* Wace, *Roman de Rou* iii, 15–16: *Engleterre Bretainne out nun / e primes out nun Albiun.*

93. *HE* xi.2 (Chibnall 6:16): *Rex autem in omnibus prosperitate uigens admodum sullimatus est, et longe lateque de illo fama uolitante per quattuor climata mundi inter maximos reges nominatus est. Nullus eo fuit rex in Albionis regno potentior, nec amplitudine terrarum infra insulam locupletior, nec abundantia omnium rerum quæ mortalibus suppetunt felicior.*

94. For Henry's marriage from a Scottish perspective, see G. Barrow, *Scotland*, 62–63.

95. *HE* x.16 (Chibnall 5:298, 300): *deuictis seu deletis quos modo Gualos dicunt, occupatam bello insulam . . . Angliam uocitauerunt.*

96. Davies, *Conquest, Coexistence*, 40–42.

97. *Brut y Tywysogyon*, an. 1116.

98. *HE* xi.2 (Chibnall 6:16): *Albionis regno potentior, nec amplitudine terrarum infra insulam locupletior.*

99. *HE* xi.33 (Chibnall 6:150). Orderic used the phrase to describe the subjects of some songs composed by Folcard, a monk of Saint-Bertin who later became abbot of Thorney. Folcard's known subjects include St. Oswald (mentioned by Orderic) who was of Danish ancestry, and the Saxon saints John of Beverley and Botolph. He may also have written a *vita* of Edward the Confessor (Chibnall 6:151n8; *Vita Eadwardi,* li–lix).

100. Thomas, *English and the Normans,* 264–65.

101. L. Johnson, "Etymologies," 125–36; Thomas, *English and the Normans,* 261–73.

102. Spiegel, "Genealogy."

103. Origin myths, from the Norman perspective, are also discussed in chapter 2. The classic analyses of medieval origin myths from the perspective of England, although without much discussion of the landscape, are Ingledew, "Book of Troy," and Reynolds, "Medieval *Origines Gentium.*" See also Busse, "Brutus in Albion," which, despite its title, doesn't talk much about Albion in particular. A brief topographical commentary on the English origin myths can be found in L. Johnson, "Etymologies."

104. P. Wormald, *"Engla Lond,"* 10–16.

105. Thomas notes that while England and Englishness were strong concepts both before and after the conquest it was by no means certain that the historical identity of the post-Conquest community in England would ultimately resolve itself through place rather than national origins (Thomas, *English and the Normans,* 261–65).


CHAPTER 4    Jerusalem and the Ends of the Earth


1. *Annales Uticenses,* an. 1099: *Jerusalem, gentilibus victis qui eam diu tenuerant, a sanctis peregrinis capta est idus julii. Hic Urbanus papa obiit. Cui Paschalis successit. Uticensis ęcclesia sancti Ebrulfi dedicata est.* Orderic added most of the entries to his monastery's annals from 1095 to 1139, as well as a few notes appended to earlier dates (Chibnall 1:24n1). The notation for 1099 appears in his hand in BN MS Latin 10062, fol. 154r.

2. BN MS Latin 10062, fol. 123r. Cf. *HE* v.9 (Chibnall 3:94). Also Chibnall 1:100n2.

3. *HE* ix.1 (Chibnall 5:4): *Nulla . . . unquam sophistis in bellicis rebus gloriosior materia prodiit, quam nostris nunc Dominus poetis atque librariis tradidit, dum per paucos Christicolas de paganis in oriente triumphauit.*

4. As Jacques Le Goff wrote: "Almost all medieval men moved con-tradictorily between two sets of horizons: the limited horizons of the clear-ing in which they lived, and the distant horizons of the whole of Christen-dom" (Le Goff, *Medieval Civilization*, 137).

5. *HE* viii.16 (Chibnall 4:228): *Multa intueor in diuina pagina, quæ subtiliter coaptata nostri temporis euentui uidentur similia. Ceterum alle-goricas allegationes et idoneas humanis moribus interpretationes studiosis rimandas relinquam, simplicemque Normannicarum historiam rerum adhuc aliquantulum protelare satagam.*

6. Alexander, "Jerusalem"; Higgins, "Defining the Earth's Center," 34–39.

7. John France has pointed out that the fall of Jerusalem, and the image of the terrestrial city in general, were rarely mentioned in western chronicles and annals in the eleventh century (France, "Le rôle de Jérusalem"). On the other hand, the most innovative (if not always the most accurate) historians of the eleventh century, Raoul Glaber and Ademar of Chabannes, did place Jerusalem and its fall to the Muslims at the center of their historiography. These two men may not have been representative of pre-Crusade thought as a whole, but their very innovation demonstrates the movement of Jerusalem toward the center of Christian consciousness.

8. Raoul Glaber, *Historiarum libri qvinque* i.24: *perpendendum . . . uidelicet de conuersionibus perfidarum ad fidem Christi gentium altrinsecus in aquilonaribus atque occidentalibus orbis partibus persepe fieri contigerit, nusquam talia in orientalibus atque meridianis eiusdem orbis plagis contigit audiri. . . . Nam cum retro illius uerticem suspensi tum fuisset crudus nimium populis oriens, tunc etiam in eius oculorum conspectu lumine fidei repleturus constitit occidens. Sic quoque omnipotentem ipsius dexteram ad misericordiae opus extensam sacri uerbi fide mitis suscepit septentrio, eiusque leuam gen-tibus barbarorum tumultuosus sortitur meridies.* I have used France's transla-tion, with altered capitalization.

9. For the importance of the Incarnation in the before-and-after peri-odization of Christian history, see Daniélou, "Conception of History," 129. Seymour Phillips gives an overview of the medieval traditions about the lands beyond Christendom in his "Outer World."

The notions of East and West, and to a lesser extent North and South, have a long and deeply troubled history. Throughout this study I use the words as medieval writers did (as difficult as that might be to define as well), but for a discussion of the shifting meanings of East and West especially, see Lewis and Wigen, *Myth of Continents*, 47–103.

10. The earliest traditions of Christian sacred geography have been brilliantly set out by R. A. Markus in "How on Earth" and idem, *End of Ancient Christianity*, 139–55. "If it was in their history that Christians saw themselves as distinct from other others," Markus argues, "their geography was the projection of this history on the ground" (Markus, *End of Ancient Christianity*, 139).

For the relationship between geography and history in maps, see especially Edson, *Mapping Time and Space*. David Woodward called medieval maps "as much historical as geographical" and explained "that the resulting documents blended concepts of both time and space as a context for understanding the Christian life" (Woodward, "Reality, Symbolism," 511). Catherine Delano-Smith and Roger J. P. Kain are wrong, however, to interpret this to mean that the "importance of time in a *mappamundi* reflects the unimportance of place in early Christianity, a religion of the book, in which belief was privileged over place" (Delano-Smith and Kain, *English Maps*, 37). Any religion that valued pilgrimage as much as Christianity did could never be said to view place as unimportant, and a number of studies of medieval maps and geography, including Edson's and Markus's, have shown that place was vital to Christian historical understanding.

11. For a general description of the form and history of T-O maps, see Edson, *Mapping Time and Space*, 4–5; Woodward, "Medieval *Mappaemundi*," 296; and Woodward, "Reality, Symbolism," 511. Some scholars refer to these images as T-O diagrams, rather than T-O maps, because of their lack of detail and also their lack of correlation with any actual geography (Delano-Smith and Kain, *English Maps*, 37–38). By the definition given in J. B. Harley and David Woodward's classic history of cartography, though, which characterizes maps as "graphic representations that facilitate a spatial understanding of things, concepts, conditions, processes or events in the human world," the T-O images are definitely a form of map, no matter how simple (Harley and Woodward, *History of Cartography*, 1:xvi).

12. Isidore of Seville, *Etymologiae* XIV.ii.1 and 3: *Divisus est . . . trifarie: e quibus una pars Asia, altera Europa, tertia Africa nuncupatur . . . evidenter orbem dimidium duae tenent, Europa et Africa, alium vero dimidium sola Asia.*

13. Edson, *Mapping Time and Space*, 44–45. This map, and the associated geographical text, only occurred in the longer recension of the text. The *De natura rerum* was in both versions accompanied by a number of diagrams; their influence is discussed in more detail below.

14. Esmeijer, *Divina Quaternitas*, 98.

15. Edson, *Mapping Time and Space*, 5, mentions the Ebstorf map, for instance, which depicted the circular globe with Christ's hands, head, and feet visible along the edges.

16. The Hereford map, dated to c. 1300, is one of the most glorious and most studied of all medieval maps. The Jerusalem image with the crucifix is reproduced on the frontispiece of Harvey, *Mappa Mundi.*

17. Bowman, "Mapping History's Redemption"; M. Campbell, "Object of One's Gaze." In pilgrim narratives, Campbell notes, the locales "are almost always 'places where' someone once did or said something; geography tends to be history; description comes in the form of narration" (Campbell, "Object of One's Gaze," 6).

18. Bowman, "Mapping History's Redemption," 165; Campbell, "Object of One's Gaze," 11–12; Markus, "How on Earth," 269–71.

19. The definitive study of this manuscript is Faith Wallis, "MS Oxford St John's College 17," which contains a large number of reproductions from the manuscript as well as an exhaustive study of its contents.

20. See Wallis, "Images of Order," 45, also her introduction to Bede's *De temporum ratione* in *Bede: The Reckoning of Time*, xviii–xxxiv, and Edson, "World Maps and Easter Tables," 25–27, for the importance of *computus* as a branch of science and a genre of manuscript.

21. N. Howe, "From Bede's World to 'Bede's World,'" 22–23.

22. Wallis has shown that this manuscript is a single, coherent work, not a miscellany compiled after the fact, and that the pages are still in their original order (Wallis, "MS Oxford St John's College 17," 50).

23. For a discussion, with some images, of this part of the manuscript, see Wallis "MS Oxford St John's College 17," 181–245, and also, Edson, *Mapping Time and Space*, 86–95. The Thorney *mappa mundi* has received quite a bit of attention in studies of medieval cartography, in part, no doubt, because of its unusual adaptations of common features. See Delano-Smith and Kain, *English Maps*, 12–13; Edson, *Mapping Time and Space*, 86–92; Edson, "World Maps and Easter Tables," 35–37.

24. Traditionally this central bar of the T-O map was interpreted as the conjunction of the Nile and the Black Sea, with Jerusalem labeled at or near the cross of the T, not across the entire bar as is the case with the Thorney map (Edson, *Mapping Time and Space*, 89). Woodward notes that, despite the widely-held belief that Jerusalem marked the *axis mundi*, maps were not inevitably centered around the city throughout the middle ages, though this was increasingly the case after the millennium and the crusade shifted Christian consciousness towards Jerusalem (Woodward, "Reality, Symbol-

ism," 515–17). The smaller map is found on MS Oxford St John's College 17, fol. 8r, reproduced in Wallis, "MS Oxford St John's College 17," between 246 and 247.

25. Orderic did not give a date for this trip, other than mentioning that it took place during the abbacy of Geoffrey of Crowland. This places Orderic's visit to England between 1109 and 1124. This range can be narrowed a bit further by following up on Orderic's statement that miracles started to take place at the tomb of Earl Waltheof in the third year of Geoffrey's abbacy, namely 1112, and that on account of these miracles Orderic himself was asked by the monks to compose a verse epitaph for the Earl (*HE* iv [Chibnall 2:348–50]). One possibility is that Orderic visited in 1115 when the new church at Crowland was dedicated (Chibnall 2:xxvi). Chibnall also suggests that Orderic's journey to England may have been a continuation of his trip to the council of Reims in 1119 (Chibnall, *World,* 36, 222). In any case, he most likely visited England late in the second decade of the twelfth century.

26. *HE* iv (Chibnall 2:324).

27. Orderic began his *Historia* around 1114, and he most likely visited Crowland between 1115 and 1120, more likely toward the end of that range. It was probably in the early 1120s that Orderic decided on a more ambitious plan for his *Historia.*

28. *HE* xi.33 (Chibnall 6:148–52).

29. MS Oxford St John's College 17, fol. 21v: *Hic super astra pius conscendit pastor ebrulfus.* This page is reproduced in Wallis, "MS Oxford St John's College 17," between 338 and 339. As Wallis notes, this is an extremely short and nondescript text for the identification of a hand, but for those familiar with Orderic's unique writing the recognition is immediate, despite the unusual majuscule terminal S in *pius* and *ebrulfus.* Orderic's hand, however, varied more than was typical in the late eleventh and twelfth centuries (the D's are particularly noticeable), probably because of the huge amount of writing he did, both formal and less so, and, as Wallis noticed, the majuscle S is identical with that which occurs at the beginning of certain words in the *Historia Ecclesiastica* (Wallis, "MS Oxford St John's College 17," 338n63). The rest of the word *ebrulfus* is identical with Orderic's writing. Chibnall does not doubt that this is Orderic's hand (Chibnall 1:203; Chibnall, *World,* 36), and neither do I.

30. Thorney's annals are actually no longer contained in MS Oxford St John's College 17; Sir Robert Cotton cut them from their original codex in the seventeenth century and incorporated them into the manuscript now known as MS Cotton Nero C. VII as folios 80–84. The folios of the Thorney *computus* were given their modern numbers after the annals had been

removed, but they were originally between fols. 143 and 144 (Wallis, "MS Oxford St John's College 17," 4, 25; see also *Thorney Annals*, 1–8).

31.  BN MS Latin 10062, fols. 130r–137v. Orderic's hand dominates this text, though he was not the only one to work on it.

32.  The twelfth-century catalogue at Ouche, for instance, noted a copy of Isidore of Seville's *De natura rerum*. Extracts from this classic work were included in the Thorney *computus*, and the many diagrams that often accompanied it are related to those in Thorney's book (Wallis, "MS Oxford St John's College 17," 408–9). Unfortunately, Ouche's copy of Isidore's work is no longer extant, so it is impossible to know whether it was the complete work or whether it contained the diagrams (since the diagrams were very complicated, not all manuscripts did). Therefore, when arguing for Orderic's exposure to certain ideas about creation, cosmology, and time it is better to argue from the Thorney *computus*, which is extant and which Orderic definitely read, than from a line in a library catalogue.

33.  The far-reaching importance of the cross and its association with Jerusalem during the time of the crusades has been discussed by Constable, "Jerusalem and the Sign of the Cross."

34.  *HE* ix.2 (Chibnall 5:18): *filios Ierusalem.*

35.  *HE* x.8 (Chibnall 5:230): *Crucem Saluatoris nostri qua more peregrini signatus sum non relinquam, sed in clipeo meo galeaque et in omnibus armis meis eandem faciam, et in sella frenoque meo sacræ crucis signum infigam. Tali karactere munitus in hostes pacis et rectitudinis procedam, et Christianorum regiones militando defendam. Equus itaque meus et arma mea notamine sancto signabuntur, et omnes aduersarii qui contra me insurrexerint in militem Christi præliabuntur. Confido in illo qui regit mundum, quod ipse nouit cordis mei secretum, et per eius clementiam opperiar tempus opportunum, quo possim optatum peragere uotum.* Although Orderic, like his contemporaries, invariably uses the noun *peregrinatio*, pilgrim, to refer to the crusaders, his description of Helias as signed with the cross, *crucis signum*, is an early use of the term that would subsequently become the standard designation for a crusader, *crucesignatus*. See Brundage, "Cruce Signari," 289–90, and Markowski, "*Crucesignatus.*"

36.  See Kantorowicz, "*Pro Patria Mori*," esp. 478–82, for some of these ideas, although in a more firmly legal sense than Orderic's interpretation.

37.  E. Blake, "Formation of the 'Crusade Idea,'" 24–25. Orderic wrote in the same tradition, based on the *Gesta Francorum*, that inspired Baudry of Bourgueil, Ralph of Caen, Guibert of Nogent, and Robert of Reims, who, according to Blake, "have in common the deliverance of the Holy Places as their central theme" (24).

38. *HE* ix.2 (Chibnall 5:14): *Pro conculcatione quoque Ierusalem sanctorumque locorum ubi filius Dei cum suis sanctissimis collegis corporaliter habitauit.*

39. For the Holy Land as the *haereditas* or *patrimonium* of Christ, see Riley-Smith, "Crusading as an Act of Love," 36.

40. Anna-Dorothee von den Brincken has suggested that the Thorney cartographer, working under the influence of the crusade, was attempting to depict both Jerusalem and Europe together as parts of the Latin and western Church (von den Brincken, "Europa in der Kartographie des Mittelalters," 300).

41. *HE* xii.8 (Chibnall 6:206): *fama qua nil in terra uelocius mouetur.*

42. *HE* xi.2 (Chibnall 6:16): *fama uolitante per quattuor climata mundi.*

43. *HE* xi.12 (Chibnall 6:70): *in tripartito climate orbis.*

44. For Hugh's burial *in aquilonali climate* see *HE* xii.30 (Chibnall 6:312).

45. James S. Romm has defined the ancient *oikoumene* as "a region made coherent by the intercommunication of its inhabitants, such that, within the radius of this region, no tribe or race is completely cut off from the peoples beyond it" (Romm, *Edges of the Earth,* 37).

46. *HE* i.1 (Le Prévost 1:5; Chibnall 1:134): *per omnia mundi climata.*

47. J. Williams, "Isidore, Orosius and the Beatus Map," 7–9, for an overview of the Beatus tradition. The definitive edition of the illustrated Beatus manuscripts is J. Williams, *Illustrated Beatus.*

48. Beatus of Liébana, *Beati in apocalipsin,* prologue to book II.3.17: *Hi duodecim sunt Christi discipuli, praedicatores fidei, et doctores gentium, qui dum omnes unum sunt, singuli tamen eorum ad praedicandum in mundo sortes proprias acceperunt, Petrus Roma, Andreas Acaya, Thomas India, Iacobus Spania, Iohannes Asia, Mattheus Macedonis, Filippus Gallias, Bartolomeus Licaonia, Simon Zelotes Aegyptum, Iacobus frater Domini Iersualem.* Cf. *De ortu et obitu patrum* 80.1, which has slight variations. See also J. Williams, "Isidore, Orosius and the Beatus Map," 8.

49. Mark 16:15.

50. The Beatus map, which is from the Cathedral of Burgo de Osma, Cod. 1, fols. 34v–35r, is reproduced in J. Williams, *Illustrated Beatus,* vol. 5, plate 14.5, and Edson, *Mapping Time and Space,* 152.

51. MS Oxford St John's College 17, fol. 6r: *Achaia ubi sanctus andreas.*

52. *HE* ii.4 (Le Prévost 1:269; Chibnall 1:178): *Hic in sorte predicationis Scithiam et Achaiam accepit, in qua etiam in ciuitate Patras ii kal. Decembris in cruce suspensus occubuit.*

53. Book II of the *Historia* is contained in BN MS Latin 5506 (I), fols. 65r–134r. Chibnall discusses Orderic's sources in Chibnall 1:54–56, and the

direct borrowings are catalogued in the "Index of Quotations and Allusions" to volume 1 of the *HE* (Chibnall 1:219–21). Aside from the canonical Acts of the Apostles, Orderic's most important sources included Pseudo-Abdias's *Historia apostolica*, Pseudo-Marcellus's *Passio sanctorum apostolorum Petri et Pauli*, the Pseudo-Clementine *Recognitiones*, and various anonymous *passiones* and *actae*. For the geographical significance of the apocryphal Acts, see Friedman, *Monstrous Races*, 69–70.

54. Phillips, "Outer World," 44. For the "rhetoric of Christian expansion" in early Christian historiography, which sketched out the geography of the world beyond the Roman empire, see Merrills, "Monks, Monsters, and Barbarians," 242–43.

55. *HE* ii.2 (Le Prévost 1:234, 236).

56. *HE* ii.2 (Le Prévost 1:249).

57. *HE* ii.9 (Le Prévost 1:321–22): *Indiæ tres esse ab historiographis asseruntur. . . . ad Æthiopiam mittit, secunda ad Medos, tertia finem facit; quia ex uno latere habet regionem tenebrarum et ex alio mare Oceanum.* Chibnall attributes this information to Pseudo-Abdias, *Historia apostolica* vii.1.2. For more on the widespread tradition of the three Indias, see Phillips, "Outer World," 30–31, and Wright, *Geographical Lore*, 272–73. For the association of India with the Ocean and with Africa, see G. Campbell, *Strange Creatures*, 112.

58. *HE* ii.17 (Le Prévost 1:361–81; Chibnall 1:190). The forgery of the *Vita Prolixior* of Martial of Limoges by Ademar of Chabannes is discussed in detail in Landes, *Relics*. Orderic's use of Ademar's *Vita*, which was attributed to Martial's follower Aurelian, is one of those singular borrowings that shows the breadth of his literary contacts. Orderic copied directly from the text; this was no reconstruction from memory. No Norman monastery is known to have possessed a copy of Martial's life. The circulation of the text was not restricted to Ademar's region near Limoges—King Cnut of England was known to be a follower of the apostle Martial—but neither was it extremely widespread (Landes, *Relics*, 164n52; F. Wormald, "Litany in Arundel MS. 60," 84–86). Orderic was clearly unaware that the apostolic cult of Martial based on the *Vita Prolixior* had been largely discredited, which suggests that the text came to him in a roundabout fashion. The origin of Orderic's manuscript source will probably never be known, but there is a curious link with a sixteenth-century copy of the *Vita Prolixior*, which claims to derive from a much earlier text. This manuscript links Martial's life with the accounts of Pseudo-Abdias, one of Orderic's main sources for his apostolic mapping (Landes and Paupert, *Naissance d'apôtre*, 43–44). Perhaps the texts came to Ouche together.

59. And this was not only true for Orderic. The Anglo-Saxon poet Cynewulf described in his work on the *Fates of the Apostles* how the "fame (*mærðo*), the might and the glory of the lord's servants spread widely over the earth" (translated in N. Howe, *Writing the Map*, 110). "Once he has centered the exemplary figures of Peter and Paul in Rome," Howe notes, "the speaker can expand his catalogue of apostles outward through Greece and beyond to the Holy Land, Asia, and finally to Africa" (ibid). Like Orderic, Cynewulf used the apostolic stories to map the world.

60. *HE* ii.4 (Le Prévost 1:282–83): *Illam nimirum presbyteri et diaconi ecclesiarum Achaiæ coram positi viderunt, et universis ecclesiis per quatuor climata mundi constitutis utiliter et eleganter scripserunt.*

61. Mark 16:15.

62. See the Prologue for the dates and order of composition of the *Historia*'s books.

63. Isidore of Seville, *De natura rerum* ix.1: *Mundus est uniuersitas omnis quae constat ex caelo et terra.* See also Lozovsky, *Earth is Our Book*, 20–21. Orderic's library at Ouche had a copy of Isidore's *De natura rerum*, though not of Bede's (which was, however, apparently available at Bec) (Nortier, *Les bibliothèques*, 200, 216).

64. Isidore of Seville, *De natura rerum* ix.2: *homo autem micros cosmos, id est minor mundus est appellatus.*

65. See the Prologue and *HE* xii.1 (Chibnall 6:186–88). Also Gurevich, *Categories of Medieval Culture*, chap. 3.

66. Ernst H. Kantorowicz provided an intriguing commentary on the medieval idea of a unified cosmos and the later interpretation of this theme in "Problem of Medieval World Unity."

67. See figure 1 above. Also Wallis, "MS Oxford St John's College 17," 224–27.

68. Esmeijer, *Divina Quaternitas*, 105.

69. The particular meaning of back-to-back maps has been recognized in other contexts. A small psalter map from the thirteenth century displays a detailed *mappa mundi* on one side of the page, with Jerusalem at the center, and on the other side a list map of the T-O design (Edson, *Mapping Time and Space*, 135–36 and plate VI; Birkholz, *King's Two Maps*, 17–19). Matthew Paris included a map of England on the opposite side of the Palestine map that represented the culmination of his Jerusalem itinerary; Palestine and Jerusalem clearly show through the page, linking England visually with the Holy Land (Breen, "*Habitus* and the Discipline of Reading," 173–75). The Thorney manuscript might not contain back-to-back maps, but it does contain back-to-back meaning.

An eleventh-century genealogical diagram of the descendants of Noah's sons in a manuscript of Beatus of Liébana's commentary (see above), though not an example of back-to-back illustrations, also shows the relationship between geography and genealogy by the inclusion of a small T-O map intended to map the generations onto the three divisions of the Earth (Woodward, "Medieval *Mappaemundi*," 331, fig. 18.13).

70. Byrhtferth was a monk at the nearby abbey of Ramsey known for his writings on *computus*. His name appears on the Thorney diagram in an explanation across the top of the page: "Byrhtferth, a monk at the monastery of Ramsey, produced this figure on the harmony of the months and elements" (MS Oxford St John's College 17, fol. 7v: *Hanc figuram edidit bryhtferð* [sic] *monachus ramesiensis cenobii de concordia mensium aut elementorum*). Whether or not the historical Byrhtferth actually had a hand in this image, it has come to be associated with him and continues to bear his name. For the possible links between Byrhtferth and the diagram from Thorney, see Hart, "Ramsey Computus," and Singer and Singer, "Restoration." Byrhtferth's known work has been published as *Byrhtferth's Enchiridion*.

71. See Edson, *Mapping Time and Place*, 91; Wallis, "MS Oxford St John's College 17," 221.

72. Augustine, *In Iohannis evangelium tractatus cxxiv* ix.14; Wallis, "MS Oxford St John's College 17," 221. Augustine's text was in Ouche's library (Delisle, "Notice," viii) and is now in the Bibliothèque de la ville in Rouen as MS 467 (Nortier, *Les bibliothèques*, 122). Orderic made reference to Augustine's work in *HE* i.9 and i.14 (Chibnall 1:142, 146).

73. This would not have been Orderic's first exposure to an illustrated wind diagram. Mediathèque de la communauté urbaine d'Alençon MS 12–II, a tenth-century manuscript from Ouche, has a diagram with the winds personified on fol. 58v (reproduced in Obrist, "Wind Diagrams," 69). Curiously, this manuscript is heavily glossed by Robert of Prunelai, the monk at Ouche who went on to become abbot of Thorney and was Orderic's host at that English monastery. For a description of the manuscript, see Jeudy and Riou, *Les Manuscrits classiques latins*, 1:21–22.

74. This was a common conceit in the middle ages and beyond. See Thonneau, "Terre, automne, mélancholie."

75. For *annus-mundus-homo* diagrams, see Edson, *Mapping Time and Space*, 43–44; Thonneau, "Terre, automne, mélancholie," 95–96.

76. For the importance of diagrams in medieval texts, see Obrist, "Wind Diagrams," 34, and Semper, "Doctrine and Diagrams," 125–26.

77. Iogna-Prat, *Order and Exclusion*, 178–79. See chapter 6 for more about the importance of the Eucharist for the spatial nature of Christendom.

78. *HE* x.11 (Chibnall 5:264, 6): *Deoque iuuante Vticensis basilica idus Nouembris dedicata est. Gislebertus enim Luxouiensis consecrauit principalem aram in honore sanctæ Dei gentiricis Mariæ, et sancti Petri apostolorum principis, ac sancti Ebrulfi confessoris, et Gislebertus Ebroicensis altare ad austrum in honore omnium apostolorum, Serlo autem aram in honore omnium martirum. Sequenti uero die Serlo crucifixum benedixit, et altare illius in honore sancti Saluatoris sanctique Egidii confessoris, et Gislebertus Ebroicensis aram matutinalis missæ in honore omnium sanctorum. Denique xvii° kalendas Nouembris Ebroicensis heros ad meridiem altare in honore omnium confessorum sanctificauit. Serlo Sagiensis aram in æde septentrionali ii° kalendas Ianuarii dedicauit in honore omnium uirginum.* Chibnall has noted that *xvii° kalendas Nouembris* appears to be an error. The chronology of the paragraph suggests that it should be *xvii° kalendas Decembris,* or 15 November.

79. For the altars in the church and their consecration, see *HE* x.11 (Chibnall 5:264–66). Alain Guerreau has shown how this spatial mapping of Christendom was accomplished at Cluny on a much grander scale in "Espace social, espace symbolique," 174–76.

80. Constable, "Jerusalem and the Sign of the Cross," 373–74. The rising sun and the site of Jerusalem have often been used to explain the eastern orientation. Richard Kieckhefer has noted, however, that this directionality of the churches "did not so much bring them into explicit relationship with a common geographical center: the oriented apse did not point to Jerusalem, as the *mihrab* in each mosque points it toward Mecca. Yet orientation was a kind of alignment, and common alignment could itself be a form of bonding among churches" (Kieckhefer, *Theology in Stone,* 155).

81. *Quid significent duodecim candelae 17: sciendum quod quattuor anguli basilice quattuor designant plagas mundi ad quas pervenit doctrina ecclesiastica, quae per litteras significatur in terra descriptas.* Ouche's twelfth-century copy of this text can be found in MS 1343, fols. 1–9, at the Bibliothèque de la ville, Rouen. The placement of the commentary in this manuscript immediately before a work by Remegius of Auxerre (d. c. 908) caused it to initially be attributed to Remegius, but more recent scholarship and paleological investigations have shown that it predates Remegius's time, probably dating from the early to mid-ninth century. For more on this text, and for the place and meaning of the *abecedarium* in the dedication of churches, see Repsher, *Rite of Church Dedication,* 33–35, 50–51, 82–84.

82. *HE* xii.30 (Chibnall 6:312).

83. *HE* ix.2 (Chibnall 5:8, 10): *Anno ab incarnatione Domini M°XC°V° indictione iiiᵃ pridie nonas Aprilis, feria iiiiᵃ, luna xxvᵃ in Galliis ab innumeris*

*inspectoribus uisus est tantus stellarum discursus, ut grando nisi luceret pro densitate putarentur. Gislebertus Luxouiensis episcopus, senex medicus, multarum artium peritissimus, singulis noctibus sidera diu contemplari solebat, et cursus eorum utpote sagax horoscopus callide denotabat. Is itaque prodigium astrorum phisicus sollicite prospexit, uigilemque qui curiam suam aliis dormientibus custodiebat aduocauit. Senex ait, 'Transmigratio populorum de regno in regnum ut opinor prefiguratur. Multi autem abibunt, qui nunquam redibunt, donec ad proprias absides astra redeant, unde nunc ut nobis uidetur liquido labant. Alii uero permanebunt in loco sullimi et sancto, uelut stellæ fulgentes in firmamento.'*

84. In 1095, 4 April fell on a Wednesday (the fourth day of the week, counting from Sunday). It was the third indiction. And the night of April 3–4 was the twenty-fifth day of the moon, the full moon (the fourteenth lunar day) having occurred that year on March 23. Wallis has noted that Orderic, though by no means expert, did have a functional working knowledge of *computus* and could make use of the necessary charts to provide both accuracy and atmosphere to the *Historia*'s stories (Wallis, "MS Oxford St John's College 17," 709–12).

CHAPTER 5    Haunted Landscapes

1. HE viii.17 (Chibnall 4:236): *Quid in episcopatu Lexouiensi in capite Ianuarii contigerit cuidam presbitero, pretereundum non estimo, nec comprimendum silentio.* A number of scholars have discussed this passage, in a variety of contexts. See Chibnall 4:xxxviii–xl, though her summary is diluted, in my view, by her attempt to find a rational explanation for Walchelin's "delirium." A more substantial discussion by Chibnall can be found in Chibnall, "Twelfth-Century View of the Historical Church," 130–33. See also Bouet, "La 'Mesnie Hellequin'"; Ginzburg, *Night Battles*, 48–49; B. McGuire, "Purgatory," 78–80; Mégier, "Deux exemples"; Schmitt, *Ghosts*, 93–100; Stock, "Antiqui and Moderni"; idem, *Implications of Literacy*, 495–99; Watkins, "Sin, Penance and Purgatory," 7–11. A slightly condensed translation of this passage also appears in Joynes, *Medieval Ghost Stories*, 49–53, a useful book that contains translations of many ghostly happenings.

2. *HE* viii.17 (Chibnall 4:236, 38): *In uilla quæ Bonauallis dicitur Gualchelinus sacerdos erat. Hic anno dominicæ incarnationis M°XCI° in capite Ianuarii accersitus ut ratio exigit, quendam egrotum in ultimis parochiæ suæ terminis noctu uisitauit. Vnde dum solus rediret, et longe ab hominum habitatione remotus iret, ingentem strepitum uelut maximi exercitus cepit audire.*

Orderic apparently wanted to explain why Walchelin, an innocent man, was wandering about the countryside at night. For the most part only those up to no good—criminals and ghosts—would be on the road after dark. Cf. Thietmar of Merseburg, *Chronicon* i.12, who declared that, "As day to the living, so night is conceded to the dead" (*Ut dies vivis, sic nox est concessa defunctis*).

3. For the siege of Courcy, a manifestation of the conflict between, on the one side, Robert Curthose and Robert of Bellême and, on the other, Richard of Courcy and Hugh of Grandmesnil, see *HE* viii.16 (Chibnall 4:228–36).

4. *HE* viii.17 (Chibnall 4:283): *Luna quippe octaua in signo arietis tunc clare micabat, et gradientibus iter demonstrabat.* Orderic was correct about the position of the moon on this date. Faith Wallis has suggested that he used his knowledge of *computus* to add this touch of verisimilitude to his story (Wallis, "MS Oxford St John's College 17," 709–10).

5. *HE* viii.17 (Chibnall 4:248); Mégier, "Deux exemples," 54–56.

6. *HE* viii.17 (Chibnall 4:248, 50): *Hæc ad ædificationem legentium scripsi, ut in bonis consolidentur iusti, et a malis resipiscant peruersi.*

7. *HE* viii.17 (Chibnall 4:240): *quicquid inconueniens fæx carnalis commisit purgatorio igne decoquitur, uariisque purgationibus prout æternus censor disponit emundatur.* Cf. Bede, *Homeliae* I.2, ll. 214–16, for a very similar image of the pain and purpose of the purgatorial fire, and also Le Goff, *Birth of Purgatory*, 102–3.

8. All of these accounts, and more, can be found in Gardiner, *Visions of Heaven and Hell Before Dante*. A great deal has been written about these visions of otherworldly journeys. See Carozzi, "La géographie de l'au-delà"; Gurevich, *Medieval Popular Culture*, 104–52; Le Goff, *Birth of Purgatory*, 112–22, 190–201. Watkins, "Sin, Penance and Purgatory," tells of some of the more obscure vision stories from Normandy and Norman England.

9. Nancy Caciola, in an otherwise excellent article, overgeneralizes when she claims that in order to see the "wild horde" of Hellequin's (or Harlequin's) hunt "the living had to leave behind their own bodies and encounter them on equal terms, as disembodied spirits." As discussed below, the troop seen by Walchelin was not "conceived as less corporeal than the revenants" that Caciola discusses (Caciola, "Wraiths, Revenants and Ritual," 37).

10. Carozzi, "La géographie de l'au-delà," 476; Gurevich, *Categories of Medieval Culture*, 85; idem, *Medieval Popular Culture*, 109, 136–37; Mégier, "Deux exemples," 55.

11. Caciola, "Wraiths, Revenants and Ritual," 10. Bouet, "La 'Mesnie Hellequin,'" 64, describes it as "an incoherent world" in which "time and space no longer possess their habitual niches" (*monde incohérent le temps et l'espace ne possèdent plus leurs repaires habituels*). Bouet's words are evocative, but

I think that his description of the event as a *"chaotic world"* (*monde chaotique,* his italics) and an "incoherent world" is not correct. The scene witnessed by Walchelin was extraordinary but not chaotic or incoherent; it simply responded to a less obvious coherence in medieval culture.

12. Gurevich, *Medieval Popular Culture,* 104.

13. *HE* viii.17 (Chibnall 4:238): *Prefatus presbiter erat iuuenis, audax et fortis, corpore magnus et agilis.*

14. The vision of Dryhthelm, for instance, in Bede's account actually occurred while he was dead; he was sent back to the world of the living to spread the tale (Bede, *Historia Ecclesiastica* v.12). Wetti, Tnugdal, and the monk of Evesham were also ill when they saw their visions (Gardiner, *Visions,* 65–66, 151, 197–98).

15. *HE* viii.17 (Chibnall 4:238): *Verum quidam enormis staturæ ferens ingentem maxucam presbiterum properantem preuenit, et super caput eius leuato uecte dixit, 'Sta nec progrediaris ultra.'*

16. *HE* viii.17 (Chibnall 4:238): *Ecce ingens turba peditum pertransibat, et pecudes ac uestes multimodamque suppellectilem et diuersa utensilia quæ predones asportare solent super colla scapulasque suas ferebat. Omnes nimirum lamentabantur, seseque ut festinarent cohortabantur.*

17. *HE* viii.17 (Chibnall 4:238): *Multos etiam uicinorum suorum qui nuper obierant presbiter ibidem recognouit, et merentes pro magnis suppliciis quibus ob facinora sua torquebantur audiuit.*

18. *HE* viii.17 (Chibnall 4:238): *homines parui uelut nani . . . sed magna capita ceu dolia. . . . cohors mulierum.*

19. *HE* viii.17 (Chibnall 4:240): *In hoc agmine prefatus sacerdos quasdam nobiles feminas recognouit, et multarum quæ uitales adhuc auras carpebant mannos et mulas cum sambucis muliebribus prospexit.*

20. *HE* viii.17 (Chibnall 4:240): *Multos nimirum magnæ estimationis . . . humana opinio sanctis in cœlo iam coniunctos astruit.*

21. For Hugh of Lisieux: *HE* v.3 (Chibnall 3:16): *nostro uir non reparabilis æuo.* For Gerbert of Saint-Wandrille, *HE* iv (Chibnall 2:298): *radiantes in firmamento cœli.*

22. Caciola, "Wraiths, Revenants and Ritual," 29.

23. *HE* viii.17 (Chibnall 4:242): *nullus color nisi nigredo et scintillans ignis in eis uidebatur.* For the "orders" of society, see Mégier, "Deux exemples," 55–56; Schmitt, *Ghosts,* 99; and Stock, "Antiqui and Moderni," 372–74. See also Bede, *Historia Ecclesiastica* v.12, who reported that Dryhthelm saw three souls dragged into a burning pit—"one was tonsured like a clerk, one was a layman, and one was a woman" (*quidam era adtonsus ut clericus, quidam laicus, quaedam femina*).

24. "The dead," Schmitt has noted, "also haunted the places that were familiar to them" (Schmitt, *Ghosts*, 180).

25. The origins and development of Hellequin's—or Herlechin's, or Herla's—hunt, also called the Wild Hunt, have been discussed widely. See Lecouteux, "Chasse sauvage," and Walter, "Hellequin, Hannequin et le Mannequin." Also Ginzburg, *Night Battles*, 40–68; Holm, "Hellequin Figure," though note that Holm misrepresents Orderic's story in some important ways; and Schmitt, *Ghosts*, 93–121. There were a number of variations on the medieval tale of the Wild Hunt, some contained in Joynes, *Medieval Ghost Stories*, 28–31, 58–59, 62–64.

26. For ghostly armies see, for instance, Raoul Glaber, *Historiarum libri quinque* v.6; Peter the Venerable, *De miraculis* i.28, ll. 113–16; William of Malmesbury, *Gesta regum Anglorum* ii.205.4–5; and Walter Map, *De nugis curialium* i.11.

27. *HE* viii.17 (Chibnall 4:242): *A multis eam olim uisam audiui, sed incredulus relatores derisi quia certa indicia nunquam de talibus uidi. Nunc uero manes mortuorum ueraciter uideo sed nemo michi credet cum uisa retulero, nisi certum specimen terrigenis exhibuero. De uacuis ergo equis qui sequuntur agmen unum apprehendam, confestim ascendam domum ducam, et ad fidem optinendam, uicinis ostendam.*

28. *HE* viii.17 (Chibnall 4:244): *subitoque nimium calorem uelut ignem ardentem sub pede sensit, et inedicibile frigus per manum qua lora tenebat eius precordia penetrauit.*

29. For the corporeality of certain medieval ghosts, see Schmitt, *Ghosts*, 196–200. It may just be possible—though there is no real evidence for this—that the physicality of Orderic's Norman ghosts harked back to the very corporeal phantoms of the Scandinavian tradition. See, for this tradition, Lecouteux, *Fantômes*.

30. Schmitt, *Ghosts*, 196–97.

31. *HE* viii.17 (Chibnall 4:244): '*Sinite illum, et permittite loqui mecum. . . . Audi me queso, et uxori meæ refer quæ mando.*'

32. William of Glos's family was well-known to Orderic. William's father Barnon had been the steward of William fitzOsbern's father Osbern, and had avenged Osbern's violent death during the years of Duke William's minority (Orderic Vitalis, interpolations in William of Jumièges, *Gesta Normannorum Ducum* vii.[2]). Given the connections between the abbey of Ouche and William fitzOsbern's family after 1061 William of Glos was probably a familiar figure to the older monks at Ouche.

33. *HE* viii.17 (Chibnall 4:244): *amentem deridebunt me.*

34. This is Schmitt's interpretation (Schmitt, *Ghosts*, 96).

35. Orderic never specifically stated that Walchelin was from a local family. But the name Walchelin was relatively common in the Ouche—for instance, William Giroie's brother-in-law Walchelin of Pont-Échanfray and his father-in-law Walchelin of Tannee—but nearly unknown elsewhere. Orderic named Walchelin and Robert's father as Raoul the Fair; the names Raoul and Walchelin both appear in the family of Walchelin of Pont-Échanfray (one of whose sons was named Raoul Rufus), and it's more than possible that the priest Walchelin was related to this more famous family. Bonneval was only ten kilometers from Pont-Échanfray.

36. In her study of the American ghost stories of the Hudson Valley, Judith Richardson makes this point from the opposite perspective. "Yet the fact that so many of the ghosts of that region," namely, the Hudson Valley, "are so inchoate or faded, so incapable of being identified, has aesthetic and historical implications. Embedded in these depictions of ghosts is a problem of communication, a loss of essential information, an inability to articulate" (Richardson, *Possessions*, 27).

37. *HE* viii.17 (Chibnall 4:246, 8): *Arma quæ ferimus ignea sunt, et nos fœtore teterrimo inficiunt, ingentique ponderositate nimis opprimunt, et ardore inextinguibili comburunt.* And *HE* viii.17 (Chibnall 4:248): *quam si ferrem super me Montem Sancti Michahelis.*

38. *HE* viii.17 (Chibnall 4:248): *tota septimana grauiter egrotauit.*

39. For the fatality of such encounters, see Peter the Venerable, *De miraculis* i.11, ll. 67–70: "For in these times when manifestations of the dead of such a sort often come to us, it is said that scarcely anyone who speaks with the dead defers death for very long" (*Cum enim huiusmodi defunctorum manifestationes nostris sepe temporibus prouenerint, uix aliquis mortuo collocutus, mortem longiore tempore distulisse narratur*). Cf. Raoul Glaber, *Historiarum libri quinque* v.6.

40. *HE* viii.17 (Chibnall 4:248).

41. Le Goff has argued that purgatory became a recognizable and distinct place, rather than a state, in the 1170s when the noun *purgatorium* was coined to replace such phrases as *purgatorio igne*, which was used by Orderic in his description of Walchelin's vision (Le Goff, *Birth of Purgatory*, 135, 154–67). This interpretation, with its emphasis on the word *purgatorium* rather than descriptions, has been widely criticized. See Carozzi, "La géographie de l'audelà," 480, and the discussion between Le Goff and Carozzi that follows Carozzi's paper; B. McGuire, "Purgatory," 61–66, at least in part; and Southern, "Between Heaven and Hell," in a more serious way.

42. My reference to the "very average dead," those people who tried their best but still ended up having to expurgate their sins in the purgatorial

fire, deliberately echoes Peter Brown's "very special dead," the saints who were believed to go directly to heaven without any intermediate stage (Brown, *Cult of the Saints*, 70–71). Like the very special dead, the very average dead and their places of burial still had great meaning for the living.

43. B. McGuire, "Purgatory," 79.

44. Richardson, *Possessions*, 174.

45. Richardson, *Possessions*, 27.

46. The eleventh, twelfth, and thirteenth centuries were the heyday of the genre (McLaughlin, "Communion with the Dead," 31–32). Anna Harrison has suggested that such ghost stories "are buoyed by the conviction that at least some of the claims established in this life are not rent by death, that aspects of a lifelike relationship exist between the living and the dead, and that reciprocal relationships between the living and the dead endure" (A. Harrison, "If One Member Glories," 27).

47. Raoul Glaber, *Historiarum libri quinque* ii.19: *repletus est totius eiusdem ecclesiẹ ambitus, uiris scilicet uestibus albis indutis ac purpureis stolis insignitis. . . . Qui uero eos precedebat crucem manu gestans, episcopum se esse multarum dicebat plebium, ibique die ipso sacra missarum celebrare se oportere perhibebat.*

48. Raoul Glaber, *Historiarum libri quinque* ii.19: *Interim uero percunctatus est supradictus frater qui aut unde essent, pro quaue causa illuc deuenissent. . . . sortem beatorum; sed ideo per hanc prouinciam nobis contigit habere transitum quoniam plures ex hac regione infra breue temporis spacium nostro sunt addendi collegio.*

49. Peter the Venerable, *De miraculis* ii.31 (27): *Neutrum tamen illorum dum uiuerent, puer uiderat, set ex his que ab eis audiuit, absque ulla eos ac si uidisset dubitatione, cognouit. . . .conspicit puer totum cimiterii ambitum sedibus innumeris refertum, ac supra sedes illas uiros monastico scemate indutos, sedere. . . . conspexit multum ignem proxime ante ipsam portam . . . plurimi ex illo agmine transeuntes, alii diu in illo morabantur, alii cito transibant.*

50. Iogna-Prat, *Order and Exclusion*, 252, notes of Peter the Venerable's story that "the monastery was essentially a place of transition between this world and the next, an antechamber or sieve (*sas*) that individuals had to pass through. . . . Twenty or thirty years on, this intermediate space would expand and take the name of purgatory."

51. There is no clue to the scriptorium's location in the *Historia*, in the *Monasticon Gallicanum*, vol. 2, plate 111, or the archaeological record. But see Greene, *Medieval Monasteries*, 6, for the typical use of the northern cloister walk, and Braunfels, *Monasteries of Western Europe*, 55, for a plan of Cluny II with the scriptorium marked.

52. *HE* viii.3 (Chibnall 4:142–44), for Robert of Rhuddlan's tomb.

53. *HE* viii.3 (Chibnall 4:144): *Hoc in mausoleo Robertus de Rodelento / Conditur humano more soli gremio. . . . Ense caput secuit Grithfridus et in mare iecut, / Soma quidem reliquum possidet hunc loculum.* Despite the kind eulogy that Orderic gave to Robert of Rhuddlan on the tomb the historian didn't think much of the lord of the Welsh marches. Only shortly before he included this verse in the *Historia*, Orderic referred to Robert as driven by "pride and greed" (*Superbia et cupiditas*) (*HE* viii.3 [Chibnall 4:138]).

54. Robert probably died in 1093 (Chibnall 4:140n1) and was buried at Chester. Some years later, according to Orderic, Arnaud went to retrieve the body and it was buried in Ouche's cloister during the time of Abbot Roger, so no later than 1099 (*HE* viii.3 [Chibnall 4:142]).

55. Robert: *HE* iii (Chibnall 2:81). Raoul: *HE* v.17 (Chibnall 3:164). Hugh: *HE* v.17 (Chibnall 3:166).

56. For the common practice in Norman Romanesque architecture of constructing the chapter-house with an apse like a church in miniature, see Beck, "Les salles capitulaires," 9–10.

57. Osbern: *HE* iii (Chibnall 2:134). Roger: *HE* xii.32 (Chibnall 6:326–28). Warin: *HE* xiii.31 (Chibnall 6:486–90). Of those who did not rest in the chapter-house, Abbot Thierry of Mathonville (d. 1058) was buried in Cyprus where he died on the way to Jerusalem; Abbot Robert of Grandmesnil (d. 1089) lay in the monastery of his exile, Saint-Eufemia in Sicily; Abbot Serlo of Orgères (d. 1123) was interred at his bishopric in Sées. The chapter-house, the gathering place for monks, was the typical site for abbatial graves in Normandy (Gazeau, "Le souvenir des abbés bénédictins," 220).

58. *HE* xiii.31 (Chibnall 6:488): *Hac tegitur petra Guarini puluis.et ossa, / Qui quater undenis Vtici monachus fuit annis. . . . De grege pro meritis a fratribus ad moderamen / Sumitur, ut sociis ferret speciale iuuamen.*

59. Hugh's nephew Arnaud of Rhuddlan, a monk at Ouche, was also the brother of Robert of Rhuddlan and provided Robert's tombstone in the cloister; perhaps this was an act of piety on his part. It was rather unusual for nobles who died in England to be returned to Normandy for burial (Cownie, *Religious Patronage*, 201–3, and the list of burial locations on 212–15).

60. *HE* viii.28 (Chibnall 4:336): *Ecce sub hoc titulo requiescit strenuus Hugo. . . . Guillelmi fortis Anglorum tempore regis, / Inter precipuos magnates is cluit heros.*

61. Hugh of Grandmesnil and his family: *HE* viii.28 (Chibnall 4:336–38). Hugh of Montpinçon and his son Raoul: *HE* v.17 (Chibnall 3:166). Hugh of Grandmesnil's daughter Matilda, the wife of Hugh of Montpinçon, died in

Joppa on the way home from a pilgrimage to Jerusalem with her second husband, Matthew (*HE* v.17 [Chibnall 3:166]). William Giroie (d. 1057), Hugh's uncle and a founder of Ouche, rested in the cathedral church of St. Erasmus in Gaeta, Campania, having died on his way home from Apulia. For the way in which the arrangement of family graves around that of a patriarch reflects a society's ideas about family structure, see Ames, "Ideologies in Stone," 653; R. McGuire, "Dialogues with the Dead," 447–49.

62. Galeron, "Promenade," 175.

63. In addition to the epitaphs and other poems in the *Historia*, three other free-standing poems have been attributed to Orderic. These verses are in Orderic's hand in MS 1, fols. 30v–32r, in the Mediathèque de la communauté urbaine, Alençon, and have been published by Léopold Delisle in "Vers attribués à Orderic Vital."

64. For the early Christian practices, Brown, *Cult of the Saints*, 27, 32–35; McLaughlin, *Consorting with Saints*, 30–31; Duval, *Auprès des saints corps et âme*.

65. Bouchard, *Sword, Miter, and Cloister*, 224; Cownie, *Religious Patronage*, 163–64; Geary, "Exchange and Interaction," esp. 90–92; idem, *Phantoms of Remembrance*, 76–80; Iogna-Prat, "Dead in the Celestial Bookkeeping," 349–59; McLaughlin, *Consorting with Saints*, esp. 125–32, and chap. 4; White, *Custom, Kinship, and Gifts to Saints*, 26. Emily Zack Tabateau does note that some monasteries fought to possess the bodies of their patrons but she does not suggest why (Tabuteau, *Transfers of Property*, 19–21).

66. Geary, "Exchange and Interaction," 90–92; idem, *Phantoms of Remembrance*, 76–77.

67. See McLaughlin, *Consorting with Saints*; Rosenwein, *To Be the Neighbor of Saint Peter*; Magnani S.-Christen, "Transforming Things and Persons."

68. Kieckhefer, *Theology in Stone*, 153.

69. The archaeologist Howard Williams has called for a more nuanced understanding of the relationship between burial and social memory in the middle ages, though the burials he discusses unfortunately do not have supporting narrative material like those at Ouche (H. Williams, "Remembering and Forgetting," esp. 227–33). For the importance of the name in evoking the person, particularly in the context of the *liber memorialis*, see Oexle, "Memoria und Memorialüberlieferung," 79–86; Geary, "Exchange and Interaction," 87–98; McLaughlin, *Consorting with Saints*, 98–100. Okasha, "Memorial Stones or Grave-Stones?" 99–100, has identified some Anglo-Saxon engraved stones as an example of a *liber vitae*.

70.  Michel Lauwers has noted the care that medieval monastic chroniclers took in describing the exact location of the tombs of abbots and other prominent affiliates of the community, and he associates this care with the hierarchical divisions of space within monasteries (Lauwers, *La mémoire des ancêtres*, 277–78). This hierarchy of space is not particularly noticeable in Orderic's descriptions of Ouche's funeral topography, with the exception of the division between the cloister and the chapter-house.

71.  *HE* viii.3 (Chibnall 4:144–46).

72.  *HE* viii.28 (Chibnall 4:336–38).

73.  *HE* xiii.31 (Chibnall 6:488–90).

74.  *HE* vi.8 (Chibnall 3:256–58).

75.  Memorial stones were always, of course, more meaningful to the living rather than to the dead, and they reflected the community's needs more than those of the dead individual (R. McGuire, "Dialogues with the Dead," 436).

76.  Nora, "Between Memory and History," 18–19, 23–24.

77.  Although Hugh died in England he was still made a monk of Ouche before his death. When Hugh, an old man, fell ill, Ouche's Abbot Roger of Le Sap sent the monk Geoffrey of Orléans (later abbot of Crowland) to England to tend to the founder. Geoffrey received Hugh into the monastic community he had founded on 16 February 1098, and he died six days later.

78.  The distinction between a "good death" and a "bad death" can be found in Caesarius of Heisterbach, *Dialogus miraculorum* xi.1. See also Binski, *Medieval Death*, 33–50; Caciola, "Spirits Seeking Bodies," 75, 84; idem, "Wraiths, Revenants and Ritual," 27–29. Philippe Ariès, in his intriguing but overreaching work, calls the good death a "tame" death, one that was anticipated and even welcomed (Ariès, *Hour of Our Death*, 5–28; see also idem, *Western Attitudes toward Death*, 1–14).

79.  As mentioned below, Abbot Osbern was initially buried in the cloister, but his body was moved to the chapter-house by Abbot Mainer when the new building was ready. Orderic did not mention such a translation for any other bones from the cloister.

80.  *HE* iii (Chibnall 2:122).

81.  *HE* v.17 (Chibnall 3:164–66).

82.  Being buried as near as possible to one's kin was almost as important as being buried in a holy place (Daniell, *Death and Burial*, 101).

83.  *HE* viii.3 (Chibnall 4:136) for Robert of Rhuddlan's gifts to the abbey.

84.  *HE* viii.3 (Chibnall 4:136) names Robert's two Benedictine brothers and the burial of his parents in the monastery.

85. This type of separation seems to be unique to the monastery of Ouche (although it is possible that it is the body of documentation about those buried in the abbey and their lives, rather than the practice itself, that is unusual). Orderic noted, for instance, that Avice and Gautier of Auffay, benefactors of Ouche's priory at Auffay, were buried in the cloister there; both died good deaths, Gautier in the monastic habit (*HE* vi.8 [Chibnall 3:256–58]).

It is notable that all of those who are known to have died during the abbacy of Osbern—namely, Robert Giroie, Arnaud of Échauffour, and Osbern himself—were buried in the cloister, while after the construction of the new chapter-house it became the favored site for tombs. Robert of Rhuddlan and Hugh of Montpinçon, however, both died well after the chapter-house was complete and were still consigned to the cloister.

86. Daniell, *Death and Burial,* 103.

87. For the continued importance of the communion between the living and the dead, see B. McGuire, "Purgatory," 67. Orderic, though, lived at a time that was becoming increasingly uncomfortable in this relationship; the violence of Robert of Rhuddlan's death may have made his presence more disruptive than most. For this increasing discomfort, which by the turn of the thirteenth century prompted the statement that "we [the living] do not communicate with the dead," see McLaughlin, "On Communion with the Dead," passim, but especially 31–32.

88. Caciola, "Wraiths, Revenants and Ritual," 28–29.

89. For the distastefulness of beheading, see Daniell, *Death and Burial,* 79–80. As Daniell notes, martyrs were often beheaded as well. But in such cases, such as that of the English St. Edmund, the head was often miraculously reattached to the body. Daniell also discusses the importance of the position of the head in medieval burial. Stones or a niche in the coffin were often used to position the head facing up, apparently so the deceased would be able to see the coming of the Lord (Daniell, *Death and Burial,* 180–81). Robert of Rhuddlan, headless, would not have been able to do so.

90. Caciola has noted how much more difficult it was for a community to assimilate a bad death. "With good deaths, community boundaries were effortlessly fractured and immediately reconstituted as the dead left the community of the living. . . . In cases of bad death, however, the process of placing the dead was more complex and gradual. . . . Not only did these dead have to make their initial entry among the dead too suddenly, while still desperately attached to life; but those left behind likely experienced a heady mixture of ambivalence, titillation and vague guilt in recalling the violent ends of murder victims or executed criminals. Collective memories of such deaths would

linger as a mental apparition that could become vividly present" (Caciola, "Spirits Seeking Bodies," 84).

91. *HE* viii.1 (Chibnall 4:112): *Beati qui bene mortui sunt.*

92. As Richardson has noted, "a haunting is by definition an intervention, an occupation, a claim of priority and possession—if shadowy then all the more difficult to refute" (Richardson, *Possessions*, 174).

## CHAPTER 6    Historians, Heretics, and the Body of Christ

1. The most recent biography of Lanfranc is Cowdrey, *Lanfranc*. The archepiscopal appointment is discussed on 78–82. Also Gibson, *Lanfranc of Bec*, 114–15.

2. John of Worcester, *Chronica* an. 1070: *operam dante rege ut quamplures ex Anglis suo honore priuarentur, in quorum locum sue gentis personas subrogaret, ob confirmationem scilicet sui quod nouiter adquisierata regni.*

3. *HE* iv (Chibnall 2:250): *Profecto Beringerium Turonensem quem nonnulli heresiarcham putabant, et eius dogma damnabant, quo de salutis hostia mortem animabus propinabat, spiritualis eloquii mucrone confodit in sinodo Romana et Vercellensi.*

4. The controversy over Berengar of Tours's eucharistic views has received quite a bit of scholarly attention, but it has for the most part been scattered in bits and pieces in more general studies. The two standard and comprehensive monographs on the debates are Macdonald, *Berengar*, and Montclos, *Lanfranc et Bérenger*.

5. *HE* iv (Chibnall 2:250, 2): *Ibi sanctissime exposuit, ueracissime comprobauit, panem et uinum quæ dominicæ mensæ superponuntur, post consecrationem esse ueram carnem et uerum sanguinem Domini redemptoris.*

6. *HE* iv (Chibnall 2:252): *dilucido edidit uenustoque stilo libellum, sacris auctoritatibus ponderosum, et indissolubiliter constantem consequentiis rationum, ueræ intelligentiæ astructione de Eucharistia copiosum, facundo sermone luculentum, nec prolixitate tediosum.*

7. Lanfranc, *De corpore et sanguine Domini*. Orderic's description of Berengar's heresy as a sect (*sectas*) echoed Lanfranc's condemnation (*Patrologia Latina* 150:430A). Ouche's catalogue does not list Lanfranc's work, but Orderic could easily have seen it at Bec, Jumièges, or Saint-Ouen, all of which had copies in the twelfth century (Nortier, *Les bibliothèques*, 220). Chibnall does not doubt that Orderic had read Lanfranc's work (Chibnall, *World*, 162).

8. William of Malmesbury, *Gesta regum Anglorum* iii.284.1–288.2. Stein, "Making History English," 102.

9. Guitmund of Aversa, *De corpore et sanguine Domini*. See also Shaughnessy, *Eucharistic Doctrine of Guitmund of Aversa* and the papers collected in Orabona, *Guitmondo di Aversa*. Norman clerics seem to have responded with particular vehemence to Berengar's thought. Durand, abbot of Troarn just north of Orderic's Ouche, also wrote against Berengar (Heurtevent, *Durand de Troarn*).

10. *HE* iv (Chibnall 2:270–78). Guitmund of Aversa's *De corpore et sanguine Domini* was often bound with Lanfranc's treatise and was also available at Bec, Jumièges, and Saint-Ouen (Nortier, *Les bibliothèques*, 213). Both works were quite popular, and had a wide circulation both inside and outside of Normandy. Cluny's Abbot Peter the Venerable was familiar with both works (and ranked Guitmund's above Lanfranc's), as was William of Malmesbury (Peter the Venerable, *Contra Petrobrusianos hereticos* 153; William of Malmesbury, *Gesta regum Anglorum* iii.284.2). Cowdrey, "Papacy and the Berengarian Controversy," 134–35 discusses how an anti-Berengarian statement became part of the oath of consecration for Norman bishops.

11. *HE* iv (Chibnall 2:272): "*Scrutamini scripturas et uidete si qua lege sancitur ut Dominico gregi pastor ab inimicis electus uiolenter imponatur.*"

12. Beckwith, *Christ's Body*; Constable, "Ideal of the Imitation of Christ"; Kobialka, *This is My Body*; Rubin, *Corpus Christi*; idem, "Eucharist and the Construction of Medieval Identities"; Stein, *Reality Fictions*, 27–34.

13. 1 Corinthians 12:27. Cf. *HE* viii.7 (Chibnall 4:166–68): "the body of Christ that is the Church" (*corpore Christi quod est æcclesia*).

14. Both Miri Rubin and Sarah Beckwith, relying on the cultural anthropology of Clifford Geertz, have studied the late medieval body of Christ as a symbol within a cultural system, and in doing so have brought the study of the Eucharist and Jesus's bodily humanity out of the purely intellectual and theological realm and into the study of medieval social practice. But, while I agree with Beckwith that the medieval body of Christ without a doubt "*makes meaning* for its practitioners and interlocutors" (original italics), the methodological definition of Christ's body as a symbol—that is, again to quote Beckwith, "the communicative context through which social worlds are imagined, invented, and changed," which is "unimaginable outside the context of social relations"—cannot fully account for the eleventh- and twelfth-century insistence on the physicality and historicity of Christ's body. See Beckwith, *Christ's Body*, 1–6, with the quotations taken from 2, 3, and Rubin, *Corpus Christi*, 5–11.

15. Historiography on the millennium has provoked some extreme positions. See, for a recent polarized summary, Landes, "Introduction," and idem, "Fear of an Apocalyptic Year 1000." Less shrill analyses are coming

to the fore, however, which see the passing of the millennium as a way of organizing and provoking thought rather than as an impetus for terror. See especially Fulton, *From Judgment to Passion*, 60–106.

16. Chenu has noted that: "Nature and history—the two sources merged finally in the symbolism of the sacraments, and from their merger one can infer and understand something of the basic texture of sacramental symbolism. At the same time that each was a ritual representation of the historic mystery and the historic acts of Christ, every sacrament from baptism on, and every smallest sacred gesture, became involved with some element of nature—water, bread, oil, salt, ash, and the like. The constant blending of the historic and the natural sources of symbolism, disparate in their points of origin, their objects, and their operation and structure, would be managed in countless different ways by zealous theologians and liturgists" (Chenu, *Nature, Man, and Society*, 117–18).

17. *HE* xiii.45 (Chibnall 6:554): *xxxiii ætatis meæ anno Guillelmus archiepiscopus Rotomagi xii kalendas Ianuarii onerauit me sacerdotio.*

18. *HE* xiii.45 (Chibnall 6:556): *cum alacritate mentis.*

19. Hans Wolter noted, though not in much detail, that Orderic's life as a monk-priest shaped his historiographical vision by providing it with a Christocentric focus congruent with the monastic and scholastic thought of the time (Wolter, *Ordericus Vitalis*, 128 and 228nn581–82). Roger Ray's critique of this idea takes Wolter's comments and Orderic's thought too narrowly (Ray, "Monastic Historiography," 251 and n. 1).

20. For the importance of the daily mass for the religious life of monk-priests, see Häussling, *Mönchskonvent und Eucharistiefeier*, and also Van Engen, *Rupert of Deutz*, 60–65.

21. Fulton, *From Judgment to Passion*, 118–19.

22. Orderic mentions Christ's birth as the beginning of the sixth age in *HE* i.1 and i.4 (Le Prévost 1:6, 13). For Orderic's *Vita Christi*, and the meaning of Christ for Orderic's historical thought, see Mégier, "*Cotidie Operatur.*"

23. See chapter 2.

24. Gregory VII, *Registrum* III.17a: *Ego Berengarius corde credo et ore confiteor panem et vinum, quę ponuntur in altari, per misterium sacrę orationis et verba nostri redemptoris substantialiter converti in veram, et propriam, vivificatricem carnem et sanguinem Iesu Christi domini nostri et post consecrationem esse verum Christi corpus, quod natum est de virgine et quod pro salute mundi oblatum in cruce pependit et quod sedet ad dextram Patris, et verum sanguinem Christi, qui de latere eius effusus est.* This oath was also transcribed by Hugh of Flavingy in his *Chronicon* (*Patrologia Latina* 154:316C–D) and was interpolated into Lanfranc, *De corpore* (*Patrologia*

*Latina* 150:411B-C). See also Macdonald, *Berengar,* 191–97; Cowdrey, "Papacy and the Berengarian Controversy," 126–30.

25. The oath sworn by Berengar in 1079 (and the earlier and less-sophisticated version from 1059) were concocted by the Church's elite, but they were not authoritative canonical statements of eucharistic belief, and they did not prevent Christian theologians and Berengarian opponents from proposing alternative visions of the Eucharist's salvific powers. Even after the Fourth Lateran Council of 1215, which has long been considered to have laid down the Christian law on the issue by declaring transubstantiation to be the Church's official view, theologians continued to reinterpret the sacramental body of Christ by questioning exactly what this transubstantiation entailed. For discussions of the continuing, and generally acceptable, diversity in eucharistic thought, see Macy, "Theological Fate of Berengar's Oath of 1059," and idem, "Dogma of Transubstantiation."

26. The Berengarian controversy was to some extant a revival of the debates between Paschasius Radbertus and Ratramnus of Corbie, who both wrote works entitled—what else?—*De corpore et sanguine Domini* in the ninth century, Paschasius in favor of the Real Presence and Ratramnus advocating a figurative view. This earlier manifestation of the debate lays outside the discussion here, but see, among many others, Chazelle, *Crucified God,* 209–38; Fulton, *From Judgment to Passion,* 9–59; Macy, *Theologies of the Eucharist,* 44–72; and summaries in most accounts of the Berengarian controversy. For the eucharistic sentiments attributed to the other eleventh- and twelfth-century heretics, see Iogna-Prat, *Order and Exclusion,* 182–218; Lambert, *Medieval Heresy,* 15–16, 55–56; Moore, *Origins of European Dissent,* 103–5.

27. Berengar of Tours, *In Purgatoria,* p. 534, ll. 76–80: *Mea vel potius scripturarum causa ita erat: panem et vinum mensae dominicae non sensualiter, sed intellectualiter, non per absumptionem, sed per assumptionem, non in portiunculam carnis, contra scripturas, sed, secundum scripturas, in totum converti Christi corpus et sanguinem.* My translation owes a debt to that of Cowdrey, "Papacy and the Berengarian Controversy," 134.

28. The question of when, or whether, medieval thought has been predominantly dualist or antidualist had received some attention, but all of it dealing with the twelfth century and later and most probably prompted, although not always explicitly, by the focus on dualist heresies in the later middle ages. See, for one of the most thorough critiques of an unvaryingly dualist middle ages, Bynum, "Why All the Fuss," 251. Also, drawing on Bynum's work, Biernoff, *Sight and Embodiment,* esp. 23–39. There is a widespread assumption, without any justification, that the earlier middle ages was unthinkingly dualist

(Boureau, "Sacrality of One's Own Body," 12; D'Avray, "Some Franciscan Ideas about the Body," 161). I challenge this assumption here.

29. Macy, *Theologies of the Eucharist*, 39, and idem, "Berengar's Legacy," 67.

30. Berengar of Tours, *Rescriptum contra Lanfrannum* (*De sacra coena*) i.2253–58: *Homo de duabus substantiis constat, anima et corpore, superiori et inferiori: superior reficitur Christi corpore ad vitam eternam pane interiore, pane spirituali, inferior ad temporalem pane senuali.* See Macdonald, *Berengar,* 298–99, for a similar, though not identical, distinction made by St. Augustine based not on any differentiation within the Eucharist but in the mind of the recipient.

31. Berengar of Tours, *Rescriptum contra Lanfrannum* (*De sacra coena*) i.2260–63: *panem sensualem, quo reficitur corpus, substantialem, panem spiritualem, id est Christi corpus quo reficitur anima, supersubstantialem.*

32. Heinrich Fichtenau characterized this philosophical difference between Berengar and Lanfranc as the difference between a Platonic perspective that viewed the material world as inferior to the spiritual and an Aristotelian approach grounded in the material realm of substances and accidents (Fichtenau, *Heretics and Scholars*, 291–93). This perspective draws on Richard Southern's argument that Lanfranc used Aristotle's *Categories,* known in the schools since the tenth century, to formulate a theory of physical change of the eucharistic bread and wine into the body and blood of Christ, although Lanfranc used the word *essentia* rather than *substantia* (Southern, "Lanfranc of Bec and Berengar of Tours," 39–41, and idem, *Saint Anselm,* 47–50; see also Gibson, *Lanfranc of Bec,* 90–91). Southern's argument has been challenged by Montclos and Holopainen who see Platonist rather than Aristotelian tendencies in Lanfranc's talk of essences (Holopainen, *Dialectic and Theology,* 67–76; Montclos, *Lanfranc et Bérenger,* 445–48). From a purely philosophical standpoint their arguments have some merit. However, when looking at the eucharistic debate as a whole and the intellectual climate of the age, as Southern and Fichtenau did, the claim that Lanfranc chose to argue from an Aristotelian perspective based in the necessity of the physical world and physical change is more convincing, especially when considered in conjunction with Guitmund of Aversa's contemporary text, which argues explicitly with the language of substance and accidents.

33. Lambert, *Medieval Heresy,* 14–21; Moore, *Origins of European Dissent,* 25–30.

34. Berengar of Tours, *In Purgatoria,* p. 531: *nunquam manichaeorum admisisse sententiam. Illi enim fantasticum, ego verum et humanum corpus Christi fuisse et tenui et teneo.* The structure of this sentence makes it un-

clear whether Berengar is referring to Manichees in the past, similar heretics in the present, or both.

35. Quite a bit has been written about the application of the term Manichees to medieval heretics. Runciman, *Medieval Manichee*, is the classic account of the affiliation between the late antique and medieval dualist heresies. This has been challenged and reconstructed in more recent times, and the literature is too vast to summarize here. But see, for summaries and some of the more important statements, Lambert, *Medieval Heresy*, 37–39; Moore, *Origins of European Dissent*, 139–76; Pegg, *Corruption of Angels*, 15–19; idem, "On Cathars," esp. 181–85; Taylor, "Letter of Héribert of Périgord," 317–18.

36. For the medieval distinction between "flesh" and "body," see Biernoff, *Sight and Embodiment*, 26 ff; Boureau, "Sacrality of One's Own Body,"; and Schmitt, "Le corps en Chrétienté," 346–47. The first two of these focus in large part on later literature; the eleventh century, while very different in its acceptance of the body, did not make a strong linguistic differentiation between flesh and body. For the very particular and physical reality of the bodily resurrection, see Bynum, *Resurrection of the Body*.

37. Berengar of Tours, *In Purgatoria*, p. 534: *non sensualiter, sed intellectualiter*; and p. 532: *fidei et intellectui*.

38. *HE* vi.1 (Chibnall 3:214): *De cursu tamen seculi et rebus humanis ueraciter scribendum est atque ad laudem creatoris et omnium rerum iusti gubernatoris cronographya pangenda est.*

39. Kieckhefer, *Theology in Stone*, 149, focuses on the liturgical rather than the material aspects of the Eucharist, coming to the same end.

40. Constable, "A Living Past," 68; Frank, *Memory of the Eyes*, 112–13, 118–33.

41. Guitmund of Aversa, *De corpore* (*Patrologia Latina* 149:1428B): *diu vocis lentissimo quodam quasi plangore.* For the grammatical nuances of Berengar's thought, see Holopainen, *Dialectic and Theology*, 77–118; Southern, "Lanfranc of Bec and Berengar of Tours"; Stock, *Implications of Literacy*, 273–81.

42. Lambert, *Medieval Heresy*, does not mention Berengar of Tours at all; Moore, *Origins*, refers to him only once (245), but without any detail about the controversy he provoked.

43. Fulton, *From Judgment to Passion*, 9.

44. This profession is edited in Somerville, "Case Against Berengar of Tours," 68: *substantialiter transmutatum in verum corpus et in verum sanguinem Christi—in ipsum scilicet corpus quod natum est de Maria virgine, quod passum est et crucifixum pro nobis, quod surrexit a mortuis, quod sedet ad dexteram Dei patris, et in ipsum eundem sanguinem qui de latere illius*

*pendentis in cruce emanavit.* Lanfranc's letter to Reginald abbot of St. Cyprian in Poitiers, Sewinus the monk, and the canon Henry, which mentioned Berengar but dealt primarily with issues of the Incarnation, was apparently related to this council (Lanfranc, *Epistola* 46). A very similar statement, and quite a bit earlier, can be found in the *Acta* of the synod held in Arras in 1025 at which a group of heretics was condemned by Bishop Gerard. See Moore, *Birth of Popular Heresy*, 18, for a translation.

45. Guitmund of Aversa, *De corpore* (*Patrologia Latina* 149:1481A): *Christum pani et vino commiscentes.*

46. Chadwick, "Ego Berengarius," 429. Accusations of impanation would have a long history in Catholic disputations. Rupert of Deutz was accused of this heresy by Alger of Liège and William of St. Thierry, and the term was flung at Martin Luther in the sixteenth century to vilify his ideas of consubstantiation (Van Engen, *Rupert of Deutz*, 139–40; Pohle, "Impanation," 694–95).

47. Pegg, "On Cathars," 184.

48. Constable has discussed this persistent relationship between past and present, though with a primary focus on art rather than liturgy, in his article "A Living Past."

49. *HE* i.1 (Chibnall 1:134; Le Prévost 1:6): *Anno itaque Cesaris Augusti xlii, ab interitu uero Cleopatræ et Antonii quando et Ægiptus in prouinciam uersa est xxviii, olimpiadis uero centesimæ nonagesimæ tertiæ anno tertio, ab urbe autem condita septingentesimo quinquagesimo secundo, id est eo anno quo compressis cunctarum per orbem terræ gentium motibus, firmissimam uerissimamque pacem ordinatione Dei Cesar Octauianus composuit, Iesus Christus filius Dei sextam mundi ætatem aduentu suo consecrauit.* Taken from Bede, *Chronica Maiora*, an. 3952.

50. Iogna-Prat, *Order and Exclusion*, 197; Stock, *Implications of Literacy*, 306.

51. Iogna-Pratt, *Order and Exclusion*, 194. The importance and place of words within medieval sacramental ideas is discussed in Häring, "Berengar's Definitions of *Sacramentum*."

52. The Eucharist and the liturgical year were for the people of medieval Christendom what a common language or the morning newspaper are for modern society: a way of bringing otherwise unconnected people together into an "imagined community," as Benedict Anderson has termed it (Anderson, *Imagined Communities*, 6, 35).

53. Karl Leyser has noted this personal tone in the work of the eleventh-century historians Thietmar of Merseburg, Ademar of Chabannes, and Raoul Glaber (Leyser, *Ascent of Latin Europe*, 21).

54. Martin Heinzelmann sees this as one of the structuring themes of Gregory of Tours's historical vision. See Heinzelmann, *Gregory of Tours,* 36–38; also Goffart, *Narrators of Barbarian History,* 191–97, esp. 194.

55. Bede, *Historia Ecclesiastica* v.24.

56. *HE* v.1 (Chibnall 3:6): *A prefato nempe anno placet inchoare presens opusculum, quo in hanc lucem xiiii° kal' Martii matris ex utero profusus sum, sabbatoque sequentis Paschæ apud Etingesham in æcclesia sancti confessoris Eattæ quæ sita est super Sabrinam fluuium, per ministerium Ordrici sacerdotis sacro fonte renatus sum.*

57. *HE* v.14 (Chibnall 3:150): *Parce queso bone lector, nec molestum tibi sit precor, si de patre meo aliquid memoriæ tradiderim litterarum, quem non uidi ex quo me uelut exosum sibi priuignum, et pro amore creatoris pepulit in exilium.*

58. *HE* xiii.45 (Chibnall 6:552).

59. In addition to the passage from Ademar of Chabannes discussed below, see Raoul Glaber, *Historiarum libri quinque* v.2–5, where he discussed his childhood and a vision of a demon he experienced. Thietmar of Merseburg, writing slightly earlier than Raoul, shows elements both of Gregory of Tours's institutional style in his frequent remarks about his illustrious and active noble family and his life as a bishop, and the more personal revelations of the eleventh and twelfth centuries in his admission of his faults (including simony) and his revelations about visions and dreams. See Thietmar of Merseburg, *Chronicon* vi.43, vi.45, vi.59, vi.79, viii.10, viii.12, for the more personal recollections, and passim for his family and episcopal duties.

60. Ademar of Chabannes, *Chronicon;* iii.46: *vidit in austrum in altitudine celi magnum cruxifixum quasi confixum in celo et Domini pendentem figuram in cruce, multo flumine lacrimarum plorantem. . . . Vidit vero tam ipsam crucem quam figuram Cruxifixi colore igneo et nimis sanguineo totam per dimidiam noctis horam.* See also Landes, *Relics,* 87–91.

61. Alexander, "Jerusalem," 104–19; Wilken, *Land Called Holy,* 11–12, 230.

62. Callahan, "Jerusalem," 122–23; Landes, *Relics,* 40–49, 87–91.

63. Ademar of Chabannes, *Chronicon;* Raoul Glaber, *Historiarum libri quinque* iii.24.

64. Urban II's speech at Clermont, which set off the First Crusade, exists in a number of versions, none definitive. It seems unlikely, given the culture of the day, that Urban actually intended for the crusade to be a "popular" movement. What is certain is that the crusade, whatever Urban's intentions and no matter how many people actually took part, provoked a greater imaginative attention to the earthly city of Jerusalem and its Christological import.

See France, "Le rôle de Jérusalem," 160–61, and also Constable, "Jerusalem and the Sign of the Cross."

65. *HE* ix.1 (Chibnall 5:4): *Hæc ideo medullitus considero, meditatusque meos litteris assigno, quia temporibus nostris insperata fit permutatio, et insigne thema referendi mira prestruitur dictatorum studio. En Ierosolimitanum iter diuinitus initur, a multis occidentalium populis unus grex miro modo congeritur, et contra ethnicos in Eoas partes unus exercitus conducitor. . . . Nulla ut reor unquam sophistis in bellicis rebus gloriosior materia prodiit, quam nostris nunc Dominus poetis atque librariis tradidit, dum per paucos Christicolas de paganis in oriente triumphauit, quos de propriis domibus dulci desiderio peregrinandi exciuit.*

66. John O. Ward has argued that "the first crusade functions as the keystone of the arch of historical interpretation for many of the most learned twelfth century historians," who regarded it not as "a digression from their theme, but a kind of *summa* or manifest sign of it" (Ward, "Some Principles of Rhetorical Historiography," 119).

67. Iogna-Pratt, *Order and Exclusion*, 178–79; Kieckhefer, *Theology in Stone*, 64–70.

68. Lanfranc, *De corpore et sanguine Domini* (*Patrologia Latina* 150:411B): *panem et vinum, quae ponuntur in altari.*

69. Cosgrove, *Apollo's Eye*, 56–57. Also—although without, I believe, sufficient attention paid to the importance of historical and spatial distance as a part of the miraculousness of the Eucharist—see Cavanaugh, "World in a Wafer."

70. Kieckhefer, *Theology in Stone*, 137: "The focus of liturgical symbolism is on the connectedness of historical particularity with the particularities of present experience: the relevance of a sacrificial deal on a day in ancient Palestine to concrete particulars of life here and now."

71. For the church building as microcosm, see chapter 4.

72. Peter the Venerable, *Contra Petrobrusianos*, Epistola.5: *templorum uel ecclesiarum fabricam fieri non debere, factas insuper subrui oportere, nec esse necessaria Christianis sacra loca ad orandum, quoniam eque in taberna et in ecclesia, in foro et in templo, ante altare uel ante stabulum, inuocatus Deus audit, et eos qui merentur exaudit.* See also Moore, *Origins of European Dissent*, 103; idem, *First European Revolution*, 106–7; and Iogna-Pratt, *Order and Exclusion*, 180–81.

73. *HE* iv (Chibnall 2:302): *Sicut mare nunquam tutum certa soliditate quiescit, sed inquietudine iugi turbatum more suo defluit, et quamuis aliquando tranquillum obtutibus spectantium appareat, solita tamen flucuatione et instabilitate nauigantes territat, sic præsens sæculum uolubili-*

*tate sua iugiter uexatur, innumerisque modis tristibus seu lætis euidenter uariatur.*

74. Caroline Walker Bynum has discussed the increased concern with change, focusing mostly on bodily change in the late twelfth and thirteenth centuries, in her *Metamorphosis and Identity*, especially in the introduction, "Change in the Middle Ages."

75. The "Twelfth-Century Renaissance" as a concept traces its origins to 1927 and Charles Homer Haskins's book *The Renaissance of the Twelfth Century*, and has more recently been reinforced, with recognition of the problems of the term, by the essays in Benson and Constable, *Renaissance and Renewal in the Twelfth Century*, and also Chenu, *Nature, Man, and Society*; see also Swanson, *Twelfth-Century Renaissance*. For an important reevaluation, see Jaeger, "Pessimism in the Twelfth-Century 'Renaissance,'" with 1151n1 for a good overview of recent literature.

76. Bynum, "Why all the Fuss," 251.

77. This historiography has some parallels with Peter Abelard's assertion that human makers do not create, but simply make accidental changes to the substances already created by God (Marenbon, *Philosophy of Peter Abelard*, 118–29).

78. *HE* viii.24 (Chibnall 4:290): *En uolubilis fortuna cotidie rotatur, et mundi status uariabiliter agitatur.* Orderic's understanding of *fortuna* as "worldly instability" (*irdische Unbeständigkeit*) compatible with the will of God has been examined in detail by Mégier, "Fortuna," 52–57.

79. Gillian Evans has noted a similar tendency in the historical thought of Anselm of Canterbury, who viewed change as the force that would bring history to its ultimate state of permanent stillness in God at the end of time (Evans, "St. Anselm and Sacred History," 192–200).

80. *HE* ix.1 (Chibnall 5:4): *Vicissitudines temporum et rerum æternus conditor sapienter salubriterque ordinat, nec ad libitus infrunitorum res humanas disponit ac uariat, sed in manu potenti et brachio excelso pie seruat, congrue prouehit ac dispensat.*

81. *HE* xiii.16 (Chibnall 6:436): *latentes rerum causas.*

82. *HE* ix.18 (Chibnall 5:190): *ut coessentibus sibi ad ædificationem seu delectationem retexere possint labentis seculi casus preteritos.*

83. An example of this incompatibility can be found in the recent collection *Historiography in the Middle Ages*, edited by Deborah Deliyannis, which tried to introduce more flexibility into the study of medieval historiography by discarding genres in favor of subject matter as an organizing principle for the various contributions. This method, however, was still unable to account for the exploratory historians, who were barely mentioned.

Epilogue

1. *HE* v.1 (Chibnall 3:8): *Antichristi tempus appropinquat, ante cuius faciem ut dominus beato Iob insinuat, præcedet egestas miraculorum, nimiumque in his qui carnaliter amant se ipsos grassabitur rabies uiciorum.* Orderic was referring to Job 41:13 (Vulgate), *faciem eius praecedit egestasi.*

2. Gregory the Great, *Moralia in Iob* XXXIV.iii.5–7. See also Chenu, *Nature, Man, and Society,* 192–93; McGinn, *Antichrist,* 80–81; Straw, *Gregory the Great,* 14–15.

3. *HE* v.1 (Chibnall 3:4): *Maiorum exempla sectantes lætale ocium indesinenter debemus deuitare, utilique studio et salubri exercitio feruenter insudare, quibus intenta mens a uiciis emundatur, et in omne nefas uitali disciplina gloriose armatur.*

4. *HE* prologue (Chibnall 1:130; Le Prévost 1:1): *Anteriores nostri ab antiquis temporibus labentis seculi excursus prudenter inspexerunt, et bona seu mala mortalibus contingentia pro cautela hominum notauerunt, et futuris semper prodesse uolentes scripta scriptis accumulauerunt.*

5. *HE* prologue (Chibnall 1:130; Le Prévost 1:2–3): *Decet utique ut sicut nouæ res mundo cotidie accidunt, sic ad laudem Dei assidue scripto tradantur, et sicut ab anterioribus preterita gesta usque ad nos transmissa sunt, sic etiam presentia nunc a presentibus futuræ posteritati litterarum notamine transmittantur.*

6. A full listing of occurrences of *posteri* and *posteritas*—future generations—can be found on 346–47 of Chibnall's *Index Verborum* at the back of volume 1 of the *HE*. Orderic also used the word *futura*, which is not indexed by Chibnall.

7. This notion found reflection in the thought of Walter Benjamin. "There is a secret agreement between past generations and the present one. Our coming was expected on earth. Like every generation that preceded us, we have been endowed with a *weak* Messianic power, a power to which the past has a claim. That claim cannot be settled cheaply" (Benjamin, "Theses on the Philosophy of History," 254).

8. Henry of Huntingdon, *Historia Anglorum* viii.epilogue.4: *Ad uos igitur iam loquar qui in tercio millenario, circa centesimum tricesimum quintum annum, eritis. Cogitate de nobis, qui modo clari uidemur, quia scilicet, quidam miseri, nos reuerentur. Cogitate, inquam, quo deuenerimus. Dicite, precor, quid nobis profuerit, si magni uel clari fuerimus? Nichil prorsus nisi in Deo claruerimus. . . . Nunc autem qui tanto tempore antequam nascamini de uobis mentionem iam uestro tempore puluis in hoc opere feci, si contigerit—*

*quod ualde desiderat anima mea—uestras ut in manus hoc opus meum prodeat, precor ut Dei clementiam inexcogitabilem pro me miserrimo exoretis. Sic et pro uobis orent et impetrent qui quarto uel quinto millenario cum Deo ambulabunt, si generatio mortalium tamdiu protelabitur.* For a discussion of this passage, see Otter, *"Prolixitas Temporum,"* 55–61. A similar, though less detailed and much less striking, passage can be found in Thietmar of Merseburg, *Chronicon* viii.12.

9. Henry of Huntingdon, *Historia Anglorum* viii.epilogue.5: *mundi terminum cotidie trementes expectemus.*

10. *HE* vi.1 (Chibnall 3:212): *Ex beniuolentia laborant, et preterita posteris sine inuidia manifestant.*

11. Cf. Thietmar of Merseburg, *Chronicon* viii.6: "No one should despair of the coming of the last day or wish that it might happen more quickly, since it is fearful even to the just and so much greater so to all those needing to be set right" (*Nemo ultimae diei adventum aut venire diffidat aut celeriter contingere exoptet, quia timendus est iustis ac multo magis corrigibilibus cunctis*). Sabina Flanagan has suggested that a belief in the immanence of Antichrist correlated more strongly with personal religious beliefs and milieu than with any widespread societal expectation of the end. Flanagan points out in her study of Norbert of Xanten, Bernard of Clairvaux, Hildegard of Bingen, and Elisabeth of Schönau that concern with Antichrist paralleled a belief that the Devil intervened personally in the world, an assertion that could be made about Orderic Vitalis as well. See Flanagan, "Twelfth-Century Apocalyptic Imaginations."

12. Otto of Freising, *Historia* VIII.

13. *HE* i.15 (Le Prévost 1:66): *Ille percunctantibus de fine respondit mala plurima præcessura, gentium bella, terræ motus per loca, pestilentias et fames, terroresque de cœlo et signa magna.*

14. Mark 13:32. Bynum, *Resurrection of the Body,* esp. 200–225.

15. *HE* vi.1 (Chibnall 3:214): *De miraculis uero prodigiisque sanctorum, quia nimia nunc in terris est penuria eorum, modo scriptoribus in referendo non est insudandum.*

16. *HE* xi.prologue (Chibnall 6:10): *Cornua dena gerens mala bestia iam dominatur,* and (Chibnall 6:8): *Lucida sanctorum iuste magnalia cessant. / Preuaricatores qui legem transgrediuntur, / Iræ celestis penas non signa merentur.*

17. This realization struck me after reading Moore, "Between Sanctity and Superstition," and idem, *First European Revolution,* 23.

18. Two of these drawings are reproduced in *Orderic Vital.* Plate XIV shows an image which can also be found in Sicotière and Poulet-Malassis,

*Le départment de l'Orne;* a version of this image can also be found in *Saint-Évroult,* 27. Plate XV in *Orderic Vital* is a drawing of the ruins by Émile Vaucanu from 1886, from a private collection. Comparing both images to the ruins as they exist today shows how much they deteriorated before steps were taken in the 1960s and 1970s to preserve the monastery's remains.

19. Freeman, *Sketches,* 160.

20. Freeman, *Sketches,* 162–63.

21. Freeman, *Sketches,* 163–64.

22. For the relative size, see Chibnall, *World,* 18. The history of the later church is summarized in Hincker, "Histoire," 23–27. For the community's fate during the Revolution, see Gobillot, "Notes d'histoire," 105–6.

23. *Monasticon Gallicanum,* vol. 2, plate 111.

24. Galeron, "Promenade," 176: "un énorme four à chaux, ménagé dans les murs de l'ancien chœur. C'est dans cet abîme que l'infatigable entrepreneur de cette destruction engloutit froidement, à toute heure, les riches chapiteaux, les corniches à délicates dentelures, les ogives gracieuses, et jusqu'aux débris des statues de ces saints et de ces martyrs qu'adorèrent si long-temps nos pères."

25. Medieval Flanders, as David Wallace notes, has been similarly overshadowed by the twentieth-century carnage of World War I (Wallace, *Premodern Places,* 92). This ability of the landscape to hold deeply contradictory pasts struck Nicholas Howe on a visit to Jarrow, now both "Bede's World" (the name of a historical recreation depicting the historian's world) and a community struggling to come to terms with its fading industrial past (N. Howe, "From Bede's World to 'Bede's World,'" 37–39.

26. Haskins, *Normans in European History.*

27. *HE* xiii.27 (Chibnall 6:476): *Vicissitudines presentis uitæ quam mutabiles sunt. Secularia gaudia cito transeunt, eosque a quibus summopere affectantur in puncto deserunt. Mundanus honor instar bullæ subito crepat ac deficit, sibique inhiantibus insultat atque decipit.*

28. *HE* xiii.27 (Chibnall 6:476): *Omnipotens itaque creator terrigenas instruit, et pluribus modis salubriter erudit, ne in hoc fragilis seculi pelago anchoram suæ spei figant, neque transitoriis delectationibus siue lucris letaliter inhereant. Non habemus hic manentem ciuitatem ut dicit apostolus sed futuram inquirimus.*

29. *HE* vi.10 (Chibnall 3:346): *nec optimis uiris melior neque malis deterior.*

30. BN MS Latin 10062, fol. 19v.

31. For the list of *souscripteurs,* see *Orderic Vital,* xi–xviii.

# Bibliography

## MANUSCRIPT SOURCES

*Bibliothèque de la ville, Rouen*

1174: Orderic Vitalis's copy, with important interpolations, of William of Jumièges's *Gesta Normannorum Ducum* is contained on ff. 116r–139v. From the library at Ouche. First half of the twelfth century.

1343: Bede's *Historia Ecclesiastica gentis Anglorum* copied in Orderic's hand, along with the Gospel of Nicodemus (with corrections by Orderic) and the life and translation of St. Martin of Tours (copied by Orderic). Also *Quid significent duodecim candelae*. From the library at Ouche. First half of the twelfth century.

*Bibliothèque nationale, Paris*

Latin 5506 (I): Autograph of Orderic Vitalis, *Historia Ecclesiastica*, books I and II, from the library at Ouche. First half of the twelfth century.

Latin 5506 (II): Autograph of Orderic Vitalis, *Historia Ecclesiastica*, books III–VI, from the library at Ouche. First half of the twelfth century.

Latin 10062: The "chapter-book" of Saint-Evroult; includes the *Liber Memorialis*, a necrology, a calender, parts of Bede's *De temporum ratione*, the monastery's annals, the Rule of St. Benedict, a catalogue of the library, and some other miscellaneous documents from the library at Ouche. Twelfth century.

Latin 10913: Autograph of Orderic Vitalis, *Historia Ecclesiastica*, books IX–XIII, from the library at Ouche. First half of the twelfth century.

*Library of St John's College, Oxford*

17: *Computus* manuscript from the abbey of Thorney (England) containing mathematical and medical texts, *computus* materials, cosmology, Bede's scientific works, a calendar and annals, and various charts, including a

*mappa mundi* (fol. 6r) and an *annus-mundus-homo* diagram known as
Byrhtferth's Diagram (fol. 7v). Completed 1110.

*Mediathèque de la communauté urbaine, Alençon*

1: From the library at Ouche. Contains the Prophets, but folios 30v–32r contain verses composed in whole or in part by Orderic Vitalis. First half of
the twelfth century.

12, part I: Boethius's *Consolation of Philosophy,* a table of human knowledge,
and a chart of the personified winds. From the library at Ouche. Eleventh
century, with twelfth- and thirteenth-century glosses.

14: Various *vitae,* and other texts from Ouche. Folio 38r–v contains Orderic's
copy of the charter of Charles the Simple given to the original foundation of Saint-Evroult in 900. Late eleventh–early twelfth century.

## PUBLISHED SOURCES

Adam of Bremen. *Gesta Hammaburgensis ecclesiae pontificum.* Edited by
Bernhard Schmeidler in *Hamburgische Kirchengeschichte.* Monumenta
Germaniae Historica, Scriptores rerum Germanicarum, 3rd ed. Hannover:
Hahn, 1917.

Ademar of Chabannes. *Chronicon.* Edited by P. Bourgain with Richard Landes
and Georges Pon in *Ademar Cabannensis Chronicon.* Part I: *Ademari
Cabannensis Opera Omnia.* Corpus Christianorum: Continuatio Mediaevalis 129. Turnhout: Brepols, 1999.

Ælfric of Eynsham. *Lives of Three English Saints.* Edited by G. I. Needham.
Methuen's Old English Library. London: Methuen, 1966.

Aelred of Rievaulx. *Genealogia regum anglorum. Patrologia Latina*
195:711–37.

Amatus of Montecassino. *History of the Normans.* Translated by Prescott N.
Dunbar and revised with introduction and notes by Graham A. Loud.
Woodbridge: Boydell Press, 2004.

*Anglo-Saxon Chronicle.* Translated and edited by Michael Swanton. New
York: Routledge, 1998.

*Annales Uticenses.* In *Orderici Vitalis Historiæ Ecclesiasticæ libri tredecim,*
5:139–73. Edited by Auguste Le Prévost. Société de l'histoire de France.
Paris: Julius Renouard et socios, 1855.

Ascelin of Chartres. *Epistola ad Berengarium.* In *Serta Mediaevali: Textus varii
saeculorum X-XIII in unum collecti,* 150–54. Edited by R. B. C. Huygens.
Corpus Christianorum: Continuatio Mediaevalis 171. Turnhout: Brepols,
2000.

Athanasius. *Vita Antonii,* Translated and edited by Carolinne White in *Early Christian Lives,* 1–70. Harmondsworth: Penguin, 1998.

Augustine of Hippo. *De civitate Dei libri xxii.* Corpus Christianorum: Series Latina 47 and 48. Turnholt: Brepols, 1955.

———. *In Iohannis evangelium tractatus cxxiv.* Patrologia Latina 35:1379–1976.

Baudry of Bourgueil. *Hierosolymitanae historiae libri quatuor. Patrologia Latina* 166:1057–1152.

Beatus of Liébana. *Beati in apocalipsin libri duodecim.* Edited by Henry A. Sanders. Papers and Monographs of the American Academy in Rome 7. Rome: American Academy in Rome, 1930.

Bede. *Chronica Maiora.* Edited by Charles W. Jones in *Bedae Venerabilis Opera,* part 6, *Opera Didascalica 2,* 461–544. Corpus Christianorum: Series Latina 123B. Turnholt: Brepols, 1977.

———. *De temporum ratione.* Edited by Charles W. Jones in *Bedae Venerabilis Opera,* part 6, *Opera Didascalica 2,* 263–460. Corpus Christianorum: Series Latina 123B. Turnholt: Brepols, 1977. Translated by Faith Wallis in *Bede: The Reckoning of Time,* Translated Texts for Historians (Liverpool: Liverpool University Press, 1999).

———. *Historia Ecclesiastica gentis Anglorum.* Edited and translated by Bertram Colgrave and R. A. B. Mynors in *Bede's Ecclesiastical History of the English People.* Oxford Medieval Texts. Oxford: Clarendon Press, 1969.

———. *Homeliae.* Edited by D. Hurst in *Bedae Venerabilis Opera,* part 3, *Opera Homiletica.* Corpus Christianorum: Series Latina 122. Turnholt: Brepols, 1995.

———. *Nomina regionvm atqve locorvm de actibvs apostolorvm.* Edited by M. L. W. Laistner in *Bedae Venerabilis Opera,* part 2, *Opera Exegetica 4,* 165–78. Corpus Christianorum: Series Latina 121. Turnholt: Brepols, 1983.

———. *The Old English Version of Bede's "Ecclesiastical History of the English People."* Edited and translated by Thomas Miller. The Early English Text Society 95. London: Oxford University Press, 1890. Reprinted 1959.

Benedict of Nursia. *Regula.* Edited and translated by Timothy Fry in *The Rule of St. Benedict: In Latin and English with Notes.* Collegeville, MN: Liturgical Press, 1981.

Berengar of Tours. *In Purgatoria epistola contra Almannum.* In Montclos, *Lanfranc et Bérenger,* 531–38.

———. *Rescriptum contra Lanfrannum (De sacra coena).* Edited by R. B. C. Huygens. Corpus Christianorum: Continuatio Mediaevalis 84. Turnhout: Brepols, 1988.

*Brut y Tywysogyon.* Translated by Thomas Jones in *Brut y Tywysogyon or The Chronicle of the Princes: Peniarth MS. 20 Version.* Board of Celtic Studies, University of Wales, History and Law Series 11. Cardiff: University of Wales Press, 1952.

Byrhtferth of Ramsey. *Enchiridion.* Edited by Peter S. Baker and Michael Lapidge in *Byrhtferth's Enchiridion.* Early English Text Society, Original Series, 15. Oxford: Oxford University Press, 1995.

Caesarius of Heisterbach. *Dialogus miraculorum.* Edited by Joseph Strange. 2 vols. Reprint edition. Ridgewood, NJ: Gregg Press, 1966.

*Cartularium Saxonicum: A Collection of Charters Relating to Anglo-Saxon History.* Edited by Walter de Gray Birch. 3 vols. London: Whiting and Co., Charles H. Clark, 1885–93.

Cassiodorus. *Variae.* Edited by Theodore Mommsen. Monumenta Germaniae Historica, Auctores antiquissimi 12. Berlin: Weismann, 1970.

*Charters of Abingdon Abbey.* Edited by S. E. Kelly. 2 parts. Anglo-Saxon Charters 7 and 8. Oxford: Oxford University Press, 2000.

Chaucer, Geoffrey. "The Compleint of Chaucer to his Empty Purse." In *The Complete Works of Geoffrey Chaucer,* vol. 1, *Romaunt of the Rose, Minor Poems,* 405–6. Edited by Walter W. Skeat. 2nd edition. Oxford: Clarendon Press, 1899.

*Codex Diplomaticus Aevi Saxonici.* Edited by J. M. Kemble. Publications of the English Historical Society. 6 vols. London: Sumptibus Societatis, 1839–48.

*Councils and Synods with Other Documents Relating to the English Church,* vol. 1, *A.D. 871–1204.* Edited by D. Whitelock, M. Brett, and C. N. L. Brooke. Oxford: Clarendon Press, 1981.

*De obitu Willelmi.* Edited and translated by Elisabeth M. C. Van Houts in *The "Gesta Normannorum Ducum" of William of Jumièges, Orderic Vitalis, and Robert of Torigni,* 2:184–90. Oxford Medieval Texts. Oxford: Clarendon Press, 1995.

*De origine gigantum.* Edited by James P. Carley and Julia Crick in "Constructing Albion's Past: An Annotated Edition of *De origine gigantum,*" *Arthurian Literature* 13 (1995): 41–114. Translated by Ruth Evans in "Gigantic Origins: An Annotated Translation of *De origine gigantum,*" *Arthurian Literature* 16 (1998): 197–211.

*De ortu et obitu patrum.* Edited and translated into Spanish by César Chaparro Gómez in *Isidoro de Sevilla, De Ortu et Obitu Patrum.* Auteurs latins du moyen âge. Paris: Société d'éditions "les belles lettres," 1985.

*Des Grantz Geanz.* Edited by Georgine E. Brereton in *Des Grantz Geanz: An Anglo-Norman Poem.* Medium aevum monographs 2. Oxford: Basil

Blackwell for the Society for the Study of Mediæval Languages and Literature, 1937.

*De translatione SS. Ebrulfi abbatis Uticensis et Ansberti.* Edited by Jean Mabillon in *Acta Sanctorum ordinis S. Benedicti in sæculorum classes distributa,* saec. V, 7:227–28. Venice: S. Coleti & J. Bettinelli, n.d.

Dicuil. *Liber de mensura orbis terrae.* Edited and translated by J. J. Tierney and L. Bieler. Scriptores Latini Hiberniae 6. Dublin: Dublin Institute for Advanced Studies, 1967.

*Domesday Book: A Complete Translation.* Edited by Ann Williams and G. H. Martin. Alecto Historical Editions. Harmondsworth: Penguin, 1992.

Dudo of Saint-Quentin. *De moribus et actis primorum Normanniae ducum.* Edited by Jules Lair. Société des antiquaires de Normandie. Caen: F. Le Blanc-Hardel, 1865. Translated by Eric Christiansen in *History of the Normans* (Woodbridge: Boydell Press, 1998).

Eadmer. *Historia novorum in Anglia.* Edited by Martin Rule. Rolls Series 81. London: Longman et al., 1884.

———. *Vita Anselmi.* Edited and translated by Richard W. Southern in *The Life of St. Anselm by Eadmer.* Oxford Medieval Texts. Oxford: Clarendon Press, 1972.

Flodoard of Reims. *Annales.* Edited by Philippe Lauer. Collection de textes pour servir à l'étude et à l'enseignement de l'histoire 39. Paris: A. Picard et fils, 1905.

Fulcher of Chartres. *Historia Hierosolymitana.* Patrologia Latina 155:823–942.

Gardiner, Eileen, ed. *Visions of Heaven and Hell Before Dante.* New York: Italica Press, 1989.

Geoffrey Malaterra. *De rebus gestis Rogerii Calabriae et Siciliae comitis et Roberti Guiscardi ductis fratris eius.* Edited by Ernesto Pontieri. Rerum Italicarum Scriptores 5, part 1. Bologna: Nicola Zanichelli, 1927–28.

Geoffrey of Monmouth. *Historia regum Brittaniae.* Edited by Neil Wright in *The "Historia Regum Britannie" of Geoffrey of Monmouth,* vol. 1, *Bern, Burgerbibliothek, MS. 568.* Cambridge: D. S. Brewer, 1984. Translated by Lewis Thorpe in *The History of the Kings of Britain* (Harmondsworth: Penguin, 1966).

Gerald of Wales. *Expugnatio Hibernica.* Edited and translated by A. B. Scott and F. X. Martin in *Expugnatio Hibernica: The Conquest of Ireland.* A New History of Ireland, Ancillary Publications 3. Dublin: Royal Irish Academy, 1978.

———. *Topographica Hibernica.* Edited by James F. Dimock in *Giraldi Cambrensis Opera,* 5:1–204. Rolls Series 21. London: Longmans, Green,

Reader, and Dyer, 1867. Translated by J. O'Meara in *The History and Topography of Ireland* (Harmondsworth: Penguin, 1982).

*Gesta Francorum et aliorum Hierosolimitanorum.* Edited and translated by Rosalind Hill in *The Deeds of the Franks and the Other Pilgrims to Jerusalem.* Medieval Texts. London: Thomas Nelson and Sons, 1962.

Gregory VII, Pope. *Registrum.* Edited by Erich Caspar in *Das Register Gregors VII.* Monumenta Germaniae Historica Epp 2. 2 vols. Berlin: Weidmann, 1955.

Gregory the Great. *Dialogues.* Edited by Adalbert de Vogüe. 2 vols. Sources chrétiennes 260. Paris: Éditions du Cerf, 1979.

———. *Moralia in Iob.* Edited by Marcus Adriaen. Corpus Christianorum: Series Latina 143. 3 vols. Turnholt: Brepols, 1979–85.

Guitmund of Aversa. *De corpore et sanguine Domini.* Edited and translated into Italian by Luciano Orabona in *La "verità" dell'eucharistia: De corporis et sanguinis Christi veritate.* Chiese del mezzogiorno, Fonti e studi 6. Naples: Edizioni scientifiche italiane, 1995. Latin text also in *Patrologia Latina* 149:1427–1508.

Guy of Amiens. *Carmen de Hastingae proelio.* Edited and translated by Frank Barlow in *The "Carmen de Hastingae proelio" of Guy Bishop of Amiens.* 2nd edition. Oxford Medieval Texts. Oxford: Clarendon Press, 1999.

Henry of Huntingdon. *Historia Anglorum.* Edited and translated by Diana Greenway in *Historia Anglorum: The History of the English People.* Oxford Medieval Texts. Oxford: Clarendon Press, 1996.

Hugh of Flavingy. *Chronicon. Patrologia Latina* 154:9–404.

Hugh of Saint-Victor. *De tribus maximis circumstantiis gestorum.* Edited by William M. Green in "Hugo of St. Victor: *De Tribus Maximis Circumstantiis Gestorum.*" *Speculum* 18, no. 4 (1943): 484–93.

Isidore of Seville. *De natura rerum.* Edited by Jacques Fontaine in *Isidore de Séville, Traité de la nature.* Bibliothèque de l'école des hautes études hispaniques 28. Bordeaux: Féret et fils, 1960.

———. *Etymologiarum libri xx.* Edited and translated into Spanish by Jose Oroz Reta and Manuel A. Marcos Casquero in *Etimologías.* Biblioteca de Autores Cristianos 433–34. 2 vols. Madrid: Editorial Catolica, 1982–83.

Jerome. *Vita S. Pauli eremitae.* Translated and edited by Carolinne White in *Early Christian Lives,* 71–84. Harmondsworth: Penguin, 1998.

John of Worcester. *Chronica.* Edited and translated in *The Chronicle of John of Worcester,* vols. 2 and 3. Vol. 2 edited by R. R. Darlington and P. McGurk

and translated by Jennifer Bray and P. McGurk. Vol. 3 edited and translated by P. McGurk. Oxford Medieval Texts. Oxford: Clarendon Press,
1995–98.

Jordanes. *Getica*. Edited by Theodore Mommsen. Monumenta Germaniae Historica, Auctores antiquissimi, vol. 5, part 1, 51–138. Berlin: Weidmann,
1882.

Joynes, Andrew, ed. *Medieval Ghost Stories: An Anthology of Miracles, Marvels and Prodigies*. Woodbridge: Boydell Press, 2001.

Landes, Richard, and Catherine Paupert, eds. *Naissance d'apôtre: la vie de saint
Martial de Limoges*. Turnhout: Brepols, 1991.

Lanfranc. *De corpore et sanguine Domini*. Patrologia Latina 150:407–42.

———. *Epistolae*. Edited and translated by Helen Clover and Margaret Gibson in *The Letters of Lanfranc Archbishop of Canterbury*. Oxford Medieval Texts. Oxford: Clarendon Press, 1979.

Laȝamon. *Brut*. Edited by G. L. Brook and R. F. Leslie. 2 vols. Early English
Text Society, Original Series, 250 and 277. London: Oxford University
Press, 1963.

*Liber Eliensis*. Edited by E. O. Blake. Camden Third Series 92. London: Royal
Historical Society, 1962.

Moore, R. I., ed. and trans. *The Birth of Popular Heresy*. Medieval Academy
Reprints for Teaching 33. Toronto: University of Toronto Press, 1995.

Orderic Vitalis. *Historia Ecclesiastica*. Edited and translated by Marjorie Chibnall in *The Ecclesiastical History of Orderic Vitalis*. Oxford Medieval
Texts. 6 vols. Oxford: Clarendon Press, 1969–80.

———. *Historia Ecclesiastica*. Edited by Auguste Le Prévost in *Orderici Vitalis Historiæ Ecclesiasticæ libri tredecim*. Société de l'histoire de France.
5 vols. Paris: Julius Renouard et socios, 1838–55.

———. Interpolations in William of Jumièges, *Gesta Normannorum Ducum*.
Edited and translated by Elisabeth M. C. Van Houts in *The "Gesta Normannorum Ducum" of William of Jumièges, Orderic Vitalis, and Robert of Torigni*. Oxford Medieval Texts. 2 vols. Oxford: Clarendon Press,
1992–95.

———. "Vers attribués à Orderic Vital." Edited by Léopold Delisle. *Annuaire-
bulletin de la Société de l'histoire de France* 1 (1863): 1–13.

Orosius. *Historiarum adversus paganos libri septem*. Edited by Marie-Pierre
Arnaud-Lindet in *Orose: Histoires (Contre les Païens)*. 3 vols. Paris: Les
Belles Lettres, 1990. Translated by Roy J. Deferrari in *The Seven Books
of History Against the Pagans*, Fathers of the Church 50 (Washington,
DC: The Catholic University of America Press, 1964).

Otto of Freising. *Historia de duabus civitatibus.* Edited by Adolf Hofmeister in
*Ottonis episcopi Frisingensis Chronica: sive, Historia de duabus civitati-*
*bus.* Monumenta Germaniae Historica, Scriptores rerum Germanicarum,
45. Reprint. Hanover: Hahn, 1984. Translated by Charles Christopher
Mierow in *The Two Cities: A Chronicle of Universal History to the Year*
*1146 A.D., by Otto, Bishop of Freising,* edited by Austin P. Evans and
Charles Knapp, Records of Western Civilization (New York: Columbia
University Press, 2002).

*Patrologia Latina.* Ed. J.-P. Migne. 217 vols. Paris: Apud Garnieri Fratres,
1844–64.

Paul the Deacon. *Historia Langobardorum.* Edited by Ludwig Berthemann
and Georg Waitz. Monumenta Germaniae Historica, Scriptores rerum
Germanicarum. Hannover: Hahn, 1878.

Peter the Venerable. *Contra Petrobrusianos hereticos.* Edited by James Fearns.
Corpus Christianorum: Continuatio Mediaevalis 10. Turnholt: Brepols,
1968.

———. *De miraculis.* Edited by Dyonisia Bouthillier. Corpus Christianorum:
Continuatio Mediaevalis 83. Turnholt: Brepols, 1988.

Pliny the Elder. *Naturalis historia.* Edited and translated by H. Rackham,
W. H. S. Jones, and D. E. Eichholz. Loeb Classical Library. 10 vols. Cambridge, MA: Harvard University Press, 1938–63.

*Quid significent duodecim candelae.* Edited by Cyrille Vogel and Reinhard
Elze in *Le pontifical Romano-Germanique du dixième siècle,* vol. 1, *Le*
*texte,* 90–121. Studi e testi 226. Vatican City: Biblioteca Apostolica Van-
ticana, 1963. Translated by Brian Repsher in *The Rite of Church Dedi-*
*cation in the Early Medieval Era* (Lewiston: Edwin Mellen Press, 1998),
171–93.

Raoul Glaber. *Historiarum libri quinque.* Edited and translated by John France
in *Rodulfus Glaber Opera.* Oxford Medieval Texts. Oxford: Clarendon
Press, 1989.

———. *Vita Domni Willelmi Abbatis.* Edited by Neithard Bulst and translated by John France and Paul Reynolds in *Rodulfus Glaber Opera.* Oxford Medieval Texts. Oxford: Clarendon Press, 1989.

*Recueil des actes de Charles III le Simple, Roi de France (893–923).* Edited
by Philippe Lauer. Chartes et diplômes relatifs à l'histoire de France 9.
Paris: Imprimerie nationale, 1949.

*Recueil des actes des ducs de Normandie (911–1066).* Edited by Marie Fau-
roux. Mémoires de la Société des antiquaires de Normandie 36. Caen: Société des antiquaires de Normandie, 1961.

Richer of Reims. *Historiarum libri quatuor.* Edited by Hartmut Hoffman in *Richer von Saint-Remi: Historiae.* Monumenta Germaniae Historica, Scriptores rerum Germanicarum, 38. Hannover: Hahn, 2000.

Robert of Torigni. Interpolation in William of Jumièges, *Gesta Normannorum Ducum.* Edited and translated by Elisabeth M. C. Van Houts in *The "Gesta Normannorum Ducum" of William of Jumièges, Orderic Vitalis, and Robert of Torigni.* Oxford Medieval Texts. 2 vols. Oxford: Clarendon Press, 1992–95.

Sandqvist, Sven, ed. *La vie de saint Évroul: Poème normand du XIVe siècle, publié avec introduction, notes et glossaire.* Études romanes de Lund 48. Lund: Lund University Press, 1992.

Saxo Grammaticus. *Gesta Danorum.* Edited by J. Olrik and H. Ræder in *Saxonis Gesta Danorum.* 2 vols. Copenhagen: Levin and Munksgaard, 1931–57.

Thietmar of Merseburg. *Chronicon.* Edited by Robert Holtzmann in *Die Chronik des Bischofs Thietmar von Merseburg und ihre Korveier Überarbeitung.* Monumenta Germaniae Historica, Scriptorum rerum Germanicarum, n.s. 9. Berlin: Weidmann, 1935. Translated into English by David A. Warner in *Ottonian Germany: The "Chronicon" of Thietmar of Merseburg,* Manchester Medieval Sources (Manchester: Manchester University Press, 2001).

*The Thorney Annals, 963–1412 A.D.: An Edition and Translation.* Edited and translated by Cyril Hart. Lewiston: Edwin Mellen Press, 1997.

*Vita Eadwardi.* Edited and translated by Frank Barlow in *The Life of King Edward who Rests at Westminster, attributed to a Monk of Saint-Bertin.* 2nd edition. Oxford Medieval Texts. Oxford: Clarendon Press, 1992.

Wace. *Roman de Brut.* Edited and translated by Judith Weiss in *Wace's "Roman de Brut": A History of the British.* Exeter Medieval English Texts and Studies. Exeter: University of Exeter Press, 1999.

———. *Roman de Rou.* Translated by Glyn S. Burgess with the text of Anthony J. Holden and notes by Glyn S. Burgess and Elisabeth Van Houts. St. Helier: Société Jersiaise, 2002.

Walter Map. *De nugis curialium.* Edited and translated by M. R. James in *De nugis curialium = Courtiers' Trifles.* Revised by C. N. L. Brooke and R. A. B. Mynors. Oxford Medieval Texts. Oxford: Clarendon Press, 1983.

William of Apulia. *Gesta Roberti Wiscardi.* Edited and translated into French by Marguerite Mathieu in *La Geste de Robert Guiscard.* Testi e monumenti 4. Palermo: Istituto siciliano di studi bizantini e neoellenici, 1961.

William of Conches. *Dragmaticon Philosophiae.* Edited by Italo Ronca. Corpus
  Christianorum: Continuatio Mediaevalis 152. Turnholt: Brepols, 1997.
  Translated into English by Italo Ronca and Matthew Curr in *A Dialogue
  on Natural Philosophy,* Notre Dame Texts in Medieval Culture 2 (Notre
  Dame, IN: University of Notre Dame Press, 1997).
William of Jumièges. *Gesta Normannorum Ducum.* Edited and translated by
  Elisabeth M. C. Van Houts in *The "Gesta Normannorum Ducum" of Wil-
  liam of Jumièges, Orderic Vitalis, and Robert of Torigni.* Oxford Medieval
  Texts. 2 vols. Oxford: Clarendon Press, 1992–95.
William of Malmesbury. *Gesta Pontificum Anglorum.* Edited by N. E. S. A.
  Hamilton. Rolls Series 52. London: Longman et al., 1870. Translated by
  David Preest in *The Deeds of the Bishops of England* (Woodbridge: Boy-
  dell Press, 2002).
———. *Gesta regum Anglorum.* Edited and translated in *Gesta Regum An-
  glorum: The History of the English Kings.* 2 vols. Vol. 1: *Gesta Regum
  Anglorum: The History of the English Kings.* Edited and translated by
  R. A. B. Mynors. Completed by R. M. Thomson and M. Winterbottom.
  Vol. 2: *General Introduction and Commentary.* By R. M. Thomson with
  M. Winterbottom. Oxford Medieval Texts. Oxford: Clarendon Press,
  1998–99.
William of Newburgh. *Historia rerum Anglicarum.* Edited and translated by
  P. G. Walsh and M. J. Kennedy. Warminster: Aris & Phillips, 1988.
William of Poitiers. *Gesta Guillelmi.* Edited and translated by R. H. C. Davis
  and Marjorie Chibnall in *The "Gesta Guillelmi" of William of Poitiers.*
  Oxford Medieval Texts. Oxford: Clarendon Press, 1998.

## SECONDARY SOURCES

*Les abbayes de Normandie, actes du XIIIe congrès des sociétés historiques et
  archéologiques de Normandie.* Rouen: Imprimerie LECERF, 1979.
Abrams, Lesley. "England, Normandy and Scandinavia." In *A Companion
  to the Anglo-Norman World,* ed. Christopher Harper-Bill and Elisabeth
  Van Houts, 43–62. Woodbridge: Boydell Press, 2003.
Abulafia, David. "The Norman Kingdom of Africa and the Norman Expedi-
  tions to Majorca and the Muslim Mediterranean." *Anglo-Norman Studies* 7 (1985): 26–49.
Ahmad, S. Maqbul. "Cartography of al-Sharīf al-Idrīsī." In Harley and Woodward, *History of Cartography,* vol. 2, book 1, 156–74.

Aigrain, René. *L'hagiographie: Ses sources—ses méthodes—son histoire.* Subsidia hagiographica 80. Reprint, with additional bibliography by Robert Godding. Brussels: Société des Bollandistes, 2000.

Albu, Emily. *The Normans and their Histories: Propaganda, Myth, and Subversion.* Woodbridge: Boydell Press, 2001.

Alexander, Philip S. "Jerusalem as the *Omphalos* of the World: On the History of a Geographical Concept." In Levine, *Jerusalem: Its Sanctity and Centrality to Judaism, Christianity, and Islam,* 104–19.

Althoff, Gerd, Johannes Fried, and Patrick J. Geary, eds. *Medieval Concepts of the Past: Ritual, Memory, Historiography.* Publications of the German Historical Institute. Cambridge: Cambridge University Press, 2002.

Ames, Kenneth L. "Ideologies in Stone: Meanings in Victorian Gravestones." *Journal of Popular Culture* 14, no. 4 (1981): 641–56.

Anderson, Benedict. *Imagined Communities: Reflections on the Origin and Spread of Nationalism.* Revised edition. London: Verso, 1983.

Ariès, Philippe. *The Hour of Our Death.* Translated by Helen Weaver. New York: Alfred A. Knopf, 1981.

———. *Western Attitudes toward Death: From the Middle Ages to the Present.* Translated by Patricia M. Ranum. Johns Hopkins Symposia in Comparative History. Baltimore: Johns Hopkins University Press, 1974.

Arnoux, Mathieu. *Mineurs, férons et maîtres de forge: étude sur la produciton du fer dans la Normandie du Moyen Âge, Xie–XVe siècles.* Mémoires de la Section d'histoire des sciences et des techniques 1. Paris: Éditions du CTHS, 1993.

Asbridge, Thomas S. *The Creation of the Principality of Antioch, 1098–1130.* Woodbridge: Boydell Press, 2000.

Ashe, Geoffrey. *Camelot and the Vision of Albion.* London: Heinemann, 1971.

Ashley, Kathleen, and Pamela Sheingorn. "The Translations of Foy: Bodies, Texts and Places." In Ellis and Tixier, *Medieval Translator,* 29–49.

Bachelard, Gaston. *The Poetics of Space.* Translated by Maria Jolas. Reprint. Boston: Beacon Press, 1994.

Baker, Alan R. H. *Geography and History: Bridging the Divide.* Cambridge Studies in Historical Geography 36. Cambridge: Cambridge University Press, 2003.

Barlow, Frank. *Edward the Confessor.* English Monarchs. Berkeley and Los Angeles: University of California Press, 1970.

Barnes, Trevor J., and James S. Duncan. "Introduction: Writing Worlds." In *Writing Worlds: Discourse, Text, and Metaphor in the Representation of Landscape,* ed. Trevor J. Barnes and James S. Duncan, 1–17. London: Routledge, 1992.

Barrow, G. W. S. *Scotland and Its Neighbours in the Middle Ages.* London: Hambledon, 1992.

Barrow, Julia. "Chester's Earliest Regatta?: Edgar's Dee-Rowing Revisited." *Early Medieval Europe* 10, no. 1 (2001): 81–93.

Bartlett, Robert. *Gerald of Wales, 1146–1223.* Oxford: Clarendon Press, 1982.

———. *The Making of Europe: Conquest, Colonization, and Cultural Change, 950–1350.* Princeton: Princeton University Press, 1993.

———. "Medieval and Modern Concepts of Race and Ethnicity." *Journal of Medieval and Early Modern Studies* 31, no. 1 (2001): 39–56.

Basso, Keith H. *Wisdom Sits in Places: Landscape and Language Among the Western Apache.* Albuquerque: University of New Mexico Press, 1996.

Bates, David. "The Conqueror's Adolescence." *Anglo-Norman Studies* 25 (2002): 1–18.

———. *Normandy Before 1066.* London: Longman, 1982.

———. *William the Conqueror.* Stroud: Tempus, 1989.

Bauduin, Pierre. "Le baron, le château et la motte: baronnage et maîtrise du territoire châtelain dans la seigneurie de Breteuil (XIe–XIIe siècles)." In Fajal, *"Autour du château médiéval,"* 37–53.

———. "Une famille châtelaine sur les confins normanno-manceaux: les Géré (Xe–XIIIe s.)." *Archéologie médiévale* 22 (1992): 309–56.

———. *La première Normandie (Xe–XIe siècles): Sur les frontières de la haute Normandie: identité et construction d'une principauté.* Caen: Press universitaires de Caen, 2004.

Beck, Bernard. "Les salles capitulaires des abbayes de Normandie: éléments originaux de l'architecture monastique médiévale." *L'information d'histoire de l'art* 18, no. 5 (1973): 204–15.

Beckerman, John S. "Succession in Normandy, 1087, and in England, 1066: The Role of Testamentary Custom." *Speculum* 47, no. 2 (1972): 258–60.

Beckwith, Sarah. *Christ's Body: Identity, Culture, and Society in Late Medieval Writings.* London: Routledge, 1993.

Benjamin, Walter. "Theses on the Philosophy of History." In *Illuminations,* ed. with an introduction by Hannah Arendt, trans. Harry Zohn, 253–64. New York: Schocken Books, 1968.

Bennett, Matthew. *Campaigns of the Norman Conquest.* Essential Histories. Oxford: Osprey Publishing, 2001.

———. "Norman Naval Activity in the Mediterranean, c. 1060–c. 1108." *Anglo-Norman Studies* 15 (1992): 41–58.

———. "Violence in Eleventh-Century Normandy: Feud, Warfare and Politics." In *Violence and Society in the Early Medieval West*, edited by Guy Halsall, 126–40. Woodbridge: Boydell Press, 1998.

Benson, Robert L., and Giles Constable, eds., with Carol D. Lanham. *Renaissance and Renewal in the Twelfth Century*. UCLA Center for Medieval and Renaissance Studies. Cambridge, MA: Harvard University Press, 1982.

Bickerman, Elias J. "*Origines Gentium*." *Classical Philology* 47 (1952): 65–81.

Biernoff, Suzannah. *Sight and Embodiment in the Middle Ages*. New York: Palgrave Macmillan, 2002.

Bindoff, S. T. "The Stuarts and Their Style." *English Historical Review* 60, no. 237 (1945): 192–216.

Binski, Paul. *Medieval Death: Ritual and Representation*. Ithaca: Cornell University Press, 1996.

Birkholz, Daniel. *The King's Two Maps: Cartography and Culture in Thirteenth-Century England*. Studies in Medieval History and Culture. New York: Routledge, 2004.

Blacker, Jean. *The Faces of Time: Portrayal of the Past in Old French and Latin Historical Narrative of the Anglo-Norman* Regnum. Austin: University of Texas Press, 1994.

Blake, E. O. "The Formation of the 'Crusade Idea.'" *Journal of Ecclesiastical History* 21, no. 1 (1970): 11–31.

Blake, William. *A Descriptive Catalogue*. In Keynes, *Complete Writings of William Blake*, 563–86.

———. *King Edward the Third*. In Keynes, *Complete Writings of William Blake*, 17–33.

———. *A Vision of The Last Judgment*. In Keynes, *Complete Writings of William Blake*, 604–17.

Boesch Gajano, Sofia. "Des *Loca sanctorum* aux espaces de la sainteté étapes de l'historiographie hagiographique." *Revue d'histoire ecclésiastique* 95, no. 3 (2000): 48–70.

Bouchard, Constance Brittain. *Sword, Miter, and Cloister: Nobility and the Church in Burgundy, 980–1198*. Ithaca: Cornell University Press, 1987.

Bouet, Pierre. "La 'Mesnie Hellequin' dans l'*Historia Ecclesiastica* d'Ordéric Vital." In *Mélanges François Kerlouégan*, ed. Danièle Conso, Nicole Fick, and Bruno Poulle, 61–78. Annales littéraires de l'Université de Besançon 515. Institut Félix Graffiot 15. Paris: Université de Besançon, 1994.

Boureau, Alain. "The Sacrality of One's Own Body in the Middle Ages." Translated by Benjamin Semple. *Yale French Studies* 86 (1994): 5–17.

Bourgne, Florence. "Translating Saints' Lives into the Vernacular: *Translatio Studii* and *Furta Sacra* (Translation as Theft)." In Ellis and Tixier, *Medieval Translator,* 50–63.

Bowman, Glenn. "'Mapping History's Redemption': Eschatology and Topography in the *Itinerarium Burdigalense.*" In Levine, *Jerusalem: Its Sanctity and Centrality to Judaism, Christianity, and Islam,* 163–87.

Bozóky, Edina. "Voyages de reliques et démonstration du pouvoir aux temps féodaux." In *Voyages et voyageurs au moyen âge: XXVIe congrès de la S.H.M.E.S.,* 267–280. Société des historiens médiévistes de l'enseignement supérieur public, Série histoire ancienne et médiévale 39. Paris: Publications de la Sorbonne, 1996.

Brague, Rémi. *The Wisdom of the World: The Human Experience of the Universe in Western Thought.* Translated by Teresa Lavender Fagan. Chicago: University of Chicago Press, 2003.

Braude, Benjamin. "The Sons of Noah and the Construction of Ethnic and Geographical Identities in the Medieval and Early Modern Periods." *William and Mary Quarterly,* 3rd ser., 54, no. 1 (1997): 103–42.

Braudel, Fernand. *The Mediterranean and the Mediterranean World in the Age of Philip II.* Translated by Siân Reynolds. 2 vols. 2nd ed. Berkeley and Los Angeles: University of California Press, 1995.

Braunfels, Wolfgang. *Monasteries of Western Europe: The Architecture of the Orders.* Translated by Alastair Laing. London: Thames and Hundon, 1972.

Breen, Katharine. "*Habitus* and the Discipline of Reading in Late Medieval England." Ph.D. diss., University of California, Berkeley, 2003.

Breisach, Ernst, ed. *Classical Rhetoric and Medieval Historiography.* Studies in Medieval Culture 19. Kalamazoo, MI: Medieval Institute Publications, 1985.

Brown, Peter. *The Body and Society: Men, Women, and Sexual Renunciation in Early Christianity.* Lectures on the History of Religion, n. s., 13. New York: Columbia University Press, 1988.

———. *The Cult of the Saints: Its Rise and Function in Latin Christianity.* The Haskell Lectures on History of Religions, n. s., 2. Chicago: University of Chicago Press, 1981.

Brundage, James A. "'Cruce Signari': The Rite for Taking the Cross in England." *Traditio* 22 (1966): 289–310.

Busse, Wilhelm G. "Brutus in Albion: Englands Gründungssage." In *Herkunft und Ursprung: Historische und mythische Formen der Legitimation,* ed. Peter Wunderli, 207–23. Sigmaringen: Jan Thorbecke Verlag, 1994.

Bynum, Caroline Walker. *Metamorphosis and Identity.* New York: Zone Books, 2001.

———. "Miracles and Marvels: The Limits of Alterity." In *Vita religiosa im Mittelalter: Festschrift für Kaspar Elm zum 70. Geburtstag,* ed. Franz J. Felten and Nikolas Jaspert with Stephanie Haarländer, 799–817. Berlin: Duncker & Humblot, 1999.

———. *The Resurrection of the Body in Western Christianity, 200–1336.* Lectures on the History of Religions, n.s., 15. New York: Columbia University Press, 1995.

———. "Why All the Fuss about the Body? A Medievalist's Perspective." In *Beyond the Cultural Turn: New Directions in the Study of Society and Culture,* ed. Victoria E. Bonnell and Lynn Hunt, 241–80. Studies in the History of Society and Culture. Berkeley and Los Angeles: University of California Press, 1999. Originally published in *Critical Inquiry* 22 (1995): 1–33.

Caciola, Nancy. "Spirits Seeking Bodies: Death, Possession and Communal Memory in the Middle Ages." In *The Place of the Dead: Death and Remembrance in Late Medieval and Early Modern Europe,* ed. Bruce Gordon and Peter Marshall, 66–86. Cambridge: Cambridge University Press, 2000.

———. "Wraiths, Revenants and Ritual in Medieval Culture." *Past and Present* 152 (1996): 3–45.

Callahan, Daniel F. "Jerusalem in the Monastic Imaginations of the Early Eleventh Century." *The Haskins Society Journal* 6 (1994): 119–27.

Campbell, Gordon Lindsay. *Strange Creatures: Anthropology in Antiquity.* London: Duckworth, 2006.

Campbell, James. "The United Kingdom of England: The Anglo-Saxon Achievement." In *Uniting the Kingdom? The Making of British History,* ed. Alexander Grant and Keith J. Stringer, 31–47. London: Routledge, 1995.

Campbell, Mary B. "'The Object of One's Gaze': Landscape, Writing, and Early Medieval Pilgrimage." In Westrem, *Discovering New Worlds: Essays on Medieval Exploration and Imagination,* 3–15.

Carozzi, Claude. "La géographie de l'au-delà et sa signification pendant le haut moyen âge." In *Popoli e paesi nella cultura altomedievale,* 2:423–81. Settimane di studio del Centro italiano di studi sull'alto medioevo 29. Spoleto: Centro italiano di studi sull'alto medioevo, 1983.

Carruthers, Mary J. *The Book of Memory: A Study of Memory in Medieval Culture.* Cambridge Studies in Medieval Literature 10. Cambridge: Cambridge University Press, 1990.

Carter, Paul. *The Road to Botany Bay: An Exploration of Landscape and History.* New York: Alfred A. Knopf, 1988.

Cassidy-Welch, Megan. *Monastic Spaces and their Meanings: Thirteenth-Century English Cistercian Monasteries.* Medieval Church Studies 1. Turnhout: Brepols, 2001.

Cavanaugh, William T. "The World in a Wafer: A Geography of the Eucharist as Resistance to Globalization." In *Catholicism and Catholicity: Eucharistic Communities in Historical and Contemporary Perspectives,* ed. Sarah Beckwith, 69–84. Oxford: Blackwell, 1999.

Cavill, Paul, ed. *The Christian Tradition in Anglo-Saxon England: Approaches to Current Scholarship and Teaching.* Christianity and Culture: Issues in Teaching and Research. Cambridge: D. S. Brewer, 2004.

Certeau, Michel de. *The Practice of Everyday Life.* Translated by Steven Rendall. Berkeley and Los Angeles: University of California Press, 1984.

Chadwick, Henry. "Ego Berengarius." *Journal of Theological Studies,* n.s., 40, no. 2 (1989): 414–45.

Chazelle, Celia. *The Crucified God in the Carolingian Era: Theology and Art of Christ's Passion.* Cambridge: Cambridge University Press, 2001.

Chenu, M.-D. *Nature, Man, and Society in the Twelfth Century: Essays on New Theological Perspectives in the Latin West.* Selected, edited, and translated by Jerome Taylor and Lester K. Little. Chicago: University of Chicago Press, 1968.

Chibnall, Marjorie. *Anglo-Norman England, 1066–1166.* Oxford: Basil Blackwell, 1986.

———. "Charter and Chronicle: The Use of Archive Sources by Norman Historians." In *Church and Government in the Middle Ages: Essays Presented to C.R. Cheney,* ed. C. N. L. Brooke et al., 1–17. Cambridge: Cambridge University Press, 1976. Reprinted in Chibnall, *Piety, Power and History,* no. XIX.

———. *The Debate on the Norman Conquest.* Issues in Historiography. Manchester: Manchester University Press, 1999.

———. "Les droits d'héritage selon Orderic Vital." *Revue historique de droit français et étranger,* 4th ser., 48 (1970): 347.

———. "Ecclesiastical Patronage and the Growth of Feudal Estates at the Time of the Norman Conquest." *Annales de Normandie* 8 (1958): 103–18.

———. "Feudal Society in Orderic Vitalis." *Anglo-Norman Studies* 1 (1979): 35–48, 199–202.

———. *The Normans.* The Peoples of Europe. Oxford: Blackwell, 2000.

———. "Orderic Vitalis on Castles." In Harper-Bill, Holdsworth, and Nelson, *Studies in Medieval History Presented to R. Allen Brown*, 43–56. Reprinted in Chibnall, *Piety, Power and History*, no. XVI.

———. *Piety, Power and History in Medieval England and Normandy.* Variorum Collected Studies Series. Aldershot: Ashgate/Variorum, 2000.

———. "Le privilège de libre élection dans les chartes de Saint-Évroult." *Annales de Normandie* 28 (1978): 341–42.

———. "A Twelfth-Century View of the Historical Church: Orderic Vitalis." In *The Church Retrospective: Papers Read at the 1995 Summer Meeting and the 1996 Winter Meeting of the Ecclesiastical History Society*, ed. Robert Swanson, 115–34. Studies in Church History 33. Woodbridge: Boydell Press for the Ecclesiastical History Society, 1997. Reprinted in Chibnall, *Piety, Power and History*, no. I.

———. *The World of Orderic Vitalis: Norman Monks and Norman Knights.* Woodbridge: Boydell Press, 1984.

Chitty, Derwas J. *The Desert a City: An Introduction to the Study of Egyptian and Palestinian Monasticism Under the Christian Empire.* Oxford: Basil Blackwell, 1966.

Clanchy, M. T. *From Memory to Written Record: England 1066–1307.* 2nd edition. Oxford: Blackwell, 1993.

Clarke, Katherine. *Between Geography and History: Hellenistic Constructions of the Roman World.* Oxford: Clarendon Press, 1999.

Classen, Peter. "*Res gestae*, Universal History, Apocalypse: Visions of Past and Future." In Benson and Constable, *Renaissance and Renewal*, 387–417.

Coleman, Janet. *Ancient and Medieval Memories: Studies in the Reconstruction of the Past.* Cambridge: Cambridge University Press, 1992.

Constable, Giles. "The Ideal of the Imitation of Christ." In Constable, *Three Studies in Medieval Religious and Social Thought*, 143–248. Cambridge: Cambridge University Press, 1995.

———. "Jerusalem and the Sign of the Cross (with particular reference to the cross of pilgrimage and crusading in the twelfth century)." In Levine, *Jerusalem: Its Sanctity and Centrality to Judaism, Christianity, and Islam*, 371–81.

———. "A Living Past: The Historical Environment of the Middle Ages." *Harvard Library Bulletin*, n.s., 1, no. 3 (1990): 49–70.

———. "Renewal and Reform in Religious Life: Concepts and Realities." In Benson and Constable, *Renaissance and Renewal*, 37–67.

Cosgrove, Denis. *Apollo's Eye: A Cartographic Genealogy of the Earth in the Western Imagination.* Baltimore: Johns Hopkins University Press, 2001.

Cowdrey, H. E. J. *The Age of Abbot Desiderius: Montecassino, the Papacy and the Normans in the Eleventh and Early Twelfth Centuries.* Oxford: Clarendon Press, 1983.

———. *Lanfranc: Scholar, Monk, and Archbishop.* Oxford: Oxford University Press, 2003.

———. "Lanfranc, the Papacy, and the See of Canterbury." In *Lanfranco di Pavia e l'Europa del secolo XI: nel IX centenario della morte (1089–1989),* ed. Giulio D'Onofrio, 439–500. Italia sacra (Herder editrice e libreria) 51. Rome: Herder, 1993. Reprinted in H. E. J. Cowdrey, *Popes and Church Reform in the Eleventh Century,* Variorum Collected Studies, no. X (Aldershot: Ashgate/Variorum, 2000).

———. "The Papacy and the Berengarian Controversy." In Ganz, Huygens, and Niewöhner, *Auctoritas und Ratio,* 109–38.

Cownie, Emma. *Religious Patronage in Anglo-Norman England, 1066–1135.* Royal Historical Society Studies in History, New Series. Woodbridge: Boydell Press, 1998.

Crouch, David. *The Beaumont Twins: The Roots and Branches of Power in the Twelfth Century.* Cambridge Studies in Medieval Life and Thought, 4th ser., 1. Cambridge: Cambridge University Press, 1986.

Curtius, Ernst Robert. *European Literature and the Latin Middle Ages.* Translated by Willard R. Trask. Bollingen Series 36. Princeton: Princeton University Press, 1953.

Dabon, Emmanuelle. "Saint-Évroult en pays d'Ouche." In *Saint-Évroult-Notre-Dame-du-Bois,* 1–13.

Dalché, Patrick Gautier. *Géographie et culture: la représentation de l'espace du VIe au XIIe siècle.* Variorum Collected Studies. Aldershot: Ashgate/Variorum, 1997.

Damian-Grint, Peter. *The New Historians of the Twelfth-Century Renaissance: Inventing Vernacular Authority.* Woodbridge: Boydell Press, 1999.

Damon, S. Foster. *A Blake Dictionary: The Ideas and Symbols of William Blake.* Rev. ed. Hanover: University Press of New England for Brown University Press, 1988.

Daniell, Christopher. *Death and Burial in Medieval England, 1066–1550.* London: Routledge, 1997.

Daniélou, Jean. "The Conception of History in the Christian Tradition," *Journal of Religion* 30 (1950): 171–79.

Daniels, Stephen, and Denis Cosgrove. "Introduction: Iconography and Landscape." In *The Iconography of Landscape: Essays on the Symbolic Rep-*

resentation, Design and Use of Past Environments, ed. Denis Cosgrove and Stephen Daniels, 1–10. Cambridge Studies in Historical Geography 9. Cambridge: Cambridge University Press, 1998.

Davies, R. R. Conquest, Coexistence, and Change: Wales, 1063–1415. The History of Wales 2. Oxford: Clarendon Press, University of Wales Press, 1987.

———. Domination and Conquest: The Experience of Ireland, Scotland and Wales, 1100–1300. The Wiles Lectures given at the Queen's University of Belfast, 1988. Cambridge: Cambridge University Press, 1990.

———. The First English Empire: Power and Identities in the British Isles, 1093–1343. The Ford Lectures delivered in the University of Oxford in Hilary Term 1998. Oxford: Oxford University Press, 2000.

Davis, R. H. C. The Normans and their Myth. London: Thames and Hudson, 1976.

D'Avray, David. "Some Franciscan Ideas about the Body." In Modern Questions about Medieval Sermons: Essays on Marriage, Death, History and Sanctity, ed. Nicole Bériou and David L. D'Avray, 155–74. Biblioteca di medioevo latino 11. Spoleto: Centro italiano di studi sull'alto medioevo, 1994.

Debord, André. "Remarques à propos des châtelains normands aux XIe et XIIe s." In Recueil d'études offert à Gabriel Désert, 327–36. Cahier des annales de Normandie 24. Caen: Musée de Normandie, 1992.

Decaëns, Joseph. "Les châteaux du XIe au XIIIe siècle dans l'actuel département de l'Orne: Essai d'inventaire et de classement." In Fajal, "Autour du château médiéval," 25–35.

Delano-Smith, Catherine, and Roger J. P. Kain. English Maps: A History. Toronto: University of Toronto Press, 1999.

Delisle, Léopold. Études sur la condition de la classe agricole et l'état de l'agriculture en Normandie au moyen-âge. Librairie spéciale pour l'histoire de la France et de ses anciennes provinces. Paris: Honoré Champion, 1903. Originally published Évreux: Impr. de A. Hérissey, 1851.

———. "Notes sur les manuscrits autographes d'Orderic Vital." In Matériaux pour l'édition de Guillaume de Jumièges, ed. Jules Lair, 7–27. Paris: n.p., 1910.

———. "Notice sur Orderic Vital." In Orderici Vitalis Historiæ Ecclesiasticæ libri tredecim, ed. Augustus Le Prévost, 1:i–cvi. Société de l'histoire de France. Paris: Julium Renouard et socios, 1838. Reprinted, with additional notes, in Orderic Vital et l'abbaye de Saint-Evroul, 1–77.

Deliyannis, Deborah Mauskopf, ed. *Historiography in the Middle Ages.* Leiden: Brill, 2003.

Deshays, Noël. *Mémoires pour servir à l'histoire des évêques de Lisieux.* Originally published in 1763. Reprinted as vol. 2 of H. de Formerville, *Histoire de l'ancien évêché-comté de Lisieux,* 2 vols. (Lisieux: E. Piel, 1873; repr., Brionne: Le Portulan, 1971).

Desloges, J., and Ph. Bernouis. "Milieu naturel, ressources du sol et du sous-sol: les conditions du peuplement de l'Orne." In *L'Orne,* ed. Philippe Bernouis, 44–49. Carte archéologique de la Gaule 61. Paris: Académie des inscriptions et belles-lettres, Conseil géneral de l'Orne, Ministère de la culture et de la communication, D.R.A.C. de Basse-Normandie, 1999.

Desvaux, Albert, and A.-L. Letacq. "Essai sur la bibliographie de l'abbaye de Saint-Évroult et du canton de la Ferté-Fresnel." *Bulletin de la Société historique et archéologique de l'Orne* 9, no. 1 (1890): 51–82, and 9, no. 2 (1890): 129–74.

Dodgshon, Robert A. *Society in Time and Space: A Geographical Perspective on Change.* Cambridge Studies in Historical Geography 27. Cambridge: Cambridge University Press, 1998.

Dolbeau, François. "Un vol de reliques dans le diocèse de Reims au milieu du XIe siècle." *Revue bénédictine* 91 (1981): 172–84.

Douglas, David. "Edward the Confessor, Duke William of Normandy, and the English Succession." *English Historical Review* 68, no. 269 (1953): 526–45.

———. *The Norman Achievement, 1050–1100.* Berkeley and Los Angeles: University of California Press, 1969.

———. "The Norman Episcopate Before the Norman Conquest." *Cambridge Historical Journal* 13, no. 2 (1957): 101–15. Also published in French as "Les évêques de Normandie (1035–1066)," *Annales de Normandie* 8 (1958): 87–102.

———. *The Norman Fate, 1100–1154.* Berkeley and Los Angeles: University of California Press, 1976.

———. "Rollo of Normandy." *English Historical Review* 57, no. 228 (1942): 417–36.

———. *William the Conqueror: The Norman Impact Upon England.* Berkeley and Los Angeles: University of California Press, 1967.

Draelants, Isabelle. "Le temps dans les textes historiographiques du Moyen Âge." In *Le temps qu'il fait au Moyen Âge: Phénomènes atmosphériques dans la littérature, la pensée scientifique et religieuse,* ed. Claude Thomasset and Joëlle Ducos, 91–138. Cultures et civilisations médiévales 15. Paris: Presses de l'Université de Paris-Sorbonne, 1998.

Drell, Joanna H. "Cultural Syncretism and Ethnic Identity: The Norman 'Conquest' of Southern Italy and Sicily." *Journal of Medieval History* 25, no. 3 (1999): 187–202.

Dumville, David N. "Between Alfred the Great and Edgar the Peacemaker: Æthelstan, First King of England." In Dumville, *Wessex and England from Alfred to Edgar: Six Essays on Political, Cultural, and Ecclesiastical Revival*, 141–71. Studies in Anglo-Saxon History. Woodbridge: Boydell Press, 1992.

———. "'Nennius' and the *Historia Brittonum*." *Studia Celtica* 10–11 (1975–76): 78–95.

Dutton, Paul Edward. *Charlemagne's Mustache and Other Cultural Clusters of a Dark Age*. The New Middle Ages. New York: Palgrave Macmillan, 2004.

Duval, Yvette. *Auprès des saints corps et âme: l'inhumation "ad sanctos" dans la chrétienté d'Orient et d'Occident du IIIe au VIIe siècle*. Paris: Études Augustiniennes, 1988.

Edson, Evelyn. *Mapping Time and Space: How Medieval Mapmakers Viewed Their World*. The British Library Studies in Map History 1. London: The British Library, 1997.

———. "World Maps and Easter Tables: Medieval Maps in Context." *Imago Mundi* 48 (1996): 25–42.

Edson, E., and E. Savage-Smith. *Medieval Views of the Cosmos*. Oxford: Bodleian Library, University of Oxford, 2004.

Ellis, Roger, and René Tixier, eds. *The Medieval Translator/Traduire au Moyen Âge*. Vol. 5. Proceedings of the International Conference of Conques (26–29 July 1993). Turnhout: Brepols, 1996.

Englisch, Brigitte. *Ordo orbis terrae: Die Weltsicht in den* Mappae mundi *des frühen und hohen Mittelalters*. Orbis mediaevalis, Vorstellungswelten des Mittelalters 3. Berlin: Akademie Verlag, 2002.

Esmeijer, Anna C. *Divina Quaternitas: A Preliminary Study in the Method and Application of Visual Exegesis*. Assen: Van Gorcum, 1978.

Evans, Gillian. "St. Anselm and Sacred History." In *The Writing of History in the Middle Ages: Essays Presented to Richard William Southern*, ed. R. H. C. Davis and J. M Wallace-Hadrill, with R. J. A. I. Catto and M. H. Keen, 187–209. Oxford: Clarendon Press, 1981.

Fajal, Bruno, ed. *"Autour du château médiéval": Actes de rencontres historiques et archéologiques de l'Orne tenues à Alençon le 5 avril 1997.*

Mémoires et documents 1. Alençon: Société historique et archéologique de l'Orne, 1998.

Fanning, Steven. "Bede, Imperium, and the Bretwaldas." *Speculum* 66, no. 1 (1991): 1–26.

Farmer, Sharon. *Communities of Saint Martin: Legend and Ritual in Medieval Tours.* Ithaca: Cornell University Press, 1991.

Fichtenau, Heinrich. *Heretics and Scholars in the High Middle Ages, 1000–1200.* Translated by Denise A. Kaiser. University Park: Pennsylvania State University Press, 1998.

Finamore, Daniel, ed. *Maritime History as World History: New Perspectives on Maritime History and Nautical Archaeology.* Gainesville: University Press of Florida; Salem, MA: Peabody Essex Museum, 2004.

Flanagan, Sabina. "Twelfth-Century Apocalyptic Imaginations and the Coming of the Antichrist." *Journal of Religious History* 24, no. 1 (2000): 57–69.

Formeville, H. de. *Histoire de l'ancien évêché-comté de Lisieux.* 2 vols. Lisieux: E. Piel, 1873. Reprinted Brionne: Le Portulan, 1971.

France, John. "The Occasion of the Coming of the Normans to Southern Italy." *Journal of Medieval History* 17, no. 3 (1991): 185–205.

———. "Le rôle de Jérusalem dans la piété du XIe siècle." In *Le partage du monde: échanges et colonisation dans la Méditerranée médiévale*, ed. Michel Balard and Alain Ducellier, 150–61. Byzantina sorbonensia 17. Paris: Publications de la Sorbonne, 1998.

Frank, Georgia. *The Memory of the Eyes: Pilgrims to Living Saints in Christian Late Antiquity.* Transformation of the Classical Heritage 30. Berkeley and Los Angeles: University of California Press, 2000.

Freeman, E. A. *The History of the Norman Conquest of England.* 6 vols. Oxford: Clarendon Press, 1867–79.

———. *Sketches of Travel in Normandy and Maine.* London: Macmillan, 1897.

———. *William the Conqueror.* Twelve English Statesmen. London: Macmillan, 1890.

Friedman, John Block. *The Monstrous Races in Medieval Art and Thought.* Cambridge, MA: Harvard University Press, 1981.

Fulton, Rachel. *From Judgment to Passion: Devotion to Christ and the Virgin Mary, 800–1200.* New York: Columbia University Press, 2002.

Gaddis, John Lewis. *The Landscape of History: How Historians Map the Past.* Oxford: Oxford University Press, 2002.

Galbraith, V. H. *Historical Research in Medieval England.* The Creighton Lecture in History, 1949. London: University of London, Athlone Press, 1951.

Galeron, Frédéric. "Promenade aux ruines du monastère de Saint-Évroult." *Revue normande* 1 (1830): 172–86.

*Gallia Christiana in provincias ecclesiasticas distributa: qua series et historia archiepiscoporum, episcoporum, et abbatum franciae vicinarumque ditionum.* . . . 16 vols. Reprint. Farnsborough: Gregg International, 1970. Orig. pub. Paris: Ex typographia regia, and others, 1715–1865.

Ganz, Peter, R. B. C. Huygens, and Friedrich Niewöhner, eds. *Auctoritas und Ratio: Studien zu Berengar von Tours.* Wolfenbütteler Mittelalter Studien 2. Weisbaden: Otto Harrassowitz, 1990.

Gazeau, Véronique. "Le souvenir des abbés bénédictins dans les abbayes normandes à la période ducale." In *Autour des morts: mémoire et identité; Actes du Ve colloque international sur la sociabilité Rouen, 19–21 novembre 1998,* ed. Olivier Dumoulin and Françoise Thelamon, 215–21. Publications de l'Université de Rouen 296. Rouen: Université de Rouen, 2001.

Geary, Patrick J. "Exchange and Interaction between the Living and the Dead in Early Medieval Society." In Geary, *Living with the Dead in the Middle Ages,* 77–92.

————. *Furta Sacra: Thefts of Relics in the Central Middle Ages.* Revised edition. Princeton: Princeton University Press, 1990.

————. "Land, Language and Memory in Europe, 700–1100." *Transactions of the Royal Historical Society,* 6th ser., 9 (1999): 169–84.

————. *Living with the Dead in the Middle Ages.* Ithaca: Cornell University Press, 1994.

————. "Oblivion Between Orality and Textuality in the Tenth Century." In Althoff, Fried, and Geary, *Medieval Concepts of the Past,* 111–22.

————. *Phantoms of Remembrance: Memory and Oblivion at the End of the First Millennium.* Princeton: Princeton University Press, 1994.

————. "Sacred Commodities: The Circulation of Medieval Relics." In Geary, *Living with the Dead in the Middle Ages,* 194–218. Originally published in *The Social Life of Things: Commodities in Cultural Perspective,* ed. Arjun Appadurai, 169–91 (Cambridge: Cambridge University Press, 1986).

Gibson, Margaret. *Lanfranc of Bec.* Oxford: Clarendon Press, 1978.

Gilles, Sealy. "Territorial Interpolations in the Old English Orosius." In Tomasch and Gilles, *Text and Territory,* 79–96.

Gillingham, John. "The Foundations of a Disunited Kingdom." In Gillingham, *The English in the Twelfth Century: Imperialism, National Identity and Political Values,* 93–109. Woodbridge: Boydell Press, 2000.

Ginzburg, Carlo. *The Night Battles: Witchcraft and Agrarian Cults in the Sixteenth and Seventeenth Centuries.* Translated by John and Anne Tedeschi. Baltimore: Johns Hopkins University Press, 1983.

Given-Wilson, Chris. *Chronicles: The Writing of History in Medieval England.* London: Hambledon and London, 2004.

Glacken, Clarence J. *Traces on the Rhodian Shore: Nature and Culture in Western Thought from Ancient Times to the End of the Eighteenth Century.* Berkeley and Los Angeles: University of California Press, 1967.

Glenn, Jason. *Politics and History in the Tenth Century: The Work and World of Richer of Reims.* Cambridge Studies in Medieval Life and Thought, Fourth Series, 60. Cambridge: Cambridge University Press, 2004.

Gobillot, René. "Notes d'histoire et d'archéologie sur l'abbaye de Saint-Évroul." In *Orderic Vital et l'abbaye de Saint-Evroul,* 103–16.

Goehring, James E. "The Dark Side of Landscape: Ideology and Power in the Christian Myth of the Desert." *Journal of Medieval and Early Modern Studies* 33, no. 3 (2003): 437–51.

Goetz, Hans-Werner. "The Concept of Time in the Historiography of the Eleventh and Twelfth Century." In Althoff, Fried, and Geary, *Medieval Concepts of the Past,* 139–65.

Goffart, Walter. *The Narrators of Barbarian History (A.D. 550–800): Jordanes, Gregory of Tours, Bede, and Paul the Deacon.* Princeton: Princeton University Press, 1988. Reprinted Notre Dame, IN: University of Notre Dame Press, 2005.

Goodman, Nelson. *Ways of Worldmaking.* Indianapolis: Hackett Publishing Company, 1978.

Gransden, Antonia. *Historical Writing in England, c. 550 to c. 1307.* London: Routledge & Kegan Paul, 1974.

Greene, J. Patrick. *Medieval Monasteries.* The Archaeology of Medieval Britain. Leicester: Leicester University Press, 1992.

Greenway, Diana. "Authority, Convention and Observation in Henry of Huntingdon's *Historia Anglorum.*" *Anglo-Norman Studies* 18 (1995): 105–21.

Gregory, Derek. *Geographical Imaginations.* Cambridge, MA: Blackwell, 1994.

Grierson, Ph. "L'origine des comtes d'Amiens, Valois et Vexin." *Le Moyen Âge* 49, no. 2 (1939): 81–125.

Grundmann, Herbert. *Geschichtsschreibung im Mittelalter: Gattungen—Epochen—Eigenart.* 4th edition. Göttingen: Vandenhoeck & Ruprecht, 1987; first published 1965.

Guenée, Bernard. *Histoire et culture historique dans l'Occident médiéval.* Collection historique. Paris: Aubier Montaigne, 1980.

Guerreau, Alain. "Espace social, espace symbolique: à Cluny au XIe siècle." In *L'ogre historien: autour de Jacques Le Goff,* ed. Jacques Revel and Jean-Claude Schmitt, 167–91. Paris: Gallimard, 1998.

Guizot, F. P. G. Introduction to Orderic Vital, *Histoire de Normandie.* Edited by F. P. G. Guizot. Translated into French by Louis Dubois. 4 vols. Collection des Mémoires relatifs à l'histoire de France 25–28. Paris: 1825–27. English translation in Thomas Forester, ed., *The Ecclesiastical History of England and Normandy by Orderic Vitalis,* vol. 1, pp. vii–xvi (London: Henry G. Bohn, 1853; reprinted New York: AMS Press, 1968).

Gurevich, A. J. *Categories of Medieval Culture.* Translated by G. L. Campbell. London: Routledge & Kegan Paul, 1985.

———. *Medieval Popular Culture: Problems of Belief and Perception.* Translated by János M. Bak and Paul A. Hollingsworth. Cambridge Studies in Oral and Literate Culture 14. Cambridge: Cambridge University Press, 1988.

Hanawalt, Barbara A., and Michal Kobialka, eds. *Medieval Practices of Space.* Medieval Cultures 23. Minneapolis: University of Minnesota Press, 2000.

Hanning, Robert W. *The Vision of History in Early Britain: From Gildas to Geoffrey of Monmouth.* New York: Columbia University Press, 1966.

Häring, N. M. "Berengar's Definitions of *Sacramentum* and Their Influence on Mediaeval Sacramentology." *Mediaeval Studies* 10 (1948): 109–46.

Harley, J. B., and David Woodward, eds. *The History of Cartography.* Vol. 1, *Cartography in Prehistoric, Ancient, and Medieval Europe and the Mediterranean.* Chicago: University of Chicago Press, 1987.

———. *The History of Cartography.* Vol. 2, Book 1, *Cartography in the Traditional Islamic and South Asian Societies.* Chicago: University of Chicago Press, 1992.

Harper-Bill, Christopher, Christopher J. Holdsworth, and Janet L. Nelson, eds. *Studies in Medieval History Presented to R. Allen Brown.* Woodbridge: Boydell Press, 1989.

Harper-Bill, Christopher, and Elisabeth Van Houts, eds. *A Companion to the Anglo-Norman World.* Woodbridge: Boydell Press, 2003.

Harrison, Anna. "'If One Member Glories . . .': Community Between the Living and the Saintly Dead in Bernard of Clairvaux's *Sermons for the Feast of All Saints.*" In *History in the Comic Mode: Medieval Communities and the Matter of Person,* ed. Rachel Fulton and Bruce W. Holsinger, 25–35. New York: Columbia University Press, 2007.

Harrison, Dick. *Medieval Space: The Extent of Microspatial Knowledge in Western Europe during the Middle Ages.* Lund Studies in International History 34. Lund: Lund University Press, 1996.

Hart, Cyril. "The Ramsey Computus." *English Historical Review* 85, no. 334 (1970): 29–44.

Harvey, David C. "Constructed Landscapes and Social Memory: Tales of St. Samson in Early Medieval Cornwall." *Environment and Planning D—Society and Space* 20, no. 2 (2002): 231–48.

Harvey, P. D. A. *Mappa Mundi: The Hereford World Map.* Toronto: University of Toronto Press, 1996.

———. *Medieval Maps.* London: The British Library, 1991.

Haskins, Charles Homer. *Norman Institutions.* Harvard Historical Studies 24. Cambridge, MA: Harvard University Press, 1918.

———. *The Normans in European History.* Reprint. New York: W. W. Norton, 1966. Originally published 1915.

———. *The Renaissance of the Twelfth Century.* Reprint. New York: Meridian Books, 1957. Originally published 1927.

Häussling, Angelus Albert. *Mönchskonvent und Eucharistiefeier: Einer Studie über die Messe in der abendländischen Klosterliturgie des frühen Mittelalters und zur Geschichte der Meßhäufigkeit.* Liturgiewissenschaftliche Quellen und Forschungen 58. Münster: Aschendorffsche, 1973.

Heinzelmann, Martin. *Gregory of Tours: History and Society in the Sixth Century.* Translated by Christopher Carroll. Cambridge: Cambridge University Press, 2001. Original published as *Gregor von Tours (538–594): 'Zehn Bücher Geschichte', Historiographie und Gesellschaftskonzept im 6. Jahrhundert* (Darmstadt: Wissenschaftliche Buchgesellschaft, 1994).

———. *Translationsberichte und andere Quellen des Reliquienkultes.* Typologie des sources du Moyen Âge occidental 33. Turnhout: Brepols, 1979.

Héliot, Pierre and M.-L. Chastang. "Quêtes et voyages de reliques au profit des églises françaises du moyen âge." *Revue d'histoire ecclésiastique* 59 (1964): 789–822, and 60 (1965): 5–32.

Heurtevent, Raoul. *Durand de Troarn et les origines de l'hérésie bérengarienne.* Études de théologie historique 5. Paris: Gabriel Beauchesne, 1912.

Higgins, Iain Macleod. "Defining the Earth's Center in a Medieval 'Multi-Text': Jerusalem in *The Book of John Mandeville.*" In Tomasch and Gilles, *Text and Territory,* 29–53.

Hincker, Vincent. "Histoire de l'abbaye de Saint-Évroult." In *Saint-Évroult-Notre-Dame-du-Bois,* 14–32.

Hirsch, Eric. "Landscape: Between Place and Space." In Hirsch and O'Hanlon, *The Anthropology of Landscape*, 3–30.

Hirsch, Eric, and Michael O'Hanlon, eds. *The Anthropology of Landscape: Perspectives on Place and Space.* Oxford Studies in Social and Cultural Anthropology. Oxford: Clarendon Press, 1995.

Holdsworth, Christopher J. "Orderic, Traditional Monk and the New Monasticism." In *Tradition and Change: Essays in Honour of Marjorie Chibnall,* ed. Diana Greenway, Christopher Holdsworth, and Jane Sayers, 21–34. Cambridge: Cambridge University Press, 1985.

Holinshed, Raphael. *Chronicles: England, Scotland, Ireland.* 6 vols. New York: AMS Press, 1965. Originally published 1577.

Holm, Bent. "The Hellequin Figure in Medieval Custom." In *Custom, Culture and Community in the Later Middle Ages: A Symposium,* ed. Thomas Pettitt and Leif Søndergaard, 105–24. Odense: Odense University Press, 1994.

Holopainen, Toivo J. *Dialectic and Theology in the Eleventh Century.* Studien und Texte zur Geistesgeschichte des Mittelalters 54. Leiden: E. J. Brill, 1996.

Hommey, Louis. *Histoire générale ecclésiastique et civile du diocèse de Séez ancien et nouveau et du territoire qui forme aujourd'hui le Département de l'Orne.* 5 vols. Alençon: E. Renaut-De Broise, 1899–1900.

Horden, Peregrine, and Nicholas Purcell. *The Corrupting Sea: A Study of Mediterranean History.* Oxford: Blackwell, 2000.

———. "The Mediterranean and 'the New Thalassology.'" *American Historical Review* 111, no. 3 (2006): 722–40.

Houben, Hubert. *Roger II of Sicily: A Ruler Between East and West.* Translated by Graham A. Loud and Diane Milburn. Cambridge: Cambridge University Press, 2002.

Howe, John. "Creating Symbolic Landscapes: Medieval Development of Sacred Space." In J. Howe and Wolfe, *Inventing Medieval Landscapes,* 208–23.

Howe, John, and Michael Wolfe, eds. *Inventing Medieval Landscapes: Senses of Place in Western Europe.* Gainesville: University Press of Florida, 2002.

Howe, Nicholas. "From Bede's World to 'Bede's World.'" In Stein and Prior, *Reading Medieval Culture,* 21–44.

———. *Writing the Map of Anglo-Saxon England: Essays in Cultural Geography.* New Haven: Yale University Press, 2008.

Ingledew, Francis. "The Book of Troy and the Genealogical Construction of History: The Case of Geoffrey of Monmouth's *Historia regum Britanniae.*" *Speculum* 69, no. 3 (1994): 665–704.

Ingold, Tim. "The Temporality of the Landscape." *World Archaeology* 25, no. 2 (1993): 152–74.

Insley, Charles. "Where Did All the Charters Go? Anglo-Saxon Charters and the New Politics of the Eleventh Century." *Anglo-Norman Studies* 24 (2001): 109–27.

Iogna-Prat, Dominique. "Constructions chrétiennes d'un espace politique." *Le Moyen Âge* 107, no. 1 (2001): 49–69.

———. "The Dead in the Celestial Bookkeeping of the Cluniac Monks Around the Year 1000." In *Debating the Middle Ages: Issues and Readings,* ed. Lester K. Little and Barbara H. Rosenwein, 340–62. Oxford: Blackwell, 1998.

———. *Order and Exclusion: Cluny and Christendom Face Heresy, Judaism, and Islam (1000–1150).* Translated by Graham Robert Edwards. Conjunctions of Religion and Power in the Medieval Past. Ithaca: Cornell University Press, 2002.

Jaeger, C. Stephen. "Pessimism in the Twelfth-Century 'Renaissance.'" *Speculum* 78, no. 4 (2003): 1151–83.

Jankulak, Karen. *The Medieval Cult of St Petroc.* Studies in Celtic History 19. Woodbridge: Boydell Press, 2000.

Jeudy, Colette and Yves-François Riou. *Les Manuscrits classiques latins de bibliothèques publiques de France.* Vol. 1, *Agen-Evreux.* Documents, études, répertoires (Institut de recherche et d'histoire de textes [France]). Paris: Éditions du Centre national de la recherche scientifique, 1989.

John, Eric. "Edward the Confessor and the Norman Succession." *English Historical Review* 94, no. 371 (1979): 241–67.

———. *Orbis Britanniae and Other Studies.* Studies in Early English History 4. Leicester: Leicester University Press, 1966.

———. "'Orbis Britanniae' and the Anglo-Saxon Kings." In John, *Orbis Britanniae and Other Studies,* 1–63.

———. "Some Alleged Charters of King Edgar for Ely." In John, *Orbis Britanniae and Other Studies,* 210–33.

Johnson, Ewan. "Normandy and Norman Identity in Southern Italian Chronicles." *Anglo-Norman Studies* 27 (2004): 85–100.

Johnson, Lesley. "Etymologies, Genealogies, and Nationalities (Again)." In *Concepts of National Identity in the Middle Ages,* ed. Simon Forde, Lesley Johnson, and Alan V. Murray, 125–36. Leeds Texts and Monographs, n. s., 14. Leeds: University of Leeds, 1995.

———. "Return to Albion." *Arthurian Literature* 13 (1995): 19–40.

Jordan, William Chester. "Why 'Race'?" *Journal of Medieval and Early Modern Studies* 31, no. 1 (2001): 165–73.

Jungmann, Joseph A. *The Mass of the Roman Rite: Its Origins and Development.* Translated by Francis A. Brunner. 2 vols. New York: Benziger Brothers, 1951–55.

Kantorowicz, Ernst H. *The King's Two Bodies: A Study in Mediaeval Political Theology.* Princeton: Princeton University Press, 1957.

———. "The Problem of Medieval World Unity." In Kantorowicz, *Selected Studies,* 76–81. Locust Valley, NY: J. J. Augustin, 1965.

———. "*Pro Patria Mori* in Medieval Political Thought." *American Historical Review* 56, no. 3 (1951): 472–92.

Keynes, Geoffrey, ed. *The Complete Writings of William Blake, with Variant Readings.* London: Oxford University Press, 1966.

Keynes, Simon. "Ely Abbey 672–1109." In *A History of Ely Cathedral,* ed. Peter Meadows and Nigel Ramsay, 3–58. Woodbridge: Boydell Press, 2003.

Kieckhefer, Richard. *Theology in Stone: Church Architecture from Byzantium to Berkeley.* Oxford: Oxford University Press, 2004.

Kline, Naomi Reed. *Maps of Medieval Thought: The Hereford Paradigm.* Woodbridge: Boydell Press, 2001.

Kobialka, Michal. *This is My Body: Representational Practices in the Early Middle Ages.* Ann Arbor: University of Michigan Press, 1999.

Koht, Halvdan. "The Dawn of Nationalism in Europe." *American Historical Review* 52, no. 2 (1947): 265–80.

Koziol, Geoffrey. "Monks, Feuds, and the Making of Peace in Eleventh-Century Flanders." In *The Peace of God: Social Violence and Religious Response in France around the Year 1000,* ed. Thomas Head and Richard Landes, 239–58. Ithaca: Cornell University Press, 1992.

Lair, Jules, ed. *Matériaux pour l'édition de Guillaume de Jumièges.* Preface and notes by Léopold Delisle. Paris, 1910.

Lambert, Elie. "L'architecture des bénédictins en Normandie." *Cahiers Léopold Delisle* 3 (1949): 3–11.

Lambert, Malcolm. *Medieval Heresy: Popular Movements from the Gregorian Reform to the Reformation.* 3rd edition. Oxford: Blackwell, 2002.

Lamouroux, Jean-Marie. "L'abbaye de Saint-Évroult au XIe siècle." In *La Normandie bénédictine au temps de Guillaume le Conquérant (XIe siècle),* 249–61.

Landes, Richard. "The Fear of an Apocalyptic Year 1000: Augustinian Historiography, Medieval and Modern." *Speculum* 75, no. 1 (2000): 97–145.

———. "Introduction: The *Terribles espoirs* of 1000 and the Tacit Fears of 2000." In *The Apocalyptic Year 1000: Religious Expectation and Social Change, 950–1050*, ed. Richard Landes, Andrew Gow, and David C. van Meter, 3–15. Oxford: Oxford University Press, 2003.

———. *Relics, Apocalypse, and the Deceits of History: Ademar of Chabannes, 989–1034*. Harvard Historical Studies 117. Cambridge, MA: Harvard University Press, 1995.

Lauer, Philippe. *Le règne de Louis IV d'Outre-Mer*. Annales de l'histoire de France à l'époque carolingienne. Bibliothèque de l'École des hautes études 127. Paris: Librairie Émile Bouillon, 1900.

Lauwers, Michel. *La mémoire des ancêtres, le souci des morts: morts, rites et société au Moyen Âge (diocèse de Liège, XIe-XIIIe siècles)*. Théologie historique 103. Paris: Beauchesne, 1997.

Lavezzo, Kathy. *Angels on the Edge of the World: Geography, Literature, and English Community, 1000–1534*. Ithaca: Cornell University Press, 2006.

Leclercq, Jean. *The Love of Learning and the Desire for God: A Study of Monastic Culture*. Translated by Catharine Misrahi. 3rd edition. New York: Fordham University Press, 1982.

Lecouteux, Claude. "Chasse sauvage/Armée furieuse: quelques reflexions." In Walter, *Le mythe de la chasse sauvage dans l'Europe médiévale*, 13–32.

———. *Fantômes et revenants au moyen âge*. L'arbre à mémoire. Paris: Imago, 1986.

Lefebvre, Henri. *The Production of Space*. Translated by Donald Nicholson-Smith. Malden, MA: Blackwell, 1991.

Le Goff, Jacques. *The Birth of Purgatory*. Translated by Arthur Goldhammer. Chicago: University of Chicago Press, 1984.

———. *Medieval Civilization, 400–1500*. Translated by Julia Barrow. New York: Barnes and Noble, 2000.

———. "The Wilderness in the Medieval West." In Le Goff, *The Medieval Imagination*, trans. Arthur Goldhammer, 47–59. Chicago: University of Chicago Press, 1988.

Legris, Chanoine. "L'exode des corps saints au diocèse de Rouen." *Revue catholique de Normandie* (May 1919): 125–36; (July 1919): 168–74; (September 1919): 209–21.

Le Patourel, John. *The Norman Empire*. Oxford: Clarendon Press, 1976.

———. "The Norman Succession, 996–1135." *English Historical Review* 86, no. 339 (1971): 225–50.

Levine, Lee I., ed. *Jerusalem: Its Sanctity and Centrality to Judaism, Christianity, and Islam*. New York: Continuum, 1999.

Lewis, Martin W., and Kären E. Wigen. "A Maritime Response to the Crisis in Area Studies." *Geographical Review* 89, no. 2 (1999): 161–68.

———. *The Myth of Continents: A Critique of Metageography.* Berkeley and Los Angeles: University of California Press, 1997.

Leyser, Karl. *The Ascent of Latin Europe: An Inaugural Lecture Delivered Before the University of Oxford on 7 November 1984.* Oxford: Clarendon Press, 1986.

Lifshitz, Felice. "Beyond Positivism and Genre: 'Hagiographical' Texts as Historical Narrative." *Viator* 25 (1994): 95–113.

———. "The 'Exodus of Holy Bodies' Reconsidered: The Translation of the Relics of St. Gildard of Rouen to Soissons." *Analecta Bollandiana* 110 (1992): 329–40.

———. "The Migration of Neustrian Relics in the Viking Age: The Myth of Voluntary Exodus, the Reality of Coercion and Theft." *Early Medieval Europe* 4, no. 2 (1995): 175–92.

Lindow, John. "Wild Hunt." In *Medieval Folklore: A Guide to Myths, Legends, Tales, Beliefs, and Customs,* ed. Carl Lindahl, John McNamara, and John Lindow, 432–33. Oxford: Oxford University Press, 2002.

Lloyd, J. E. "Wales and the Coming of the Normans (1039–1093)." *Transactions of the Honourable Society of Cymmrodorion* (1901): 122–64.

Lot, Ferdinand. "La *mesnie Hellequin* et le comte Ernequin de Boulogne." *Romania* (1903): 422–41.

Loud, G. A. *The Age of Robert Guiscard: Southern Italy and the Norman Conquest.* The Medieval World. Harlow: Longman, 2000.

———. *Conquerors and Churchmen in Norman Italy.* Variorum Collected Studies. Aldershot: Ashgate/Variorum, 1999.

———. "The *Gens Normannorum*—Myth or Reality?" *Anglo-Norman Studies* 4 (1981): 104–16, 204–9. Reprinted in Loud, *Conquerors and Churchmen in Norman Italy,* no. I.

———. "How 'Norman' was the Norman Conquest of Southern Italy?" *Nottingham Medieval Studies* 25 (1981): 13–34. Reprinted in Loud, *Conquerors and Churchmen in Norman Italy,* no. II.

———. "Norman Italy and the Holy Land." In *The Horns of Hattin: Proceedings of the Second Conference of the Society for the Study of the Crusades and the Latin East, Jerusalem and Haifa, 2–6 July 1987,* ed. Benjamin Z. Kedar, 49–62. Jerusalem: Yad Izhak Ben-Zvi, Israel Exploration Society, 1992. Reprinted in Loud, *Conquerors and Churchmen in Norman Italy,* no. XIV.

———. "The Papacy and the Rulers of Southern Italy, 1058–1198." In Loud and Metcalfe, *Society of Norman Italy,* 151–84.

Loud, G. A., and A. Metcalfe, eds. *The Society of Norman Italy.* The Medieval Mediterranean: Peoples, Economies, Cultures, 400–1500, vol. 38. Leiden: Brill, 2002.

Louise, Gérard. "La mise en place du réseau castral sur les confins de la Normandie et du Maine dans le cadre du futur territoire du département de l'Orne (Xe-XIIIe siècles)." In Fajal, *"Autour du château médiéval,"* 9–24.

———. *La seigneurie de Bellême, Xe-XIIe siècles: dévolution des pouvoirs territoriaux et construction d'une seigneurie de frontière aux confins de la Normandie et du Maine à la charnière de l'an mil.* 2 vols. *Le pays bas-normand* 83, nos. 3–4 (1990) and 84, nos. 1–2 (1991).

Loyn, H. R. *The Governance of Anglo-Saxon England, 500–1087.* The Governance of England 1. London: Edward Arnold, 1984.

———. "The Imperial Style of the Tenth Century Anglo-Saxon Kings." *History* 40, no. 138–39 (1955): 111–15.

———. *The Norman Conquest.* 3rd edition. London: Hutchinson, 1982.

Lozovsky, Natalia. *"The Earth is Our Book": Geographical Knowledge in the Latin West ca. 400–1000.* Recentiores: Later Latin Texts and Contexts. Ann Arbor: University of Michigan Press, 2000.

Luria, A. R. *The Mind of a Mnemonist: A Little Book about a Vast Memory.* Translated by Lynn Solotaroff. Cambridge, MA: Harvard University Press, 1968.

Lynch, Kevin. *The Image of the City.* Cambridge, MA: M. I. T. Press, 1960.

Macdonald, A. J. *Berengar and the Reform of Sacramental Doctrine.* London: Longmans, Green and Co., 1930.

Macy, Gary. "Berengar's Legacy as Heresiarch." In Ganz, Huygens, and Niewöhner, *Auctoritas und Ratio,* 47–67. Reprinted in Macy, *Treasures from the Storeroom,* 59–80.

———. "The Dogma of Transubstantiation in the Middle Ages," *Journal of Ecclesiastical History* 45 (1994): 11–41. Reprinted in Macy, *Treasures from the Storeroom,* 81–120.

———. "The Theological Fate of Berengar's Oath of 1059: Interpreting a Blunder Become Tradition." In *Interpreting Tradition: The Art of Theological Reflection,* ed. Jane Kopas, 27–38. Proceedings of the Annual Convention of the College Theology Society, 1983. Chico, CA: Scholars Press, 1984. Reprinted in Macy, *Treasures from the Storeroom,* 20–35.

———. *The Theologies of the Eucharist in the Early Scholastic Period: A Study of the Salvific Function of the Sacrament according to the Theologians, c. 1080–c. 1220.* Oxford: Clarendon Press, 1984.

————. *Treasures from the Storeroom: Medieval Religion and the Eucharist.* Collegeville, MN: Liturgical Press, 1999.

Magnani S.-Christen, Eliana. "Transforming Things and Persons: The Gift *pro anima* in the Eleventh and Twelfth Centuries." In *Negotiating the Gift: Pre-Modern Figurations of Exchange,* ed. Gadi Algazi, Valentin Groebner, and Bernhard Jussen, 269–84. Verofftentlichungen des Max-Planck-Instituts fur Geschichte 188. Göttingen: Vandenhoeck & Ruprecht, 2003.

Maillefer, Jean-Marie. "Une famille aristocratique aux confins de la Normandie: Les Géré au XIe siècle." In *Autour du pouvoir ducal normand Xe–XIIe siècles,* ed. Lucien Musset, Jean Michel Bouvris, and Jean-Marie Maillefer, 175–206. Cahiers des annales de Normandie 17. Caen: Annales de Normandie, 1985.

Marenbon, John. *The Philosophy of Peter Abelard.* Cambridge: Cambridge University Press, 1997.

Markowski, Michael. "*Crucesignatus*: The Origins and Early Usage." *Journal of Medieval History* 10 (1984): 157–65.

Markus, R. A. *The End of Ancient Christianity.* Cambridge: Cambridge University Press, 1990.

————. "How on Earth Could Places Become Holy? Origins of the Christian Idea of Holy Places." *Journal of Early Christian Studies* 2, no. 3 (1994): 257–71.

McGinn, Bernard. *Antichrist: Two Thousand Years of the Human Fascination with Evil.* New York: HarperCollins; San Francisco: HarperSanFrancicisco, 1994.

McGuire, Brian Patrick. "Purgatory, the Communion of Saints, and Medieval Change." *Viator* 20 (1989): 61–84.

McGuire, Randall H. "Dialogues with the Dead: Ideology and the Cemetery." In *The Recovery of Meaning: Historical Archaeology in the Eastern United States,* ed. Mark P. Leone and Parker B. Potter, Jr., 435–80. Washington: Smithsonian Institution Press, 1988.

McKitterick, Rosamund. *History and Memory in the Carolingian World.* Cambridge: Cambridge University Press, 2004.

McLaughlin, Megan. "Communion with the Dead." *Journal of Medieval History* 17 (1991): 23–34.

————. *Consorting with Saints: Prayer for the Dead in Early Medieval France.* Ithaca: Cornell University Press, 1994.

Mégier, Elisabeth. "*Cotidie Operatur*: Christus und die Geschichte in der *Historia Ecclesiastica* des Ordericus Vitalis." *Revue Mabillon,* n.s., 10 (1999): 169–204.

———. "Deux exemples de 'prépurgatoire' chez les historiens: à propos de *La naissance du Purgatoire* de Jacques Le Goff." *Cahiers de civilisation médiévale* 28, no. 1 (1985): 45–62.

———. "*Divina Pagina* and the Narration of History in Orderic Vitalis' *Historia Ecclesiastica*." *Revue bénédictine* 110, no. 1–2 (2000): 106–23.

———. "*Fortuna* als Kategorie der Geschichtsdeutung im 12. Jahrhundert am Beispiel Ordericus' Vitalis und Ottos von Freising." *Mittellateinisches Jahrbuch* 32, no. 1 (1997): 49–70.

Merrills, A. H. *History and Geography in Late Antiquity.* Cambridge Studies in Medieval Life and Thought, Fourth Series, 64. Cambridge: Cambridge University Press, 2005.

———. "Monks, Monsters, and Barbarians: Re-defining the African Periphery in Late Antiquity." *Journal of Early Christian Studies* 12 (2004): 217–44.

Metcalfe, Alex. "The Muslims of Sicily Under Christian Rule." In Loud and Metcalfe, *Society of Norman Italy,* 289–317.

Miller, Patricia Cox. "Jerome's Centaur: A Hyper-Icon of the Desert." *Journal of Early Christian Studies* 4, no. 2 (1996): 209–33.

*Monasticon Gallicanum: Collection de 168 planches de vues topographiques représentant les monastères de l'Ordre de Saint-Benoît Congrégation de Saint-Maur avec deux cartes des établissements bénedictins en France.* Drawings reproduced by Achille Peigné-Delacourt. Preface by Léopold Delisle. 2 vols. Paris: Victor Palmé, 1871.

Monnet, Pierre. "La *patria* médiévale vue d'Allemagne, entre construction impériale et identités régionales." *Le Moyen Âge* 107, no. 1 (2001): 71–99.

Montclos, Jean de. *Lanfranc et Bérenger: la controverse eucharistique du XIe siècle.* Études et documents 37. Leuven: Spicilegium sacrum lovaniense, 1971.

Moore, R. I. "Between Sanctity and Superstition: Saints and their Miracles in the Age of Revolution." In *The Work of Jacques Le Goff and the Challenges of Medieval History,* ed. Miri Rubin, 55–67. Woodbridge: Boydell Press, 1997.

———. *The First European Revolution, c. 970–1215.* The Making of Europe. Oxford: Blackwell, 2000.

———. *The Origins of European Dissent.* Reissue. New York: Basil Blackwell, 1985.

Morphy, Howard. "Landscape and the Reproduction of the Ancestral Past." In Hirsch and O'Hanlon, *Anthropology of Landscape,* 184–209.

Morrison, Karl F. *History as a Visual Art in the Twelfth-Century Renaissance*. Princeton: Princeton University Press, 1990.

Murray, Alan V. "How Norman was the Principality of Antioch? Prolegomena to a Study of the Origins of the Nobility of a Crusader State." In *Family Trees and the Roots of Politics: The Prosopography of Britain and France from the Tenth to the Twelfth Century*, ed. K. S. B. Keats-Rohan, 349–59. Woodbridge: Boydell Press, 1997.

Musset, Lucien. "Les abbayes normandes au moyen-âge: position de quelques problèmes." In *Les Abbayes de Normandie, actes du XIIIe congrès des sociétés historiques et archéologiques de Normandie*, 13–26.

———. "Aux origines d'une classe dirigeante: Les Tosny, grands barons normands du Xe au XIIIe siècle." *Francia* 5 (1977): 45–80.

———. "Essai sur le peuplement de la Normandie (Vie-XIIe siècle)." In Musset, *Nordica et Normannica*, 389–402.

———. "Évroul." In *Dictionnaire d'histoire et de géographie ecclésiastiques*, ed. R. Aubert, 16:219. Paris: Letouzey et Ane, 1967.

———. "L'exode des reliques du diocèse de Sées au temps des invasions Normandes." *Bulletin de la Société historique et archéologique de l'Orne* 88 (1970): 3–22.

———. "L'image de la Scandinavie dans les œuvres normandes de la période ducale (911–1204)." In Musset, *Nordica and Normannica*, 213–31.

———. *Nordica et Normannica: Recueil d'études sur la Scandinavie ancienne et médiévale, les expéditions des Vikings et la fondation de la Normandie*. Studia nordica. Paris: Société des études nordiques, 1997.

———. "L'origine de Rollon." In Musset, *Nordica et Normannica*, 383–87.

———. "Les translations de reliques en Normandie (IXe–XIIe siècles)." In *Les Saints dans la Normandie médiévale*, ed. Pierre Bouet and François Neveux, 97–108. Colloque de Cerisy-la-Salle (26–29 Septembre 1996). Caen: Presses Universitaires de Caen, 2000.

Nelson, Janet L. "Inauguration Rituals." In *Early Medieval Kingship*, ed. P. H. Sawyer and I. N. Wood, 50–71. Leeds: University of Leeds, 1977.

———. "The Rites of the Conqueror." *Anglo-Norman Studies* 4 (1981): 117–32, 210–21.

Newman, Barbara. "What Did It Mean to Say 'I Saw'? The Clash between Theory and Practice in Medieval Visionary Culture." *Speculum* 80, no. 1 (2005): 1–43.

Nicolet, Claude. *Space, Geography, and Politics in the Early Roman Empire*. Translated by Hélène Leclerc. Ann Arbor: University of Michigan Press, 1991.

Noisette, Patrice. "Usages et représentations de l'espace dans la *Regula Benedicti*: une nouvelle approche des significations historiques de la Règle." *Regulae Benedicti Studia* 14/15 (1985/6): 69–80.

Nora, Pierre. "Between Memory and History: *Les Leiux de Mémoire.*" Translated by Marc Roudebuch. *Representations* 26 (1989): 7–24.

*La Normandie bénédictine au temps de Guillaume le Conquérant (XIe siècle).* Lille: Facultés catholiques, 1967.

Nortier, Geneviève. *Les bibliothèques médiévales des abbayes bénédictines de Normandie.* New edition. Bibliotheque d'histoire et de archéologie chretiennes. Paris: Editions P. Lethielleux, 1971.

Norwich, John Julius. *The Normans in Sicily: The Magnificent Story of 'the Other Norman Conquest.'* Harmondsworth: Penguin, 1992.

Obrist, Barbara. "Wind Diagrams and Medieval Cosmology." *Speculum* 72, no. 1 (1997): 33–84.

Oexle, Otto Gerhard. "Memoria und Memorialüberlieferung im früheren Mittelalter." *Frühmittelalterliche Studien* 10 (1976): 70–95.

Okasha, Elisabeth. "Memorial Stones or Grave-Stones?" In Cavill, *Christian Tradition in Anglo-Saxon England*, 91–101.

Oleson, T. J. "Edward the Confessor's Promise of the Throne to Duke William of Normandy." *English Historical Review* 72, no. 283 (1957): 221–28.

Olwig, Kenneth Robert. *Landscape, Nature, and the Body Politic: From Britain's Renaissance to America's New World.* Madison: University of Wisconsin Press, 2002.

———. "Recovering the Substantive Nature of Landscape." *Annals of the Association of American Geographers* 86, no. 4 (1996): 630–53.

Orabona, Luciano, ed. *Guitmondo di Aversa, la cultura europea e la riforma gregoriana nel Mezzogiorno.* Vol. 2, *Corpo mistico e teologia trinitaria, esegesi biblica, fonti patristiche, dialettica ed eucaristia.* Chiese del mezzogiorno—Fonti e studi, 14. Naples: Edizioni scientifiche italiane, 2000.

*Orderic Vital et l'abbaye de Saint-Evroul: Notices et travaux publiés en l'honneur de l'historien normand, moine de cette abbaye.* Société historique et archéologique de l'Orne. Alençon: Imprimerie Alençonnaise, 1912.

Otter, Monika. *Inventiones: Fiction and Referentiality in Twelfth-Century English Historical Writing.* Chapel Hill: University of North Carolina Press, 1996.

———. "*Prolixitas Temporum*: Futurity in Medieval Historical Narratives." In Stein and Prior, *Reading Medieval Culture*, 45–67.

Partner, Nancy F. "The New Cornificius: Medieval History and the Artifice of Words." In Breisach, *Classical Rhetoric and Medieval Historiography*, 5–59.

———. *Serious Entertainments: The Writing of History in Twelfth-Century England.* Chicago: University of Chicago Press, 1977.

Pegg, Mark Gregory. *The Corruption of Angels: The Great Inquisition of 1245–1246.* Princeton: Princeton University Press, 2001.

———. "On Cathars, Albigenses, and Good Men of Languedoc." *Journal of Medieval History* 27, no. 2 (2001): 181–95.

Pelatan, Jean. "Milieu naturel." In Pelatan, *Orne*, 269–337. Encyclopédies régionales. Paris: Éditions Bonneton, 1995.

Phillips, Seymour. "The Outer World of the European Middle Ages." In *Implicit Understandings: Observing, Reporting, and Reflecting on the Encounters between Europeans and Other Peoples in the Early Modern Era*, ed. Stuart B. Schwartz, 23–63. Studies in Comparative Early Modern History. Cambridge: Cambridge University Press, 1994.

Picot, Émile. "Liste des abbés de Saint-Évroul." In *Orderic Vital et l'abbaye de Saint-Evroul*, 79–101.

Pohle, J. "Impanation." *Catholic Encyclopedia*, 7:694–95. New York: Robert Appleton, 1910.

Post, Gaines. "Two Notes on Nationalism in the Middle Ages." *Traditio* 9 (1953): 281–320.

Potts, Cassandra. "*Atque unum ex diversis gentibus populum effecit*: Historical Tradition and the Norman Identity." *Anglo-Norman Studies* 18 (1995): 139–52.

———. *Monastic Revival and Regional Identity in Early Normandy.* Studies in the History of Medieval Religion 11. Woodbridge: Boydell Press, 1997.

Power, Daniel. *The Norman Frontier in the Twelfth and Early Thirteenth Centuries.* Cambridge Studies in Medieval Life and Thought, Fourth Series, 62. Cambridge: Cambridge University Press, 2004.

Pred, Allan. "Place as Historically Contingent Process: Structuration and the Time-Geography of Becoming Places." *Annals of the Association of American Geographers* 74, no. 2 (1984): 279–97.

Radding, Charles M., and Francis Newton. *Theology, Rhetoric, and Politics in the Eucharistic Controversy, 1078–1079: Alberic of Monte Cassino Against Berengar of Tours.* New York: Columbia University Press, 2003.

Ray, Roger. "Bede's *Vera Lex Historiae*." *Speculum* 55, no. 1 (1980): 1–21.

————. "The Monastic Historiography of Orderic Vitalis." Ph.D. diss., Duke University, 1968.

Remensnyder, Amy G. *Remembering Kings Past: Monastic Foundation Legends in Medieval Southern France*. Ithaca: Cornell University Press, 1995.

————. "Topographies of Memory: Center and Periphery in High Medieval France." In Althoff, Fried, and Geary, *Medieval Concepts of the Past*, 193–214.

Repsher, Brian. *The Rite of Church Dedication in the Early Medieval Era*. Lewiston: Edwin Mellen Press, 1998.

Reynolds, Susan. *Kingdoms and Communities in Western Europe, 900–1300*. 2nd edition. Oxford: Clarendon Press, 1997.

————. "Medieval *Origines Gentium* and the Community of the Realm." *History* 68 (1983): 375–90.

Richardson, Judith. *Possessions: The History and Uses of Haunting in the Hudson Valley*. Cambridge, MA: Harvard University Press, 2003.

Riley-Smith, Jonathan. "Crusading as an Act of Love." *History* 65 (1980): 177–92.

Romm, James S. *The Edges of the Earth in Ancient Thought: Geography, Exploration, and Fiction*. Princeton: Princeton University Press, 1992.

Rosenwein, Barbara H. *To Be the Neighbor of Saint Peter: The Social Meaning of Cluny's Property, 909–1049*. Ithaca: Cornell University Press, 1989.

Rubenstein, Jay. *Guibert of Nogent: Portrait of a Medieval Mind*. New York: Routledge, 2002.

Rubin, Miri. *Corpus Christi: The Eucharist in Late Medieval Culture*. Cambridge: Cambridge University Press, 1991.

————. "The Eucharist and the Construction of Medieval Identities." In *Culture and History, 1350–1600: Essays on English Communities, Identities and Writing*, ed. David Aers, 43–63. Detroit: Wayne State University Press, 1992.

Rumsey, Alan. "Tracks, Traces, and Links to Land in Aboriginal Australia, New Guinea, and Beyond." In Rumsey and Weiner, *Emplaced Myth*, 19–42.

Rumsey, Alan, and James Weiner, eds. *Emplaced Myth: Space, Narrative, and Knowledge in Aboriginal Australia and Papua New Guinea*. Honolulu: University of Hawai'i Press, 2001.

Runciman, Steven. *The Medieval Manichee: A Study of the Christian Dualist Heresy*. Cambridge: Cambridge University Press, 1947.

*Saint-Évroult-Notre-Dame-du-Bois: Une abbaye bénédictine en terre normande*. Condé-sur-Noireau: Éditions NEA, 2001.

Sawyer, P. H. *Anglo-Saxon Charters: An Annotated List and Bibliography.* Royal Historical Society Guides and Handbooks 8. London: Royal Historical Society, 1968.

Schama, Simon. *Landscape and Memory.* New York: Alfred A. Knopf, 1995.

Scherb, Victor I. "Assimilating Giants: The Appropriation of Gog and Magog in Medieval and Early Modern England." *Journal of Medieval and Early Modern Studies* 32, no. 1 (2002): 59–84.

Schmidt, H. D. "The Idea and Slogan of 'Perfidious Albion.'" *Journal of the History of Ideas* 14, no. 4 (1953): 604–16.

Schmitt, Jean-Claude. "Le corps en Chrétienté." In *Le corps, le rites, les rêves, le temps: essais d'anthropologie médiévale,* 344–59. Paris: Gallimard, 2001.

———. *Ghosts in the Middle Ages: The Living and the Dead in Medieval Society.* Translated by Teresa Lavender Fagan. Chicago: University of Chicago Press, 1998.

Searle, Eleanor. *Predatory Kinship and the Creation of Norman Power, 840–1066.* Berkeley and Los Angeles: University of California Press, 1988.

Semper, Philippa. "Doctrine and Diagrams: Maintaining the Order of the World in *Byrhtferth's Enchiridion.*" In Cavill, *Christian Tradition in Anglo-Saxon England,* 121–37.

Shaughnessy, Patrick. *The Eucharistic Doctrine of Guitmund of Aversa.* Rome: Scuola Salesiana del Libro, 1939.

Sheldrake, Philip. *Spaces for the Sacred: Place, Memory, and Identity.* Baltimore: Johns Hopkins University Press, 2001.

Sheppard, Alice. *Families of the King: Writing Identity in the "Anglo-Saxon Chronicle."* Toronto: University of Toronto Press, 2004.

Shopkow, Leah. "Dynastic History." In Deliyannis, *Historiography in the Middle Ages,* 217–48.

———. *History and Community: Norman Historical Writing in the Eleventh and Twelfth Centuries.* Washington, DC: Catholic University of America Press, 1997.

Short, Ian. "*Tam Angli quam Franci*: Self-Definition in Anglo-Norman England." *Anglo-Norman Studies* 18 (1995): 153–75.

Sicotière, Leon de la, and Auguste Poulet-Malassis. *Le département de l'Orne archéologique et pittoresque.* L'Aigle: Beuzelin, 1845.

Sigal, Pierre-André. "Les voyages de reliques aux XIe et XIIe siècles." In *Voyage, quête, pèlerinage dans la littérature et la civilisation médiévale,* 75–104. Senefiance 2. Aix-en-Provence: Editions CUER MA; Paris: H. Champion, 1976.

Singer, Charles, and Dorothea Singer. "A Restoration: Byrhtferd of Ramsey's Diagram of the Physical and Physiological Fours." *Bodleian Quarterly Review* 2, no. 14 (1917): 47–51.

Smail, Daniel Lord. *Imaginary Cartographies: Possession and Identity in Late Medieval Marseille.* Ithaca: Cornell University Press, 1999.

Smalley, Beryl. *Historians in the Middle Ages.* New York: Charles Scribner's Sons, 1974.

Smith, Anthony D. "Culture, Community and Territory: The Politics of Ethnicity and Nationalism." *International Affairs* 72, no. 3 (1996): 445–58.

———. "Were There Nations in Antiquity?" In *Power and the Nation in European History,* ed. Len Scales and Oliver Zimmer, 33–53. Cambridge: Cambridge University Press, 2005.

Smith, Julia M. H. "Oral and Written: Saints, Miracles, and Relics in Brittany, c. 850–1250." *Speculum* 65, no. 2 (1990): 309–43.

Snoek, G. J. C. *Medieval Piety from Relics to the Eucharist: A Process of Mutual Interaction.* Studies in the History of Christian Thought 63. Leiden: E. J. Brill, 1995.

Somerville, Robert. "The Case Against Berengar of Tours—A New Text." *Studi Gregoriani* 9 (1972): 53–75.

Southern, Richard W. "Aspects of the European Tradition of Historical Writing: 1. The Classical Tradition from Einhard to Geoffrey of Monmouth." *Transactions of the Royal Historical Society,* 5th ser., 20 (1970): 173–96.

———. "Aspects of the European Tradition of Historical Writing: 2. Hugh of St Victor and the Idea of Historical Development." *Transactions of the Royal Historical Society,* 5th ser., 21 (1971): 159–79.

———. "Aspects of the European Tradition of Historical Writing: 3. History as Prophecy," *Transactions of the Royal Historical Society,* 5th ser., 22 (1972): 159–80.

———. "Aspects of the European Tradition of Historical Writing: 4. The Sense of the Past," *Transactions of the Royal Historical Society,* 5th ser., 23 (1973): 245–56.

———. "Between Heaven and Hell." *Times Literary Supplement* (18 June 1982): 651–52.

———. "Lanfranc of Bec and Berengar of Tours." In *Studies in Medieval History Presented to Frederick Maurice Powick,* ed. R. W. Hunt, W. A. Pantin, and R. W. Southern, 27–48. Oxford: Clarendon Press, 1948.

———. *Medieval Humanism.* New York: Harper & Row, 1970.

———. *Saint Anselm: A Portrait in a Landscape.* Cambridge: Cambridge University Press, 1990.

Spiegel, Gabrielle M. "Genealogy: Form and Function in Medieval Historiography." In Spiegel, *The Past as Text*, 99–110. Originally published as "Genealogy: Form and Function in Medieval Historical Narrative," *History and Theory* 22, no. 1 (1983): 43–53.

———. "History, Historicism, and the Social Logic of the Text." In Spiegel, *The Past as Text*, 3–28. Originally published in *Speculum* 65, no. 1 (1990): 59–86.

———. *The Past as Text: The Theory and Practice of Medieval Historiography*. Parallax: Re-Visions of Culture and Society. Baltimore: Johns Hopkins University Press, 1997.

———. "Political Utility in Medieval Historiography: A Sketch." In Spiegel, *The Past as Text*, 83–98. Originally published in *History and Theory* 14, no. 3 (1975): 314–25.

Stafford, Pauline. *Unification and Conquest: A Political and Social History of England in the Tenth and Eleventh Centuries*. London: Edward Arnold, 1989.

Stein, Robert M. "Making History English: Cultural Identity and Historical Explanation in William of Malmesbury and Laʒamon's *Brut*." In Tomasch and Gilles, *Text and Territory*, 97–115.

———. *Reality Fictions: Romance, History, and Governmental Authority, 1025–1180*. Notre Dame, IN: University of Notre Dame Press, 2006.

Stein, Robert M., and Sandra Pierson Prior, eds. *Reading Medieval Culture: Essays in Honor of Robert W. Hanning*. Notre Dame, IN: University of Notre Dame Press, 2005.

Stenton, F. M. *Anglo-Saxon England*. 3rd edition. Oxford: Oxford University Press, 1971.

Stewart, Pamela J. and Andrew Strathern. "Origins versus Creative Powers: The Interplay of Movement and Fixity." In Rumsey and Weiner, *Emplaced Myth*, 79–98.

Stock, Brian. "Antiqui and Moderni as 'Giants' and 'Dwarfs': A Reflection of Popular Culture?" *Modern Philology* 76, no. 4 (1979): 370–74.

———. *The Implications of Literacy: Written Language and Models of Interpretation in the Eleventh and Twelfth Centuries*. Princeton: Princeton University Press, 1983.

Straw, Carole. *Gregory the Great: Perfection in Imperfection*. Transformation of the Classical Heritage 14. Berkeley and Los Angeles: University of California Press, 1988.

Summit, Jennifer. "Topography as Historiography: Petrarch, Chaucer, and the Making of Medieval Rome." *Journal of Medieval and Early Modern Studies* 30, no. 2 (2000): 211–46.

Swanson, R. N. *The Twelfth-Century Renaissance.* Manchester: Manchester University Press; New York: St. Martin's Press, 1999.

Tabuteau, Emily Zack. *Transfers of Property in Eleventh-Century Norman Law.* Studies in Legal History. Chapel Hill: University of North Carolina Press, 1988.

Taylor, Claire. "The Letter of Héribert of Périgord as a Source for Dualist Heresy in the Society of Early Eleventh-Century Aquitaine." *Journal of Medieval History* 26, no. 4 (2000): 313–49.

Thomas, Hugh M. *The English and the Normans: Ethnic Hostility, Assimilation, and Identity, 1066–c. 1220.* Oxford: Oxford University Press, 2003.

Thompson, Kathleen. "Family and Influence to the South of Normandy in the Eleventh Century: The Lordship of Bellême." *Journal of Medieval History* 11, no. 3 (1985): 215–26.

———. *Power and Border Lordship in Medieval France: The County of the Perche, 1000–1226.* Royal Historical Society Studies in History, New Series. Woodbridge: Boydell Press, 2002.

Thonneau, Marie-José. "Terre, automne, mélancholie: Âges de la vie humaine et tempéraments." In *La ronde des saisons: Les saisons dans la littérature et la société anglaises au Moyen Âge,* ed. Léo Carruthers, 91–100. Paris: Presses de l'Université de Paris-Sorbonne, 1998.

Thoreau, Henry David. *Walden: or, Life in the Woods.* New York: Signet Classic, 1960. Originally published Boston: Ticknor and Fields, 1854.

Thornton, David E. "Edgar and the Eight Kings, AD 973: *textus et dramatis personae.*" *Early Medieval Europe* 10, no. 1 (2001): 49–79.

Tomasch, Sylvia, and Sealy Gilles, eds. *Text and Territory: Geographical Imagination in the European Middle Ages.* The Middle Ages Series. Philadelphia: University of Pennsylvania Press, 1998.

Tuan, Yi-Fu. "Foreword." In *Geography and the Human Spirit,* by Anne Buttimer. Baltimore: Johns Hopkins University Press, 1993.

———. *Space and Place: The Perspective of Experience.* Minneapolis: University of Minnesota Press, 1977.

———. *Topophilia: A Study of Environmental Perception, Attitude, and Values.* New York: Columbia University Press, 1974.

Twain, Mark. "As Concerns Interpreting the Deity." In *What is Man? And Other Philosophical Writings,* ed. Paul Baender, 109–20. The Works of Mark Twain 19. Berkeley and Los Angeles: University of California Press for the Iowa Center for Textual Studies, 1973.

Van Engen, John H. *Rupert of Deutz.* Publications of the UCLA Center for Medieval and Renaissance Studies 18. Berkeley and Los Angeles: University of California Press, 1983.

Van Houts, Elisabeth. "Historical Writing." In Harper-Bill and Van Houts, *Companion to the Anglo-Norman World*, 103–21.

―――. "The Norman Conquest through European Eyes." *English Historical Review* 110, no. 438 (1995): 832–53.

―――. "Scandinavian Influence in Norman Literature of the Eleventh Century." *Anglo-Norman Studies* 6 (1984): 107–21.

von den Brincken, Anna-Dorothee. "Europa in der Kartographie des Mittelalters." *Archiv für Kulturgeschichte* 55, no. 2 (1973): 289–304.

Wagner, Roy. "Condensed Mapping: Myth and the Folding of Space/Space and the Folding of Myth." In Rumsey and Weiner, *Emplaced Myth*, 71–78.

Walker, Barbara MacDonald. "The Grandmesnils: A Study in Norman Baronial Enterprise." Ph.D. diss., University of California, Santa Barbara, 1968.

Wallace, David. *Premodern Places: Calais to Surinam, Chaucer to Aphra Behn*. Oxford: Blackwell, 2004.

Wallis, Faith. "Images of Order in the Medieval *Computus*." In *Ideas of Order in the Middle Ages*, ed. Warren Ginsberg, 45–68. The Center for Medieval and Early Renaissance Studies, Acta 15. Binghamton: State University of New York at Binghamton, 1990.

―――. "MS Oxford St John's College 17: A Mediaeval Manuscript in its Context." Ph.D. diss., University of Toronto, 1985.

Walter, Philippe. "Hellequin, Hannequin et le Mannequin." In Walter, *Le mythe de la chasse sauvage dans l'Europe médiévale*, 33–72.

―――, ed. *Le mythe de la chasse sauvage dans l'Europe médiévale*. Essais sur le Moyen Âge 19. Paris: Honoré Champion, 1997.

Ward, Benedicta. "The Desert Myth: Reflections on the Desert Ideal in Early Cistercian Monasticism." In *One Yet Two: Monastic Tradition, East and West; Orthodox-Cistercian Symposium, Oxford University, 26 August–1 September 1973*, ed. M. Basil Pennington, 183–99. Cistercian Studies Series 29. Kalamazoo: Cistercian Publications, 1976.

Ward, John O. "Some Principles of Rhetorical Historiography in the Twelfth Century." In Breisach, *Classical Rhetoric and Medieval Historiography*, 103–65.

Warner, William. *Albion's England*. Anglistica and Americana 131. Hildesheim, NY: Georg Olms, 1971. Facsimile of the 1612 edition.

Warren, W. L. *Henry II*. English Monarchs. Berkeley and Los Angeles: University of California Press, 1973.

Watkins, Carl. "Memories of the Marvellous in the Anglo-Norman Realm." In *Medieval Memories: Men, Women and the Past, 700–1300*, ed. Elisabeth Van Houts, 92–112. Women and Men in History. New York: Pearson Education Limited, Longman, 2001.

————. "Sin, Penance and Purgatory in the Anglo-Norman Realm: The Evidence of Visions and Ghost Stories." *Past and Present* 175 (2002): 3–33.

Webber, Nick. *The Evolution of Norman Identity, 911–1154.* Woodbridge: Boydell Press, 2005.

Werner, Karl-Ferdinand. "Qu'est-ce que la Neustrie?" In *La Neustrie: les pays au nord le la Loire de Dagobert à Charles le Chauve (VIIe–IXe siècles),* ed. Patrick Périn and Laure-Charlotte Feffer, 29–38. Rouen: Musées et monuments départementaux de Seine-Maritime, 1985.

Westrem, Scott D. "Against Gog and Magog." In Tomasch and Gilles, *Text and Territory,* 54–75.

————, ed. *Discovering New Worlds: Essays on Medieval Exploration and Imagination.* Garland Reference Library in the Humanities 1436. Garland Medieval Casebooks 2. New York: Garland, 1991.

White, Stephen D. *Custom, Kinship, and Gifts to Saints: The* Laudatio Parentum *in Western France, 1050–1150.* Studies in Legal History. Chapel Hill: University of North Carolina Press, 1988.

Wilken, Robert L. *The Land Called Holy: Palestine in Christian History and Thought.* New Haven: Yale University Press, 1992.

Williams, Ann. *Kingship and Government in Pre-Conquest England, c. 500–1066.* British History in Perspective. New York: St. Martin's Press, 1999.

Williams, George H. *Wilderness and Paradise in Christian Thought: The Biblical Experience of the Desert in the History of Christianity and the Paradise Theme in the Theological Idea of the University.* New York: Harper, 1962.

Williams, Howard. "Remembering and Forgetting the Medieval Dead: Exploring Death, Memory and Material Culture in Monastic Archaeology." In *Archaeologies of Remembrance: Death and Memory in Past Societies,* ed. Howard Williams, 227–54. New York: Kluwer Academic/Plenum Publishers, 2003.

Williams, John. *The Illustrated Beatus: A Corpus of the Illustrations of the Commentary on the Apocalypse.* 5 vols. London: Harvey Miller Publishers, 1994–2003.

————. "Isidore, Orosius and the Beatus Map." *Imago Mundi* 49 (1997): 7–32.

Wolf, Kenneth Baxter. *Making History: The Normans and Their Historians in Eleventh-Century Italy.* Middle Ages Series. Philadelphia: University of Pennsylvania Press, 1995.

Wolter, Hans. *Ordericus Vitalis: Ein Beitrag zur kluniazensischen Geschichtsschreibung.* Veröffentlichungen des Instituts für Europäische Geschichte, Mainz 7. Wiesbaden: Franz Steiner Verlag, 1955.

Woodward, David. "Medieval *Mappaemundi.*" In Harley and Woodward, *The History of Cartography,* 1:286–370.

———. "Reality, Symbolism, Time, and Space in Medieval World Maps." *Annals of the Association of American Geographers* 75, no. 4 (1985): 510–21.

Wormald, Francis. "The Litany in Arundel MS. 60: Appendix." *Analecta Bollandiana* 64 (1946): 84–86.

Wormald, Patrick. "Bede, the *Bretwaldas* and the Origins of the *Gens Anglorum.*" In *Ideal and Reality in Frankish and Anglo-Saxon Society: Studies Presented to J. M. Wallace-Hadrill,* ed. Patrick Wormald with Donald Bullough and Roger Collins, 99–129. Oxford: Basil Blackwell, 1983.

———. "*Engla Lond*: The Making of an Allegiance." *Journal of Historical Sociology* 7, no. 1 (1994): 1–24.

Wright, John Kirtland. *The Geographical Lore of the Time of the Crusades: A Study in the History of Medieval Science and Tradition in Western Europe.* Reprint. New York: Dover Publications, 1965. Originally published 1925.

Yver, Jean. "Les châteaux-forts en Normandie jusqu'au milieu du XIIe siècle: contribution à l'étude du pouvoir ducal." *Bulletin de la Société des antiquaires de Normandie* 53 (1955–56): 28–115.

Zumthor, Paul. *La measure du monde: représentation de l'espace au moyen âge.* Poétique. Paris: Éditions du Seuil, 1993.

# Index

epitaphs written by, 102–6
epitaphs written for, 135–36
father. *See* Odelarius of
  Orléans
knowledge of *computus*, 77–78,
  90–91
maps and, 48, 77–78, 91
memorial to, 136
motives for writing, xv,
  xx–xxi, 116
Norman myth allegedly
  perpetuated by, 35
perceptions of home, xxii
presence in the *Historia
  Ecclesiastica*, 120–21
priesthood, 112
relevance, xxi
saw Thorney *computus*, 77–78
thoughts on the crusades,
  70–71
travels, 16, 42, 50, 74, 77,
  185n25
*See also Historia Ecclesiastica*
  (Orderic Vitalis)
Orderic Vitalis, interpolations in
  William of Jumièges's
  *Gesta Normannorum
  Ducum*, xviii, 4
*De origine gigantum. See Des
  Grantz Geanz*
Orkney Islands, 47, 48
Orléans, 12, 14, 114, 115
Orne (river), 1
Orosius, *Historiarum adversus
  paganos libri septem*,
  19, 21–22, 27, 37, 38,
  47, 113
geographical introduction,
  20, 21
Old English version of, 48

Osbern, abbot of Ouche, 103, 107
Otherworld
  local landscape overlaid by,
    93–94, 98, 100–102
  visions of, 93–94
  —Dryhthelm, 93, 99
  *See also* purgatorial suffering
Otto of Freising. *See De duabus
  civitatibus* (Otto of
  Freising)
Ouche, Benedictine abbey of
  chapter–house, 103
  church of Saint-Peter at, 6, 15
  —built by St. Evroul, 9
  —St. Evroul buried in, 9
  earlier abbey at site of, 6,
    10–14
  foundation of, 4–5, 16
  geography of, 3
  —ecclesiastical, 2–3
  —monastic, 3–4
  —physical, 6, 8–9
  —political, 2
  history of, 3–16
  as key to Orderic's geographical
    vision, 3
  library, 19, 75, 78,
  named for the region, 2
  —name used instead of Saint-
    Évroult, xvi, 142n27
  new church consecrated at,
    70, 86–89, 91, 123
  as a place of holiness, 11–16
  punished, 12–13
  revealed to St. Evroul, 5–6,
    12
  ruins of, 132–34
  tombs at, 102–9
Ouche (region), 1–2
Ouche (town), 2

Pachomius, 7

Paul the Deacon. *See Historia Langobardorum* (Paul the Deacon)

Paul the Hermit, 7

Perche (region), 1

Peter of Bruis, 114, 124, 125

Peter the Venerable
*De miraculis*
—ghosts in, 101–2
*Contra Petrobrusianos*, 114

Picts, 26, 44

place, xv, xxii, 69
as an anchor for history, 3, 4, 6, 18, 29, 53, 63, 70–72, 85, 104–5, 109, 118, 122, 132
as a repository of holiness, 6, 11–13, 15–16, 73, 124–25, 132
*See also* geography; maps

place-names, 29, 51–69

Platonism, 206n32

Pompeius Trogus, 19

Pomponius Mela, 36

Pont-Échanfray, 2. *See also* Walchelin of Pont-Échanfray

Poole, R. L., 136

portents, xi–xiv, 49, 89–91, 131–32, 138n5, 139nn7, 9

Ptolemy, 36, 37

purgatorial suffering, 92–102, 108
emplaced, 99, 196n41

*Quid significent duodecim candelae,* 88–89

Raoul Glaber, 72–73, 122, 127, 182n7
Christianization in, 72–73, 74, 83
ghosts in, 100–102

Raoul of Drachy, 150n50
relics of St. Evroul stolen by, 11–12
relics of St. Evroul taken to Rebais by, 14

Raoul of Montpinçon, 103, 107

Real Presence, 114, 115

Rebais-en-Brie, monastery, 10, 11, 14

relics, 10–16, 51, 104, 118
theft of, 10–15, 148n41, 149nn43, 46

Restold, 15

revenants, 95–96

Richard of Bienfaite, 96

Richer of Reims, xiv, 27–28

Risle (river), 1

Robert I, king of France, 11

Robert I the Magnificent, duke of Normandy, 32

Robert II of Grandmesnil, 4–5, 16

Robert II the Pious, king of France, 11

Robert, brother of Walchelin, 98–99

Robert Curthose, duke of Normandy, 33, 40, 64, 66, 92

Robert Giroie, 103, 106, 107

Robert Guiscard, 30–31, 43

Robert of Beaumont, earl of Leicester, 8

Robert of Bellême, 92, 94

Robert of Prunelai, abbot of Thorney, 77

Robert of Rhuddlan, 65
bad death of, 103, 106–9
Orderic's epitaph for, 102–3, 105
tomb of, 102–3, 106, 107

Robert of Toringi, 20

Roger I of Sicily, 30–31

Roger II of Montgomery, xvii, 65

# AMANDA JANE HINGST

is an independent scholar in Madison, Wisconsin.